THE MARKET ECONOMY:

A Reader

S0-AFF-394

Edited by

James L. Doti
Chapman College

Dwight R. Lee
The University of Georgia

ROXBURY PUBLISHING COMPANY

Library of Congress Cataloging-in-Publication Data

The Market Economy: A Reader / [edited by] James L. Doti, Dwight R. Lee.
        p.   cm.
        1. Free Enterprise. 2. Capitalism. 3. Economic policy.
I. Doti, James L., 1946-   . II. Lee, Dwight R., 1941-   .
HB95.M36   1991
338.9 – dc20   90-19524
                                                                        CIP

The Market Economy: A Reader

Executive Editor: Claude Teweles
Cover Design: Allan Miller

Printed in the United States of America   10 9 8 7 6 5 4

Hardcover ISBN 0-935732-25-X
Paperback ISBN 0-935732-26-8

ROXBURY PUBLISHING COMPANY
P. O. Box 491044
Los Angeles, California 90049
(213) 653-1068

About the Editors

James L. Doti is a graduate of the University of Chicago where he earned his A.M. and Ph.D. in Economics. He has taught at Chapman College since 1974, where he has also served as Director of the Center for Economic Research, Dean of the School of Business and Economics and Acting President. Dr. Doti is currently Professor of Economics and Director of Business Forecasting at Chapman College.

The author of many scholarly articles, Dr. Doti has recently coauthored a textbook entitled *Econometric Analysis — An Applications Approach*. He was a recipient of the Faculty Recognition Award for Teaching and Research at Chapman College, the Freedoms Foundation George Washington Honor Medal, and the Paul Harris Award for distinguished contributions in the area of education. He has also served on the Editorial Review Board of the *Midwestern Journal of Business and Economics* and the Board of Directors of the Association for University Business and Economic Research.

Dwight R. Lee received his B.A. in Economics from San Diego State University and his Ph.D. in Economics from the University of California, San Diego. He has taught at the University of Colorado, Virginia Polytechnic and State University, and George Mason University. Dr. Lee is currently the Bernard B. and Eugenia A. Ramsey Professor of Private Enterprise at the University of Georgia.

Dr. Lee has published over 50 articles in professional economic journals. He has also coauthored five books and is the contributing editor of another. He is an adjunct scholar to the Center for Study of Public Choice at George Mason University and the Center for the Study of American Business at Washington University. He is on the editorial board of the journal *Defence Economics*, is a Senior Associate of the Foundation for Research on Economics and the Environment, and serves on the Executive Committee of the Association of Private Enterprise Education.

To George Stigler and Milton Friedman.

J.L.D.

To Bernard B. and Eugenia A. Ramsey.

D.R.L.

Preface

*I have known Adam Smith slightly, Ricardo
well, and Malthus intimately. Is it not something
to say for a science that its three greatest
masters were about the three best men I ever
knew.*

Mackintosh to Empson

The Market Economy: A Reader is intended, as the title suggests, to outline
the characteristics and philosophical underpinnings of the market economy and
its usefulness in the allocation of resources.

This anthology offers a comprehensive set of authentic, primary source selections that demonstrate how the tenets of classical economic liberalism provide
the foundation for an efficient economic system – while also maximizing individual freedom. The readings also provide a structure for analyzing economic
and philosophical issues.

We felt that students of economics ought to be given the opportunity to read
writers like Adam Smith, David Ricardo, and Milton Friedman firsthand – as
opposed to reading other writers' interpretations of their work. We included
the writings of several authors who are not economists but whose work is
important in terms of their contribution to economic thought: Henry David
Thoreau and Ayn Rand.

The Market Economy: A Reader features classic readings such as Adam
Smith's invisible hand from his *Wealth of Nations*, David Ricardo's original
explanation of comparative advantage from *Principles of Political Economy and
Taxation*, and John Stuart Mill's eloquent expression of the limits of government
in *On Liberty*.

Latter day proponents of private enterprise include Friedrich Hayek, Ludwig von Mises, and Milton Friedman. These authors and others address how
the market economy responds to such topical issues as the environment, income
distribution, and free trade.

It may seem presumptuous of us to include our own articles with those of such a select group of notable writers. Our defense is that the logical basis of our articles is rooted in the classical liberal philosophy so well articulated in the other writings included in this book. In drawing heavily from these writings, our own articles demonstrate the contemporary applicability of the basic tenets of classical liberalism. In addition, we hope our articles will serve as useful introductory pieces before immersing the reader into the writings of other authors.

A special note of thanks is due our assistant, Ann Cameron, who was invaluable in so many ways to the publication of this anthology. We also wish to thank our colleagues Donald Booth, Lynne P. Doti, Esmael Adibi, George Selgin, Larry White, and Richard Timberlake, who made useful suggestions regarding the readings and structure of the book. Dwight Lee also expresses his appreciation to the Philip M. McKenna Foundation for the general support it has provided his work over the years.

We are grateful to the publishers that allowed us permission to reprint the readings included here. We would also like to thank the following members of the Editorial Advisory Board appointed for this project, whose comments on the manuscript were most helpful.

William R. Allen
University of California, Los Angeles

Fred Kiesner
Loyola Marymount University

Fred R. Glahe
University of Colorado, Boulder

C. D. Macaulay
University of Michigan, Ann Arbor

Robert Higgs
Seattle University

Abu N. M. Wahid
Eastern Illinois University

Frank P. Jozsa, Jr.
Allentown College

Our attempt to bring together a representative set of readings in the market economy proved an extremely rewarding task. There can be few pleasures greater than sharing the readings that were so influential in shaping one's own intellectual development. We hope they will stimulate others as much as they have affected us.

James L. Doti and Dwight R. Lee

Table of Contents

SECTION THREE
Imperfect Markets

SECTION FOUR
Governmental Regulation

SECTION FIVE
The Proper Role of Government

SECTION SIX
Scarcity, Conflict, and Social Cooperation

SECTION SEVEN
The Distribution of Income

SECTION EIGHT
International Trade

Section ONE

The Invisible Hand

It is not from the benevolence of the butcher, the brewer, or the baker, that we expect our dinner, but from their regard to their own self-interest.

Adam Smith

Perhaps the most illuminating topic to be learned in economics is the process in which self-interested behavior on the part of individuals results in the public good. Knowing how this process works is critical in understanding how an economic system functions. This process was likened to an invisible hand by Adam Smith (1723–90) in his magnum opus published in 1776, *The Wealth of Nations:*

He generally, indeed, neither intends to promote the public interest nor knows how much he is promoting it. By preferring the support of domestic to that of foreign industry, he intends only his own security; and by directing that industry in such a manner as its produce may be of the greatest value, he intends only his own gain; and he is in this, as in many other cases, led by an invisible hand to promote an end which was no part of his intention.

Although Adam Smith was not the first to refute the then prevailing view that every gain for an individual involves a corresponding loss for another, his refutation and alternative thesis was the most complete and logically drawn. Smith believed there is a harmonious order in society where the natural and almost instinctive self-interested urges and desires of individuals are channeled into the interests of society. This channeling, according to Smith and other proponents of free markets, is best done through the forces of competition rather than through the laws or edicts of a society.

The invisible hand philosophy underlying these beliefs pervades the various readings included in this section. In the first selection, James Doti (1946–) compares and contrasts Christian dogma with that of capitalism. Doti concludes that self-interest is a more effective motivating force than altruism for maximizing utility in a highly specialized economy. This reading is the first of seven articles by Doti included in this book that initially appeared in *The Freeman*. All these articles use the sights, sounds and characters of Chicago's Little Italy as a backdrop for telling various economic lessons.

Milton Friedman (1912–), the author of the second selection, won the Nobel Prize in Economics in 1976. Recently voted by *Life* magazine as one of the "100 Most Influential Americans of the 20th Century," Friedman's writings have had a significant impact in moving many of the world's economies towards more reliance on free markets. In this, the first of four selections included in this book from his classic *Capitalism and Freedom* (1962), Friedman turns the tables on those arguing for greater social responsibility on the part of business leaders. While the prevailing views of society may make Friedman's views appear radical, he cogently argues that it is not only wrong but subversive to believe that corporate officials have a social responsibility other than maximizing profits.

Although Ayn Rand (1905–82) is not considered an economist, her objectivist philosophy that forms the core of her many novels, essays, and teachings provides a compelling moral argument for reliance on the market economy. In a selection from Rand's powerful novel, *Atlas Shrugged*, the principal character, Hank Rearden, presents a strong argument for the morality of self-interest.

In an exploration of the vital link between economic failure and progress, Dwight Lee (1941–) refutes the view that governments should come to the aid of those who fail in a market economy. Lee argues that without failure there can be no progress.

Friedrich A. Hayek (1899–), our second Nobel laureate (1974) in this section, earned his early reputation as a leading critic of Keynesianism and an advocate of Austrian business cycle theory. With the publication of *The Road to Serfdom* (1944), however, Hayek's fame as a leading advocate of the market system spread. This fame was given impetus with the publication of *Individualism and Economic Order* (1948) and his founding of the Mount Pelerin Society, a society of scholars established to defend the efficacy of the market system. Hayek's essay in this section involves a familiar Hayekian theme of the importance of a freely moving price system as a very efficient means for communicating information in a free society.

The philosophical core of all the readings in this book is rooted in the passages from Adam Smith's *Wealth of Nations* included as the final reading in this section. Indeed, *The Wealth of Nations* represents the intellectual cornerstone of the market economy and classical liberalism and was instrumental in establishing economics as an autonomous academic discipline. Smith's discussion of the pin factory as an illustration of the gains resulting from specialization and his concept of the invisible hand as a metaphor for how private vice leads to public virtue are classics of world literature. In reading Smith, one should take time to digest his many illustrations of eighteenth century life.

Born in Kirkcaldy, Scotland, a small fishing and mining village near Edinburg, Smith received his M.A. degree from the University of Glasgow where he later held a professorship in moral philosophy. While living a rather contemplative life as a teacher and scholar with his widowed mother for most of his years, Smith's travels in France as the tutor of the young Duke of Baccleuch gave him a broad perspective to draw upon in framing the ideas contained in *Wealth of Nations* — a book he wrote after retiring from academe, a retirement made possible by a life pension he had been awarded by the Duke of Baccleuch.

The modern reader should be alerted to the fact that many of the digressions contained in *The Wealth of Nations* not only make Smith's reasoning persuasive, they also teach a great deal about history, political science, psychology, and other social sciences, besides making it a very interesting book to read. ●

1. Capitalism and Greed

James L. Doti

Before economics became a science of economic models, theoretical proofs, and irrational rationality it was called moral philosophy and dealt with how individuals live their lives. A comprehensive philosophy of life was presented during the latter part of the eighteenth century by Adam Smith. In his path breaking work, *The Wealth of Nations*, Adam Smith described an economic system based on self-interest. This system which later became known as capitalism is described in this famous passage:

> It is not from the benevolence of the butcher, the brewer, or the baker, that we expect our dinner, but from their regard to their own interest. We address ourselves, not to their humanity but to their self-love, and never talk to them of our own necessities but of their advantages.*

Thus, the forces of self-interest determine individual actions. It is difficult to reconcile this practical religion of capitalistic societies, however, with any system of thought or morality that can be described as Christian. Surely, an underlying theme in Christ's teachings is that love and charity toward one's neighbors rather than self-interest should guide an individual's actions:

> But I say this to you who are listening: Love your enemies, do good to those who hate you, bless those who curse you, pray for those who treat you badly. To the man who slaps you on the cheek, present the other cheek too; to the man who takes your cloak from you, do not refuse your tunic. Give to everyone who asks you, and do not ask for your property back from the man who robs you. Treat others as you would like them to

---

*   Adam Smith, *The Wealth of Nations*, Modern Library Edition (New York: Random House, 1937), p. 14.

Reprinted from *The Freeman*, November, 1982, pp. 673-677, by permission of the Foundation for Economic Education.

treat you. And if you lend to those from whom you hope to receive, what thanks can you expect? Even sinners lend to sinners to get back the same amount. Instead, love your enemies and do good, and lend without any hope of return.*

Christ also taught us to ". . . be on your guard against avarice of any kind, for a man's life is not made secure by what he owns, even when he has more than he needs."**

Christ's message certainly seems to conflict with Adam Smith's belief that striving for personal gain is a natural human trait which should be given almost free reign in society. But though the underlying moral basis of Christianity and capitalism may contrast sharply, it can be argued that the outcome of an economic system based on capitalism has socially redeeming characteristics.

The Challenge

To understand this argument, let us set the following goal: To better society and benefit our fellow human beings. Attaining this goal by living a Christian life seems straightforward. But how can one achieve such a goal in a capitalistic society where self-interest is the ruling economic dogma?

Adam Smith answers this question in the most famous passage from the *Wealth of Nations*:

> . . . every individual necessarily labors to render the annual revenue of the society, as great as he can. He generally, indeed, neither intends to promote the public interest, nor knows how much he is promoting it . . . he intends only his own gain, and he is in this, as in many other cases, led by an invisible hand to promote an end which was no part of his intention. Nor is it always the worse for the society that it was no part of it. By pursuing his own interest he frequently promotes that of the society more effectually than when he really intends to promote it.***

This principle was vividly demonstrated to me when I was an undergraduate student in Chicago during the "Great Snowstorm" of 1967—a storm not to be confused with the "Great Chicago Snowstorms" of 1968, 69, 70 . . . 81.

At the time, I was living in what generously could be described as a hovel. It would not be wide of the mark to conjure up images of the bleaker passages in a Dickens novel to have a reasonably correct impression of the place. My routine in life consisted of going to school or work and studying endlessly, or so it seemed. One of the simple joys in life that helped to break the monotony was

---

*   *La Bible de Jerusalem*, Revised Version, Luke VI: 34-38.
**   *La Bible de Jerusalem*, Revised Version, Luke VII: 15-18.
***   Smith, p. 423.

my noon day trip to the local deli where the greatest Italian beef sandwiches in the world were made.

During one weekend in January, as I crammed for final exams, I anxiously awaited my noon day repast. At 12:00 sharp, as I opened the door for what would be a short stroll to "Salvatore's Deli," a solid wall of snow blocked my path. Now for anyone who has lived in Chicago for, at least, a couple of years, this kind of experience is not uncommon. What made this situation unique, however, was my discovery so late in the day of the snowstorm's occurrence. Since my windows were boarded up to prevent cold from entering (a sort of makeshift storm window), I had no idea a massive storm hit the city the previous night.

Quickly sizing up the situation, I chortled as it dawned on me that final exams would be cancelled, and I would have another week before I again would have to start cramming. Upon further reflection, my initial elation was dampened as I looked at my inventory of foodstuffs and realized that restocking would be my first order of business. Worse yet, "Salvatore's Deli" would undoubtedly be closed since Sal would never be able to make it in from the suburb where he lived. My only recourse would be to shovel myself out and go to the nearest "Mom and Pop" grocery store.

After a good deal of shoveling and trekking through the snow, I finally reached the store. But what I found looked like "The Twilight Zone." Shelves were emptied and all that remained were several tins of anchovies and cans of artichoke hearts. Panic was beginning to set in and a cold sweat that defied the elements broke out over my face. There was only one other grocery store in the area, but I held out little hope that the scene would be much different. You can well imagine my surprise, therefore, when I entered the store to find an adequate, albeit depleted, supply of groceries on the shelves.

It was like a scene from a Keystone Cops movie as I sped around the aisles stocking up on Cokes, Twinkies, Snickers, and other necessities of life. But, again, my brief moment of joy was dashed as I entered the checkout line and saw a sign that read: "Prices for all groceries are temporarily doubled." My joy gave way to outrage as I stormed out the door empty-handed.

Several feet from the door, however, as I gazed upon miles of snow and drew several breathfuls of icy air, principles and ideals gave way to reason and survival. I returned to selectively purchase my needed provisions. The only "idealism" that remained within me was my ability to muster up some grumbling as I trekked back home through the snow.

A footnote to this story is that the store stayed open and was somehow able to sell groceries during the entire week that normal deliveries were cut off. It was only later that I found out that the grocery store owner had paid children to take their sleds to the closest vegetable and meat warehouse to stock up on whatever the children could buy and fit on their sleds.

Capitalism in Action

The Wealth of Nations is replete with examples like my snowstorm experience. But, perhaps because of the eighteenth-century setting, Adam Smith's examples never affected me as much as my first-hand experience with the workings of a capitalistic system. What greater support could I have for the theory that private vice leads to public virtue? Here we have one store owner who in the interest of fair play does not change his prices but quickly sells all his merchandise and closes shop for the rest of the week. I am sure he experienced a great feeling of self-satisfaction because he had done the decent and proper thing by not exploiting his customers during a time of urgent need.

In sharp contrast to this example of high-minded idealism, we have the case of a capitalist who would seize upon any opportunity to maximize profits. Yet, in doing so, he forced people to limit their purchases to what they really needed. In addition, the higher prices allowed the greedy grocery owner to pay children to put their sleds to a new use, thereby increasing the supply of food available for sale. As Adam Smith stated in the quote noted earlier, "By pursuing his own interest he frequently promotes that of society more effectually than when he really intends to promote it."

It could be argued that high prices, while admittedly containing some inherent benefits, discriminate against the poor. In addressing this argument, I can assure you that no one in the neighborhood was poorer than I. Yet I benefited greatly from the forces of self-interest. I should also note that high prices give way to low prices as capitalists scramble to supply more of the high-priced goods to increase their profits.

What we see here is capitalism in action, and at first glance, it is not a pretty sight. Capitalists motivated by greed seek their own gain by maximizing profits. The forces of the market place, however, convert this private vice into public virtue. Thus, living a life based on greed, which appears to be the antithesis of Christian morality, can do quite well in accomplishing the goal set forth above — that is, to better society and benefit our fellow human beings. In fact, Adam Smith's contribution in the history of intellectual thought was not inventing capitalism but providing theoretical insight into how self-interested individuals ultimately benefit society more than they benefit themselves.

I would now like to carry the argument one step further. Not only do I believe that self-interest benefits society, but I also contend that it is the only efficient way goods can be produced and distributed in a modern economic system.

To see this, think of all the goods purchased in our society. Think of all the goods we consume on a daily basis. Do we know who produced these goods? Do we even know how or where they were produced? Probably not. A modern society requires specialization of labor with millions of individuals contributing to the production of goods and services. This contribution on the part of laborers does not come about as a result of an altruistic desire to serve society, but from a basic desire to serve oneself.

At times, of course, altruism can serve as the prime motivating force for individuals. This force is strongest in relationships between family members or friends, but it can also exist for others. An example of this is someone who contributes to "Food for the Hungry." Indeed, contributing to help relieve world hunger is a charitable act that embodies the love, compassion and respect that a person can feel for humanity. Yet, such a charitable act is essentially a voluntary redistribution of income. It does not, however, represent the actual production of the charitable good. Ultimately, any relief of world hunger comes about as a result of countless farmers, food processors, distributors, shippers, and other disinterested individuals producing the food that charitable individuals may purchase for the hungry.

Adam Smith said all of this in a more lucid and eloquent way in my favorite quote from *The Wealth of Nations*: "In civilized society he [man] stands at all times in need of the co-operation and assistance of great multitudes, while his whole life is scarce sufficient to gain the friendship of a few persons."*

It is unfortunate indeed that "greed" has acquired such a bad connotation. Without it, we would not have indoor plumbing, clock radios, or even water in Southern California. Alas, that means some of us would be in Chicago suffering through a few more "Great Snowstorms"! ●

---

*   Smith, p. 14.

2. Social Responsibility of Business and Labor

Milton Friedman

The view has been gaining widespread acceptance that corporate officials and labor leaders have a "social responsibility" that goes beyond serving the interest of their stockholders or their members. This view shows a fundamental misconception of the character and nature of a free economy. In such an economy, there is one and only one social responsibility of business — to use its resources and engage in activities designed to increase its profits so long as it stays within the rules of the game, which is to say, engages in open and free competition, without deception or fraud. Similarly, the "social responsibility" of labor leaders is to serve the interests of the members of their unions. It is the responsibility of the rest of us to establish a framework of law such that an individual in pursuing his own interest is, to quote Adam Smith again, "led by an invisible hand to promote an end which was no part of his intention. Nor is it always the worse for the society that it was no part of it. By pursuing his own interest, he frequently promotes that of the society more effectually than when he really intends to promote it. I have never known much good done by those who affected to trade for the public good."*

Few trends could so thoroughly undermine the very foundations of our free society as the acceptance by corporate officials of a social responsibility other than to make as much money for their stockholders as possible. This is a fundamentally subversive doctrine. If businessmen do have a social responsibility other than making maximum profits for stockholders, how are they to know what it is? Can self-selected private individuals decide what the social interest is? Can they decide how great a burden they are justified in placing on themselves

---

* Adam Smith, *The Wealth of Nations* (1776), Bk. IV, Chapter ii (Cannan ed. London, 1930), p. 421.

Reprinted from *Capitalism and Freedom*, pp. 133-136, by permission of The University of Chicago Press. Copyright © 1962 by The University of Chicago.

or their stockholders to serve that social interest? Is it tolerable that these public functions of taxation, expenditure, and control be exercised by the people who happen at the moment to be in charge of particular enterprises, chosen for those posts by strictly private groups? If businessmen are civil servants rather than the employees of their stockholders then in a democracy they will, sooner or later, be chosen by the public techniques of election and appointment.

And long before this occurs, their decision-making power will have been taken away from them. A dramatic illustration was the cancellation of a steel price increase by U.S. Steel in April 1962 through the medium of a public display of anger by President Kennedy and threats of reprisals on levels ranging from anti-trust suits to examination of the tax reports of steel executives. This was a striking episode because of the public display of the vast powers concentrated in Washington. We were all made aware of how much of the power needed for a police state was already available. It illustrates the present point as well. If the price of steel is a public decision, as the doctrine of social responsibility declares, then it cannot be permitted to be made privately.

The particular aspect of the doctrine which this example illustrates, and which has been most prominent recently, is an alleged social responsibility of business and labor to keep prices and wage rates down in order to avoid price inflation. Suppose that at a time when there was upward pressure on prices — ultimately of course reflecting an increase in the stock of money—every businessman and labor leader were to accept this responsibility and suppose all could succeed in keeping any price from rising, so we had voluntary price and wage control without open inflation. What would be the result? Clearly product shortages, labor shortages, gray markets, black markets. If prices are not allowed to ration goods and workers, there must be some other means to do so. Can the alternative rationing schemes be private? Perhaps for a time in a small and unimportant area. But if the goods involved are many and important, there will necessarily be pressure, and probably irresistible pressure, for governmental rationing of goods, a governmental wage policy, and governmental measures for allocating and distributing labor.

Price controls, whether legal or voluntary, if effectively enforced would eventually lead to the destruction of the free-enterprise system and its replacement by a centrally controlled system. And it would not even be effective in preventing inflation. History offers ample evidence that what determines the average level of prices and wages is the amount of money in the economy and not the greediness of businessmen or of workers. Governments ask for the self-restraint of business and labor because of their inability to manage their own affairs — which includes the control of money — and the natural human tendency to pass the buck.

One topic in the area of social responsibility that I feel dutybound to touch on, because it affects my own personal interests, has been the claim that business should contribute to the support of charitable activities and especially to universities. Such giving by corporations is an inappropriate use of corporate funds in a free-enterprise society.

The corporation is an instrument of the stockholders who own it. If the corporation makes a contribution, it prevents the individual stockholder from himself deciding how he should dispose of his funds. With the corporation tax and the deductibility of contributions, stockholders may of course want the corporation to make a gift on their behalf, since this would enable them to make a larger gift. The best solution would be the abolition of the corporate tax. But so long as there is a corporate tax, there is no justification for permitting deductions for contributions to charitable and educational institutions. Such contributions should be made by the individuals who are the ultimate owners of property in our society.

People who urge extension of the deductibility of this kind of corporate contribution in the name of free enterprise are fundamentally working against their own interest. A major complaint made frequently against modern business is that it involves the separation of ownership and control—that the corporation has become a social institution that is a law unto itself, with irresponsible executives who do not serve the interests of their stockholders. This charge is not true. But the direction in which policy is now moving, of permitting corporations to make contributions for charitable purposes and allowing deductions for income tax, is a step in the direction of creating a true divorce between ownership and control and of undermining the basic nature and character of our society. It is a step away from an individualistic society and toward the corporate state. ●

3. The Moral Meaning of Capitalism

Ayn Rand

This is a statement made by the fictitious character, Hank Rearden, from the novel, Atlas Shrugged, *at his trial for an illegal sale of a metal alloy which he had created and which has been placed under government rationing and control.*

"I do not want my attitude to be misunderstood. I shall be glad to state it for the record. . . . I work for nothing but my own profit—which I make by selling a product they need to men who are willing and able to buy it. I do not produce it for their benefit at the expense of mine, and they do not buy it for my benefit at the expense of theirs; I do not sacrifice my interests to them nor do they sacrifice theirs to me; we deal as equals by mutual consent to mutual advantage—and I am proud of every penny that I have earned in this manner. I am rich and I am proud of every penny I own. I have made my money by my own effort, in free exchange and through the voluntary consent of every man I dealt with—the voluntary consent of those who employed me when I started, the voluntary consent of those who work for me now, the voluntary consent of those who buy my product. I shall answer all the questions you are afraid to ask me openly. Do I wish to pay my workers more than their services are worth to me? I do not. Do I wish to sell my product for less than my customers are willing to pay me? I do not. Do I wish to sell it at a loss or give it away? I do not. If this is evil, do whatever you please about me, according to whatever standards you hold. These are mine. I am earning my own living, as every honest man must. I refuse to accept as guilt the fact of my own existence and the fact that I must work in order to support it. I refuse to accept as guilt the fact that I am able to do it and to do it well. I refuse to accept as guilt the fact that I am able to do it better than most people — the fact that my work is of greater value than the work of my neighbors and that more men are willing to pay me. I refuse to apologize for my ability — I refuse to apologize for my success — I refuse to apologize for my money. If this is evil, make the most of it. If this is what the public finds harmful to its interests let the public destroy me. This is my code — and I will accept no other. I could say to you that I have done more good for my fellow man than you can ever hope to accomplish — but I will not say it, because I do not seek the good of others as a sanction for my right to exist, nor do I recognize the good of others as a justification for their seizure of my property or their destruction of my life. I will not say that the good of others was the purpose of my work — my own good was my purpose, and I despise the man who surrenders his. I could say to you that you do not serve the public good — that nobody's good can be achieved at the price of human sacrifices — that when you violate the rights of one man, you have violated the rights of all, and a public of rightless creatures is doomed to destruction. I could say to you that you will and can achieve nothing but universal devastation — as any looter must, when he runs out of victims. I could say it, but I won't. It is not your particular policy that I challenge, but your moral premise. If it were true that men could achieve their good by means of turning some men into sacrificial animals, and I were asked to immolate myself for the sake of creatures who wanted to survive at the price of my blood, if I were asked to serve the interests of society apart from, above and against my own — I would refuse, I would reject it as the most contemptible evil, I would fight it with every power I possess, I would fight the whole of mankind, if one minute were all I could last before I were murdered, I would fight in the full confidence of the justice of my battle and of a living being's right to exist. Let there be no misunderstanding about me. If it is now the belief of my fellow men, who call themselves the public, that their good requires victims, then I say: The public good be damned, I will have no part of it!" ●

4. Freedom and Failure

Dwight R. Lee

During good times and bad, the economic landscape seems always littered with firms that have failed, workers who have become unemployed, farmers who have lost their land, and the residue of entire industries in the process of withering away. The natural tendency is to see these failures, and the genuine human hardships that result, as a flaw of the economic system that produces them. Even those who consider themselves supporters of the market economy call for government action to buffer society against the harsh failures of unfettered capitalism.

It is certainly the case that when viewed in isolation the consequences of economic failure appear cruel, harsh, and unfair. Because of events over which they have little or no control, many hard-working, law-abiding citizens experience serious economic hardships in a system of free market capitalism. No one can argue with credibility that all, or even a significant minority, of these victims of economic failure are getting what they deserve in any particular instance of adversity. But economic outcomes that in isolation seem unjustified may be the necessary consequence of a system that is generating an overall, long-run pattern of outcomes that is entirely justified. As Henry Hazlitt has warned repeatedly, the major source of error in economic understanding comes from the tendency "to concentrate on ... short-run effects on special groups and to ignore ... the long-run effects on the community as a whole."*

Hazlitt's warning cannot be overemphasized when considering economic failure and the fairness of free market capitalism. Each market failure is an inseparable part of a wider web of interactions and outcomes that provides everyone the maximum opportunity for success in the world of scarcity. Scarcity is an unfortunate fact of life, and it is easy to see scarcity itself as unfair. But

---

*   Henry Hazlitt, *Economics in One Lesson*, (New York: Arlington House Publishers, 1979), p. 17.

Reprinted from *The Freeman*, October, 1986, pp. 392-395, by permission of the Foundation for Economic Education.

unless one is prepared to argue that making the best of an unfortunate situation is also unfair, there can be nothing unfair about free market capitalism. And because instances of failure are necessary companions to the general success of the free market process, it would require a sharp twist of logic to characterize as unfair the failures that arise from free market activity.

Economic failure is inevitable if we are to have economic progress. One explanation for this link between failure and progress was provided by Joseph Schumpeter when he described capitalism as a "process of creative destruction."* The discovery of improved products, and better ways of producing existing products, necessarily means that many established products and technologies are valued less. Those who have committed their resources to these now obsolete products and technologies will suffer a decline in wealth as their investments turn sour and their skills become less employable. They will experience economic failure. But this destruction of wealth, or economic failure, is only part of a larger picture of wealth creation and economic success. The loss of wealth experienced by some is (1) a transfer of resources to those who will put them to more valuable use, and (2) a compelling incentive to redirect efforts into more productive employment. The process of "creative destruction" is our best hope for economic success.

Entrepreneurial Freedom and Failure

There is another vital link between economic failure and progress. Economic progress that expands opportunities for all is clearly a force for fairness. Such broad-based economic progress depends on what is best described as the entrepreneurial spirit. Without those with visions of what might be, and the dedication and courage to pursue those visions, few of the technologies and products that provide the foundation for our current wealth would be available. It is only because individual entrepreneurs have had the freedom to attempt what the more "sensible" among us would never have attempted that economic development has been possible.**

This does not mean that most entrepreneurial ventures contribute to our economic well-being. Quite the opposite is true. A relatively small percentage of the projects promoted by entrepreneurs adds more to our wealth than it consumes in time, talent, and resources. Most entrepreneurial ventures turn out to be exactly what most of us would have predicted in advance — impractical fan-

---

*   Joseph A. Schumpeter, *Capitalism, Socialism and Democracy*, (New York: Harper Torch Books, 1962), pp. 81-86.

**   The benefits from freedom are clearly not confined to those who choose to exercise it. As F. A. Hayek has said, "The benefits I derive from freedom are thus largely the result of the uses of freedom by others, and mostly of those uses of freedom that I could never avail myself of. If is therefore not necessarily freedom that I can exercise myself that is most important for me." See F. A. Hayek, *The Constitution of Liberty*, (Chicago: The University of Chicago Press, 1960), p. 32.

tasies. But, it is impossible to know in advance which entrepreneurial gambles will be an economic step forward. The only one way to discover these economic successes is to give entrepreneurs the freedom to snub their noses at the conventional wisdom and venture forth in pursuit of their "impossible" dreams.

This freedom to attempt success in the face of daunting odds requires an accompanying freedom to fail. And the freedom to fail has to be sufficiently painful that it cannot be ignored. The entrepreneur whose project is rejected by the consumer will remain convinced that it is the consumer who is mistaken. Unless such entrepreneurial confidence is sternly subordinated to consumer preferences, the losses from the many entrepreneurial mistakes would persist and overwhelm the gains from the relatively few entrepreneurial successes. Without the discipline of failure forcing accountability to consumer preferences, entrepreneurial ventures would be economically destructive and entrepreneurial freedom could not be tolerated. The economic system that cannot condone failure cannot risk freedom.

Communication, Honesty, and Concern

There is only one economic system that turns failure into a force for the type of accountability that makes freedom possible. That system is free market capitalism. It is a system that allows freedom because it is a system that motivates people, both when they succeed and when they fail, to deal with each other with honesty and fairness.

Consider the characteristics of a system of human interaction that would be ideal from the perspective of economic accountability and fairness. First, this system would have each of us in constant communication with everyone else. If there is to be any hope of being accountable to the preferences of others in our use of resources, each of us will need to receive information from others on their preferences. Second, the communication that took place would be honest. Transmitting inaccurate information on the value derived from resources would make it impossible to direct resources into their highest valued uses. Third, each individual would give the preferences of others the same weight one gives one's own. No matter how much a person may desire one economic outcome, if others communicate to that person that they value another outcome even more, that person would accommodate their preferences.

It is possible to achieve a real world approximation to this ideal system – free market capitalism. The key to understanding this approximation is in recognizing the incentives established by the private property system which forms the foundation of the market.

In the private property system, resources are transferred from one individual to another through voluntary exchanges. The market prices that arise from these exchanges are the means by which all market participants communicate their preferences to each other. There exist strong incentives for people to communicate honestly through prices. It is in the interest of all market participants to assess carefully the value realized from different resources, and to communicate their desire for more of a particular resource only if it is honestly worth more to them than the prevailing market price. The temptation sellers would otherwise have to overstate the values of their products with excessive prices is controlled by market competition.

Finally, each market participant is motivated to act *as if* he has the same concern for the preferences of others as he has for his own. When an individual reduces his use of a product in response to a higher price, he is in effect saying, "Others are telling me that this product is worth more to them than it is to me, so I will consume less so that they can consume more." Similarly, economic failures such as bankruptcies and unemployment can be thought of as people saying, "Others are telling me that my resources would be more valuable in other activities, so I will respond to their preferences." These "failures" reflect the success of free market capitalism in getting people to cooperate with each other freely, fairly, and honestly.

Focusing on Failure

Unfortunately, few people heed Henry Hazlitt's warning and look beyond the isolated trees of economic failure to see the overall forest of economic success. This oversight is explained in part by the fact that it is easier to concentrate on particular outcomes than to comprehend the larger pattern of which these outcomes are only a part. But this is far from a complete explanation. The fact is that there is more for people to gain as members of organized interest groups by concentrating on the isolated failures than by considering the overall success of free market capitalism.

When individuals suffer losses from the operation of free market capitalism, they are in fact making a necessary contribution to the working of an economic system that serves the long-run interest of all. From the perspective of each individual, however, the best possible situation would be to receive protection against personal economic failure while benefiting from the contributions the failures of others make to economic progress. The fundamental fairness of the free market is that it does not provide anyone a free ride on the contributions of others. In the free market everyone has to contribute to the general economic prosperity by accepting the failures as well as the successes that come one's way.

It is the legitimate function of government to enforce the private property rights upon which the fair and honest cooperation of the free market depends. When property rights are enforced no one can avoid making the cooperative adjustments required by economic failure while benefiting from the cooperative adjustments economic failures force on others.

Unfortunately, government power, though justified as a means of protecting property rights, can be destructive of these rights. This abuse of government power is sure to occur when, as has been the case in recent decades, government ceases to be viewed as a necessary evil and instead is seen as the primary source of social progress. Once it becomes widely believed that the discretionary use of government power is an acceptable means of solving particular economic problems, economic failure will become a useful justification for the politically organized to receive unfair advantages at the expense of the politically unorganized.

The negative consequences of economic failure are highly visible because at any one time they tend to be concentrated on a relatively few. The positive consequences of economic failure are largely invisible because they are indirect and spread over the entire population. When the few who experience economic failure are organized they will see it to their advantage to lobby government for relief. By granting this relief, politicians receive the gratitude of the benefiting few by imposing a diffused cost on the entire population. This imparts a clear political bias in favor of substituting unfair government force for the fairness of market cooperation. This bias, however, although generated by the political muscle of organized special interests, ultimately rests on perceptions of fairness.

If protecting a particular group against the consequences of economic failure is widely considered to be an unjust use of government power, then politicians will be very reluctant to provide such protection. Special interest groups lobbying government for relief from an economic failure cannot rely solely on the organizational advantage they have over the general public. Success depends crucially on the perception that justice is served by indemnifying particular groups against failure. There is much to be gained by those that are, or would be, politically influential from portraying their economic failures as unfair. No one should be surprised that as government has grown, the focus on economic failures has increased, as has the perception that these failures are unfair. With government standing ready to transfer wealth to those whom the economy has treated "unfairly," the private payoff is in lamenting the "unfairness" of failure rather than celebrating the fairness of the cooperation, wealth, and freedom that this failure makes possible.

Conclusion

The fact is that government cannot reduce economic failure. It can only protect some against failure by increasing the overall level of failure and imposing it on others. As Hayek warned over 40 years ago: "The more we try to provide full security by interfering with the market system, the greater the insecurity becomes; and, what is worse, the greater becomes the contrast between the security of those to whom it is granted as a privilege and the ever increasing insecurity of the underprivileged."*

The special favors granted by government are not only unfair, they become the justification for yet more futile government attempts to provide security against economic failure.

Once government starts down the road of buffering people against the

---

*   F. A. Hayek, *The Road to Serfdom*, (Chicago: The University of Chicago Press, 1944), p. 130.

failures of market activity it becomes difficult to turn back. And the ultimate destination if we remain on this road is a politicized economy lacking both fairness and prosperity because it cannot provide the accountability nor tolerate the freedom which are essential for economic success and honest cooperation. The best hope for preserving the market process is by advancing public understanding of how this process works to promote a broad-based prosperity. Only through economic understanding can we pierce the rhetorical facade of fairness used by organized special interests to acquire political favors. Once this facade has been stripped away, it will be difficult for political opportunists to undermine the freedom and prosperity of all under the pretense of concern and justice. ●

5. The Use of Knowledge in Society

Friedrich A. Hayek

If we can agree that the economic problem of society is mainly one of rapid adaptation to changes in the particular circumstances of time and place, it would seem to follow that the ultimate decisions must be left to the people who are familiar with these circumstances, who know directly of the relevant changes and of the resources immediately available to meet them. We cannot expect that this problem will be solved by first communicating all this knowledge to a central board which, after integrating all knowledge, issues its orders. We must solve it by some form of decentralization. But this answers only part of our problem. We need decentralization because only thus can we insure that the knowledge of the particular circumstances of time and place will be promptly used. But the "man on the spot" cannot decide solely on the basis of his limited but intimate knowledge of the facts of his immediate surroundings. There still remains the problem of communicating to him such further information as he needs to fit his decisions into the whole pattern of changes of the larger economic system.

Fundamentally, in a system in which the knowledge of the relevant facts is dispersed among many people, prices can act to co-ordinate the separate actions of different people in the same way as subjective values help the individual to co-ordinate the parts of his plan. It is worth contemplating for a moment a very simple and commonplace instance of the action of the price system to see what precisely it accomplishes. Assume that somewhere in the world a new opportunity for the use of some raw material, say, tin, has arisen, or that one of the sources of supply of tin has been eliminated. It does not matter for our purpose – and it is significant that it does not matter – which of these two causes has made tin more scarce. All that the users of tin need to know is that

Abridged from "The Use of Knowledge in Society," *American Economic Review*, XXXV, Number 4, September, 1945, pp. 519-530, by permission of the American Economic Association.

some of the tin they used to consume is now more profitably employed else-where and that, in consequence, they must economize tin. There is no need for the great majority of them even to know where the more urgent need as arisen, or in favor of what other needs they ought to husband the supply. If only some of them know directly of the new demand, and switch resources over to it, and if the people who are aware of the new gap thus created in turn fill it from still other sources, the effect will rapidly spread throughout the whole economic sys-tem and influence not only all the uses of tin but also those of its substitutes and the substitutes of these substitutes, the supply of all the things made of tin, and their substitutes, and so on; and all this without the great majority of those in-strumental in bringing about these substitutions knowing anything at all about the original cause of these changes. The whole acts as one market, not because any of its members survey the whole field, but because their limited individual fields of vision sufficiently overlap so that through many intermediaries the relevant information is communicated to all. The mere fact that there is one price for any commodity—or rather that local prices are connected in a man-ner determined by the cost of transport, etc.—brings about the solution which (it is just conceptually possible) might have been arrived at by one single mind possessing all the information which is in fact dispersed among all the people involved in the process.

We must look at the price system as such a mechanism for communicating information if we want to understand its real function—a function which, of course, it fulfils less perfectly as prices grow more rigid. (Even when quoted prices have become quite rigid, however, the forces which would operate through changes in price still operate to a considerable extent through changes in the other terms of the contract.) The most significant fact about this system is the economy of knowledge with which it operates, or how little the individual participants need to know in order to be able to take the right action. In abbre-viated form, by a kind of symbol, only the most essential information is passed on and passed on only to those concerned. It is more than a metaphor to describe the price system as a kind of machinery for registering change, or a sys-tem of telecommunications which enables individual producers to watch merely the movements of a few pointers, as an engineer might watch the hands of a few dials, in order to adjust their activities to changes of which they may never know more than is reflected in the price movement.

Of course, these adjustments are probably never "perfect" in the sense in which the economist conceives of them in his equilibrium analysis. But I fear that our theoretical habits of approaching the problem with the assumption of more or less perfect knowledge on the part of almost everyone has made us somewhat blind to the true function of the price mechanism and led us to apply rather misleading standards in judging its efficiency. The marvel is that in a case like that of a scarcity of one raw material, without an order being issued, without more than perhaps a handful of people knowing the cause, tens of thousands of people whose identity could not be ascertained by months of investigation, are made to use the material or its products more sparingly; that is, they move in the right direction. This is enough of a marvel even if, in a constantly changing world, not all will hit it off so perfectly that their profit rates will always be maintained at the same even or "normal" level.

I have deliberately used the word "marvel" to shock the reader out of the complacency with which we often take the working of this mechanism for granted. I am convinced that if it were the result of deliberate human design, and if the people guided by the price changes understood that their decisions have significance far beyond their immediate aim, this mechanism would have been acclaimed as one of the greatest triumphs of the human mind. Its misfortune is the double one that it is not the product of human design and that the people guided by it usually do not know why they are made to do what they do. But those who clamor for "conscious direction" — and who cannot believe that anything which has evolved without design (and even without our understanding it) should solve problems which we should not be able to solve consciously — should remember this: The problem is precisely how to extend the span of our utilization of resources beyond the span of the control of any one mind; and, therefore, how to dispense with the need of conscious control and how to provide inducements which will make the individuals do the desirable things without anyone having to tell them what to do.

The problem which we meet here is by no means peculiar to economics but arises in connection with nearly all truly social phenomena, with language and with most of our cultural inheritance, and constitutes really the central theoretical problem of all social science. As Alfred Whitehead has said in another connection, "It is a profoundly erroneous truism, repeated by all copy-books and by eminent people when they are making speeches, that we should cultivate the habit of thinking what we are doing. The precise opposite is the case. Civilization advances by extending the number of important operations which we can perform without thinking about them." This is of profound significance in the social field. We make constant use of formulas, symbols, and rules whose meaning we do not understand and through the use of which we avail ourselves of the assistance of knowledge which individually we do not possess. We have developed these practices and institutions by building upon habits and institutions which have proved successful in their own sphere and which have in turn become the foundation of the civilization we have built up.

The price system is just one of those formations which man has learned to use (though he is still very far from having learned to make the best use of it) after he had stumbled upon it without understanding it. Through it not only a division of labor but also a co-ordinated utilization of resources based on an equally divided knowledge has become possible. The people who like to deride any suggestion that this may be so usually distort the argument by insinuating that is asserts that by some miracle just that sort of system has spontaneously grown up which is best suited to modern civilization. It is the other way round: man has been able to develop that division of labor on which our civilization is based because he happened to stumble upon a method which made it possible. Had he not done so, he might still have developed some other, altogether different, type of civilization, something like the "state" of the termite ants, or some other altogether unimaginable type. All that we can say is that nobody has yet succeeded in designing an alternative system in which certain features of the existing one can be preserved which are dear even to those who most violently assail it — such as particularly the extent to which the individual can choose his pursuits and consequently freely use his own knowledge and skill. ●

6. Of the Division of Labour and Restraints Upon Importation

Adam Smith

The greatest improvement in the productive powers of labour, and the greater part of the skill, dexterity, and judgment with which it is any where directed, or applied, seem to have been the effects of the division of labour.

To take an example, therefore, from a very trifling manufacture; but one in which the division of labour has been very often taken notice of, the trade of the pin-maker; a workman not educated to this business (which the division of labour has rendered a distinct trade), nor acquainted with the use of the machinery employed in it (to the invention of which the same division of labour has probably given occasion), could scarce, perhaps, with his utmost industry, make one pin in a day, and certainly could not make twenty. But in the way in which this business is now carried on, not only the whole work is a peculiar trade, but it is divided into a number of branches, of which the greater part are likewise peculiar trades. One man draws out the wire, another straights it, a third cuts it, a fourth points it, a fifth grinds it at the top for receiving the head; to make the head requires two or three distinct operations; to put it on, is a peculiar business, to whiten the pins is another; it is even a trade by itself to put them into the paper; and the important business of making a pin is, in this manner, divided into about eighteen distinct operations, which, in some manufactories, are all performed by distinct hands, though in others the same man will sometimes perform two or three of them. I have seen a small manufactory of this kind where ten men only were employed, and where some of them consequently performed two or three distinct operations. But though they were very poor, and therefore but indifferently accommodated with the necessary machinery, they could, when they exerted themselves, make among them about twelve pounds of pins in a day. There are in a pound upwards of four thousand pins of a middling size. Those ten persons, therefore, could make among them upwards of forty-eight

---

Abridged from *The Wealth of Nations*, Modern Library Edition (New York: Random House, 1937), pp. 3-21 and 422-423.

thousand pins in a day. Each person, therefore, making a tenth part of forty-eight thousand pins, might be considered as making four thousand eight hundred pins in a day. But if they had all wrought separately and independently, and without any of them having been educated to this peculiar business, they certainly could not each of them have made twenty, perhaps not one pin in a day; that is, certainly, not the two hundred and fortieth, perhaps not the four thousand eight hundredth part of what they are at present capable of performing, in consequence of a proper division and combination of their different operations.

In every other art and manufacture, the effects of the division of labour are similar to what they are in this very trifling one; though, in many of them, the labour can neither be so much subdivided, nor reduced to so great a simplicity of operation. The division of labour, however, so far as it can be introduced, occasions, in every art, a proportionable increase of the productive powers of labour. The separation of different trades and employments from one another, seems to have taken place, in consequence of this advantage. This separation too generally carried furthest in those countries which enjoy the highest degree of industry and improvement; what is the work of one man in a rude state of society, being generally that of several in an improved one.

This great increase of the quantity of work, which, in consequence of the division of labour, the same number of people are capable of performing, is owing to three different circumstances; first, to the increase of dexterity in every particular workman; secondly, to the saving of the time which is commonly lost in passing from one species of work to another; and lastly, to the invention of a great number of machines which facilitate and abridge labour, and enable one man to do the work of many.

First, the improvement of the dexterity of the workman necessarily increases the quantity of the work he can perform; and the division of labour, by reducing every man's business to some one simple operation, and by making this operation the sole employment of his life, necessarily increases very much the dexterity of the workman. A common smith, who, though accustomed to handle the hammer, has never been used to make nails, if upon some particular occasion he is obliged to attempt it, will scarce, I am assured, be able to make above two or three hundred nails in a day, and those too very bad ones. A smith who has been accustomed to make nails, but whose sole or principal business has not been that of a nailer, can seldom with his utmost diligence make more than eight hundred or a thousand nails in a day. I have seen several boys under twenty years of age who had never exercised any other trade but that of making nails, and who, when they exerted themselves, could make, each of them, upwards of two thousand three hundred nails in a day. The making of a nail, however, is by no means one of the simplest operations. The same person blows the bellows, stirs or mends the fire as there is occasion, heats the iron, and forges every part of the nail: In forging the head too he is obliged to change his tools. The different operations into which the making of a pin, or of a metal button, is subdivided, are all of them much more simple, and the dexterity of the person, of whose life it has been the sole business to perform them, is usually much greater. The rapidity with which some of the operations of those manufactures are performed, exceeds what the human hand could, by those who had never seen them, be supposed capable of acquiring.

Secondly, the advantage which is gained by saving the time commonly lost in passing from one sort of work to another, is much greater than we should at first view be apt to imagine it. It is impossible to pass very quickly from one kind of work to another, that is carried on in a different place, and with quite different tools. A country weaver, who cultivates a small farm, must lose a good deal of time in passing from his loom to the field, and from the field to his loom. When the two trades can be carried on in the same workhouse, the loss of time is no doubt much less. It is even in this case, however, very considerable. A man commonly saunters a little in turning his hand from one sort of employment to another. When he first begins the new work he is seldom very keen and hearty; his mind, as they say, does not go to it, and for some time he rather trifles than applies to good purpose. The habit of sauntering and of indolent careless application, which is naturally, or rather necessarily acquired by every country workman who is obliged to change his work and his tools every half hour, and to apply his hand in twenty different ways almost every day of his life; renders him almost always slothful and lazy, and incapable of any vigorous application even on the most pressing occasions. Independent, therefore, of his deficiency in point of dexterity, this cause alone must always reduce considerably the quantity of work which he is capable of performing.

Thirdly, and lastly, every body must be sensible how much labour is facilitated and abridged by the application of proper machinery. It is unnecessary to give any example. I shall only observe, therefore, that the invention of all those machines by which labour is so much facilitated and abridged, seems to have been originally owing to the division of labour. Men are much more likely to discover easier and readier methods of attaining any object, when the whole attention of their minds is directed towards that single object, than when it is dissipated among a great variety of things. But in consequence of the division of labour, the whole of every man's attention comes naturally to be directed towards some one very simple object. It is naturally to be expected, therefore, that some one or other of those who are employed in each particular branch of labour should soon find out easier and readier methods of performing their own particular work, wherever the nature of it admits of such improvement. A great part of the machines made use of in those manufactures in which labour is most subdivided, were originally the inventions of common workmen, who, being each of them employed in some very simple operation, naturally turned their thoughts towards finding out easier and readier methods of performing it. Whoever has been much accustomed to visit such manufactures, must frequently have been shewn very pretty machines, which were the inventions of such workmen, in order to facilitate and quicken their own particular part of the work. In the first fire-engines, a boy was constantly employed to open, and shut alternately the communication between the boiler and the cylinder, according as the piston either ascended or descended. One of those boys, who loved to play with his companions, observed that, by tying a string from the handle of the valve which opened this communication to another part of the machine, the valve would open and shut without his assistance, and leave him at liberty to divert himself with his play-fellows. One of the greatest improvements that has been made upon this machine, since it was first invented, was in this manner the discovery of a boy who wanted to save his own labour.

All the improvements in machinery, however, have by no means been the inventions of those who had occasion to use the machines. Many improvements have been made by the ingenuity of the makers of the machines, when to make them became the business of a peculiar trade; and some by that of those who are called philosophers or men of speculation, whose trade it is not to do any thing, but to observe every thing; and who, upon that account, are often capable of combining together the powers of the most distant and dissimilar objects. In the progress of society, philosophy or speculation becomes, like every other employment, the principal or sole trade and occupation of a particular class of citizens. Like every other employment too, it is subdivided into a great number of different branches, each of which affords occupation to a peculiar tribe or class of philosophers; and this subdivision of employment in philosophy, as well as in every other business, improves dexterity, and saves time. Each individual becomes more expert in his own peculiar branch, more work is done upon the whole, and the quantity of science is considerably increased by it.

It is the great multiplication of the productions of all the different arts, in consequence of the division of labour, which occasions, in a well-governed society, that universal opulence which extends itself to the lowest ranks of the people. Every workman has a great quantity of his own work to dispose of beyond what he himself has occasion for; and every other workman being exactly in the same situation, he is enabled to exchange a great quantity of his own goods for a great quantity, or, what comes to the same thing, for the price of a great quantity of theirs. He supplies them abundantly with what they have occasion for, and they accommodate him as amply with what he has occasion for, and a general plenty diffuses itself through all the different ranks of the society.

Observe the accommodation of the most common artificer or day-labourer in a civilized and thriving country, and you will perceive that the number of people of whose industry a part, though but a small part, has been employed in procuring him this accommodation, exceeds all computation. The woolen coat, for example, which covers the day-labourer, as coarse and rough as it may appear, is the produce of the joint labour of a great multitude of workmen. The shepherd, the sorter of the wool, the wool-comber or carder, the dyer, the scribbler, the spinner, the weaver, the fuller, the dresser, with many others, must all join their different arts in order to complete even this homely production. How many merchants and carriers, besides, must have been employed in transporting the materials from some of those workmen to others who often live in a very distant part of the country! How much commerce and navigation in particular, how many ship-builders, sailors, sail-makers, rope-makers, must have been employed in order to bring together the different drugs made use of by the dyer, which often come from the remotest corners of the world! What a variety of labour too is necessary in order to produce the tools of the meanest of those workmen! To say nothing of such complicated machines as the ship of the sailor, the mill of the fuller, or even the loom of the weaver, let us consider only what a variety of labour is requisite in order to form that very simple machine, the shears with which the shepherd clips the wool. The miner, the builder of the furnace for smelting the ore, the feller of the timber, the burner of the charcoal to be made use of in the smelting-house, the brick-maker, the brick-layer, the workmen who attend the furnace, the mill-wright, the forger, the smith, must all of them join their different arts in order to produce them. Were we to examine, in the same manner, all the different parts of his dress and household furniture, the coarse linen shirt which he wears next his skin, the shoes which cover his feet, the bed which he lies on, and all the different parts which compose it, the kitchengrate at which he prepares his victuals, the coals which he makes use of for that purpose, dug from the bowels of the earth, and brought to him perhaps by a long sea and a long land carriage, all the other utensils of his kitchen, all the furniture of his table, the knives and forks, the earthen or pewter plates upon which he serves up and divides his victuals, the different hands employed in preparing his bread and his beer, the glass window which lets in the heat and the light, and keeps out the wind and the rain, with all the knowledge and art requisite for preparing that beautiful and happy invention, without which these northern parts of the world could scarce have afforded a very comfortable habitation, together with the tools of all the different workmen employed in producing those different conveniencies; if we examine, I say, all these things, and consider what a variety of labour is employed about each of them, we shall be sensible that without the assistance and co-operation of many thousands, the very meanest person in a civilized country could not be provided, even according to, what we very falsely imagine, the easy and simple manner in which he is commonly accommodated. Compared, indeed, with the more extravagant luxury of the great, his accommodation must no doubt appear extremely simple and easy; and yet it may be true, perhaps, that the accommodation of an European prince does not always so much exceed that of an industrious and frugal peasant, as the accommodation of the latter exceeds that of many an African king, the absolute master of the lives and liberties of ten thousand naked savages.

This division of labour, from which so many advantages are derived, is not originally the effect of any human wisdom, which foresees and intends that general opulence to which it gives occasion. It is the necessary, though very slow and gradual, consequence of a certain propensity in human nature which has in view no such extensive utility; the propensity to truck, barter, and exchange one thing for another.

Whether this propensity be one of those original principles in human nature, of which no further account can be given; or whether, as seems more probable, it be the necessary consequence of the faculties of reason and speech, it belongs not to our present subject to enquire. It is common to all men, and to be found in no other race of animals, which seem to know neither this nor any other species of contracts. Two greyhounds, in running down the same hare, have sometimes the appearance of act-ing in some sort of concert. Each turns her towards his companion, or endeavours to intercept her when his companion turns her towards himself. This, however, is not the effect of any contract, but of the accidental concurrence of their passions in the same object at that particular time. Nobody ever saw a dog make a fair and deliberate exchange of one bone for another with another dog. Nobody ever saw one animal by its gestures and natural cries signify to another, this is mine, that yours; I am willing to give this for that. When an animal wants to obtain something either of a man or of another animal, it has no other means of persuasion but to gain the favour of those whose service it requires. A puppy fawns upon its dam, and a spaniel endeavours by a thousand attractions to engage the attention of its master who is at dinner, when it wants to be fed by him. Man sometimes uses the same arts with his brethren, and when he has no other means of engaging them to act according to his inclinations, endeavors by every servile and fawning attention to obtain their good will. He has not time, however, to do this upon every occasion. In civilized society he stands at all times in need of the co-operation and assistance of great multitudes, while his whole life is scarce sufficient to gain the friendship of a few persons. In almost every other race of animals each individual, when it is grown up to maturity, is entirely independent, and in its natural state has occasion for the assistance of no other living creature. But man has almost constant occasion for the help of his brethren, and it is in vain for him to expect it from their benevolence only. He will be more likely to prevail if he can interest their self-love in his favour, and shew them that it is for their own advantage to do for him what he requires of them. Whoever offers to another a bargain of any kind, proposes to do this. Give me that which I want, and you shall have this which you want, is the meaning of every such offer; and it is in this manner that we obtain from one another the far greater part of those good offices which we stand in need of. It is not from the benevolence of the butcher, the brewer, or the baker, that we expect our dinner, but from their regard to their own interest. We address ourselves, not to their humanity but to their self-love, and never talk to them of our own necessities but of their advantages. Nobody but a beggar chuses to depend chiefly upon the benevolence of his fellow-citizens. Even a beggar does not depend upon it entirely. The charity of well-disposed people, indeed, supplies him with the whole fund of his subsistence. But though this principle ultimately provides him with all the necessities of life which he has occasion for, it neither does nor can provide him with them as he has occasion for them. The greater part of his occasional wants are supplied in the same manner as those of other people, by treaty, by barter, and by purchase. With the money which one man gives him he purchases food. The old cloaths which another bestows upon him he exchanges for other old cloaths which suit him better, or for lodging, or for food, or for money, with which he can buy either food, cloaths, or lodging, as he has occasion.

As it is by treaty, by barter, and by purchase, that we obtain from one another the greater part of those mutual good offices which we stand in need of, so it is this same trucking disposition which originally gives occasion to the division of labour. In a tribe of hunters or shepherds a particular person makes bows and arrows, for example, with more readiness and dexterity than any other. He frequently exchanges them for cattle or for venison with his companions; and he finds at last that he can in this manner get more cattle and venison, than if he himself went to the field to catch them. From a regard to his own interest, therefore, the making of bows and arrows grows to be his chief business, and he becomes a sort of armourer. Another excels in making the frames and covers of their little huts or moveable houses. He is accustomed to be of use in this way to his neighbours, who reward him in the same manner with cattle and with venison, till at last he finds it his interest to dedicate himself entirely to this employment, and to become a sort of house-carpenter. In the same manner a third becomes a smith or a brazier; a fourth a tanner or dresser of hides or skins, the principal part of the clothing of savages. And thus the certainty of being able to exchange all that surplus part of the produce of his own labour, which is over and above his own consumption, for such parts of the produce of other men's labour as he may have occasion for, encourages every man to apply himself to a particular occupation, and to cultivate and bring to perfection whatever talent or genius he may possess for that particular species of business.

The difference of natural talents in different men is, in reality, much less than we are aware of; and the very different genius which appears to distinguish men of different professions, when grown up to maturity, is not upon many occasions so much the cause, as the effect of the division of labour. The difference between the most dissimilar characters, between a philosopher and a common street porter, for example, seems to arise not so much from nature, as from habit, custom, and education. When they came into the world, and for the first six or eight years of their existence, they were, perhaps, very much alike, and neither their parents nor playfellows could perceive any remarkable difference. About that age, or soon after, they come to be employed in very different occupations. The difference of talents comes then to be taken notice of, and widens by degrees, till at last the vanity of the philosopher is willing to acknowledge scarce any resemblance. But without the disposition to truck, barter, and exchange, every man must have procured to himself every necessary and conveniency of life which he wanted. All must have had the same duties to perform, and the same work to do, and there could have been no such difference of employment as could alone give occasion to any great difference of talents.

As it is this disposition which forms that difference of talents, so remarkable among men of different professions, so it is this same disposition which renders that difference useful. Many tribes of animals acknowledged to be all of the same species, derive from nature a much more remarkable distinction of genius, than what, antecedent to custom and education, appears to take place among men. By nature a philosopher is not in genius and disposition half so different from a street porter, as a mastiff is from a greyhound, or a greyhound from a spaniel, or this last from a shepherd's dog. Those different tribes of animals, however, though all of the same species, are of scarce any use to one another. The strength of the mastiff is not in the least supported either by the swiftness of the greyhound, or by the sagacity of the spaniel, or by the docility of the shepherd's dog. The effects of those different geniuses and talents, for want of the power or disposition to barter and exchange, cannot be brought into a common stock, and do not in the least contribute to the better accommodation and conveniency of the species. Each animal is still obliged to support and defend itself, separately and independently, and derives no sort of advantage from that variety of talents with which nature has distinguished its fellows. Among men, on the contrary, the most dissimilar geniuses are of use to one another; the different produces of their respective talents, by the general disposition to truck, barter, and exchange, being brought, as it were, into a common stock, where every man may purchase whatever part of the produce of other men's talents he has occasion for.

As it is the power of exchanging that gives occasion to the division of labour, so the extent of this division must always be limited by the extent of that power, or, in other words, by the extent of the market. When the market is very small, no person can have any encouragement to dedicate himself entirely to one employment, for want of the power to exchange all that surplus part of the produce of his own labour, which is over and above his own consumption, for such parts of the produce of other men's labour as he has occasion for.

There are some sorts of industry, even of the lowest kind, which can be carried on no where but in a great town. A porter, for example, can find employment and subsistence in no other place. A village is by much too narrow a sphere for him; even an ordinary market town is scarce large enough to afford him constant occupation. In the lone houses and very small villages which are scattered about in so desert a country as the Highlands of Scotland, every farmer must be butcher, baker and brewer for his own family. In such situations we can scarce expect to find even a smith, a carpenter, or a mason, within less than twenty miles of another of the same trade. The scattered families that live at eight or ten miles distance from the nearest of them, must learn to perform themselves a great number of little pieces of work, for which, in more populous countries, they would call in the assistance of those workmen. Country workmen are almost every where obliged to apply themselves to all the different branches of industry that have so much affinity to one another as to be employed about the same sort of materials. A country carpenter deals in every sort of work that is made of wood: a country smith in every sort of work that is made of iron. The former is not only a carpenter, but a joiner, a cabinet maker, and even a carver in wood, as well as a wheelwright, a ploughwright, a cart and waggon maker. The employments of the latter are still more various. It is impossible there should be such a trade as even that of a nailer in the remote and inland parts of the Highlands of Scotland. Such a workman at the rate of a thousand nails a day, and three hundred days in the year, will make three hundred thousand nails in the year. But in such a situation it would be impossible to dispose of one thousand, that is, of one day's work in the year.

The general industry of the society never can exceed what the capital of the society can employ. As the number of workmen that can be kept in employment by any particular person must bear a certain proportion to his capital, so the number of those that can be continually employed by all the members of a great society, must bear a certain proportion to the whole capital of that society, and never can exceed that proportion. No regulation of commerce can increase the quantity of industry in any society beyond what its capital can maintain. It can only divert a part of it into a direction into which it might not otherwise have gone; and it is by no means certain that this artificial direction is likely to be more advantageous to the society than that into which it would have gone of its own accord.

Every individual is continually exerting himself to find out the most advantageous employment for whatever capital he can command. It is his own advantage, indeed, and not that of the society, which he has in view. But the study of his own advantage naturally, or rather necessarily leads him to prefer that employment which is most advantageous to the society.

The produce of industry is what it adds to the subject or materials upon which it is employed. In proportion as the value of this produce is great or small, so will likewise be the profits of the employer. But it is only for the sake of profit that any man employs a capital in the support of industry; and he will always, therefore, endeavour to employ it in the support of that industry of which the produce is likely to be of the greatest value, or to exchange for the greatest quantity either of money or of other goods.

But the annual revenue of every society is always precisely equal to the exchangeable value of the whole annual produce of its industry, or rather is precisely the same thing with that exchangeable value. As every individual, therefore, endeavours as much as he can both to employ his capital in the support of domestic industry, and so to direct that industry that its produce may be of the greatest value; every individual necessarily labours to render the annual revenue of the society as great as he can. He generally, indeed, neither intends to promote the public interest, nor knows how much he is promoting it. By preferring the support of domestic to that of foreign industry, he intends only his own security; and by directing that industry in such a manner as its produce may be of the greatest value, he intends only his own gain, and he is in this, as in many other cases, led by an invisible hand to promote an end which was no part of his intention. Nor is it always the worse for the society that it was no part of it. By pursuing his own interest he frequently promotes that of the society more effectually than when he really intends to promote it. I have never known much good done by those who affected to trade for the public good. It is an affectation, indeed, not very common among merchants, and very few words need be employed in dissuading them from it. ●

Section TWO

The Market and Individual Freedom

So long as effective freedom of exchange is maintained, the central feature of the market organization of economic activity is that it prevents one person from interfering with another in respect of most of his activities.

Milton Friedman

The private enterprise system is far superior to socialism in creating wealth. This is no small advantage, given the desire we all have for more goods and services. But the important argument in favor of private enterprise is not that it generates more material wealth. Even if the private enterprise system was no more efficient at transforming limited resources into valued products than socialism, there would still be a compelling case for private enterprise. Our individual freedoms are far more secure under a decentralized economic system based on private property than they are under a centralized economic system based on government control.

While we all agree that our freedom is important, few of us ever take time to reflect on how important. Like good health, freedom is seldom appreciated until we are deprived of it. The world is unfortunately full of examples of people who, deprived of freedom in their homeland, have been willing to forsake their material possessions, their family and friends, and often their very lives in the attempt to gain their freedom.

As valuable as freedom is for its own sake, however, it is important to recognize that it is no accident that freedom and prosperity typically go together. Indeed, freedom is a necessary ingredient for economic progress. It may be possible to have freedom without economic progress, but it is impossible to have genuine economic progress without freedom. The key to insuring that freedom is a force for prosperity is the existence of private property rights. When private property rights are protected and contracts enforced, individuals will exercise their freedom in ways that are responsive to the concerns of others. In the absence of effective private property rights, individuals cannot be depended upon to use their freedom responsibly, and social tolerance for individual freedom will erode. This goes a long way in explaining why our freedoms are more secure in an economic system based on private property and exchange than in an economic system that attempts to minimize the role of private property.

The unifying theme of the readings in this section is that the private market not only excels at producing wealth but is indispensible in the protection of freedom.

In the opening selection, James Doti provides for the reader a sense of the joy and wonder with which people who are not used to the freedom offered in America feel when they first experience it. Doti puts the reader in the shoes of an immigrant from Italy in the 1930s with a bittersweet exchange of letters between the immigrant and his Italian parents back home.

Dwight Lee considers the connection between individual responsibility and liberty in his article. Individual liberty can be tolerated only when the pursuit of self-interest promotes the general interest, as it is when subjected to the responsibility imposed by free market competition. Without the responsibility of the market place, individual freedom is not possible.

In the next selection, Milton Friedman argues that when economic freedom is denied by the state, as it necessarily is under socialism, political freedom is almost sure to be suppressed as well.

James Gwartney (1940–), a professor of economics at Florida State University in Tallahassee, traces in his writing the growth of freedom and prosperity associated with western civilization to the importance of private property in western traditions. By dispersing economic power and motivating productive use of scarce resources, private property has fostered a record of prosperity and freedom that is unmatched in human history. Yet, private property has been the object of numerous criticisms. Gwartney presents these criticisms fairly and refutes them convincingly.

While visiting at the University of Chicago during the 1950s, Hayek continued his writing on some of the central issues of economics: what are the economic and political institutions that allow free individuals to cooperate productively with one another, how did those institutions come into being, and how are they maintained? During this time Hayek wrote *The Constitution of Liberty* which stands as a major contribution to our understanding of political economy. Hayek's selection here, which is taken from *The Constitution of Liberty*, explains why we realize far more from freedom than most of us realize. As Hayek points out, "The benefits I derive from freedom are thus largely the result of the uses of freedom by others, and mostly of those uses of freedom that I could never avail myself of."

Ludwig von Mises (1881–1973) had a long and productive career as an economist, both in Europe and the United States where he immigrated in 1940. He was a major contributor to what is known as the Austrian School of Economics, so named because it grew out of the work of Austrian economists. A major tenet of Austrian economics is that the information necessary to make economic decisions appropriately is based on the subjective evaluations of individuals and can never be collected and quantified in ways that allow central authorities to direct economic activity efficiently. In the last selection of this section, von Mises considers how private property protects freedom and provides the necessary information, in the form of monetary prices, for people to pursue their own objectives efficiently and in harmony with others pursuing their objectives. This information is impossible for socialist economic planners to obtain and utilize for reasons von Mises explains. ●

7.   Io Leggo e Scrivo

James L. Doti

Giuseppe Doti was a reader and writer. He had other jobs that paid money, but when asked what he did for a living, he would say, "Io leggo e scrivo."

After emigrating to America, he found his ability to read and write a rare talent in the Chicago community known as Little Italy. Illiterate immigrants needed a sympathetic soulmate to read and write letters passing to and from the old country. His letters arranged marriages, kept waiting wives and lovers content and, in general, soothed the ravaged nerves and aching anxieties of disconnected people.

In reading and writing letters, Giuseppe grew to understand the very soul of a person. His ability in conveying a person's passions and petty pretentions with dignity and spirit made him a reader and writer of the first rank. Giuseppe was conscious of his high calling and devoted following, and he dressed the part.

Upon returning home in the evening after work, Giuseppe had his dinner and then his toilet. After meticulously grooming himself and spending an inordinate amount of time trimming a Hitleresque-style mustache instead of the hair he no longer had, he would put on a freshly laundered white shirt and starched collar. Giuseppe always wore a maroon tie that he felt complimented his piercing blue eyes. The double-breasted tweed suit he generally wore made him appear even shorter and stouter than he actually was. And although he had a noticeable limp from a stroke he suffered several years earlier when he was 63, Giuseppe forsook the use of a cane which he felt to be more suitable for a person much older than he.

Every evening he listened to the phonograph that invariably played a Puccini or Verdi opera between seven thirty and eight o'clock, but at eight o'clock sharp, he retired to a back room of his humble flat to receive his clients.

They would come and sit expectantly in the kitchen, clutching their letters, anxiously awaiting the reading that would relieve or justify their heaviest anxieties. Upon entering the back room, they would clasp Giuseppe's hand in

Reprinted from *The Freeman*, August, 1990, pp. 284-288, by permission of the Foundation for Economic Education.

both of theirs and then silently present a nonmonetary offering. Feigning surprise, Giuseppe would refuse acceptance of the offering until the giver's insistence reached the appropriate level of intensity. At that point, the charade would end by Giuseppe humbly tilting his head and bowing in acceptance.

The abundant quantities of homemade wines, basement cured salami, prosciutto and mortadella, dried pepperulo, canned giardiniera, and aged provolone cheese amassed by Giuseppe were ceremoniously doled out by his wife Irena to their children and grandchildren. Irena drew the line once when she refused to admit into their flat a recent immigrant who brought a live chicken as a token of appreciation. When word of this spread through Little Italy, the neighbors reinforced their opinion that Irena's noble lineage made her too proud to dress a chicken.

Giuseppe had already taken care of three clients when he got up to greet Bruno Pucci, a recent immigrant, bearing a crumpled letter and bottle of homemade chianti. For once, Giuseppe was greatly pleased to receive an offering. It was well known that Bruno Pucci's family made the finest wine in Little Italy.

Bruno sat and looked at the room around him. Unlike most Italian-decorated rooms that were thick with a plethora of heavy furniture and religious ornamentation, this room was sparsely furnished with a card table and two chairs. The room was illuminated by a single light bulb dangling at the end of a three foot cord. Two yellowed etchings, one of Marcus Aurelius and the other of Dante Alighieri, ornamented the heavily cracked walls.

Handing the letter to Giuseppe, Bruno said, "I'm worried about Italia, Signore Doti. They vote for Mussolini, and who knows what that jackass is gonna do."

After carefully unfolding the letter and slowly putting on his wire-rimmed reading glasses, Giuseppe read the letter to himself. If there were deaths or other tragedies to report, Giuseppe wanted to be prepared. This was a practice he learned several months earlier after reporting the death of a woman's ninety-eight year old aunt. Upon hearing of her aunt's untimely demise, the lady fell to the floor and began a rhythmic wailing that continued even as her relatives dragged her out of the flat.

The letter from Bruno Pucci's father to Giuseppe's relief had no deaths to report. He poured Bruno a glass of wine and pushed a platter of freshly baked biscotti toward him. Giuseppe then read in Italian:

March 13, 1936

My dear son,

Italia is changing. We don't have to put up with King Victor Emmanuel and his national assembly. We voted for Il Duce Mussolini and his party and hope things will change for the better. He made the trains run on time, won the war in Abyssinia and now that his party controls the national assembly, we think he will make our country work. You should return to your homeland and family and be part of a new Italia.

Giuseppe recognized the work of another reader and writer, Vito Abboduto, a competent writer to be sure but one whose maudlin style injected into the letters a more depressing mood than even the dour Italian peasants were inclined to exhibit. Giuseppe continued reading to Bruno.

Mussolini's party bosses came to our town last week and told us we can increase our wine production by everyone working together. So instead of each family making wine, we will all work together. The party bosses promised us that the government will buy all the wine our town makes at top dollar if we turn over all our equipment to the state. A workers' representative will be in charge of making the wine, but each family will have one vote to reelect him or throw him out at the end of the year.

I have been told to work on the grape-crushing unit. I will miss making our family wine, but we will make more money by working with the government.

Your mother misses you and cannot understand why you left us. She is worried you are not eating enough, and it is too cold in Chicago. You are too young at 34 years old to be away from home. The women here in Italia make better wives and are not so independent as in America. We heard of a woman in America who left her husband because she would not shine his shoes. What kind of world is that?

Come home my son. Our cousin, Tito Cimino, the local constable, promised me he can get you an easy job that pays well on the grape-picking unit. Your mother and father need you, my son. We are sending you a large photograph of us so you don't forget us.

Your loving father

When Giuseppe stopped reading he looked and saw in Bruno Pucci's catatonic stare the burden of guilt that seemed to smother the lives of so many recent immigrants. Giuseppe said nothing and waited for Bruno to speak. When he did, he spoke slowly and softly with his tear-filled eyes pointed toward the floor.

"Signore Doti, I look at that picture they send me and my father looks at me like I killed somebody and my mother looks like she's gonna die. But I can't go back. Please write a letter for me."

Giuseppe picked up his Schaeffer fountain pen and began to write the words Bruno spoke in Italian.

April 23, 1936

My dear Mama and Papa,

I eat well. Uncle Rocco and Aunt Maria take good care of me. It is good to be with family here. I help Uncle Rocco make wine at night and work at his grocery store during the day.

Yesterday we threw out a batch of wine when we found dead rats that fell in the fermenting vat and drowned. I told Uncle Rocco that no one would know any difference when they taste the wine, but Uncle Rocco said our family honor is at stake.

Bruno caught Giuseppe suspiciously eyeing the bottle of wine he had brought and said, "No Signore Doti, don't worry. I brought you good wine. We dumped the bad wine down the sewer."

Giuseppe raised his hands deferentially to indicate no concern on his part but at the same time decided to tell Irena to give the gift bottle of wine to his newest son-in-law, Fiore.

Bruno took out a folded money order from his wallet and sliding it over to Giuseppe continued his letter.

Because we lost so much wine with the rats, I can only send you a little money this time. Next time I send you more.

Your loving son,
Bruno

•   •   •

Giuseppe had almost forgotten about wine, Mussolini, and rats when Bruno returned letter in hand more than half a year later. This time Bruno did not bring wine but two tickets to the Friday night fights that he inserted in the palm of Giuseppe's hand. Giuseppe who hated violence of any kind, including boxing, was thinking of what son-in-law to pass the tickets onto as he led Bruno to the back room.

Giuseppe silently accepted the letter that Bruno had shakily handed to him. The fact that there were no stamps on the envelope was an indication that the letter had been smuggled out of Italy. This was a common practice ever since Mussolini's secret police started routinely censoring letters mailed out of the country.

As he read the letter to himself, Giuseppe decided to prepare Bruno for the unhappy contents by sighing audibly and shaking his head several times in disbelief. Giuseppe was not being inconsiderate. He had long ago discovered that people are much happier receiving news that was not as bad as they had imagined after observing his exaggerated lamentations.

Then he began to read to Bruno.

October 2, 1936

My dear son,

Things are terrible here. Food and coal are scarce. Thank God our cousin Tito Cimino gives us extra rations or else I don't know how we would survive.

We increased wine production this year, but the government did not pay us much for it. I don't blame them. It is terrible wine. We picked the grapes too early when they were still watery. We told the workers' representative that this would make terrible wine with no character. But we make more wine that way, and he has a production quota to fill.

Now we can't get rid of the workers' representative. We all vote for him even though he is an idiot. He controls all the jobs, wages and favors. So what can we do? Nobody can travel anywhere even to find work in other cities without his approval. We can't even make our own wine anymore since we gave our press, grinder and fermentation vats to the government. So nothing is ours anymore. That is why we bow and scrape to all the party officials so our meager existence does not become even worse than it already is.

Poor Italia is going to the dogs. And we keep voting to give that jackass Il Duce more and more power. To get anything nowadays, you have to know people in the government, and then when they do you a favor, you belong to them and they have your vote.

Since the secret police censor all the letters now, I had to wait for a friend who was returning to America to bring this letter to you. The government also owns all the newspapers now. That is how they control everything that is written. The big crowds that cheer "Duce" are there because the party bosses force the owners to let their workers attend the rallies. But things keep getting worse and worse.

Cousin Tito can still use his pull to get you a job if you want to come back. Your mother does the wash for the local party official, so we can also get favors from him. Mother worries about you being away from us. But as bad as things are here, maybe it is better that you stay in America.

Our love to your Zio Rocco and Zia Maria. I don't know what your mother would do if she didn't know you were being taken care of by family.

Your loving father

When Giuseppe had finished reading the letter, he left the room to leave Bruno with his private thoughts. He returned with a bowl of chestnuts that Irena had just roasted.

After grabbing several chestnuts, Bruno said, "Our family makes the best wine in Italia. Now wadda they gonna do?"

Realizing that Bruno did not want his questions answered, Giuseppe asked if he wanted to send a letter.

"Si, Signore Doti. But please you write the letter. Tell them that you have opportunity in America. Tell them that I love America and cannot go back."

He gave Giuseppe a money order to enclose with the letter and then he left the flat after placing a handful of chestnuts in his pocket.

Giuseppe would be able to write the letter for Bruno. For like Bruno, he had left his own parents to make a new home in America. He knew the pain and guilt one felt in leaving one's parents and homeland. He knew the fear and isolation one felt in arriving in a new land where an unknown language was spoken and an unknown people lived. And he knew both the exhilaration and intimidation one felt in experiencing a new found freedom that made it possible to succeed or fail on a grand scale. So he knew what Bruno was feeling and he wrote.

December 2, 1936

My dear Mama and Papa,

I cry when I hear of your struggle. Sometimes I dream how good it would be if you were here to share our lives together in my new country, America. I dream you are here to taste the freedom I have tasted and see the opportunities I have seen.

America is a nation of justice. Like Italia, there are crooked politicians and government bureaucrats with their palms out asking for favors. But we have rights that protect us from their injustice.

America is a nation of hope. Like Italia, there are people who look down on others because of their family background and education. But we have opportunities that make it possible to improve ourselves so we can live better lives.

Life is not easy here. I have a job, go to school, help Uncle Rocco make wine and take extra work when I can get it. But for the first time in my life I don't feel the system holding me back. So while you say Tito Cimino can get me a job, he cannot give me the hope and dreams I have for a better life. A job in Italia is a way to put food on the table, but a job in America is a way to get a better job.

When Mussolini came to power, you had dreams for a better Italia, an Italia where the government would help the people lead better lives. I too remember the rising expectations of people every time we had a new national assembly under King Victor Emmanual. But I grew frustrated when each government took more from the people than it gave.

In America, we rely on ourselves, not a government, to improve ourselves. We are in control of our destiny. And while this freedom places additional responsibility on us for what we do with our lives, it is better than placing false hopes in others.

Many people say America is great because everyone has the right to vote. But I remember we voted in Italia and things always got worse instead of better. What makes America great is not our right to vote but the rights we have that protect us from those for whom we vote.

I hope and pray you will understand why I will not return to our beloved homeland. Please always know that my love and thoughts are with you.

Your loving son,
Bruno

Giuseppe lit his pipe and began reading the letter to himself. As he read, distant memories of his parents and homeland were reawakened. Giuseppe found it strange that though his parents had died long ago, he still felt a heavy burden of guilt for having left them.

It was late. The rest of the flat was dark and quiet. Giuseppe wearily got up and turned down the space heater before joining Irena in bed. As he fell asleep, his last waking thoughts were his hope that Vito Abboduto would read the letter to Bruno's mother and father with the same intensity and emotion that it was written. ●

8. Liberty and Individual Responsibility

Dwight R. Lee

Liberty is both a highly valued outcome of a beneficent political economy and an essential ingredient into it. In some respects a consideration of the role of liberty as both output and input is straightforward. Limited government, serving to maintain the legal environment necessary for an economic order based on private property and voluntary exchange, provides fertile ground for individual liberty. And the lifeblood of a political economy characterized by limited government, private property, and voluntary exchange, is the flow of information that can be provided only when individuals possess a full measure of political and economic liberty.

However, a careful examination of how a political economy based on classical liberal principles both nourishes, and is nourished by, individual liberty reveals a complicated interaction between the social institutions necessary for liberty and the exercise of liberty. The exercise of liberty, unless tempered by a responsibility that can never be imposed entirely by a force external to the ethical convictions of the individual, will with time undermine the social institutions upon which liberty depends. A careful study of the political economy of liberty contains within it a warning of just how fragile is the foundation upon which liberty stands.

Scarcity, Rules, and Liberty

In order to examine the connections between economics, politics, and liberty, it is useful to consider first the most fundamental of economic problems. That problem is scarcity. In a world without scarcity each of us could be entirely independent of others. Each individual could exercise complete freedom in a broad range of activities and have no impact whatsoever on anyone else. Because we live in a world of scarcity, individuals must interact with one

---

Reprinted from *The Freeman*, April, 1987, pp. 126-133, by permission of the Foundation for Economic Education.

another, and this interaction is shaped by rules of social conduct. Such rules impose restrictions on the activities of individuals and establish the important distinction between liberty and license. Without the restrictions imposed by such rules, scarcity itself would impose on us an even more confining set of restrictions.

Consider the fact that although scarcity makes cooperation desirable, it makes competition inevitable. Each of us wants more than he has, and the only way to get more is by competing against others for control over limited resources. Competition is commonly seen as the source of a host of social ills, with the replacement of competition by cooperation suggested as necessary for social improvement. What this view fails to recognize is that competition is not the cause, but rather the consequence, of the ultimate social ill, namely scarcity. With no way to eliminate scarcity, the important question is not how to prevent competition, but how to provide rules for social conduct that motivate the type of competitive behavior which leads to productive and cooperative outcomes. Competition can be either productive or destructive, depending on the rules that define permissible limits in our dealings with one another.

Consider the possibility of no rules, or more accurately the rule of force. Everyone would be free to do whatever he wanted as long as he possessed the power to force his will on others. In this setting, people would be forced to compete through the exercise of unrestrained brute strength and there would be no freedom in the meaningful sense of "independence of the arbitrary will of another."*

If one person had enough physical power he could force others to work for him without compensation, to be his slave. But the master today has no assurance that he will not be someone else's slave tomorrow.

Neither is the rule of force likely to motivate productive and cooperative outcomes. There would be little motivation to devote one's effort to the production of wealth since there would exist no protections against its forcible expropriation by others. Competing successfully would depend more on developing the skills needed for plundering and defending against plunder than on developing the skills needed to produce wealth. Even if one were able to survive in such a social environment, one's standard of living would be low. With resources being devoted overwhelmingly to predation and protection from the predatory activity of others, little would be produced and poverty would be the norm. Life in such a Hobbesian jungle would indeed be "solitary, poor, nasty, brutish, and short."

Freedom from rules is simply not a viable social possibility. In a society without rules there would be little prosperity and no genuine freedom.

---

*   The usefulness of this definition of freedom is explained by F. A. Hayek in his *The Constitution of Liberty* (The University of Chicago Press, 1960). See especially chapters 1 and 2.

Social Order at the Sacrifice of Liberty

Emergence from the Hobbesian jungle, which finds a "war of each against all," is necessary if we are to realize the benefits of a civil social order. Underlying any beneficent social order are rules that will impose limits on individual behavior. All rules serve to limit freedom of action. However, when rules are applied generally they can, by limiting the actions of each in predictable ways, expand the liberty of all.*

On the other hand, when they become too numerous and detailed, rules can destroy liberty just as surely and effectively as no rules. And the tendency is in the direction of too many rules. Traditionally the obsession within societies has been the horrors of disorder. With plunder, riot, rape, mayhem, and murder the common experience, the loss of liberty has been seen as the unavoidable cost of escaping disorder. The prevalent human condition throughout history has been subjugation to rigid and brutally enforced rules that specify the type and location of one's work, travel, religious practices, and even social status. The overriding problem of society has been that of maintaining order, and only the most limited amount of liberty has been considered compatible with this objective.

While a rigid social order based on detailed rules concerning every aspect of behavior may be preferred to the chaos that would prevail in the absence of all rules, the shortcomings of such a social order are apparent. The first problem is to find leaders who can be trusted with the power that has to be exercised in a totally controlled society. Such power is subject to enormous abuse. Those who have such power are in a position to advance their interests at the expense of their subjects, and will seldom be able to resist the temptation to do so. The only possible advantage an all powerful government has over anarchy is that the exercise of government power is visible. Moving from the anarchy of no rules to the detailed control of leviathan government is to substitute one thief in the light for many thieves in the night.

The cost in terms of sacrificed liberty is much the same regardless of whether it is sacrificed to anarchy or to unlimited government. One who finds himself forced to toil for the benefit of others is not likely to care who his masters are —

---

* In the words of John Locke, "The end of law is not to abolish or restrain but to preserve and enlarge freedom; for in all the states of created beings capable of laws, where there is no law, there is no freedom. For liberty is to be free from the restraint and violence of others, which cannot be when there is no law; but freedom is not, as we are told, a liberty for everyman to do what he lists. For who can be free, when every other man's humor might domineer over him?" See John Locke, *The Second Treatise of Government*, ed. by Thomas P. Perdon (New York: The Liberal Arts Press, Inc., 1954), pp. 32-33.

the physically dominant brutes in the "jungle" or the politically dominant brutes in the government.

So, traditionally, the social choice appeared to have been between some combination of two undesirable states: the regimentation of detailed rules or the lack of social order. Society could have less of one only at the cost of having more of the other. There appeared to be no realistic hope that individuals living together in a world of scarcity could simultaneously have both more liberty and more social order. It was in the seventeenth and eighteenth centuries that philosophers began to give serious consideration to a structure of rules that offered the possibility of overcoming this social dilemma.*

The Rule of Private Property

It was the writings of John Locke, Adam Smith, Bernard Mandeville, and other seventeenth-and eighteenth-century philosophers that gave modern birth to the ideal of compatibility between individual liberty and social order. Crucial to this ideal was a fundamental conceptual shift regarding the role of rules. Social rules were traditionally seen as necessary to force particular outcomes which were required if a productive social order was to be maintained. Fields had to be tilled, cloth had to be woven, cattle had to be tended, and particular services had to be rendered. Concentrating authority in the hands of a ruler who could require these things to be done was seen as the only guarantee that they would be done. The fundamental insight of the aforementioned philosophers was that establishing general rules of social conduct, which ignored particular outcomes, could create an environment in which desirable outcomes emerged from the exercise of individual liberty.

Crucial to this liberating view of social order are rules which clearly define individual rights by providing assurances that individuals can plan and carry out their activities without the return to their activities being arbitrarily confiscated by others. Lacking such assurances, little motivation exists for people to be productive and no basis exists for them to interact with each other in a civil manner.

The rule of private property can now be seen as crucial to the goal of a productive social order that is compatible with, indeed dependent upon, individual liberty. The rule of private property requires that individual rights to property be well defined and subject to transfer from one individual to another

---

* The first recorded awareness that individual liberty could be expanded under a set of universally applied rules (the rule of law) comes from the ancient Greeks, particularly the Athenians during the fifth and fourth centuries B.C. The Greek ideals of liberty were kept alive by Roman writers, such as Cicero, whose work was important to the modern development of classical liberal principles.

by mutual consent of both parties. When liberties are constrained only by the broad limits imposed by the rule of private property, then a system of social communication and cooperation is established within which the liberty of each individual is compatible with the liberty of all. Indeed, under the rule of private property the liberty exercised by one expands the options over which liberty can be exercised by all.*

The social cooperation facilitated by the rule of private property, though well known to all serious students of economics, is sufficiently relevant to a consideration of liberty to deserve discussion. When property is privately owned and voluntarily exchanged, market prices emerge. These prices are the means by which each market participant communicates to all other market participants the value he places on the marginal units of goods.

Property Encourages Honesty

In addition to creating a truly impressive network of communication, private property motivates an equally impressive degree of honesty. Honesty can be expected to prevail since it is in no one's interest to be dishonest about the price one is willing to pay. The self-interest of market participants ensures that they will assess carefully the value they expect to realize from an incremental unit of each good, and then communicate their desire for more only if the incremental unit is worth more to them than the prevailing market price.** Furthermore, each participant in this communication process is motivated to act *as if* one gives the concerns of others the same consideration one gives one's own. When an individual reduces consumption of a product in response to an increase in its price, that person is in effect saying, "Others are saying to me that this product is worth more to them at the margin than it is to me, so I will consume less so they can consume more."

This system of communication and cooperation obviously does not work with perfection. However, even when full recognition is given to what has become known as "market failure," any impartial evaluation must acknowledge that the benefits derived from the rule of private property, and the derivative market process, cannot even remotely be duplicated by any known alternative social rule, or set of rules. Because the information and incentives generated by market competition allow each of us to interact cooperatively and honestly with

---

*   As Hayek points out, "The benefits I derive from freedom are thus largely the result of the uses of freedom by others, and mostly of those uses of freedom that I could never avail myself of." F. A. Hayek, *op. cit.*; p. 32.

**   Under certain conditions it is obviously possible for sellers to benefit by misrepresenting their products. But just as obvious is the fact that this problem is mitigated by market forces. Also, specific market arrangements tend to develop that reduce the seller's potential to gain from fraud, because both buyer and seller can benefit from such arrangements. For a useful discussion of such arrangements, and the theory behind them, see Benjamin Kelin and Keith Leffler, "The Role of Market Forces in Assuring Contractual Performance," *Journal of Political Economy* (August 1981), pp. 615-41.

literally millions of people around the globe, we are able to specialize our efforts, direct resources into their most productive uses, and thus generate enormous wealth.

Surely more important than the wealth generated under a system of private property and market exchange is the individual liberty that this system permits. The rule of private property makes it possible to allow people a large measure of liberty because this rule makes people accountable for the consequences of their decisions. Every time an individual puts a resource to use, a cost is imposed; that cost being measured in terms of the value of the resource in the highest valued alternative use. When an individual owns a resource he is fully accountable for this cost, since his use of the resource requires the sacrifice of the highest amount someone else is willing to pay for it. Given this accountability there is no harm, and indeed much benefit, in giving individuals wide latitude to use resources as they choose.

In the absence of private property rights there is a constant clamoring, often with justification, for detailed restrictions on individual behavior. Consider, for example, the fact that it is difficult in the extreme to divide up and parcel out the atmosphere as private property. As a consequence, the atmosphere is a common property resource and individuals are not held accountable for the costs being generated when they use the atmosphere as a receptacle for their auto exhaust, or industrial smoke. The result is broad public acceptance of huge Federal and state bureaucracies imposing a host of detailed restrictions on our behavior in the name of forcing us to act in environmentally responsible ways.

Eliminate the accountability provided by the rule of private property and you eliminate the very basis upon which people can be tolerant of the freedom of others. A reduction in the scope of individual liberty, with detailed directives and regulations replacing general rules of social conduct, is the certain consequence of either the inability or the unwillingness to rely on private property and voluntary exchange to order economic activity.

The Need for Government

The advantages we realize from observing the rule of private property are general advantages. The rule of private property is not designed to generate particular outcomes or to allow particular individuals to benefit at the expense of others. Rather it allows the liberty necessary to accomplish objectives that on balance benefit us all, but which no one could have predicted or programmed ahead of time. However, unless each of us refrains from attempting to infringe upon the property rights of others, the general advantages realized from an economic process which fosters both the production of wealth and a social tolerance for liberty will be diminished for everyone.

Unfortunately, even though we become collectively worse off when property rights are violated, it is possible for each individual to improve his situation by infringing on the property of others. The only parasite on a healthy organism is in an enviable position. It is true that if there is a multitude of parasites attempting to free ride on the same organism no one benefits; the organism perishes, as do the parasites. But this elementary fact provides little motivation for any one individual to cease being a parasite and turn to productive activity. Each individual recognizes that denying oneself the immediate gains from plunder will do nothing to preserve the benefits derived from private property and voluntary exchange if there is a general failure to respect property rights. Indeed, in a world where everyone is engaged in plunder it would be the height of folly for an individual to confine one's efforts to productive activity.

In other words, the free and productive social order based on private property and voluntary exchange is a public good; a good which when available to one is available to all. As with any public good it has to be paid for by the contributions of individuals, contributions which in this case take the form of sacrificing opportunities to infringe on the property rights of others. As is the case with all public goods, each individual faces the tempting possibility of free riding on the contributions of others. Since individuals know that they can benefit from the free and productive social order that is being paid for by the restraint of others, whether they restrain themselves or not, when left entirely to individual choice we can expect too little respect for private property rights.

Faced with the problem of maintaining social order, each individual is generally willing to exercise restraint if, by agreeing to do so, everyone else is made to do the same. Such collective respect for private property rights has the potential for making everyone better off and, with good prospects for enforcement, will be agreed to almost universally. Enforcement of the social rules of the game is essential here, and it is the need for such enforcement that provides the rationale for the monopoly in coercion which is granted to government.

It is the legitimate role of government to exercise its power in order to serve as an impartial referee who knows the rules of the game, observes the play of the participants, and imposes penalties on those who violate the rules. Good government, as a good referee, does not strive for particular results, but is concerned solely with facilitating the interaction of individuals each of whom is free to pursue his own purposes as long as he operates within the limits established by the agreed upon set of rules.

By enforcing the rule of private property, government is both performing as a referee and requiring that those who benefit from a free and productive social order contribute their part in maintaining it. Those who persist in violating the property rights of others will, if government is doing its job, be denied their liberty through imprisonment. This has the effect of converting the public good provided by respect for private property into a price-excludable public good. That is, those who do not pay the price are excluded from the benefits.

Up to this point the discussion has been concerned primarily with the protective or rule enforcement role of government. The government has to enforce general rules if liberty and social order are to be maintained. In this capacity the government makes no choices in the sense of weighing the benefits and costs of alternatives. It has only to determine if the rules are being obeyed and to take predetermined measures if they are not. The discussion has, however, touched on a further function of government. Public goods other than social order exist, and the government is also the institution through which members of the community decide which of these goods to finance publicly, and how extensively they should be funded. In this capacity, government is called upon to make genuine economic choices, and to engage in directly productive activities.*

The Need to Control Government

The government is then more than the referee in the game; it is a participating player as well. In its capacity as a player, government is also subject to rules. This situation presents some rather difficult problems. The fact is that the government is necessarily exempt from certain rules that apply to all other players in the game. The government, in one sense, has the authority to violate property rights by forcing citizens to pay for certain public goods. One can argue that this is not really a violation of property rights since everyone is part of the collective process in which the decision to provide public goods is made and goods are provided in return for payments rendered. This argument notwithstanding, it remains true that government's legal power to compel people to make payments places it outside the rules that apply to private individuals and organizations.

Not only does government enter into the game under less restrictive rules than are imposed on nongovernment players, but since it is government that enforces the rules on all, it is government that enforces the rules on itself. Letting a player in any game be the judge of his own infractions creates an opportunity for abuse that few can be expected to resist. Of course, the government is not a single player but rather a collection of the members of the community. Even so, in their roles as political decision makers individuals will coalesce around certain objectives and will be tempted to take whatever action is necessary to realize their objectives. Whether acting individually or in groups, people find fewer things easier to do than justify in their minds those actions that advance their interests. As a player in the game the government has to be called to task for violations of the rules just as other players; but how can we be sure that the government will be sufficiently diligent in calling infractions and imposing penalties against itself?

The problem here was clearly seen by James Madison when, in arguing for ratification of the United States Constitution, he wrote:

If men were angels, no government would be necessary. If angels were

---

*   Buchanan makes a clear distinction between the rule of enforcement role of government and the role of government as economic decision maker in his discussion of "the protective state" and "the productive state." See James M. Buchanan, *The Limits of Liberty: Between Anarchy and Leviathan* (Chicago: The University of Chicago Press, 1975), Chapter 4.

to govern men, neither external nor internal controls on government would be necessary. In framing a government which is to be administered by men over men, the great difficulty lies in this: You must first enable the government to control the governed; and in the next place, oblige it to control itself.*

Obliging government to control itself is no easy task. Government power, unless tightly circumscribed, creates opportunities for some to benefit at the expense of others through involuntary transfers. This abuse of government power tends to feed upon itself. First, government transfers reduce the private return from producing new wealth and increase the private return from acquiring or protecting existing wealth through political influence. This shift in relative returns draws more people out of productive activity and into political activity, which shifts relative returns yet further in favor of the latter. Second, government transfer activity is destructive of the accountability that characterizes an economic order operating in accordance with the rule of private property. As this accountability is reduced, the very basis for individual liberty is also reduced, and there will be increased pressure for yet broader government control on individual behavior. The power needed by government to maintain a free social order can easily become the force that undermines that order.

Our liberty and prosperity depend on general rules of social conduct. It is government's legitimate function to enforce those rules, as well as to provide a limited number of public goods. In order for government to perform its role properly, the conduct of government also has to be disciplined by general rules. It is important that these rules on government are obeyed. No society will long remain free unless they are. But how do we impose the discipline on government to get it to enforce these rules on itself and ensure that government power is not used to destroy the very liberty it is supposed to protect?

Constitutional Limits and the Limits of Constitutions

The only genuine hope for controlling government is through constitutional limits on government activity and constitutionally grounded procedures for operating within those limits. It is only by elevating these limits and procedures to the constitutional level that there can be any real prospect of immunizing them against the special interest pressures of ordinary politics.

But while the constitutional approach is the only one that holds promise for limiting government power and for making this power a positive rather than a negative force for freedom, constitutions by no means provide an easy or assured route to responsible government. An effective constitution cannot be created simply by writing words on parchment. The U.S. Constitution, surely the most effective and durable written constitution in history, has served as the

---

*   Federalist 51, *The Federalist Papers.*

model constitution (sometimes being copied nearly verbatim) for numerous political regimes around the world. Few of these cloned constitutions have been particularly durable or effective. A successful constitution has to be derived from customs, beliefs, and ethical understandings that are rooted in a pre-existing social order. A constitution can serve effectively to guard against only those abuses of government power that are widely recognized as abuses. If battered by the force of public approval of particular government practices, constitutional barriers against those practices will soon be breached. As observed by Henry Simons: "Constitutional provisions are no stronger than the moral consensus that they articulate. At best, they can only check abuses of power until moral pressure is mobilized; and their check must become ineffective if often overtly used."*

There can be no doubt, for example, that the success of the U.S. Constitution derived from the fact that it was the product of intense and widespread public concern for individual liberty. The 55 delegates to the constitutional convention who met in Philadelphia during the summer of 1787 were not operating from a clean slate. For at least two decades interest in securing liberty had been elevated to an obsession among the American people. According to a colonist writing in 1768, "Never was there a People whom it more immediately concerned to search into the Nature and Extent of their Rights and Privileges than it does the People of America at this Day."**

Edmond Burke noted before the House of Commons in 1775 that extensive study of law and politics had made them acutely inquisitive and sensitive about their liberties.*** An outpouring of writing, taking the form of everything from political tracts by the unlettered to celebrated contributions to political philosophy by the intellectual luminaries of the day, was manifestation of the public concerns that found expression in the U.S. Constitution. The protection of liberty was the pre-eminent concern, a concern that saw government power as a necessary evil and discretionary government power as an unmitigated evil.

There is no way of shifting to a constitution the responsibility for protecting individual liberty against the abuse of government power. Liberty will not long survive the absence of effective constitutional limits on government, but constitutional limits on government will not long remain effective in the absence of public approval of those limits.

---

*   Henry C. Simons, *Economic Policy for a Free Society* (Chicago: University of Chicago Press, 1951), p. 20.
**   Quoted in Clinton Rossiter, *Seedtime of the Republic: The Origin of the American Tradition of Political Liberty* (New York: Harcourt, Brace, and World, Inc., 1953), p. 362.
***   See Gordon S. Wood, *The Creation of the American Republic, 1776-1787*, (Chapel Hill: The University of North Carolina Press, 1969), pp. 4-5.

Individual Responsibility and Political Restraint

Public approval of constitutional limits that make liberty possible depends ultimately on individuals accepting responsibility for the consequences of exercising that liberty. Responsibility has no meaning in the absence of individual liberty, but liberty has no future in the absence of individual responsibility. In the words of Hayek, "A free society will not function or maintain itself unless its members regard it as right that each individual occupy the position that results from his action and accept it as due to his own action."*

This sense of individual responsibility is not easily maintained. As Hayek also points out, liberty "can offer to the individual only chances and . . . the outcome of his efforts will depend on innumerable accidents, . . ."** When an individual suffers a setback it is always possible for him to find plausible reasons for absolving himself of responsibility. The temptation is strong to petition government for relief through exemptions from the rules of the game that apply to everyone else. The individual may recognize that if such exemptions were generalized everyone would be worse off, but still feel sincerely that in his particular case special treatment is fully justified.

When politicians begin exceeding their constitutional authority in order to provide special assistance to the few, they soon find it impossible to avoid providing special assistance to the many. The sense of individual responsibility that is the only effective bulwark against the abuse of government power will quickly break down in the face of that abuse. Few people retain a strong sense of responsibility for their actions when those around them are seeking to avoid this responsibility through political influence. The destructive dynamic here is clear. An expanding government weakens the sense of individual responsibility, and results in more demands on government and yet further government expansion. And, by increasing the opportunities for people to benefit at the expense of others, an expanding government weakens the rule of private property and thus undermines the accountability upon which individual liberty depends.

There is every reason for concern that the size of government in the western democracies has reached the point of posing a threat to the long tradition of liberty that has made these democracies beacons of hope throughout the world. Underlying this development is a fundamental shift in the way the public views government. Rather than seeing government power as a threat that is socially beneficent only when tightly circumscribed, discretionary government power in pursuit of particular ends is now widely seen as the primary force for social progress.

---

*   Hayek, *op. cit.*, p. 71.

**   Hayek, *op. cit.*, p. 71. While acknowledging here the obvious fact that no one can be in complete control of the outcomes that affect him, Hayek continues with the observation that when an individual has to accept responsibility for those outcomes, "it forcefully directs his attention to those circumstances that he can control as if they were the only ones that mattered."

The surface consequences of this shift in responsibility from the individual to the state are clear enough. Expanding budgets and chronic deficits have become ubiquitous features of the modern welfare state, and have raised concern that this fiscal irresponsibility creates the potential for economic adversity. The most troubling thing about chronic budget deficits, however, is not their adverse economic consequences, but the fact that they reflect our inability to exercise political restraint. There is much discussion of the financial burdens our lack of fiscal responsibility is imposing on future generations. But our lack of fiscal responsibility derives from a general lack of political restraint that portends a far greater burden on the yet unborn than the obligation to pay our debts. That burden is the loss of liberty that we enjoy today because of the political restraint exercised by our ancestors, but which cannot long survive our political intemperance.

Conclusion

Liberty is possible only when adherence to general rules of conduct makes the regimentation of detailed directives and restrictions unnecessary for the maintenance of social order. Liberty can never be license since the unrestrained use of liberty quickly and surely renders inoperative the general rules upon which it is based. The ideal setting for liberty is one in which individuals have internalized an ethic of responsibility and restraint that motivates voluntary compliance with society's general rules. It is because this ideal can never be fully realized, however, that government is granted the power to force compliance on those who would, in the absence of external restraint, threaten the general liberty by abusing their own liberty. Government power is necessary if liberty is to be prevented from cannibalizing itself.

Government power may be necessary to maintain liberty, but it is not sufficient. The ability of government to enforce impartially general rules *can* be sabotaged by the same lack of individual responsibility and restraint that makes government necessary in the first place. The ability of government to enforce impartially general rules *will* be sabotaged if the lack of responsibility and restraint reaches the point where government becomes the dominant source of discipline in society. The more necessary government is to the maintenance of the general rules upon which liberty depends, the more insufficient to this task it is sure to be.

There is no avoiding the fact that liberty will perish if the exercise of liberty is not tempered by an ethic of individual responsibility. The affirmation of this fact is the ethical responsibility of those of us who cherish liberty and understand the fragile foundation upon which it stands. ●

9. The Relation between Economic Freedom and Political Freedom

Milton Friedman

Fundamentally, there are only two ways of co-ordinating the economic activities of millions. One is central direction involving the use of coercion—the technique of the army and of the modern totalitarian state. The other is voluntary co-operation of individuals—the technique of the market place.

The possibility of co-ordination through voluntary co-operation rests on the elementary—yet frequently denied—proposition that both parties to an economic transaction benefit from it, *provided the transaction is bi-laterally voluntary and informed.*

Exchange can therefore bring about co-ordination without coercion. A working model of a society organized through voluntary exchange is a *free private enterprise exchange economy*—what we have been calling competitive capitalism.

In its simplest form, such a society consists of a number of independent households—a collection of Robinson Crusoes, as it were. Each household uses the resources it controls to produce goods and services that it exchanges for goods and services produced by other households, on terms mutually acceptable to the two parties to the bargain. It is thereby enabled to satisfy its wants indirectly by producing goods and services for others, rather than directly by producing goods for its own immediate use. The incentive for adopting this indirect route is, of course, the increased product made possible by division of labor and specialization of function. Since the household always has the alternative of producing directly for itself, it need not enter into any exchange unless it benefits from it. Hence, no exchange will take place unless both parties do benefit from it. Co-operation is thereby achieved without coercion.

Abridged from *Capitalism and Freedom*, pp. 13-21, by permission of The University of Chicago Press. Copyright © 1962 by the University of Chicago.

Specialization of function and division of labor would not go far if the ultimate productive unit were the household. In a modern society, we have gone much farther. We have introduced enterprises which are intermediaries between individuals in their capacities as suppliers of service and as purchasers of goods. And similarly, specialization of function and division of labor would not go very far if we had to continue to rely on the barter of product for product. In consequence, money has been introduced as a means of facilitating exchange, and of enabling the acts of purchase and of sale to be separated into two parts.

Despite the important role of enterprises and of money in our actual economy, and despite the numerous and complex problems they raise, the central characteristic of the market technique of achieving co-ordination is fully displayed in the simple exchange economy that contains neither enterprises nor money. As in that simple model, so in the complex enterprise and money-exchange economy, co-operation is strictly individual and voluntary *provided: (a)* that enterprises are private, so that the ultimate contracting parties are individuals and *(b)* that individuals are effectively free to enter or not to enter into any particular exchange, so that every transaction is strictly voluntary.

It is far easier to state these provisos in general terms than to spell them out in detail, or to specify precisely the institutional arrangements most conducive to their maintenance. Indeed, much of technical economic literature is concerned with precisely these questions. The basic requisite is the maintenance of law and order to prevent physical coercion of one individual by another and to enforce contracts voluntarily entered into, thus giving substance to "private." Aside from this, perhaps the most difficult problems arise from monopoly — which inhibits effective freedom by denying individuals alternatives to the particular exchange — and from "neighborhood effects" — effects on third parties for which it is not feasible to charge or recompense them.

So long as effective freedom of exchange is maintained, the central feature of the market organization of economic activity is that it prevents one person from interfering with another in respect of most of his activities. The consumer is protected from coercion by the seller because of the presence of other sellers with whom he can deal. The seller is protected from coercion by the consumer because of other consumers to whom he can sell. The employee is protected from coercion by the employer because of other employers for whom he can work, and so on. And the market does this impersonally and without centralized authority.

Indeed, a major source of objection to a free economy is precisely that it does this task so well. It gives people what they want instead of what a particular group thinks they ought to want. Underlying most arguments against the free market is a lack of belief in freedom itself.

The existence of a free market does not of course eliminate the need for government. On the contrary, government is essential both as a forum for determining the "rules of the game" and as an umpire to interpret and enforce the rules decided on. What the market does is to reduce greatly the range of issues that must be decided through political means, and thereby to minimize the extent to which government need participate directly in the game. The characteristic feature of action through political channels is that it tends to require or enforce substantial conformity. The great advantage of the market, on the other hand, is that it permits wide diversity. It is, in political terms, a system of proportional representation. Each man can vote, as it were, for the color of tie he wants and get it; he does not have to see what color the majority wants and then, if he is in the minority, submit.

It is this feature of the market that we refer to when we say that the market provides economic freedom. But this characteristic also has implications that go far beyond the narrowly economic. Political freedom means the absence of coercion of a man by his fellow men. The fundamental threat to freedom is power to coerce, be it in the hands of a monarch, a dictator, an oligarchy, or a momentary majority. The preservation of freedom requires the elimination of such concentration of power to the fullest possible extent and the dispersal and distribution of whatever power cannot be eliminated — a system of checks and balances. By removing the organization of economic activity from the control of political authority, the market eliminates this source of coercive power. It enables economic strength to be a check to political power rather than a reinforcement.

Economic power can be widely dispersed. There can be many millionaires in one large economy. But can there be more than one really outstanding leader, one person on whom the energies and enthusiasms of his countrymen are centered?

The force of this abstract argument can perhaps best be demonstrated by an example. Let us consider first, a hypothetical example that may help to bring out the principles involved, and then some actual examples from recent experience that illustrate the way in which the market works to preserve political freedom.

One feature of a free society is surely the freedom of individuals to advocate and propagandize openly for a radical change in the structure of the society — so long as the advocacy is restricted to persuasion and does not include force or other forms of coercion. It is a mark of the political freedom of a capitalist society that men can openly advocate and work for socialism. Equally, political freedom in a socialist society would require that men be free to advocate the introduction of capitalism. How could the freedom to advocate capitalism be preserved and protected in a socialist society?

In order for men to advocate anything, they must in the first place be able to earn a living. This already raises a problem in a socialist society, since all jobs are under the direct control of political authorities. It would take an act of self-denial whose difficulty is underlined by experience in the United States after World War II with the problem of "security" among Federal employees, for a socialist government to permit its employees to advocate policies directly contrary to official doctrine.

But let us suppose this act of self-denial to be achieved. For advocacy of capitalism to mean anything, the proponents must be able to finance their cause—to hold public meetings, publish pamphlets, buy radio time, issue newspapers and magazines, and so on. How could they raise the funds? There might and probably would be men in the socialist society with large incomes, perhaps even large capital sums in the form of government bonds and the like, but these would of necessity be high public officials. It is possible to conceive of a minor socialist official retaining his job although openly advocating capitalism. It strains credulity to imagine the socialist top brass financing such "subversive" activities.

In a capitalist society, it is only necessary to convince a few wealthy people to get funds to launch any idea, however strange, and there are many such persons, many independent foci of support. And, indeed, it is not even necessary to persuade people or financial institutions with available funds of the soundness of the ideas to be propagated. It is only necessary to persuade them that the propagation can be financially successful; that the newspaper or magazine or book or other venture will be profitable. The competitive publisher, for example, cannot afford to publish only writing with which he personally agrees; his touchstone must be the likelihood that the market will be large enough to yield a satisfactory return on his investment.

In a free market society, it is enough to have the funds. The suppliers of paper are as willing to sell it to the *Daily Worker* as to the *Wall Street Journal*. In a socialist society, it would not be enough to have the funds. The hypothetical supporter of capitalism would have to persuade a government factory making paper to sell to him, the government printing press to print his pamphlets, a government post office to distribute them among the people, a government agency to rent him a hall in which to talk, and so on.

Perhaps there is some way in which one could overcome these difficulties and preserve freedom in a socialist society. One cannot say it is utterly impossible. What is clear, however, is that there are very real difficulties in establishing institutions that will effectively preserve the possibility of dissent. So far as I know, none of the people who have been in favor of socialism and also in favor of freedom have really faced up to this issue, or made even a respectable start at developing the institutional arrangements that would permit freedom under socialism. By contrast, it is clear how a free market capitalist society fosters freedom.

A striking practical example of these abstract principles is the experience of Winston Churchill. From 1933 to the outbreak of World War II, Churchill was not permitted to talk over the British radio, which was, of course, a government monopoly administered by the British Broadcasting Corporation. Here was a leading citizen of his country, a Member of Parliament, a former cabinet minister, a man who was desperately trying by every device possible to persuade his countrymen to take steps to ward off the menace of Hitler's Germany. He was not permitted to talk over the radio to the British people because the BBC was a government monopoly and his position was too "controversial."

One may believe, as I do, that communism would destroy all of our freedoms, one may be opposed to it as firmly and as strongly as possible, and yet, at the same time, also believe that in a free society it is intolerable for a man to be prevented from making voluntary arrangements with others that are mutually attractive because he believes in or is trying to promote communism. His freedom includes his freedom to promote communism. Freedom also, of course, includes the freedom of others not to deal with him under those circumstances.

No one who buys bread knows whether the wheat from which it is made was grown by a Communist or a Republican, by a Constitutionalist or a Fascist, or, for that matter, by a Negro or a white. This illustrates how an impersonal market separates economic activities from political views and protects men from being discriminated against in their economic activities for reasons that are irrelevant to their productivity—whether these reasons are associated with their views or their color.

As this example suggests, the groups in our society that have the most at stake in the preservation and strengthening of competitive capitalism are those minority groups which can most easily become the object of the distrust and enmity of the majority—the Negroes, the Jews, the foreign-born, to mention only the most obvious. Yet, paradoxically enough, the enemies of the free market—the Socialists and Communists—have been recruited in disproportionate measure from these groups. Instead of recognizing that the existence of the market has protected them from the attitudes of their fellow countrymen, they mistakenly attribute the residual discrimination to the market. ●

10. Private Property, Freedom, and the West

James Gwartney

The architects of Western Civilization believed that protection of private property was essential for the preservation of individual freedom. When individuals do not possess secure property rights, dependency on kings, lords, and governments for the essentials of life is inevitable.

In recent decades, appreciation of private ownership has been declining in the West. High taxes, welfare transfers, regulatory restraints, and bureaucratic edicts are eroding private property. Increasingly, the political process – that is, government ownership and control – is being substituted for private property and the market process which is a natural outgrowth of private ownership.

Paradoxically, the decline in appreciation for private ownership is coming at a time when both theoretical advances and economic outcomes are strengthening the case for private ownership. Evidence is mounting that private ownership not only protects liberty, as our forefathers recognized, but it also provides for superior economic performance. In contrast, government ownership creates a perverse incentive structure which leads to a Hobbesian world of political infighting and waste of valuable resources.

Three Types of Ownership Rights

Property ownership denotes who has the right to control and benefit from a thing. There are three types of property rights: (1) communal, (2) private, and (3) state (or government).

Communal property rights grant everyone the right to use a resource as intensely as they desire. No one has exclusive ownership – the right to prohibit unauthorized use by others. Since individual resource users bear little of the costs accompanying resource exploitation, each has an incentive to use the resource before someone else does. Thus, over-utilization and failure to con-

Reprinted from *The Intercollegiate Review*, Spring/Summer, 1985, pp. 39-40, by permission of the Intercollegiate Studies Institute, Inc.

serve for the future characterize communal ownership. The case of buffalo in the early West illustrates the impact of communal ownership. Each hunter knew that a buffalo that was not captured today would probably be captured tomorrow by someone else. Since exclusive ownership was absent, so too was the motivation to exploit the buffalo in a manner that provided for the future posterity of the animal. The outcome: mass slaughter of buffalo for their hides and virtual extinction of the species. While communal ownership may appear attractive to a utopian, the system fails to make individuals accountable for their actions. Economic waste and destructive behavior are the result.

In contrast with communal rights, private ownership grants individuals and private groups the exclusive right to control, benefit from, and transfer property as long as their actions do not harm the property of others. Each party is free to do what he wants with his private property as long as his use does not violate the property rights of another. While often associated with selfishness on the part of owners, private ownership would more properly be viewed as a means by which owners are protected against the selfishness of others. Private ownership provides legal protection against the seizure of one's property via theft, violence (or threat of violence), or fraud by another party.

Finally, property may be owned by governments. The government ownership may involve either direct title to property or indirect ownership via taxation and regulation of property nominally owned by private parties. While state-owned property technically belongs to all, this does not mean everyone has the right to use it. In contrast with communal property, government ownership provides for exclusive use by designated parties. The political process determines how, by whom, and under what conditions government property may be used. Essentially, government ownership substitutes the decision-making of government officials and the political process for the choices of private owners.

Individual Freedom, Private Ownership, and the Intellectual Roots of the West

As the population of Europe grew in the sixteenth century, land became increasingly scarce. The communal ownership of grazing lands and the destructive impact of overgrazing which accompanied it eventually led to the enclosure movement. About the same time, changes in military technology expanded the optimal size of geographic area defensible against potential intruders and plunderers. This led to the nation-state as a replacement protective agency for the prior feudal order.* Simultaneously, the influence of the Reformation began to sweep across Europe. By the seventeenth century, the idea that individuals had certain God-given rights that should not be violated by anyone

---

*   See Douglass C. North, *Structure of Change in Economic History* (New York: Norton, 1981) for an excellent account of this period.

gained popularity.

It was against this background that people like John Locke and David Hume began to think seriously about human freedom, private ownership of property, and the role of government. They propagated the view that all individuals, not just those born of noblemen, were entitled to the fruits of their labor and enjoyment of their property. However, private property was constantly threatened from, as Locke put it, "the invasions of others." As a result, in his *Second Treatise of Government* (1690), Locke argued:

> [An individual] seeks out and is willing to join in society with others, who are already united, or have a mind to unite, for the mutual preservation of their lives, liberties, and estates, which I call by the general name, property.*

Hume, too, perceived that the major function of government was to protect the possessions of individuals and thereby provide for freedom and order. In his *Treatise* written in 1740, Hume stated:

> No one can doubt, that the convention of the distinction of property, and for the stability of possession, is of all circumstances the most necessary to the establishment of human society, and that after the agreement for the fixing and observing of this rule, there remains little or nothing to be done toward settling a perfect harmony and concord.**

These early English philosophers exerted a profound influence on the thinking of Thomas Jefferson, John Adams, James Madison, and other early American political leaders. The architects of the U.S. political system also believed that private property was the foundation of human freedom and that the function of government was to protect and secure the possessions of individuals from both foreign (national defense) and domestic intruders. It was John Adams's opinion that:

> Property is surely a right of mankind as real as liberty.... The moment the idea is admitted into society that property is not as sacred as the laws of God, and that there is not a force of law and public justice to protect it, anarchy and tyranny commence.***

The early American intellectuals were keenly aware of the interdependency

---

* John Locke, *Treatise of Civil Government*, Charles Sherman, ed. (New York: Appleton-Century-Crofts, 1937), 82.

** David Hume, *Treatise of Human Nature*, book III, part II, para. II.

*** John Adams, "Defense of the Constitutions of Government of the United States of America," in Charles F. Adams, ed., *The Works of John Adams* (1850-1856), VI, 8f.

of personal freedom with one's right to own property. Labor and saving are the foundation of physical property. Without physical possessions, individuals would be unable to store up the fruits of their labor or pass along gifts to family and other loved ones. Denial of one's rights to possessions justly acquired (without the use of violence, theft, or fraud) is equivalent to denying one the fruits of their labor — the very subsistence of livelihood.

Thus, without protection of one's private property other rights would have little meaning. Recognizing this point, James Madison argued that protection of private property was interwoven with the protection of other personal freedoms. While still a Congressman from Virginia, he stated:

> In its [the right to own property] larger and juster meaning, it embraced everything to which a man may attach a value and have a right, and which leaves to every one else the like advantage. In the former sense, a man's land or merchandise, or money, is called property. In the latter sense, a man has a property in his opinions and the free communication of them. He has a property of peculiar value in his religious opinions, and in the profession and practice dictated by them. He has a property very dear to him in the safety and liberty of his person. He has an equal property in the free use of his facilities, and free choice of the objects on which to employ them. In a word, as a man is said to have a right to his property, he may be equally said to have a property in his rights.*

Wisdom of Our Forefathers

Even with the benefit of the last two hundred years of history, serious scholars must be impressed with the insight possessed by the early proponents of private ownership. Even though they did not understand fully how a private-property based economic system worked, they recognized that it minimized social conflict and protected individual freedom.

Private property and market organization permit individuals to choose different occupations, consumer goods, and even lifestyles without interfering with the freedom of others to do likewise. Market organization based on private property is a system of proportional representation. Each individual casts his dollar votes for the consumer goods of his choice. Similarly, each individual is free to sell productive services to whomever he or she chooses without having to obtain permission from a king, lord, or political majority. The result is both freedom and diversity as various minorities, directed by market prices, choose varying bundles of goods and supply differing types of productive services.

Contrast this with a system of state property rights and political allocation. In the political arena the majority decides for everyone. For example, when

---

*   Statement made March 27, 1792, from *The Works of James Madison*, Vol. IV, 478-79. Also see John Locke, *A Letter Concerning Toleration* for similar views.

schooling, retirement pensions, housing, and land management are provided through the political process, we all must pay for and subscribe to the program or service favored by the dominant political coalition. The will of the individual must give way to the will of the majority. Unnecessary social conflict results as minority views are suppressed.*

Simultaneously, private property also protects individual freedom by keeping economic power dispersed. Of course, power accompanies ownership. The owner of a plot of land determines whether it will be used for a housing development, wheat farm, parking lot, or some other use. The owner of each oil pool determines whether the resource will be exploited now or preserved for the future. However, with private ownership this power is spread among literally millions of people, no one of whom has much power over another. The power of even the wealthiest property owner is limited by the presence of other property owners willing to provide similar products and services. If the Hunt brothers decide to quit selling oil or David Rockefeller gets out of the banking and real estate business, neither the earning ability nor consumer alternatives available to Americans would be altered significantly.

A recent survey by the Federal Reserve Board indicated the wealthiest two percent of American households own twenty-eight percent of the nation's physical property. At first glance, this appears to be enormous power in the hands of a few people. However, reflection should cause one to question this view. This wealth, enormous as it is, is in the hands of 1.6 million households, representing diverse political, religious, ethnic, and personal interests. Unless it is used to provide services to *others* in exchange for income, the wealth of these property owners will shrink. Compare the power of these wealthy households with the power of 536 elected federal office holders. This latter group, comprising just .0000025 percent of our population, determines how one-quarter of our national output is allocated. They tax approximately one-fifth of our national income away from earners and allocate it to nonearners. They set the dollar value of the social security benefits received by thirty-six million Americans. The regulatory power under the jurisdiction of the 536 individuals holds a life or death grip on the economic health of literally millions of businesses. In contrast with private owners, members of Congress have the power to take property, a portion of your earnings for example, without your consent. One could go on and on, but the point is clear. When government ownership

---

*   The case of schooling vividly illustrates the unnecessary social conflict that emanates from political provision. Views vary as to what constitutes a quality education. Some parents would like schools to focus on the basics; others favor a broad curriculum. Some favor highly structured organization; others prefer the open school concept. Some want their children to attend schools that emphasize moral values and religious beliefs; others oppose even so much as a moment of silent meditation. When schooling is provided in the private sector, all of these diverse views can and are satisfied. In contrast, each of the differences promotes division and conflict within the public school system.

is substituted for private property, enormous power over the lives of others is bestowed upon a small handful of political figures. One of the major virtues of private property is its ability to check the excessive concentration of economic power in the hands of the few. Widespread ownership of property is the enemy of tyranny and abusive use of power. This proposition is just as true today as it was a couple of hundred years ago.

Economic Progress and Private Ownership

While the early defenders of private ownership emphasized its importance as the cornerstone of individual liberty, economic theory indicates that private property also provides the foundation for efficient use of resources and rapid economic growth. Production does not just happen. Human decision-makers must be motivated to undertake productive activities, use resources wisely, and discover better (less costly) ways of doing things. There are five major reasons why a system of well-defined, secure private ownership rights promotes economic progress.

1. *Private ownership encourages wise stewardship.* More than 2,300 years ago Aristotle noted, "What is common to many is taken least care of, for all men have greater regard for what is their own than for what they possess in common with others." Here, as in many other areas, his insight has stood the test of time. Private owners pay close heed to how their property is used because if it is damaged, abused, or misused, they will bear the costs of the depreciating action. Simultaneously, improvements that add more to the value of their property than their costs will increase the wealth of the owner. Thus private owners have a strong incentive to undertake cost-effective property improvements.

It is often observed that private housing is better maintained than public housing, private campgrounds better cared for than public grounds, and private lands more efficiently utilized than public lands. This should not be surprising. Private owners take good care of things because they both bear the costs of irresponsible use and reap the benefits of wise stewardship.

2. *Private ownership makes people accountable for their actions and thereby promotes the general welfare.* A system of well-defined, secure private ownership rights allows individuals to reap the benefits of the positive things they do for others and simultaneously holds them responsible for costs they impose on others.* With private ownership, producers incur costs when they use resources and simultaneously they are in a position to capture the benefits

---

* Of course, in some cases it is difficult to assign property rights in a manner that permits decision-makers to capture fully the benefits of their actions and make them accountable fully for the costs they impose on others. Migrating animals and use rights to rivers, oceans, and the atmosphere provide examples. Under such circumstances, ideal economic efficiency breaks down. See James Gwartney and Richard Stroup, *Economics: Private and Public Choice,* 3rd ed. (New York: Academic Press, 1983) chapter 30 for additional detail on this topic.

(through the sale of products and services) their actions bestow upon others. When an activity generates more benefits than costs, profit-seeking entrepreneurs have an incentive to discover and undertake it. On the other hand, they have an incentive to avoid counterproductive activities for which costs exceed benefits. Private ownership makes *decision-makers* accountable. As Adam Smith noted long ago, this accountability is the genius of a private property-based system because it brings individual self-interest and social welfare into harmony.

3. *Private ownership encourages individuals to develop and employ resources in a manner that is most advantageous to others.* When private property rights are protected, people get ahead by selling productive services in exchange for income. The exchange process leads to mutual gains stemming from specialization, division of labor, and mass production methods. Positive-sum economic activities — actions that generate mutual gain for trading partners — are encouraged. Social cooperation and expansion in the size of the economic pie results.

Individuals have a strong incentive to (a) develop skills for which the demand *of others* is strong and (b) employ their resources in a manner that is most beneficial *to others* because such employment generates more income. With private ownership, the link between providing services others deem beneficial and personal income will be a close one. Individuals who provide large amounts of productive services *to others* will earn large incomes. In contrast, those who provide few productive services *to others* will experience lower incomes. In a very real sense, one's income will be directly related to one's ability to provide services that enhance the welfare of other people.

4. *Private ownership brings the widest possible range of knowledge to bear upon the problem of scarcity.* Improved knowledge and innovations provide a vital impetus for economic progress. In fact, the major difference between the modern man and the early gatherer-hunter is the amount of knowledge that we possess with regard to how resources can be transformed into desired goods. Our ancestors possessed virtually the same resources available today. But the superior knowledge we possess today permits us to squeeze a vastly larger output per person from the available resources.

No individual or elite group knows everything. Genius often comes from unexpected sources. Private property and economic freedom permit a wide variety of individuals, reflecting different combinations of creative talents, ideas, and market perceptions, to contribute knowledge to the production process. While this attribute of a free economy is often overlooked, unquestionably it is an important contributor to the dynamic growth of production under the system.*

---

*   Thomas Sowell, *Knowledge and Decisions* (New York: Basic Books, 1980), clearly articulates the importance of this factor.

5. *Private ownership encourages current resource owners to conserve for the future.* Since the current market value of property will reflect its expected future income, private ownership encourages wise conservation. Any time the present value of using a resource in the future is more valuable than the use of the resource now, the resource will be preserved for the future. For example, suppose one believes the price of a barrel of oil (or any other resource) is going to rise ten percent annually. When the expected increase in price is greater than the interest rate, resource owners (or potential purchasers who think the price of the resource will rise more rapidly than the interest rate) will gain by conserving the resource for the future.

As long as private property is transferable, even current decision-makers who do not expect to *personally* reap the future harvest of an asset will have strong incentive to take the preferences of future generations into account. Suppose a 60 year-old tree farmer is contemplating whether or not to plant Douglas fir trees which will not reach optimal cutting size for another 50 years. When ownership is transferable, the market value of the farmer's land will increase in anticipation of the future harvest as the trees grow and the expected day of harvest moves closer. Thus, the farmer will be able to capture his contribution at any time, even though the actual harvest may not take place until well after his death.

Doomsday commentators who fear we are going to use up vital minerals, cut all the trees, or eliminate all the wilderness areas do not understand the conservation ethic of the market. Should any of these things become relatively more scarce in the future, *when they are owned privately*, their prices will rise more rapidly than the interest rate. The rising price will induce individuals to cut back on their current use, preserve more of the resource for the future, and search more diligently for additional supplies of the resource (and good substitutes for it). As Dwight Lee, Professor of Economics at the University of Georgia, recently stated, "No social institution does more to motivate current decision-makers to act *as if* they cared about the future than the institution of private property."*

---

*   Dwight Lee, "Patience is a Market Virtue," *Reason*, (January, 1985), 44. Through the ages, some previous writers, including Aristotle, have argued that private parties should be granted exclusive *use* rights while the government still maintains ownership. While maintaining government ownership, several state governments granted use rights to land in early America. Fortunately, this policy was soon abandoned. As our analysis indicates, the problem with use rights without ownership is that the arrangement fails to provide an incentive to maintain and improve the property for the future since, lacking transferability rights, users are unable to capture the benefits of wise stewardship. Also see Richard Stroup and John Baden, *Natural Resources: Bureaucratic Myths and Environmental Management* (Cambridge, Mass.: Ballinger, 1983) for additional detail on the efficiency of private ownership as a protector of natural resources and the environment.

Private Ownership—The Economic Record

The linkage between private property and economic progress has been illustrated under a broad range of circumstances. First of all, there is the economic miracle of the West during the last 250 years. Since Americans tend to lack a sense of history, most fail to recognize just how well the political economy of the West has worked. Improved living standards are not something that started with, say the discovery of the wheel 5,000 years ago. Quite the contrary, the historical record is the story of a nip-and-tuck race between subsistence and starvation. Periods of economic growth have been rare exceptions. Our ancestors were keenly aware of this point. As Phelps Brown has shown, the real income of a typical English tradesman was virtually unchanged between 1215 and 1798, a period of nearly six centuries. Just as human beings had worked sunup to sundown to eke out a minimal living for 6,000 years, so too did our ancestors just 250 years ago.

However, all of this began to change about the time the new ideas on property rights and the role of government were transformed into public policy. Human creativity developed ideas that transformed the way people lived and worked. Improved farming techniques (e.g. crop rotations, fertilizers, and miracle grains) permitted our ancestors to squeeze much larger outputs from the land. Machines were developed that improved our ability to produce agriculture products and transformed resources into manufacturing goods. Petroleum, electricity, and later nuclear power replaced human and animal power as the major source of energy. Eventually, we figured out how to construct engines that revolutionized our ability to power machines and transport both people and cargo. Not only did we achieve these things, but simultaneously quality food, warm clothing, comfortable houses, and diversity of entertainment were brought within the budget constraints of the mass population. For the first time in history, millions of human beings attained living standards far above subsistence. The economic history of the West is a story of progress far beyond even the imagination of our ancestors.

Just as private ownership based systems delivered economic progress in the past, a check of recent economic performance indicates they continue to do so in the present. During the 1960-1981 period, the annual growth rate of per capita GNP of only four countries exceeded six percent. Those four countries were Japan, Hong Kong, South Korea, and Singapore—all private ownership based economies. Compare the economic record of South Korea with North Korea, West Germany with East Germany, Kenya with Ethiopia, or Taiwan and Hong Kong with mainland China. In each case, the record paints the same picture—economies that rely more fully on private property rights grow more rapidly.

Even in the Soviet Union, private ownership is associated with high productivity. Soviet families living on collective farms are permitted to cultivate a private plot, the area of which is not to exceed one acre. Although these private plots constitute only about one percent of the land under cultivation in the Soviet Union, the Soviet press reports that approximately one-quarter of the total value of agricultural output is generated on these plots.

State Property—The Alternative to Private Ownership

One cannot adequately judge the case for private ownership without considering the alternative — government ownership of property. Public ownership means that substitution of the political process for market allocation. Until recently, traditional economists and political scientists held what might be called the "benevolent despot" model of government. According to this view, government decision-makers always choose the alternative that is best for society. The political process was simply viewed as a corrective device.

Recognizing the naivete of this view, a group of economists — they are now referred to as "public choice" economists — set out to enhance our understanding of how the political process really works. While the work has not attracted wide media exposure, it may prove to be the most revolutionary breakthrough of economic analysis during the post-war era.* Public choice analysis provides insight as to what we can expect from the democratic collective decision-making process. For our purposes three of the implications are particularly important.

First, there will be a strong tendency for politicians to support positions favored by well-organized, easily identifiable special interest groups. When the cost of special interest legislation is spread widely among the voting populace, most non-special interest voters will largely ignore the issue. In fact, they are likely to be uninformed as to how the issue impacts their welfare. In contrast, special interest voters will be vitally concerned. They will let candidates (and legislators) know how strongly they feel about the issue. Many special interest voters will vote for or against politicians, almost exclusively, on the basis of this issue. Given the intensity of special interest voters and the apathy of other voters, politicians will be led as if by an "invisible hand" (to borrow Adam Smith's expression) to promote the positions of special interests.

Second, the political process will be biased toward the adoption of short-sighted policies, actions which yield payoffs prior to a forthcoming election while generating costs that are not readily observable until after the election. The pre-election benefits will enhance the politician's image with voters while the negative side effect will not generally be observable on election day. Since politicians neither capture benefits nor experience costs beyond their tenure in

---

*   For those desiring additional information on the economics of public choice see Gordon Tullock, *The Vote Motive* (London: The Institute of Economic Affairs, 1976);) Henry Lepage, *Tomorrow, Capitalism*, (LaSalle, Ill.: Open Court Publishing Co., 1978) chapters 5 and 6; James Gwartney and Richard Stroup, *Economics: Private and Public Choice*, chapters 4, 29, and 30; and Mancur Olson, *The Logic of Collective Action*, (Cambridge: Harvard University Press, 1971).

office, they have a strong incentive to choose alternatives that are attractive in the short run even though the long run effects may be quite different and highly inefficient.

Finally, allocation via the political process encourages individuals and groups to engage in redistributive and protective activities rather than production. When the government moves beyond the protection of private property and actively reallocates income and other property rights, more resources will flow into favor-seeking (economists use the term "rent-seeking"). Individuals, businesses, and interest groups will invest more heavily in political resources (lobbying, contributions, etc.) designed to yield government action that promotes their personal interest. The political ethos of "taking from others in exchange for votes and political resources" replaces the market ethic of "helping others in exchange for income." However, just as sheep do not stand still while they are sheared, neither do individuals deprived of their property. Citizens will respond to higher tax rates by expanding their tax avoidance activities.* Similarly, additional regulation will lead to additional protective action. The more a society relies upon tax, transfer, and regulatory activities to determine income shares, the closer the society will approach the Hobbesian world of political infighting and economic stagnation. As individuals and interest groups allocate more resources to fighting and clawing for a larger slice of the economic pie, the absolute size of those slices will decline. The American experience with the tax-transfer society is not inconsistent with this view.

The Invalid Charge—Private Ownership Favors the Rich

Even while recognizing many of the positive attributes of private ownership, critics often charge that it promotes inequality and works to the advantage of the rich. "The rich get richer and the poor get poorer," we are told. When analyzing the validity of this view, it is important to keep several facts in mind. First, ownership of physical property, particularly inherited property, is not a major source of income inequality. Between 81 percent and 83 percent of national income in the United States is allocated to labor and the share has been amazingly constant during the last 50 years.** Income differences stemming

---

*   See James Gwartney and James Long, "Tax Rates, Tax Shelters, and the Efficiency of Capital Formation," in Dwight Lee, ed., *The Political Economy of Capital Formation* (San Francisco: Pacific Institute, 1985) for evidence on this point.

**   Labor income is composed of employee compensation plus the earnings of self-employed workers.

from the provision of labor services are the major source of inequality in the United States. The share of national income going to physical capital in the form of interest, rents, and corporate profits is only 17 to 19 percent of our national income.* Not only is the fraction of income derived from physical wealth small, most owners of physical wealth acquire it by saving from their labor income rather than inheritance. The share of aggregate income derived from inherited property is estimated at two percent. Thus, even complete elimination of the inheritance of property would do little to promote income equality.** Given that leaving wealth to whomever one chooses provides a valuable stimulus to productive effort and that such bequeaths contribute little to inequality, the case for the elimination of inheritance is weak.

Second, we live in a dynamic world, one where there is considerable movement both up and down the economic ladder. A recent study found that of the top twenty percent of income recipients in 1971, more than half had fallen from their prior lofty position seven years later. Similarly, nearly half of those among the bottom quintile of income recipients in 1971 had moved up the income ladder by 1978.*** Studies of intergenerational income data find even more mobility — both upward and downward — in the comparative economic position of fathers and sons. Private property rewards achievers from all socioeconomic backgrounds. When property — including one's property right to fruits of his labor — is protected from oppressive taxation, achievers from all economic backgrounds have the opportunity to create, expand their wealth, and climb to the top of the economic ladder.

Third, those who charge that private ownership favors the rich generally fail to recognize that the market process is a powerful force for uplifting the mass of population. Blinded by the illusion of a static world, like Marx, they fail to understand the dynamics of economic growth and income generation. As we previously discussed, the major difference between our modern standard of living and that of our ancestors hundreds of years ago is the amount of knowledge we possess with regard to how resources can be transformed into desired goods. When property rights to innovations are protected, a market economy not only provides a strong incentive for entrepreneurs to innovate, but it also provides *a premium reward for innovations that improve the living standard of the mass population.* Successful entrepreneurs will focus on how they can bring a product or service within the grasp of the typical consumer — how they can serve

---

* As egalitarians are fond of pointing out, the richest 20 percent of income recipients own approximately 59 percent of the *physical* wealth, while the poorest 20 percent own only 8 percent of the wealth. In interpreting the significance of data on the inequality of physical wealth holdings it is important to recognize that such wealth generates less than one-fifth of our national income.

** See Alan S. Blinder, *Toward an Economic Theory of Income Distribution* (Cambridge, Mass.: MIT Press, 1974) for additional detail on this topic.

*** Greg J. Duncan, et al., *Years of Poverty, Years of Plenty* (Ann Arbor: Institute for Social Research, University of Michigan, 1984), Table 1.1.

markets where sales units are tabulated in the millions rather than the hundreds.

Most products go through two rather distinct phases. At first, they are quite expensive and purchased by only the very rich. During this phase, producers experiment with alternative designs and methods of production. The high initial price, paid primarily by the rich, serves to cover developmental costs. Entrepreneurs iron out complications and acquire valuable experience which will permit either them or their emulators to succeed in the next phase. During the second phase, production techniques and product modifications are developed making the product attractive and affordable to more and more consumers. Mass production and market penetration are the keys to success in this phase. Of course, entrepreneurs who serve a mass market often earn a fortune. But in the process of doing so, they improve the standard of living of numerous people (remember, exchange is a positive-sum activity).

You cannot have mass production without also having economic products for the mass of consumers. No one understood this point better than Harvard economist Joseph Schumpeter. Summarizing his ideas on this topic, Professor Schumpeter noted:

> . . . the capitalist engine is first and last an engine of mass production which unavoidably also means production for the masses. . . . It is the cheap cloth, the cheap cotton and rayon fabric, boots, motorcars and so on that are the typical achievements of capitalist production, and not as a rule improvements that would mean much to the rich man. Queen Elizabeth owned silk stockings. The capitalist achievement does not typically consist in providing more silk stockings for queens but in bringing them within the reach of factory girls in return for a steadily decreasing amount of effort.*

Entrepreneurs do not make fortunes by selling just to the rich. Large-scale entrepreneurs must bring their products within the budget constraint of the mass market. In the process of doing so, they uplift the living standards of the mass of consumers. This is a tremendously important point that both Marx and modern egalitarians totally fail to grasp.

Finally, it makes no sense to compare economic equality under private ownership with an unattainable standard such as perfect equality. The relevant comparison is with what one would expect from the political process. Perhaps surprising to some, there is little reason to believe that allocation via the political process promotes equality. Politicians find redistribution from widely dispersed, disorganized groups (e.g., taxpayers and consumers) to easily-identifiable, concentrated interests (e.g., labor, business, farmers, and the elderly)

---

*   Joseph Schumpeter, *Capitalism, Socialism, and Democracy*, 3rd ed. (New York: Harper and Row, 1962), 62.

far more attractive than egalitarian transfers. Similarly, politicians are attracted to transfers that provide (or appear to provide) readily identifiable *current* benefits at the expense of costs that are difficult to observe. These are the types of reshuffles one should expect from the political process and there is little reason to believe they will be egalitarian.*

At the individual level, persons who develop persuasive skills (i.e., lobbying, public speaking, public relations, media exposure), organization abilities, finances, and political knowledge will be rewarded handsomely with income, prestige, and power when resources are allocated via the political process. There is little reason to believe that the poor will possess relatively more of these characteristics. In fact, the entrepreneurs and managers in a politically dominated society are likely to be pretty much the same people as those who would excel under market organization. The people with better ideas, more creative minds, and more energy will rise to the top of a socialist bureaucracy just as they will rise to the top in the business world. Those who fare poorly under market organization are unlikely to do better, either relatively or absolutely, under socialism.

The empirical data are consistent with this view. Despite the enormous increase in the tax-transfer sector, the distribution of income in the United States has changed little since World War II. Similarly, there is little evidence that income transfers have reduced the incidence of poverty. In fact, one can build a strong case that the transfers have confronted the poor with a perverse incentive structure and have thereby actually retarded progress against poverty.**

Concluding Thoughts

Our current situation is beset with irony. The twentieth century has been characterized by the growth of government and the weakening of private ownership. Government expenditures now total nearly forty percent of our national income. More than one out of every five dollars is taxed away from its earner and transferred to another in the form of either cash payments or noncash benefits. Far from protecting property rights as envisioned by the political architects of the West, government has become the major source of attenuation in private property.

Nonetheless, the intellectual case for private ownership is stronger today than at any time in the past. History illustrates that, just as its early defenders perceived, private ownership minimizes social conflict and provides a shield

---

*   Less than 20 percent of the income transfers in the United States are means-tested — that is, targeted toward the poor. If one includes transfers stemming from regulatory actions such as trade restrictions, occupational and business entry restraints, and export subsidies, the share of transfers targeted toward the poor would be even smaller.

**   For a comprehensive analysis of this issue, see Charles Murray, *Losing Ground: American Social Policy, 1950-1980* (New York: Basic Books, 1984).

against oppressive concentration of power. Where private property is most widely respected on this planet, personal freedom is most secure and the presence of the domineering state is least observable. In addition, the evidence of a positive link between private ownership and economic progress is most impressive. Against the historical record of man's struggle for survival, clearly the development of widespread private ownership in the West was associated with something of an economic miracle. The superior performance of private-property based systems continues today as the rising living standards of modern day capitalist economies compared to their socialist counterparts illustrates. Recent work in public choice has made us more fully aware of the defects of even the democratic political process—why political allocation leads to economic stagnation while failing to promote economic equality. Only the naive continue to cling to the notion that the political process is the friend of the mythical common man.

An old Chinese proverb states: "Societies are like fish; they always begin to go rotten in the head." History illustrates the wisdom of private ownership. To the extent we fail to realize it, it merely illustrates we are going "rotten in the head." ●

11. The Creative Powers of a Free Civilization

Friedrich A. Hayek

The case for individual freedom rests chiefly on the recognition of the inevitable ignorance of all of us concerning a great many of the factors on which the achievement of our ends and welfare depends.*

If there were omniscient men, if we could know not only all that affects our present wishes but also our future wants and desires, there would be little case for liberty. And, in turn, liberty of the individual would, of course, make com-

---

* One of the few authors who has seen clearly at least part of this was F. W. Maitland, who stresses (*Collected Papers* [Cambridge: Cambridge University Press, 1911], I, 107) that "the most powerful argument is that based on the ignorance, the necessary ignorance, of our masters." See, however, B.E. Kline and N. H. Martin, "Freedom, Authority and Decentralization," *Harvard Business Review*, XXXVI (1958), esp. 70: "the chief characteristic of the command hierarchy, or any group in our society, is not knowledge but ignorance. · Consider that any one person can know only a fraction of what is going on around him. Much of what that person knows or believes will be false rather than true.... at any given time, vastly more is not known than is known, either by one person in a command chain or by all the organization. — It seems possible, then, that in organizing ourselves into a hierarchy of authority for the purpose of increasing efficiency, we may really be institutionalizing ignorance. While making better use of what the few know, we are making sure that the great majority are prevented from exploring the dark areas beyond our knowledge."

There is one important respect in which the term "ignorance" is somewhat too narrow for our purposes. There are occasions when it would probably be better to speak of "uncertainty" with reference to ignorance concerning what is right, since it is doubtful whether we can meaningfully speak about something being right if nobody knows what is right in the particular context. The fact in such instances may be that the existing morals provide no answer to a problem, though there might be some answer which, if it were known and widely accepted, would be very valuable. I am much indebted to Mr. Pierre F. Goodrich, whose comment during a discussion helped to clarify this important point for me, though I have not been persuaded to speak generally of "imperfection" where I stress ignorance.

Abridged from *The Constitution of Liberty*, pp. 29-38, with permission of The University of Chicago Press. Copyright © 1960 by The University of Chicago.

plete foresight impossible. Liberty is essential in order to leave room for the unforeseeable and unpredictable; we want it because we have learned to expect from it the opportunity of realizing many of our aims. It is because every individual knows so little and, in particular, because we rarely know which of us knows best that we trust the independent and competitive efforts of many to induce the emergence of what we shall want when we see it.

Humiliating to human pride as it may be, we must recognize that the advance and even the preservation of civilization are dependent upon a maximum of opportunity for accidents to happen.* These accidents occur in the combination of knowledge and attitudes, skills and habits, acquired by individual men and also when qualified men are confronted with the particular circumstances which they are equipped to deal with. Our necessary ignorance of so much means that we have to deal largely with probabilities and chances.

Of course, it is true of social as of individual life that favorable accidents usually do not just happen. We must prepare for them.** But they still remain chances and do not become certainties. They involve risks deliberately taken, the possible misfortune of individuals and groups who are as meritorious as others who prosper, the possibility of serious failure or relapse even for the majority, and merely a high probability of a net gain on balance. All we can do is to increase the chance that some special constellation of individual endowment and circumstance will result in the shaping of some new tool or the improvement of an old one, and to improve the prospect that such innovations will become rapidly known to those who can take advantage of them.

All political theories assume, of course, that most individuals are very ignorant. Those who plead for liberty differ from the rest in that they include among the ignorant themselves as well as the wisest. Compared with the totality of knowledge which is continually utilized in the evolution of a dynamic civilization, the difference between the knowledge that the wisest and that which the most ignorant individual can deliberately employ is comparatively insignificant.

The classical argument for tolerance formulated by John Milton and John Locke and restated by John Stuart Mill and Walter Bagehot rests, of course, on the recognition of this ignorance of ours. It is a special application of general

---

*   Cf. J. A. Wheeler, "A Septet of Sibyls: Aids in the Search for Truth," *American Scientist*, XLIV (1956), 360: "Our whole problem is to make the mistakes as fast as possible."

**   Cf. the remark of Louis Pasteur: "In research, chance helps only those whose minds are well prepared for it," quoted by R. Taton, *Reason and Chance in Scientific Discovery* (London: 1957), p. 91.

considerations to which a non-rationalist insight into the working of our mind opens the doors. We shall find throughout this book that, though we are usually not aware of it, all institutions of freedom are adaptations to this fundamental fact of ignorance, adapted to deal with chances and probabilities, not certainty. Certainty we cannot achieve in human affairs, and it is for this reason that, to make the best use of what knowledge we have, we must adhere to rules which experience has shown to serve best on the whole, though we do not know what will be the consequences of obeying them in the particular instance.*

Man learns by the disappointment of expectations. Needless to say, we ought not to increase the unpredictability of events by foolish human institutions. So far as possible, our aim should be to improve human institutions so as to increase the chances of correct foresight. Above all, however, we should provide the maximum of opportunity for unknown individuals to learn of facts that we ourselves are yet unaware of and to make use of this knowledge in their actions.

It is through the mutually adjusted efforts of many people that more knowledge is utilized than any one individual possesses or than it is possible to synthesize intellectually; and it is through such utilization of dispersed knowledge that achievements are made possible greater than any single mind can foresee. It is because freedom means the renunciation of direct control of individual efforts that a free society can make use of so much more knowledge than the mind of the wisest ruler could comprehend.

From this foundation of the argument for liberty it follows that we shall not achieve its ends if we confine liberty to the particular instances where we know it will do good. Freedom granted only when it is known beforehand that its effects will be beneficial is not freedom. If we knew how freedom would be used, the case for it would largely disappear. We shall never get the benefits of freedom, never obtain those unforeseeable new developments for which it

---

*   Cf. A. P. Lerner, "The Backward-leaning Approach to Controls," *F.P.E.*, LXV (1957), 441: "The free-trade doctrines are valid as *general rules* whose general use is generally beneficial. As with all general rules, there are particular cases where, if one knew all the attendant circumstances and the full effects in all their ramifications, it would be better for the rule not to be applied. But that does not make the rule a bad rule or give reason for not applying the rule where, as is normally the case, one does not know all the ramifications that would make the case a desirable exception."

provides the opportunity, if it is not also granted where the uses made of it by some do not seem desirable. It is therefore no argument against individual freedom that it is frequently abused. Freedom necessarily means that many things will be done which we do not like. Our faith in freedom does not rest on the foreseeable results in particular circumstances but on the belief that it will, on balance, release more forces for the good than for the bad.

It also follows that the importance of our being free to do a particular thing has nothing to do with the question of whether we or the majority are ever likely to make use of that particular possibility. To grant no more freedom than all can exercise would be to misconceive its function completely. The freedom that will be used by only one man in a million may be more important to society and more beneficial to the majority than any freedom that we all use.*

It might even be said that the less likely the opportunity to make use of freedom to do a particular thing, the more precious it will be for society as a whole. The less likely the opportunity, the more serious it will be to miss it when it arises, for the experience that it offers will be nearly unique. It is also probably true that the majority are not directly interested in most of the important things that any one person should be free to do. It is because we do not know how individuals will use their freedom that it is so important. If it were otherwise, the results of freedom could also be achieved by the majority's deciding what should be done by the individuals. But majority action is, of necessity, confined to the already tried and ascertained, to issues on which agreement has already been reached in that process of discussion that must be preceded by different experiences and actions on the part of different individuals.

The benefits I derive from freedom are thus largely the result of the uses of freedom by others, and mostly of those uses of freedom that I could never avail myself of. It is therefore not necessarily freedom that I can exercise myself that is most important for me. It is certainly more important that anything can be tried by somebody than that all can do the same things. It is not because we like to be able to do particular things, not because we regard any particular freedom as essential to our happiness, that we have a claim to freedom. The instinct that makes us revolt against any physical restraint, though a helpful ally, is not always

---

*   Cf. H. Rashdall, "The Philosophical Theory of Property," in *Property: Its Duties and Rights* (New York and London, 1915), p. 62: "The plea for liberty is not sufficiently met by insisting, as has been so eloquently and humorously done by Mr. Lowes Dickinson (*Justice and Liberty: a Political Dialogue, e.g.* pp. 129,131), upon the absurdity of supposing that the propertyless labourer under the ordinary capitalistic regime enjoys any liberty of which socialism would deprive him. For it may be of extreme importance that some should enjoy liberty — that it should be possible for some few men to be able to dispose of their time in their own way — although such liberty may be neither possible nor desirable for the great majority. That culture requires a considerable differentiation in social conditions is also a principle of unquestionable importance." See also Kline and Martin in the article quoted in n. 10, p. 69: "If there is to be freedom for the few who *will* take advantage of it, freedom must be offered to the many. If any lesson is clear from history, it is this."

a safe guide for justifying or delimiting freedom. What is important is not what freedom I personally would like to exercise but what freedom some person may need in order to do things beneficial to society. This freedom we can assure to the unknown person only by giving it to all.

The benefits of freedom are therefore not confined to the free — or, at least, a man does not benefit mainly from those aspects of freedom which he himself takes advantage of. There can be no doubt that in history unfree majorities have benefited from the existence of free minorities and that today unfree societies benefit from what they obtain and learn from free societies. Of course the benefits we derive from the freedom of others become greater as the number of those who can exercise freedom increases. The argument for the freedom of some therefore applies to the freedom of all. But it is still better for all that some should be free than none and also that many enjoy full freedom than that all have a restricted freedom. The significant point is that the importance of freedom to do a particular thing has nothing to do with the number of people who want to do it: it might almost be in inverse proportion. One consequence of this is that a society may be hamstrung by controls, although the great majority may not be aware that their freedom has been significantly curtailed. If we proceeded on the assumption that only the exercises of freedom that the majority will practice are important, we would be certain to create a stagnant society with all the characteristic of unfreedom.

The undesigned novelties that constantly emerge in the process of adaptation will consist, first, of new arrangements or patterns in which the efforts of different individuals are coordinated and of new constellations in the use of resources, which will be in their nature as temporary as the particular conditions that have evoked them. There will be, second, modifications of tools and institutions adapted to the new circumstances. Some of these will also be merely temporary adaptations to the conditions of the moment, while others will be improvements that increase the versatility of the existing tools and usages and will therefore be retained. These latter will constitute a better adaptation not merely to the particular circumstances of time and place but to some permanent feature of our environment. In such spontaneous "formations"* is embodied a perception of the general laws that govern nature. With this cumulative embodiment of experience in tools and forms of action will emerge a growth of explicit knowledge, of formulated generic rules that can be communicated by language from person to person.

This process by which the new emerges is best understood in the intellectual sphere when the results are new ideas. It is the field in which most of us are aware at least of some of the individual steps of the process, where we neces-

---

*   For the use of the term "formation," more appropriate in this connection than the usual "institution," see my study on *The Counter Revolution of Science* (Glencoe, Ill., 1952), p. 83.

sarily know what is happening and thus generally recognize the necessity of freedom. Most scientists realize that we cannot plan the advance of knowledge, that in the voyage into the unknown — which is what research is — we are in great measure dependent on the vagaries of individual genius and of circumstance, and that scientific advance, like a new idea that will spring up in a single mind, will be the result of a combination of conceptions, habits, and circumstances brought to one person by society, the result as much of lucky accidents as of systematic effort.

Because we are more aware that our advances in the intellectual sphere often spring from the unforeseen and undesigned, we tend to overstress the importance of the freedom of *doing* things. But the freedom of research and belief and the freedom of speech and discussion, the importance of which is widely understood, are significant only in the last stage of the process in which new truths are discovered. To extol the value of intellectual liberty at the expense of the value of the liberty of doing things would be like treating the crowning part of an edifice as the whole. We have new ideas to discuss, different views to adjust, because those ideas and views arise from the efforts of individuals in ever new circumstances, who avail themselves in their concrete tasks of the new tools and forms of action they have learned.

The non-intellectual part of this process — the formation of the changed material environment in which the new emerges — requires for its understanding and appreciation a much greater effort of imagination than the factors stressed by the intellectualist view. While we are sometimes able to trace the intellectual processes that have led to a new idea, we can scarcely ever reconstruct the sequence and combination of those contributions that have not led to the acquisition of explicit knowledge; we can scarcely ever reconstruct the favorable habits and skills employed, the facilities and opportunities used, and the particular environment of the main actors that has favored the result. Our efforts toward understanding this part of the process can go little further than to show on simplified models the kind of forces at work and to point to the general principle rather than the specific character of the influences that operate.* Men are always concerned only with what they know. Therefore, those features which, while the process is under way, are not consciously known to anybody are commonly disregarded and can perhaps never be traced in detail.

In fact, these unconscious features not only are commonly disregarded but are often treated as if they were a hindrance rather than a help of an essential condition. Because they are not "rational" in the sense of explicitly entering into our reasoning, they are often treated as irrational in the sense of being contrary to intelligent action. Yet, though much of the non-rational that affects our

---

*   Cf. my article "Degrees of Explanation," *British Journal for the Philosophy of Science*, Vol. VI (1955).

action may be irrational in this sense, many of the "mere habits" and "meaningless institutions" that we use and presuppose in our actions are essential conditions for what we achieve; they are successful adaptations of society that are constantly improved and on which depends the range of what we can achieve. While it is important to discover their defects, we could not for a moment go on without constantly relying on them.

The manner in which we have learned to order our day, to dress, to eat, to arrange our houses, to speak and write, and to use the countless other tools and implements of civilization, no less than the "know-how" of production and trade, furnishes us constantly with the foundations on which our own contributions to the process of civilization must be based. And it is in the new use and improvement of whatever the facilities of civilization offer us that the new ideas arise that are ultimately handled in the intellectual sphere. Though the conscious manipulation of abstract thought, once it has been set in train, has in some measure a life of its own, it would not long continue and develop without the constant challenges that arise from the ability of people to act in a new manner, to try new ways of doing things, and to alter the whole structure of civilization in adaptation to change. The intellectual process is in effect only a process of elaboration, selection, and elimination of ideas already formed. And the flow of new ideas, to a great extent, springs from the sphere in which action, often non-rational action, and material events impinge upon each other. It would dry up if freedom were confined to the intellectual sphere.

The importance of freedom, therefore, does not depend on the elevated character of the activities it makes possible. Freedom of action, even in humble things, is as important as freedom of thought. It has become a common practice to disparage freedom of action by calling it "economic liberty."* But the concept of freedom of action is much wider than that of economic liberty, which it includes; and, what is more important, it is very questionable whether there are any actions which can be called merely "economic" and whether any restrictions on liberty can be confined to what are called merely "economic" aspects. Economic considerations are merely those by which we reconcile and adjust our different purposes, none of which, in the last resort, are economic (excepting those of the miser or the man for whom making money has become an end in itself).**

The rationalist who desires to subject everything to human reason is thus faced with a real dilemma. The use of reason aims at control and predictability. But the process of the advance of reason rests on freedom and the unpredictability of human action. Those who extol the powers of human reason usually see only one side of that interaction of human thought and conduct in which

---

* See A. Director, "The Parity of the Economic Market Place," in *Conference on Freedom and the Law* ("University of Chicago Law School Conference Series," No. 13 [Chicago: 1953]).

** Cf. my book *The Road to Serfdom* (London and Chicago: 1944), chap. vii.

reason is at the same time used and shaped. They do not see that, for advance to take place, the social process from which the growth of reason emerges must remain free from its control.

There can be little doubt that man owes some of his greatest successes in the past to the fact that he has *not* been able to control social life. His continued advance may well depend on his deliberately refraining from exercising controls which are now in his power. In the past, the spontaneous forces of growth, however much restricted, could usually still assert themselves against the organized coercion of the state. With the technological means of control now at the disposal of government, it is not certain that such assertion is still possible; at any rate, it may soon become impossible. We are not far from the point where the deliberately organized forces of society may destroy those spontaneous forces which have made advance possible. ●

12. Private Property and the Government and the Impracticability of Socialism

Ludwig von Mises

Private Property and the Government

All those in positions of political power, all governments, all kings, and all republican authorities have always looked askance at private property. There is an inherent tendency in all governmental power to recognize no restraints on its operation and to extend the sphere of its dominion as much as possible. To control everything, to leave no room for anything to happen of its own accord without the interference of the authorities – this is the goal for which every ruler secretly strives. If only private property did not stand in the way! Private property creates for the individual a sphere in which he is free of the state. It sets limits to the operation of the authoritarian will. It allows other forces to arise side by side with and in opposition to political power. It thus becomes the basis of all those activities that are free from violent interference on the part of the state. It is the soil in which the seeds of freedom are nurtured and in which the autonomy of the individual and ultimately all intellectual and material progress are rooted. In this sense, it has even been called the fundamental prerequisite for the development of the individual.

There has never been a political power that voluntarily desisted from impeding the free development and operation of the institution of private ownership of the means of production. Governments tolerate private property when they are compelled to do so, but they do not acknowledge it voluntarily in recognition of its necessity. Even liberal politicians, on gaining power, have usually relegated their liberal principles more or less to the background. The tendency to impose oppressive restraints on private property, to abuse political power,

Reprinted from *The Free and Prosperous Commonwealth*, translated by Ralph Raico and edited by Arthur Goddard, pp. 67-75, by permission of Mrs. Ludwig von Mises. Copyright © 1962 by the William Volker Fund.

and to refuse to respect or recognize any free sphere outside or beyond the dominion of the state is too deeply ingrained in the mentality of those who control the governmental apparatus of compulsion and coercion for them ever to be able to resist it voluntarily. A liberal government is a *contradictio in adjecto*. Governments must be forced into adopting liberalism by the power of the unanimous opinion of the people; that they could voluntarily become liberal is not to be expected.

It is easy to understand what would constrain rulers to recognize the property rights of their subjects in a society composed exclusively of farmers all of whom were equally rich. In such a social order, every attempt to abridge the right to property would immediately meet with the resistance of a united front of all subjects against the government and thus bring about the latter's fall. The situation is essentially different, however, in a society in which there is not only agricultural but also industrial production, and especially where there are big business enterprises involving large-scale investments in industry, mining, and trade. In such a society, it is quite possible for those in control of the government to take action against private property. In fact, politically there is nothing more advantageous for a government that an attack on property rights, for it is always an easy matter to incite the masses against the owners of land and capital. From time immemorial, therefore, it has been the idea of all absolute monarchs, of all despots and tyrants, to ally themselves with the "people" against the propertied classes. The Second Empire of Louis Napoleon was not the only regime to be founded on the principle of Caesarism. The Prussian authoritarian state of the Hohenzollerns also took up the idea, introduced by Lassalle into German politics during the Prussian constitutional struggle, of winning the masses of workers to the battle against the liberal bourgeoisie by means of a policy of etatism and interventionism. This was the basic principle of the "social monarchy" so highly extolled by Schmoller and his school.

In spite of all persecutions, however, the institution of private property has survived. Neither the animosity of all governments nor the hostile campaign waged against it by writers and moralists and by churches and religions, nor the resentment of the masses — itself deeply rooted in instinctive envy — has availed to abolish it. Every attempt to replace it with some other method of organizing production and distribution has always of itself promptly proved unfeasible to the point of absurdity. People have had to recognize that the institution of private property is indispensible and to revert to it whether they liked it or not.

But for all that, they have still refused to admit that the reason for this return to the institution of free private ownership of the means of production is to be found in the fact that an economic system serving the needs and purposes of man's life in society is, in principle, impracticable except on this foundation. People have been unable to make up their minds to rid themselves of an ideology to which they have become attached, namely the belief that private property is an evil that cannot, at least for the time being, be dispensed with as long as men have not yet sufficiently evolved ethically. While governments — contrary to their intentions, of course, and to the inherent tendency of every organized center of power — have reconciled themselves to the existence of private property, they have still continued to adhere firmly — not only outwardly, but also in their own thinking — to an ideology hostile to property rights. Indeed, they consider opposition to private property to be correct in principle and any deviation from it on their part to be due solely to their own weakness or to consideration for the interests of powerful groups.

The Impracticability of Socialism

People are wont to consider socialism impracticable because they think that men lack the moral qualities demanded by a socialist society. It is feared that under socialism most men will not exhibit the same zeal in the performance of the duties and tasks assigned to them that they bring to their daily work in a social order based on private ownership of the means of production. In a capitalist society, every individual knows that the fruit of his labor is his own to enjoy, that his income increases or decreases according as the output of his labor is greater or smaller. In a socialist society, every individual will think that less depends on the efficiency of his own labor, since a fixed portion of the total output is due him in any case and the amount of the latter cannot be appreciably diminished by the loss resulting from the laziness of any one man. If, as is to be feared, such a conviction should become general, the productivity of labor in a socialist community would drop considerably.

The objection thus raised against socialism is completely sound, but it does not get to the heart of the matter. Were it possible in a socialist community to ascertain the output of the labor of every individual comrade with the same precision with which this is accomplished for each worker by means of economic calculation in the capitalist system, the practicability of socialism would not be dependent on the good will of every individual. Society would be in a position, at least within certain limits, to determine the share of the total output to be allotted to each worker on the basis of the extent of his contribution to production. What renders socialism impracticable is precisely the fact that calculation of this kind is impossible in a socialist society.

In the capitalist system, the calculation of profitability constitutes a guide that indicates to the individual whether the enterprise he is operating ought, under the given circumstances to be in operation at all and whether it is being run in the most efficient possible way, i.e., at the least cost in factors of production. If an undertaking proves unprofitable, this means that the raw materials, half-finished goods, and labor that are needed in it are employed by other enterprises for an end that, from the standpoint of the consumers, is more urgent and more important or for the same end, but in a more economical manner (i.e., with a smaller expenditure of capital and labor). When, for instance, hand weaving came to be unprofitable, this signified that the capital and labor employed in weaving by machine yield greater output and that it is consequently uneconomical to adhere to a method of production in which the same input of capital and labor yields a smaller output.

If a new enterprise is being planned, one can calculate in advance whether it can be made profitable at all and in what way. If, for example, one has the intention of constructing a railroad line, one can, by estimating the traffic to be expected and its ability to pay the freight rates, calculate whether it pays to invest capital and labor in such an undertaking. If the result of this calculation shows that the projected railroad promises no profit, this is tantamount to saying that there is other, more urgent employment for the capital and the labor that the construction of the railroad would require; the world is not yet rich enough to be able to afford such an expenditure. But it is not only when the question arises whether or not a given undertaking is to be begun at all that the calculation of value and profitability is decisive; it controls every single step that the entrepreneur takes in the conduct of his business.

Capitalist economic calculation, which alone makes rational production possible, is based on monetary calculation. Only because the prices of all goods and services in the market can be expressed in terms of money is it possible for them, in spite of their heterogeneity, to enter into a calculation involving homogeneous units of measurement. In a socialist society, where all the means of production are owned by the community, and where, consequently, there is no market and no exchange of productive goods and services, there can also be no money prices for goods and services of higher order. Such a social system would thus, of necessity, be lacking in the means for the rational management of business enterprises, viz., economic calculation. For economic calculation cannot take place in the absence of a common denominator to which all the heterogeneous goods and services can be reduced.

Let us consider a quite simple case. For the construction of a railroad from A to B several routes are conceivable. Let us suppose that a mountain stands between A and B. The railroad can be made to run over the mountain, around the mountain, or, by way of a tunnel, through the mountain. In a capitalist society, it is a very easy matter to compute which line will prove the most profitable. One ascertains the cost involved in constructing each of the three lines and the differences in operating costs necessarily incurred by the anticipated traffic on each. From these quantities it is not difficult to determine which stretch of road will be the most profitable. A socialist society could not make such calculations. For it would have no possible way of reducing to a uniform standard of measurement all the heterogeneous quantities and qualities of goods and services that here come into consideration. In the face of the ordinary, everyday problems which the management of an economy presents, a socialist society would stand helpless, for it would have no possible way of keeping its accounts.

The prosperity that has made it possible for many more people to inhabit the earth today than in the precapitalist era is due solely to the capitalist method of lengthy chains of production, which necessarily require monetary calculation. This is impossible under socialism. In vain have socialist writers labored to demonstrate how one could still manage even without monetary and price calculation. All their efforts in this respect have met with failure.

The leadership of a socialist society would thus be confronted by a problem that it could not possibly solve. It would not be able to decide which of the innumerable possible modes of procedure is the most rational. The resulting chaos in the economy would culminate quickly and irresistibly in universal impoverishment and a retrogression to the primitive condition under which our ancestors once lived.

The socialist ideal, carried to its logical conclusion, would eventuate in a social order in which all the means of production were owned by the people as a whole. Production would be completely in the hands of the government, the center of power in society. It alone would determine what was to be produced and how, and in what way goods ready for consumption were to be distributed. It makes little difference whether we imagine this socialist state of the future as democratically constituted or otherwise. Even a democratic socialist state would necessarily constitute a tightly organized bureaucracy in which everyone apart from the highest officials, though he might very well, in his capacity as a voter, have participated in some fashion in framing the directives issued by the central authority, would be in the subservient position of an administrator bound to carry them out obediently.

A socialist state of this kind is not comparable to the state enterprises, no matter how vast their scale, that we have seen developing in the last decades in Europe, especially in Germany and Russia. The latter all flourish *side by side* with private ownership of the means of production. They engage in commercial transactions with enterprises that capitalists own and manage, and they receive various stimuli from these enterprises that invigorate their own operation. State railroads, for instance, are provided by their suppliers, the manufacturers of locomotives, coaches, signal installations, and other equipment, with apparatus that has proved successful elsewhere in the operation of privately owned railroads. Thence they receive the incentive to institute innovations in order to keep up with the progress in technology and in methods of business management that is taking place all around them.

It is a matter of common knowledge that national and municipal enterprises have, on the whole, failed, that they are expensive and inefficient, and that they have to be subsidized out of tax funds just to maintain themselves in operation. Of course, where a public enterprise occupies a monopolistic position — as is, for instance, generally the case with municipal transportation facilities and electric light and power plants — the bad consequences of inefficiency need not always express themselves in visible financial failure. Under certain circumstances it may be possible to conceal it by making use of the opportunity open to the monopolist of raising the price of his products and services high enough to render these enterprises, in spite of their uneconomic management, still profitable. The lower productivity of the socialist method of production merely manifests itself differently here and is not so easily recognized as otherwise; essentially, however, the case remains the same.

But none of these experiments in the socialist management of enterprises can afford us any basis for judging what it would mean if the socialist ideal of the communal ownership of *all* means of production were to be realized. In the socialist society of the future, which will leave no room whatsoever for the free activity of private enterprises operating side by side with those owned and controlled by the state, the central planning board will lack entirely the gauge provided for the whole economy by the market and market prices. In the market, where all goods and services come to be traded, exchange ratios, expressed in money prices, may be determined for everything bought and sold. In a social order based on private property, it thus becomes possible to resort to monetary calculation in checking on the results of all economic activities. The social productivity of every economic transaction may be tested by the methods of bookkeeping and cost accounting. It yet remains to be shown that public enterprises are unable to make use of cost accounting in the same way as private enterprises do. Nevertheless, monetary calculation does give even governmental and communal enterprises some basis for judging the success or failure of their management. In a completely socialist economic system, this would be quite impossible, for in the absence of private ownership of the means of production, there could be no exchange of capital goods in the market and consequently neither money prices nor monetary calculation. The general management of a purely socialist society will therefore have no means of reducing to a common denominator the costs of production of all the heterogenous commodities that it plans to produce.

Nor can this be achieved by setting expenditures in kind against savings in kind. One cannot calculate if it is not possible to reduce to a common medium of expression hours of labor of various grades, iron, coal, building materials of every kind, machines, and all the other things needed in the operation and management of different enterprises. Calculation is possible only when one is able to reduce to monetary terms all the goods under consideration. Of course, monetary calculation has its imperfections and deficiencies, but we have nothing better to put in its place. If suffices for the practical purposes of life as long as the monetary system is sound. If we were to renounce monetary calculation, every economic computation would become absolutely impossible.

This is the decisive objection that economics raises against the possibility of a socialist society. It must forgo the intellectual division of labor that consists in the cooperation of all entrepreneurs, landowners, and workers as producers and consumers in the formation of market prices. But without it, rationality, i.e., the possibility of economic calculation, is unthinkable. ●

Section THREE

Imperfect Markets

People of the same trade seldom meet to-gether, even for merriment, and diversion, but the conversation ends in a conspiracy against the public, or in some contrivance to raise prices.

Adam Smith

The efficiency resulting from a market economy generally occurs when competitive economic conditions are present. Indeed, most theoretical models that explain private market forces assume a perfectly competitive economic environment where property rights are well defined and market participants have no effective control over the price and total quantity sold of goods and services.

Of course, such perfectly competitive markets rarely, if ever, exist in the marketplace. In spite of this, most economists contend that the assumption of perfectly competitive markets in microeconomic models is a useful approximation of the real world in that these models yield realistic predictions regarding the allocation of resources. But when imperfect markets deviate significantly from the ideal perfect market setting, alternative models may reflect more accurately the resulting economic inefficiencies and distortions.

In those instances where markets deviate significantly from the ideal, the public sector is often called in to regulate the marketplace. Such regulation is usually intended to lead to pricing and output decisions that more closely resemble the outcome of competitive rather than monopolistic market forces.

But while deviation from the ideal perfect market is often considered a justification for regulation, it should be recognized that the forces of competition are remarkably strong. So strong are the forces of competition that few, if any, monopoly agreements can withstand their pressure. Also antimonopoly regulations are often used to legally sanction monopolies and make them longer-lived than would have been the case if the forces of competition were allowed to run their course. An issue of critical importance, therefore, in normative policy evaluation is whether regulation leads to pricing and output decisions that more closely resemble monopolistic or competitive market conditions.

Another example of imperfect markets arises when private property rights to important resources do not exist, and as a consequence people are able to use these resources without paying the full cost of doing so. The external cost (the cost that is external to the decision-maker) that results can lead to serious problems, such as excessive environmental pollution. In the case of pollution, there is a strong argument for government policy to reduce pollution by internalizing the cost of engaging in polluting activities.

Unfortunately, government policy in this area of pollution control seldom addresses the problem very efficiently. By trying to reduce pollution with direct commands and controls, government policy invariably achieves less pollution reduction and higher pollution control costs than is possible by using economic incentives to motivate pollution reduction. Indeed, in some cases government pollution policy may actually increase rather than decrease the level of pollution. The problem with most pollution control policy is that special interests have often used that policy to create external costs of their own; i.e., obtain benefits by imposing costs on others. Such policies have failed to address the problem of pollution efficiently because they create political externalities that are fundamentally the same as the market externalities that cause excessive pollution in the first place.

The first reading of this section uses the game of bocce as a backdrop for a cast of characters that demonstrates the inherent instability of collusive pricing agreements unless the government gets involved.

In another selection from *Capitalism and Freedom*, Milton Friedman identifies three major sources of monopoly.

Before retiring from academic life in 1977, Friedrich Hayek spent ten very productive years in Austria at the University of Saltzburg. Our third reading in this section is a selection from Hayek's major work produced during those years: *Law, Legislation and Liberty*. A reoccurring theme in this work as well as many of his later writings is the "theory of unintended social consequences," the argument that most institutions, including the market economy, are the unconscious consequences of actions taken with other goals in mind. A corollary to this theory is the Hayekian theme that most individual actions should be freely allowed to have their unintended consequences. The Hayek reading in this section which argues that bigness on the part of business does not necessarily confer monopoly power is consistent with that theme: If firms naturally become big, one need not worry about the consequences of such bigness to competition. Moreover, it is not monopoly per se but the prevention of competition that is harmful.

In the Dwight Lee reading, attention turns to the imperfections in markets that lead to both environmental and political pollution. Lee points out that the best way of abating environmental pollution is greater rather than lesser reliance on the market economy. Unfortunately, this more optimal solution is stymied by political pollution. Lee views this pollution as occurring because the private benefits of government programs are funded by defenseless taxpayers.

Larry Ruff, in our final reading in this section, makes a strong case for putting a price on environmental pollution via an efficient tax. Ruff, who received his Ph.D. in economics from Stanford University, has taught at the University of California, San Diego as well as having held a number of appointments in the private and public arenas. While Ruff's proposed pollution tax may strike the reader as different from Lee's proposed sale of pollution rights, in actuality there is no fundamental difference between the two proposals. Both place greater reliance on the price system in a market economy as a means of providing a long-term solution to environmental pollution. •

13. Bocce and the Economics of Collusion

James L. Doti

It's all in the wrist.

That was my conclusion after learning the basic techniques of bocce from my Uncle Rocci (Si Rocco). The lessons consisted mainly of his shouting in my ear, "Don't roll the ball; you pull the ball and throw, like this."

His recommended style resulted in a jerky shot put-type toss that was known as a "pull throw." The throw looked unusual even in bocce where each player had a highly individualized approach to the sport.

However strange the pull throw appeared, it served me well. After moving to Chicago's "Little Italy" to attend a nearby university, I was recruited during my second summer in the neighborhood to play in the legendary Sons of Italy Bocce League. The four-man team I played on was called "The Undertakers," which in addition to myself consisted of three local area morticians.

Bocce was a relatively simple sport consisting mainly of trying to get a clay ball about the size of a cantaloupe near a smaller ball called a paulina. Teams take alternating throws at getting a ball as close as possible to the paulina while trying at the same time to displace those of an opponent. The rules are basically the same as lawn bowling, but the similarity ends there.

Lawn bowling is a genteel sport. I watched it played recently on the bluffs overlooking Laguna Beach, California. Men and women wearing all-white out-fits gently rolled their balls on carefully manicured lawns. No emotion was shown by the stony-faced players, and everything was so quiet that even the gentle clunk of the balls hitting each other seemed to jar the senses.

In sharp contrast to this scene was the carnival-like atmosphere that existed during the Sons of Italy League's bocce games. Players in that league gathered every Sunday on a packed clay and cinder lot in Garibaldi Park promptly after

Reprinted from *The Freeman*, March, 1986, pp. 91-95, by permission of The Foundation for Economic Education.

11 o'clock mass. Members of the league were so vocal and their gesticulations so dramatic that one could tell the movement of the bocce ball by listening to the shouts and observing the wild gyrations that accompanied most of the throws.

The games served as a backdrop to all the other social activities taking place. While the bocce teams played, families milled around. Wives discussed births, deaths and scandals; children released their energy. Betting circles resembling the trading pits of the stock exchange formed while vendors hawked their wares: freshly baked pastries, Italian lemonade, pizza, beer, and subs. A festive spirit enveloped the area as the delicious smell of Italian sausage (Salcicce) roasting on open-pit barbecues wafted through the air. Since most events of neighborhood importance took place at large and noisy gatherings, the festive atmosphere added to rather than detracted from the seriousness of the bocce games.

The importance of the bocce games was also reflected by the team's postgame meetings at the neighborhood conference center—Whitey's Tavern. After a tiring day of bocce on what was typically a hot, sunny and humid summer afternoon, the dark and natural coolness of Whitey's offered a most pleasant respite. It was there under the backdrop of moving water scenes from the "land of sky-blue waters" and crudely patched plaster walls that many business decisions in the neighborhood were made. Even in the case of our postgame wrap-up which ostensibly took place to review our team's performance, it turned out that the supply of local funeral services also hung in the balance.

After roundly attacking each other's performance at bocce, the business part of our meeting would usually start with Nick Mortadella, the youngest and most dynamic mortician of the lot, saying something like, "What are we gonna price the new fake bronze caskets at? We go too low; nobody'll buy the real ones."

It usually took a while before the Sallamagotta brothers, Vinnie and Sal, could change their thought processes from bocce to business. I also got the feeling that Vinnie and Sal considered Nick to be something of an interloper in a neighborhood business that up until six years ago had been exclusively theirs.

Nick could be described as the kind of person who carries his weight well. His large build seemed to add to his stature, but the silk shirts he left open to expose his hairy chest and inflate his sense of machismo irritated the more conservative Sallamagotta brothers.

"Well, did ya hear me? What're we gonna price it at?"

Vinnie seemed more upset by the direct query than his older brother, Sal, who spent most of his time closely examining the food he was eating. Ever since emigrating from Italy, Sal was strongly suspicious of the food served in American restaurants.

Nick persisted, "Come on you guys—what do you wanna do?"

Vinnie finally responded, "Well . . . maybe some family wants . . . to buy . . . the fake casket."

Besides his deadly slow speaking style which exasperated both his brother, Sal, and the interloper, Nick, the lack of business acumen on the part of the college-educated Vinnie and the inability for him to understand even the most basic principles of profit maximization led Sal and Nick to react with disdain to most of Vinnie's statements.

"Listen, how 'bout if we all agree that we don't buy the fake one," said Nick ignoring Vinnie's comment.

We all looked over to the elder brother, Sal, who was busily engaged in examining a fennel seed on the pizza he was eating. When he realized a reply was in order, Sal gave a characteristic shrug of acceptance.

So it was that imitation bronze caskets never made inroads in Little Italy's funeral parlors.

We were preparing to leave when Sal confronted Nick: "You say too many Hail Marys."

After blankly staring at Sal for a few moments, Nick threw some nuts in his mouth and snapped, "I dunno what you're talking about."

"You know what I'm talking about," said Sal, who at this point was fastidiously folding his napkin and making sucking sounds with his teeth to indicate the end of his meal. Sal continued, "We all agree to say five Hail Marys at ten o'clock. When we're finished with the Hail Marys, everybody knows they got to leave. But somebody told me you said Hail Marys every hour at Palucci's wake." After silently making the sign of the cross out of respect for the recently departed Angelo Palucci, Sal continued, "Now nobody knows when they got to leave. If Palucci's family wants more Hail Marys, they should go pay the priest."

Rolling his eyes and in a huff, Nick interrupted Vinnie and said, "OK you guys. I didn't know it's such a big deal to ya. From now on, one set of Hail Marys at ten o'clock."

So it was that one set of Hail Marys was said in Little Italy over the dearly departed promptly at ten o'clock every evening.

The harmony demonstrated by my team member's ability to compromise and work in consort at their weekly meetings turned out to be short-lived. War clouds were clearly evident one Friday evening when I noticed a milling of people outside Sallamagotta Bros. Funeral Home. Getting closer to investigate, I saw Nick Mortadella standing outside in the street staring daggers at the hubbub of people. When I asked Nick what was going on, he motioned for me to follow him.

Nick walked into his competitors' funeral home and led me down into the basement where coffee and cookies were generally served to the mourners. But in place of the usual aluminum tray of store-bought cookies was a "sweet table" filled with a bountiful supply of the most luscious-looking Italian pastries that I have ever seen. People wandered with delight around the table as they ogled cannoli, pasticiotti, spugliatelli and zeppoli (St. Joseph cakes).

Indeed, except for Nick who still glowered, everyone seemed to be in a festive spirit. Fiori Capputi, one of the locals known for his prodigious appetite, was heaping pastries on his platter when he nudged Nick and said, "Hey, Nick, what are ya going to do to top this? Haw Haw."

I was just about to select an especially delicious-looking cannoli from the table when Nick pulled me away and said, "We have to go and talk to Sal." Upstairs we found a stoic-looking Sal wearing a dandruff-flaked pin-stripe suit and positioned in front of the main parlor greeting mourners. When he saw the austere expression on Nick's face, he said to wait for him at his home. Since his home was attached to the funeral parlor, we only had to walk behind the curtain where some poor soul was "laid-out" to be at Sal's back door.

Mrs. Sallamagotta, a portly woman whose cheerful personality belied her association with the funeral business, greeted us warmly. After leading us into the living room, Mrs. Sallamagotta brought us coffee and cannoli, the familiarity of which intensified Nick's anger.

As we waited, I marveled at Mrs. Sallamagotta's ingenuity in covering every conceivable object of fabric in her household with plastic. In addition to the typical plastic covered sofas and chairs, Mrs. Sallamagotta had custom-made plastic coverings for lamp shades and throw pillows, strategically-placed plastic carpet-runners, and even a plastic covered pillow in the dog's sleeping basket. The sound of crinkling plastic was noticeable as the dog and I rustled uneasily when particularly strident wailing sounds were heard from the adjoining funeral parlor.

When Sal finally arrived, he looked at the uneaten cannoli on Nick's plate and said, "Whazza matter Nick, don't you like the cannoli?"

Nick exploded with several rhetorical questions: "Forget da cannoli. What do you think is going on here? Are we in the catering business or something? What's next — sausage and pepperulla?"

After several wounded protestations of innocence, Sal said, "My wife works hard to make the cakes and everybody likes 'em. Why don't you tell your wife to make some?"

Sal had obviously struck a raw nerve in bringing Nick's wife into the arguments. Everyone in the neighborhood considered Nick's wife a career woman because she recently decided to go back to school to take some accounting courses in order to help her husband with the bookkeeping. Although Nick understood the rationality of her decision, he could not help agreeing with Sal's itimation that his wife's proper place was at home making pastries. Nick's festering resentment was exacerbated by the fact that after four daughters, his wife decided to have no more children. The inability for his wife to produce a male heir was particularly grating to Nick since he had prematurely named his business, Mortadella and Sons Funeral Home — an error in judgment that became a familiar neighborhood joke.

Gritting his teeth, Nick said, "Leave my wife out of this." From here the argument quickly generated into a typical Italian shouting match where the logical basis of an argument is far less important than the decibel level in which it is carried out.

The unresolved nature of the shouting match was obvious as Nick yelled a final insult at Sal and then indicated to me that we make a rapid exit. As we left,

Mrs. Sallamagotta grabbed each of our hands and wrapped them around the strings that held a bakery box full of leftover pastries, an offering that Nick did not refuse.

Outside in the street, Nick was still seething. "Wait till he sees what I can do . . . he hasn't seen the last of this . . . two people can play his game."

As we parted ways, Nick stomped off while firmly clutching the strings of his box of pastries.

●   ●   ●

In his monumental work, *The Wealth of Nations*, Adam Smith discusses the ease in which monopolistic pricing agreements among the competitors can be made:

> People of the same trade seldom meet together, even for merriment, and diversion, but the conversation ends in a conspiracy against the public, or in some contrivance to raise prices.*

The collusion that affected the supply of funeral services in Chicago's Little Italy is the same type of collusion that has occurred at one time or another in every sector of an economic system.

During the 1950's, a conspiracy among electrical goods suppliers involving such industrial giants as General Electric and Westinghouse took place. Following a costly price war that occurred in the transformer and switchgear electrical goods industry in 1954-55, profits in that industry tumbled. As a result, pressure was placed on key executives to turn the profit picture around.

In an article that presents a detailed review of the electrical conspiracy, Richard Austin Smith explains how the collusion was facilitated over rounds of golf:

> At the Switchgear Division (General Electric), the pressure was so great that a lifelong believer in tough competition underwent a remarkable conversion. He called a department manager into his office and told him the old cartel was to be cranked up again. . . shortly thereafter, they trotted off to mix in a little conspiracy with a little golf in Bedford Springs, Pennsylvania. They formed a foursome with key men at Westinghouse... They concluded that it might take more than the combined market power of G.E. and Westinghouse (some 70 to 75 percent) to get things back to normal; other companies would have to be brought in. . . Then there was another round of golf and a couple of rounds of drinks and the competitors went their separate ways, after agreeing to keep in touch by memoran-

---

*   *The Wealth of Nations*, Modern Library edition, 1937, p. 128.

dums. Every month that year one company conspirator would initiate a memorandum to the others. . . listing every pending job whether sealed bid or open and stating what the calculated book price would be. Then the conspirators would reassemble and compare calculations to forestall any chiseling from the agreed-upon book.*

The similarity of the electrical conspiracy with my experience in Little Italy should not be surprising. Rewards from evading competitive market forces are substantial. This can be more clearly seen by considering a simple example.

Assume that a funeral home owner in Little Italy incurs $300 of additional costs to produce funeral services worth $1,000 of increased revenue. Each "customer" is therefore worth $700 ($1,000 – $300) in additional profits to a funeral home owner – a return that might explain why the Sallamagotta brothers resented the interloper, Nick, for encroaching on their business.

A new competitor in a market also means there is a greater likelihood that price-cutting will take place as each competitor strives to increase market share. Indeed, the collusion typified by the post game meetings at Whitey's Tavern and that among major electrical goods suppliers over a round of golf represent attempts by individuals to prevent competitive market forces from eating into monopolistic returns.

Fortunately, monopolistic agreements among competitors tend to be highly unstable and short-lived. One need not look far to see the reason for such instability. In the numerical example presented above, each additional "customer" to a funeral home represents $700 of additional profits – certainly a healthy inducement to violate monopolistic pricing agreements. Of course, to avoid retaliation, the initial violations tend to be hidden or, at least, less obvious than announced price cuts. Hence, the initial violations in the funeral home business of Little Italy involved additional services such as reciting more Hail Marys or providing a bountiful sweet table in place of store-bought cookies. In the case of the electrical goods conspiracy, the initial violations involved under-the-table price cuts:

> Westinghouse had proposed to Florida Power that it add all its circuit-breaker order (about a million dollars worth) to its order for Westinghouse transformers. In return, Westinghouse would take 4 per cent off circuit-breaker book and hide the discount in the transformer order. . .
> Retaliation was not long in coming. Westinghouse went to Baltimore Gas and Electric. . . and said they would give 5 per cent off on switchgear and circuit-breakers, and a week later Allis-Chalmers gave Potomac Electric 12 per cent off. A week after that, Westinghouse gave Atlantic City

---

*   *Fortune*, "The Incredible Electrical Conspiracy," April, 1961, p. 172.

Electric 20 per cent off, and it went down to much worse. . . in the winter of 1957-58 prices were 60 per cent off book. That was the end of the cartel.*

Even if one were to unrealistically assume that the participants in collusion abide by iron-clad agreements are successful in preventing violations, there is still the likely entry of new competitors into the market to consider. Of course, a new competitor could be asked to join the cartel, but that would generally mean that a given level of profits would be divided among more participants, resulting in smaller profit shares for all. In addition, a greater number of participants in the cartel increases the likelihood that the agreements will be violated and therefore increases in the enforcement costs of the cartel. The recent experience of the OPEC cartel is a case in point.

The only way a cartel can become permanently entrenched is to elicit the aid of government by making competition illegal. There are many ways a government can be used to establish and enforce monopolistic pricing agreements among competitors. Under the guise of protecting the consumer, governmental agencies such as the Interstate Commerce Commission, Federal Communications Commission, and the Civil Aeronautics Board usually end up mandating complex lists of monopolistic pricing agreements. In addition, licensing provisions and tariffs which make it more difficult for potential competitors to enter a market represent other ways a government can be used to protect long-lived cartels and monopolistic pricing agreements.

●   ●   ●

In retaliation to the Sallamagotta brothers' sweet table, Nick Mortadella's opening salvo was to distribute felt-backed holy cards at funerals instead of the cheaper and more ordinary paper ones. When this strategy failed in generating the interest he hoped for, Nick resorted to lowering his base-rate charges for funeral services.

Meanwhile, the Sallamagotta brothers found the additional number of mourners generated by their sumptuous sweet table getting out of hand. People were coming from as far as Gary, Indiana to partake in the goodies. In fact, the social life of the neighborhood seemed to hinge on the local death rate. I even found myself following the death notices rather closely as I and countless others in the neighborhood became professional mourners. When the Sallamagotta brothers finally put an end to the sweet table and followed Nick's price cuts, a funeral home price war had begun.

These events, of course, had a noticeable effect on our bocce games. Although the enjoyment of playing bocce was far too important for the team to

---

*   *Fortune*, p. 176.

break up, the rancor on our team led to a total deterioration of our team's playing performance and the demise of our post-game meetings at Whitey's.

Under such conditions, playing bocce became a burden, particularly for me since I was the middleman. Scathing remarks that were addressed to me but intended for all to hear filled our ears.

"Did you hear how some poor sucker came all the way from Milwaukee and found they took out the sweet table — Whoo-ee, was he mad."

"Hey, maybe we get the poker cards with the felt on the back. Haw Haw."

" . . . Oh, oh . . . we only have . . . one shot . . . and it's Nick's . . . we lose . . . for sure."

This time Vinnie spoke the truth. Our bocce play was so miserably bad that we were losing against even the worst teams in the league. It was obvious that the competitive zeal that had enveloped the funeral business had made inroads in our style of play. But rather than using the competitive drive to advantage against our opponents, we were using it against ourselves. I half suspected that my fellow team members were committing the unpardonable sin of intentionally hitting each other's team balls away from the paulina. There was even talk that each funeral home would sponsor separate teams in next year's league.

It is difficult to imagine where events would have turned were it not for an unforeseen business development in the neighborhood. The change was evident during an unusually peaceful bocce game that was devoid of the acrimonious display of insults which had characterized recent play. More surprising still was the fact that my teammates shouted words of encouragement to each other.

"Thatta way, Sal."

"Good shot, Nick."

"This time . . . we win."

Something was definitely in the wind as we all agreed to meet together at Whitey's. It was like old times sitting in our usual red vinyl booth. This time, though, we skipped the bocce talk as Nick moved immediately to the business at hand.

"OK, ya all know that Frenchy is going to open up a new funeral home in the neighborhood. What're we gonna do?"

Frenchy, a neighborhood local of questionable French ancestry, owned a funeral home in nearby Greektown. Evidently, Frenchy's move to expand his market share was behind the team's renewed spirit of cooperation.

"We've already dropped our prices," said Nick diplomatically avoiding mention of the factors that led to this turn of events. The intensity of Nick's feeling was evident when in a highly charged and emotional tone he said, "If we get another funeral home, we won't feed our families."

Although the Sallamagotta brothers were still silent, it was obvious from their reactions that the weight of Nick's last comment struck home. The prospect of not adequately feeding one's family throws fear into the hearts of Italians.

"I checked with the Alderman's boys. We pay three grand; they won't give

Frenchy a license — simple as that," said Nick in the self-satisfied manner of a person who had obviously done one's homework. He added that the payoff would be made next week to Alderman Cooley's local precinct captain after the bocce game.

"But three . . . thousand . . . that's a lot of money."

"Aw shut up, Vinnie," shouted Sal who suddenly interrupted a careful examination of some gristle in his beef sandwich. "We pay the money."

"There's one hitch," cautioned Nick whose sly smile implied there was no hitch at all. "The alderman is catching heat from Alderman Czebinski; I guess the funeral homes in his ward don't much like our prices. We make peace and go back to our old prices, or Frenchy gets the license."

A round of their clinking beer steins suggested that peace and order was again restored in the funeral trade of Little Italy.

The following week, after a brilliant round of bocce with my pull throw in top form, I looked forward with silent anticipation to celebrating our bocce victory. As we walked towards Whitey's, Nick in an obviously embarrassed and self-conscious tone said, "The precinct captain don't want you to be there when we pay em the money. Meet us later at Sal's."

I understood. The precinct captain's pull in City Hall was far more important than the bocce pull I learned from Uncle Rocco. ●

14. The Sources of Monopoly

Milton Friedman

Competition has two very different meanings. In ordinary discourse, competition means personal rivalry, with one individual seeking to outdo his known competitor. In the economic world, competition means almost the opposite. There is no personal rivalry in the competitive market place. There is no personal haggling. The wheat farmer in a free market does not feel himself in personal rivalry with, or threatened by, his neighbor, who is, in fact, his competitor. The essence of a competitive market is its impersonal character. No one participant can determine the terms on which other participants shall have access to goods or jobs. All take prices as given by the market and no individual can by himself have more than a negligible influence on price though all participants together determine price by the combined effect of their separate actions.

Monopoly exists when a specific individual or enterprise has sufficient control over a particular product or service to determine significantly the terms on which other individuals shall have access to it. In some ways, monopoly comes closer to the ordinary concept of competition since it does involve personal rivalry.

The Sources of Monopoly

There are three major sources of monopoly: "technical" considerations, direct and indirect governmental assistance, and private collusion.

1. *Technical Considerations.* Monopoly arises to some extent because technical considerations make it more efficient or economical to have a single enterprise rather than many. The most obvious example is a telephone system, water system, and the like in an individual community. There is unfortunately no good solution for technical monopoly. There is only a choice among three evils: private unregulated monopoly, private monopoly regulated by the state, and government operation.

It seems impossible to state as a general proposition that one of these evils

---

Reprinted from *Capitalism and Freedom*, pp. 119-132, by permission of The University of Chicago Press. Copyright © 1962 by The University of Chicago.

is uniformly preferable to another. The great disadvantage of either governmental regulation or governmental operation of monopoly is that it is exceedingly difficult to reverse. In consequence, I am inclined to urge that the least of the evils is private unregulated monopoly wherever this is tolerable. Dynamic changes are highly likely to undermine it and there is at least some chance that these will be allowed to have their effect. And even in the short run, there is generally a wider range of substitutes than there seems to be at first blush, so private enterprises are fairly narrowly limited in the extent to which it is profitable to keep prices above cost. Moreover, as we have seen, the regulatory agencies often tend themselves to fall under the control of the producers and so prices may not be any lower with regulation than without regulation.

Fortunately, the areas in which technical considerations make monopoly a likely or a probable outcome are fairly limited. They would offer no serious threat to the preservation of a free economy if it were not for the tendency of regulation, introduced on this ground, to spread to situations in which it is not so justified.

2. *Direct and Indirect Government Assistance.* Probably the most important source of monopoly power has been government assistance, direct and indirect. Numerous examples of reasonably direct government assistance have been cited above. The indirect assistance to monopoly consists of measures taken for other purposes which have as a largely unintended effect the imposition of limitations on potential competitors of existing firms.

Tariffs have of course been imposed largely to "protect" domestic industries, which means to impose handicaps on potential competitors. They always interfere with the freedom of individuals to engage in voluntary exchange. After all, the liberal takes the individual, not the nation or citizen of a particular nation, as his unit. Hence he regards it just as much a violation of freedom if citizens of the United States and Switzerland are prevented from consummating an exchange that would be mutually advantageous as if two citizens of the United States are prevented from doing so. Tariffs need not produce monopoly. If the market for the protected industry is sufficiently large and technical conditions permit many firms, there can be effective competition domestically in the protected industry, as in the United States in textiles. Clearly, however, tariffs do foster monopoly. It is far easier for a few firms than for many to collude to fix prices, and it is generally easier for enterprises in the same country to collude than for enterprises in different countries.

A major source of labor monopoly has been government assistance. Licensure provisions, building codes, and the like, discussed above have been one source. Legislation granting special immunities to labor unions, such as exemption from the antitrust laws, restrictions on union responsibility, the right to appear before special tribunals, and so on, are a second source. Perhaps of equal or greater importance than either is a general climate of opinion and law enforcement applying different standards to actions taken in the course of a labor dispute than to the same actions under other circumstances. If men turn cars over, or destroy property, out of sheer wickedness or in the course of exacting private vengeance, not a hand will be lifted to protect them from the legal consequences. If they commit the same acts in the course of labor dispute, they may well get off scot free. Union actions involving actual or potential physical violence or coercion could hardly take place if it were not for the unspoken acquiescence of the authorities.

3. *Private Collusion.* The final source of monopoly is private collusion. As Adam Smith says, "People of the same trade seldom meet together, even for merriment and diversion, but the conversation ends in a conspiracy against the public, or in some contrivance to raise prices."* Such collusion or private cartel arrangements are therefore constantly arising. However, they are generally unstable and of brief duration unless they can call government to their assistance. The establishment of the cartel, by raising prices, makes it more profitable for outsiders to enter the industry. Moreover, since the higher price can be established only by the participants' restricting their output below the level that they would like to produce at the fixed price, there is an incentive for each one separately to undercut the price in order to expand output. Each one, of course, hopes that the others will abide by the agreement. It takes only one or at most a few "chiselers" — who are indeed public benefactors — to break the cartel. In the absence of government assistance in enforcing the cartel, they are almost sure to succeed fairly promptly.

The major role of our antitrust laws has been to inhibit such private collusion. Their main contribution in this respect has been less through actual prosecutions than by their indirect effects. They have ruled out the obvious collusive devices — such as the public get-together for this specific purpose — and have therefore made collusion more expensive. More important, they have reaffirmed common law doctrine that combinations in restraint of trade are unenforceable in the courts. In various European countries, the courts will enforce an agreement entered into by a group of enterprises to sell only through a joint selling agency, committing the enterprises to pay specified penalties if they violate the agreement. In the United States, such an agreement would not be enforceable in the courts. This difference is one of the major reasons why cartels have been more stable and widespread in European countries than in the United States. ●

---

*   *The Wealth of Nations* (1776), Bk. I, chap. x, Pt. II (Cannan ed. London, 1930), p. 130.

15. Government Policy and the Market

Friedrich A. Hayek

The Achievements of the Free Market

What, then, is it that we want competition to bring about and which it normally does bring about if it is not prevented from doing so? It is a result so simple and obvious that most of us are inclined to take it for granted; and we are wholly unaware that it is a remarkable thing which is brought about and which never could be achieved by any authority telling the individual producer what to do. Competition, if not prevented, tends to bring about a state of affairs in which: *first*, everything will be produced which somebody knows how to produce and which he can sell profitably at a price at which buyers will prefer it to the available alternatives; *second*, everything that is being produced is produced by persons who can do so at least as cheaply as everybody else who in fact is not producing it;* and *third*, that everything will be sold at prices lower than, or at least as low as, those at which it could be sold by anybody who in fact does not do so.

There are three points which have to be considered if one wants to see the significance of such a state in its proper light: first, that this is a state of affairs which no central direction could ever bring about; second, that this state is approached remarkably closely in all fields where competition is not prevented by government or where governments do not tolerate such prevention by private persons or organizations; third, that in very large sectors of economic activity this state has never been closely approached because governments have restricted competition or allowed and often assisted private persons or organizations

---

* See Gilbert Ryle, 'Knowing how and knowing that', *Proceedings of the Aristotelian Society*, 1945-6, and *The Concept of Mind* (London: 1949), ch. 2; see also my essay 'Rules, perception and intelligibility', *Proceedings of the British Academy*, xlviii, 1962, reprinted in my *Studies in Philosophy, Politics and Economics* (London and Chicago: 1967) *(S.P.P.E.)*.

Reprinted from *Law, Legislation and Liberty*, pp. 74-83, by permission of The University of Chicago Press. Copyright © 1976 by F. A. Hayek.

to restrict competition.

Modest as these accomplishments of competition may at first appear, the fact is that we do not know of any other method that would bring about better results; and wherever competition is prevented or impeded the conditions for their achievement are usually very far from being satisfied. Considering that competition has always been prevented in many fields by the deliberate policies of government from achieving this, while the result is very closely approximated wherever competition is allowed to operate, we should certainly be more concerned to make it generally possible than to make it operate in accordance with an unachievable standard of 'perfection'.

To what a great extent in a normally functioning society the result described is in fact achieved in all sectors where competition is not prevented is demonstrated by the difficulty of discovering opportunities for making a living by serving the customers better than is already being done. We know only too well how difficult this in fact is and how much ingenuity is needed in a functioning catallaxy to discover such opportunities.* It is also instructive to compare in this respect the situation in a country which possesses a large commercially alert class, where most of the existing opportunities will have been taken advantage of, and in a country where people are less versatile or enterprising and which in consequence will often offer to one with a different outlook great opportunities for rapid gain.** The important point here is that a highly developed commercial spirit is itself as much the product as the condition of effective competition, and that we know of no other method of producing it than to throw competition open to all who want to take advantage of the opportunities it offers.

Competition and Rationality

Competition is not merely the only method which we know for utilizing the knowledge and skills that other people may possess, but it is also the method by which we all have been led to acquire much of the knowledge and skills we do possess. This is not understood by those who maintain that the argument for

---

*   See Sten Gagnèr, *Studien zur Ideengeschichte der Gesetzgebung* (Uppsala: 1960); Alan Gewirt, *Marsilius of Padua, Defender of Peace* (New York: 1951 and 1956); and T. F. T. Plucknett, *Statutes and their Interpretation in the First Half of the Fourteenth Century* (Cambridge: 1922).

**   See my essay on 'Notes on the evolution of rules of conduct,' in *S.P.P.E.*

competition rests on the assumption of rational behaviour of those who take part in it. But rational behaviour is not a premise of economic theory, though it is often presented as such. The basic contention of theory is rather that competition will make it necessary for people to act rationally in order to maintain themselves. It is based not on the assumption that most or all the participants in the market process are rational, but, on the contrary, on the assumption that it will in general be through competition that a few relatively more rational individuals will make it necessary for the rest to emulate them in order to prevail.* In a society in which rational behaviour confers an advantage on the individual, rational methods will progressively be developed and be spread by imitation. It is no use being more rational than the rest if one is not allowed to derive benefits from being so. And it is therefore in general not rationality which is required to make competition work, but competition, or traditions which allow competition, which will produce rational behaviour.** The endeavour to do better than can be done in the customary manner is the process in which that capacity for thinking is developed which will later manifest itself in argument and criticism. No society which has not first developed a commercial group within which the improvement of the tools of thought has brought advantage to the individual has ever gained the capacity of systematic rational thinking.

This should be remembered particularly by those who are inclined to argue that competition will not work among people who lack the spirit of enterprise: let merely a few rise and be esteemed and powerful because they have successfully tried new ways, even if they may be in the first instance foreign intruders, and let those tempted to imitate them be free to do so, however few they may

---

*   The best documented and most fully studied instance of the development of distinct 'cultural' traditions among separated groups of animals of the same species is that of the Japanese macaque monkeys which in comparatively recent times were split by the extension of human cultivation into distinct groups which appear in a short time to have acquired clearly distinguishable cultural traits. See also on this J. E. Frisch, 'Research on primate behaviour in Japan', *American Anthropoligist*, lxi, 1959; F. Imanishi, 'Social behavior in Japanese monkeys: "Macaca fuscata",' *Psychologia*, I. 1957; and S. Kawamura, 'The process of sub-cultural propagation among Japanese macaques,' in C. H. Southwick (ed), *Primate Social Behavior* (Princeton: 1963).

**   V. C. Wynne-Edwards, *Animal Dispersion in Relation to Social Behaviour* (Edinburgh: 1966), p. 456; see also ibid., p. 12: "The substitution of a parcel of ground as the object of competition in place of the actual food it contains so that each individual or family unit has a separate holding of the resource to exploit, is the simplest and most direct kind of limiting convention it is possible to have. . . . Much space is devoted in later chapters to studying the almost endless variety of density limiting factors . . . The food territory just considered is concrete enough. . . . We shall find that abstract goals are especially characteristic of gregarious species." And ibid., p. 190: "There is little new in this situation so far as mankind is concerned, except in degree of complexity; all conventional behaviour is inherently social and moral in character; and so far from being an exclusively human attribute, we find that the primary code of conventions evolved to prevent population density from exceeding the optimum, stems not only from the lowest vertebrate classes, but appears well established among the invertebrate phyla as well."

be in the first instance, and that spirit of enterprise will emerge by the only method which can produce it. Competition is as much a method for breeding certain types of mind as anything else: the very cast of thinking of the great entrepreneurs would not exist but for the environment in which they developed their gifts. The same innate capacity to think will take a wholly different turn according to the task it is set.

Such a development will be possible only if the traditionalist majority does not have power to make compulsory for everyone those traditional manners and mores which would prevent the experimentation with new ways inherent in competition. This means that the powers of the majority must be limited to the enforcement of such general rules as will prevent the individuals from encroaching on the protected domains of their fellows, and should not extend to positive prescriptions of what the individuals must do. If the majority view, or any *one* view, is made generally to prevail concerning how things must be done, such developments as we have sketched by which the more rational procedures gradually replace the less rational ones become impossible. The intellectual growth of a community rests on the views of a few gradually spreading, even to the disadvantage of those who are reluctant to accept them; and though nobody should have the power to force upon them new views because he thinks they are better, if success proves that they are more effective, those who stick to their old ways must not be protected against a relative or even absolute decline in their position. Competition is, after all, always a process in which a small number makes it necessary for larger numbers to do what they do not like, be it to work harder, to change habits, or to devote a degree of attention, continuous application, or regularity to their work which without competition would not be needed.

If in a society in which the spirit of enterprise has not yet spread, the majority has power to prohibit whatever it dislikes, it is most unlikely that it will allow competition to arise. I doubt whether a functioning market has ever newly arisen under an unlimited democracy, and it seems at least likely that unlimited democracy will destroy it where it has grown up. To those with whom others compete, the fact that they have competitors is always a nuisance that prevents a quiet life; and such direct effects of competition are always much more visible than the indirect benefits which we derive from it. In particular, the direct effects will be felt by the numbers of the same trade who see how competition is operating, while the consumer will generally have little idea to whose actions the reduction of prices or the improvement of quality is due.

Size, Concentration and Power

The misleading emphasis on the influence of the individual firm on prices, in combination with the popular prejudice against bigness as such, with various 'social' considerations supposed to make it desirable to preserve the middle class, the independent entrepreneur, the small craftsman or shopkeeper, or quite generally the existing structure of society, has acted against changes caused by economic and technological development. The 'power' which large corporations can exercise is represented as in itself dangerous and as making necessary special governmental measures to restrict it. This concern about size and power of individual corporations more often than perhaps any other consideration produces essentially antiliberal conclusions drawn from liberal premises.

We shall presently see that there are two important respects in which monopoly may confer on its possessor harmful power. But neither size in itself, nor ability to determine the prices at which all can buy their product is a measure of their harmful power. More important still, there is no possible measure or standard by which we can decide whether a particular enterprise is too large. Certainly the bare fact that one big firm in a particular industry 'dominates' the market because the other firms of the industry will follow its price leadership, is no proof that this position can in fact be improved upon in any way other than by the appearance of an effective competitor — an event which we may hope for, but which we cannot bring about so long as nobody is available who does enjoy the same (or other compensating) special advantages as the firm that is now dominant.

The most effective size of the individual firm is as much one of the unknowns to be discovered by the market process as the prices, quantities or qualities of the goods to be produced and sold. There can be no general rule about what is the most desirable size since this will depend on the ever-changing technological and economic conditions; and there will always be many changes which will give advantages to enterprises of what on past standards will appear to be an excessive size. It is not to be denied that the advantages of the size will not always rest on facts which we cannot alter, such as the scarcity of certain kinds of talents or resources (including such accidental and yet unavoidable facts as that somebody has been earlier in the field and therefore has had more time to acquire experience and special knowledge); they will often be determined by institutional arrangements which happen to give an advantage to size which is artificial in the sense that it does not secure smaller social costs of the unit of output. In so far as tax legislation, the law of corporations, or the greater influence on the administrative machinery of government, give to the larger unit differential advantages which are not based on genuine superiority of performance, there is indeed every reason for so altering the framework as to remove such artificial advantages of bigness. But there is as little justification for discrimination by policy against large size as such as there is for assisting it.

The argument that mere size confers harmful power over the market behavior of competitors possesses a degree of plausibility when we think in terms of one 'industry' within which there may indeed sometimes be room only for one specialised big firm. But the growth of the giant corporation has made largely meaningless the conception of separate industries which one corporation, because of the magnitude of its resources, can dominate. One of the unforeseen results of the increase of size of the individual corporations which the theorists have not yet quite digested is that large size has brought diversification far beyond the bounds of any definable industry. In consequence, the size of the corporations in other industries has become the main check on the power which size might give a single large corporation in one industry. It may well be that, say in the electrical industry of one country, no other corporation has the strength or staying power to 'take on' an established giant intent upon defending its *de facto* monopoly of some of the products. But as the development of the great automobile or chemical concerns in the USA shows, they have no compunction about encroaching on such fields in which the backing of large resources is essential to make the prospects of entry promising. Size has thus become the most effective antidote to the power of size: that will control the power of large aggregations of capital are other large aggregations of capital, and such control will be much more effective than any supervision by government, whose permission of an act carries its authorization, if not outright protection. As I cannot repeat too often, government-supervised monopoly always tends to become government-protected monopoly; and the fight against bigness only too often results in preventing those very developments through which size becomes the antidote of size.

I do not intend to deny that there are real social and political (as distinct from merely economic) considerations which make a large number of small enterprises appear as more desirable or 'healthy' structures than a smaller number of large ones. We have already had occasion to refer to the danger arising from the fact that constantly increasing numbers of the population work in ever larger corporations, and as a result are familiar with the organizational type of order but strangers to the working of the market which co-ordinates the activities of the several corporations. Considerations like this are often advanced in justification of measures designed to curb the growth of individual enterprise or to protect the less efficient smaller firms against their displacement or absorption into a big one.

Yet, even granting that such measures might in some sense be desirable, it is one of those things which, even though in themselves desirable, cannot be achieved without conferring a discretionary and arbitrary power on some authority, and which therefore must give way to the higher consideration that no authority should be given such power. We have already stressed that such a limitation on all power may make impossible the achievement of some particular aims which may be desired by a majority of the people, and that generally, to avoid greater evils, a free society must deny itself certain kinds of power even if the foreseeable consequences of its exercise appear only beneficial and constitute perhaps the only available method of achieving that particular result.

The Political Aspects of Economic Power

The argument that the great size of an individual corporation confers great power on its management, and that such power of a few men is politically dangerous and morally objectionable, certainly deserves serious consideration. Its persuasiveness derives, however, in a great measure from a confusion of the different meanings of the word 'power', and from a constant shifting from one of the senses in which the possession of great power is desirable to another in which it is objectionable: power over material things and power over the conduct of other men. These two kinds of power are not necessarily connected and can to a large extent be separated. It is one of the ironies of history that socialism, which gained influence by promising the substitution of the administration of things for the power over men, inevitably leads to an unbounded increase of the power exercised by men over other men.

So long as large aggregations of material resources make it possible to achieve better results in terms of improved or cheaper products or more desirable services than smaller organizations provide, every extension of this kind of power must be regarded as in itself beneficial. The fact that large aggregations of resources under a single direction often increase power of this kind more than in proportion to size is often the reason for the development of very large enterprises. Although size is not an advantage in every respect, and though there will always be a limit to the increase of size which still brings an increase of productivity, there will at all times exist fields in which technological change gives an advantage to units larger than those which have existed before. From the replacement of the cottage weaver by the factory to the growth of the continuous process in steel production and to the supermarket, advances in technological knowledge have again and again made larger units more efficient. But if such increase in size leads to more effective use of resources, it does not necessarily increase the power over the conduct of the people, except the limited power which the head of an enterprise wields over those who join it for their benefit. Even though a mail-order house like Sears Roebuck & Co. has grown to be one of the 100 largest corporations in the world and far exceeds in size any comparable enterprise, and although its activities have profoundly affected the standards and habits of millions, it cannot be said to exercise power in any sense other than that of offering services which people prefer when they become available. Nor would a single corporation gain power over the conduct of other men if it were so efficient in the production of a piece of mechanical equipment as universally employed as, say, ball bearings, that it would drive out all competition: so long as it stood ready to supply everyone awaiting its product on the same terms, even though it thereby made a huge profit, not only would all its customers be better off for its existence, but they could also not be said to be dependent on its power.

In modern society it is not the size of the aggregate of resources controlled by an enterprise which gives it power over the conduct of other people, so much as its capacity to withhold services on which people are dependent. It is therefore also not only simply power over the price of their products but the power to exact different terms from different customers which confers power over conduct. This power, however, is not directly dependent on size and not even an inevitable product of monopoly – although it will be possessed by the monopolist of any essential product, whether he be big or small, so long as he is free to make a sale dependent on terms not exacted from all customers alike. We shall see that it is not only the power of the monopolist to discriminate, together with the influence he may exercise on government possessing similar powers, which is truly harmful and ought to be curbed. But this power, although often associated with large size, is neither a necessary consequence of size nor confined to large organizations. The same problem arises when some small enterprise, or a labour union, which controls an essential service can hold the community to ransom by refusing to supply it.

Before we consider further the problem of checking these harmful actions of monopolists we must, however, consider some other reasons why size as such is often regarded as harmful.

The fact that the welfare of many more people is affected by the decisions of a big enterprise rather than by those of a small one does not mean that other considerations should enter into those decisions, or that it is desirable or possible in the case of the former to safeguard against mistakes by some sort of public supervision. Much of the resentment against the big corporations is due to the belief that they do not take consequences into account which we think that they could because they are big, although a smaller firm admittedly could not do so: if a large concern closes down an unprofitable local plant, there will be an outcry because it 'could have afforded' to run it at a loss in order to preserve the jobs, while if the same plant had been an independent enterprise everybody would accept its closing down as inevitable. It is, however, no less desirable that an uneconomical plant be closed down if it belongs to a large concern, although it could be kept going out of the profits of the rest of the concern, than if it is an enterprise which cannot draw on such other sources of revenue.

There exists a widespread feeling that a big corporation, because it is big, should take more account of the indirect consequences of its decisions, and that it should be required to assume responsibilities not imposed upon smaller ones. But it is precisely here that there lies the danger of a big enterprise acquiring objectionably large powers. So long as the management has the one overriding duty of administering the resources under its control as trustees for the shareholders and for their benefit, its hands are largely tied; and it will have no arbitrary power to benefit this or that particular interest. But once the management of a big enterprise is regarded as not only entitled but even obliged to consider in its decisions whatever is regarded as the public or social interest, or to support good causes and generally to act for the public benefit, it gains indeed an uncontrollable power — a power which could not long be left in the hands of private managers but would inevitably be made the subject of increasing public control.*

---

*   David Lack, *The Life of the Robin*, revised edition (London: 1946), p. 35.

In so far as corporations have power to benefit groups of individuals, mere size will also become a source of influencing government, and thus beget power of a very objectionable kind. We shall see presently that such influence, much more serious when it is exerted by the organized interests of groups than when exerted by the largest single enterprise, can be guarded against only by depriving government of the power of benefiting particular groups.

We must finally mention another instance in which it is undeniable that the mere fact of bigness creates a highly undesirable position: namely where, because of the consequences of what happens to a big enterprise, government cannot afford to let such an enterprise fail. At least in so far as the expectation that it will thus be protected makes investment in very big corporations appear less risky than investment in smaller ones, this will produce one of the 'artificial' advantages of bigness which are not based on better performance and which policy ought to eliminate. It seems clear that this can be done only by effectively depriving government of the power of providing such protection, for as long as it has such power it is vulnerable to pressure.

The chief point to remember, which is often obscured by the current talk about monopoly, is that it is not monopoly as such but only the prevention of competition which is harmful. These are so very far from being the same thing that it ought to be repeated that a monopoly that rests entirely on superior performance is wholly praiseworthy—even if such a monopolist keeps prices at a level at which he makes large profits and only just low enough to make it impossible for others to compete with him successfully, because he still uses a smaller amount of resources than others would do if they produced the same quantity of the product. Nor can there be a legitimate claim that such a monopolist is under a moral obligation to sell his product as cheaply as he still could while making a 'normal' profit — as little as we are under a moral obligation to work as hard as possible, or to sell a rare object at a moderate gain. Just as nobody dreams of attacking the 'monopoly' price of the unique skill of an artist or surgeon, so there is no wrong in the 'monopoly' profit of an enterprise capable of producing more cheaply than anybody else.

That it is not monopoly but only the prevention of competition (and all prevention of competition, whether it leads to monopoly or not) which is morally wrong should be specially remembered by those 'neo-liberals' who believe that they must show their impartiality by thundering against all enterprise monopoly as much as against labour monopolies, forgetting that much enterprise monopoly is the result of better performance, while all labour monopoly is due to the coercive suppression of competition. Where enterprise monopoly is based on a similar prevention of competition, it is as reprehensible and in as much need of prevention as those of labour and ought to be severely dealt with. But neither the existence of monopoly nor size as such are on economic or moral grounds undesirable or comparable with any acts aiming at the prevention of competition. ●

16. Environmental Versus Political Pollution

Dwight R. Lee

It is widely accepted that the use of private property in the pursuit of private advantage has led to excessive pollution. It is as widely accepted that the solution to this problem requires an expansion of government control over market decisions. Both views are completely at variance with fact. Pollution is excessive not because of too much reliance on private property but because of too little. Furthermore, attempts to control pollution with direct government control over polluting activities are badly flawed, for they are not guided by the information that can be provided only when property is privately owned. In fact, the problem with government attempts to reduce pollution is completely analogous to the problem that leads to excessive pollution in the first place.

The problem of environmental pollution cannot be adequately understood until it is recognized as fundamentally an economic problem; that is, a problem of scarcity. Our resources simply are not sufficient to satisfy all our demands. We want clean air, pure water, and unspoiled landscapes in order to sustain life and health, and indulge our aesthetic sensitivities. But equally important for maintaining life and enhancing its quality is the use of our environment as a waste-sink. Every productive act we engage in — whether breathing in and out, growing wheat, or generating electricity — creates unwanted by-products that have to be discharged, in one form or another, into the environment. One of the costs of producing more man-made goods is sacrifice of some environmental quality. Similarly, the cost of a cleaner environment has to be reckoned in terms of the resulting sacrifice of some manmade goods. To say that we all value a cleaner environment gives no guidance in deciding whether or not the environment should be a little bit cleaner, or a little bit dirtier. Although we want a cleaner environment, we also want more housing, entertainment, medical research, schooling, fine wines, fast-acting detergent, warmth in the winter, air

Reprinted from International Institute for Economic Research (IIER), Original Paper 39, September, 1982, by permission of IIER.

conditioning in the summer, convenient and safe transportation, attractive clothing, etc. The relevant question is, what is the appropriate combination of environmental purity and all the other desirable things we enjoy, given that we can have more of one only at the cost of sacrificing some of the others?

Honest Communication and Consideration for Others

In an ideal world (ideal except for scarcity), every resource decision would be guided by information on the value of the resource in all possible employments. One way of realizing this ideal, at least conceptually, would be first to arrange for everyone to communicate with everyone else the value they place on different resource uses. In addition, we would have to insure that people communicate with each other honestly and that no one would give greater weight to personal benefits than to the benefits of others. Under these circumstances, resources would be directed into their highest valued employments. If someone communicated to you that a particular resource was worth more to him than to you, you would know this was an honest statement and, in your concern for his interest, you would let him have the resource.

Of course, what we have here may appear to be nothing more than a utopian dream. It would be hard even to imagine the technological advances necessary to allow all users and potential users of a particular resource to communicate simultaneously with each other. And even if the technological problems of communication were solved, we would still be left with the moral or ethical problems of motivating people to communicate honestly and to give the interests of others consideration equal to their own. If avoiding the horrors of Hell and achieving the ecstasy of Heaven have not been sufficient motivation to ensure honesty and brotherly love, there is little reason to believe that the mundane goal of efficient resource allocation will inspire the realization of these noble virtues.

But as utopian as it may appear, we should not completely dismiss the idea that resources can be allocated efficiently as a consequence of people communicating their values to each other, both honestly and with full regard for the interests of others. Indeed, this is a quite accurate description of exactly what happens with most of the resources we use. For a wide range of our resource-using activities, this system of information and consideration is coordinating our actions and interests with the actions and interests of literally millions of others in such a way that an amazingly efficient pattern of resource use emerges. In addition, this system of communication and consideration works so smoothly that few have either awareness of, or appreciation for, the truly astonishing task that is being performed.

Interestingly, the social institution upon which the system of communication and consideration is based is private property, an institution that has long been criticized by people who often claim great concern with promoting social communication and cooperation. The fact that private property can be the source of enormous private wealth is surely seen by some as a major problem. To the economist, however, it is the fact that individuals can profit from private property that explains one of its major advantages. When individuals own resources and are thus able to capture most, if not all, of the value from their use, they have a strong motivation to use them carefully and to direct them into their most productive employments. People use resources they own more wisely than resources that are commonly owned. If you want to find graffiti on a bathroom wall, you are well-advised to look in public restrooms, not privately owned bathrooms.

But if you are interested in efficient resource allocation, it is not enough to have individuals simply putting the resources they own into those uses they value most. The best use the owner had for a resource may be less valuable than the best use someone else has for it. How can each individual be informed as to the value of his resources to others, and then be motivated to take this value fully into consideration? The answer is provided by an activity that is made possible by private ownership – exchange.

Only when people have well-defined and enforced ownership rights in resources is exchange possible. No one is going to pay you for a resource unless you have a transferable property right entitling you to control and use that resource. Not until transferable property rights exist in a resource will a market develop in which the resource can be bought and sold. A market price will emerge. The price will reflect the fact that if you want to purchase the resource you will have to pay at least as much as it is worth to the owner, and this can be no less than the value others place on the resource and are therefore willing to pay the owner. In other words, market exchange results in resource prices that honestly communicate to everyone the value of those resources to others. This is a communication process that not only provides an enormous amount of information, but provides it in such a way that all relevant decisionmakers are motivated to take it fully into consideration.

Whether you already own a resource or will have to purchase it, its market price reflects its cost to you. If you already own it and retain it, the market price reflects the value you have to forego in not selling it, just as it would if you had to purchase the resource. People will be motivated to use resources that are privately owned and easily exchanged only as long as these resources are worth at least as much to them as they are to others. In other words, people are motivated to make economic decisions as if they considered the interests of others as their own.

This discussion of resource allocation through a system of communication and consideration, and the examination of the institutions or property rights and market exchange necessary for this system to function properly, may seem something of a digression from our main focus on the problem of environmental pollution. But having looked carefully at the allocative efficiencies that result from a properly functioning system of communication and consideration, it is possible to better understand the problems that arise when such a system is not working properly. This leads us back to the pollution problem.

Too Little Private Property—Too Much Pollution

We are now in a position to explain why pollution is excessive. Those environmental resources, such as waterways and airsheds that, among other things, necessarily serve as repositories for pollutants, are not easily parcelled out to individuals as privately owned and controlled property. Because these receptor resources are not privately owned, market exchange does not govern the uses to which they are put. All of us make use of commonly owned receptor resources for dumping our waste, and we do so in the absence of the information and consideration that guide most of our resource-use decisions. The institutional foundation of the system of information and consideration that serves us so well in most of our economic activities, is defective when it comes to using many of our environmental resources, because these resources are not subject to private ownership.

Consider, for example, your decision to drive your car to work. Doing so requires the use of resources that are valued by others, such as oil, gasoline, and the labor required for automotive upkeep. But because these resources are privately owned and easily exchanged on markets, you give full consideration to the value of these resources to others in the prices you pay. This is not the case with the clean air you use to vent your exhaust into as you drive. The value that others place on the clean air you foul is not made known to you, because clean air is not rationed by market exchange. There is no price on clean air that informs you of its value to others. And even if somehow you did know this value, in the absence of a price you have to pay there would be little motivation to take it into consideration. The harmful effects generated by your polluting activity are imposed almost entirely on others. Not surprisingly, it can be expected that you will put much greater weight on the benefits of your pollution than on its costs.

With privately owned resources, people have the information and motivation to employ more of each resource only so long as the value it provides to them is at least as great as the value it would otherwise provide to others. With commonly owned receptor resources, people are motivated to employ these resources as waste-sinks as long as the value to them of doing so is positive, regardless of the value that others forego as a consequence. From the perspective of the efficient allocation of our resources, our receptor resources are over-used as waste-sinks relative to their use for providing environmental quality. Pollution is excessive.

Creating Private Property Rights

Before discussing the approach that most economists recommend for solving the problem of excessive pollution, it would be useful to identify just what it is that the ideal solution would accomplish. First, and most obviously, we want pollution reduced to that level consistent with the efficient allocation of our resource, the allocation which maximizes the value generated by our resources.

Put differently, we want to reduce pollution as long as reducing pollution by one more unit provides more value in improved environmental quality than it costs in terms of the value of sacrificed man-made goods.

A second objective is to reduce pollution as cheaply as possible. There are two separate considerations here. Each pollution source has to be abated at minimum cost. There are many ways to cut back a given amount on pollution, but in general there will be only one least-cost way. But even if all polluters are abating pollution as cheaply as possible, it is not necessarily the case that pollution overall is being reduced at least cost. How far do the individual sources go in abating pollution? The least-cost pattern of pollution abatement will find the cost of reducing pollution by one more unit (the marginal abatement cost) the same for all polluters.* Since some polluters will be more efficient at pollution reduction than others, the least-cost pattern of pollution abatement will require different abatement levels for different polluters.

A third objective of a pollution management program is to establish incentives that will motivate advances in pollution abatement technology. This dynamic aspect of pollution control is as important as the point-in-time, or static, considerations discussed in the previous two paragraphs.

These three objectives — (1) achieving the efficient level of pollution, (2) achieving the least-cost pattern of pollution reduction, and (3) motivating advances in the technology of pollution control — probably will never be fully realized. This is particularly true of the first objective. Not being able to own and control identifiable and isolated portions of the atmosphere, for example, no one is in a position to let a polluter foul his, and only his, clean air in exchange for a claim on other desirable things (this claim generally being money). Without such exchange possibilities, prices do not spring up that reflect the value people place on clean air, and without this information there is no way of determining the efficient level of air pollution.

Likewise, private ownership of identifiable and isolated portions of water in our lakes, rivers, and oceans is not possible, and thus there is no accurate way of determining the efficient level of water pollution. With it impossible to determine the efficient level of pollution through the information provided by market exchange, we have to rely upon the political process for this determination. In a democratic political order, there is the presumption that the information

---

*   If the marginal abatement costs are not the same for all polluters, then it is possible to reduce the cost of pollution abatement without increasing the level of pollution. Assume, for example, that the marginal abatement cost of polluter A is $5 and the marginal abatement cost of B is $10: reducing pollution by one more unit will cost A $5 and B $10. Obviously, if A abates one unit more and B one unit less, the level of pollution remains the same, but abatement costs are reduced by $5. The abatement costs of realizing the given level of pollution will continue to be lowered by having A increase abatement and B reduce abatement until the marginal cost of abatement is the same for both. This equality will eventually occur, making the realistic assumption that marginal abatement cost increases as abatement increases.

provided by voting and lobbying will keep the political process responsive to the preferences of the citizens. There is some hope, then, that political decision makers will arrive at a level of pollution that is not too far removed from the efficient level.

Assuming that the politically acceptable level of pollution has been determined, the last two objectives of a pollution control program have to be considered. It is possible to move a long way in realizing these objectives by having the government create and enforce a system of property rights in the use of the environment as a waste-sink. The essential idea is simply to have the government issue transferable pollution rights which give the holder the right to discharge one unit of pollution each week, for example. The total number of rights issued would conform to the targeted level of pollution as determined by the political process. This scheme, assuming adequate enforcement, would serve to limit pollution to the acceptable level. Also each polluter, having to reduce pollution to the level allowed by the number of rights held, will be motivated to do so at the minimum cost. But the crucial advantage in the pollution rights approach comes from the fact that the rights are transferable.

Because the pollution rights would be transferable, a market would develop for them, and the resulting exchanges would determine a market price for rights. The cost of discharging another unit of pollution per week would then equal the price of a pollution right — the value others place on the ability to increase their pollution. People would be motivated to increase their use of the environment as a waste-sink only if the additional pollution benefits them at least as much as it would benefit others. A pattern of polluting activities results that maximizes the value realized from the allowable level of pollution. Another way of stating this is that the reduction in pollution necessary to realize the acceptable level is achieved with the least cost (minimum sacrifice in valuable alternatives) pattern of abatement.

Faced with a positive price for pollution rights, each polluter has every motivation to discover the cheapest way to reduce pollution and to apply it. Each polluter will be motivated also to reduce pollution as long as the cost of reducing one more unit is less than the price of a pollution right. With all polluters facing the same market price for pollution rights, the cost of abating one more unit of pollution will be the same for all polluters. This is another way of stating the requirement for the least-cost abatement pattern. The information and incentives generated by private ownership and market exchange automatically lead to the desirable pattern of pollution abatement.

The pollution rights approach also creates an incentive for polluters to develop improved abatement technologies. History is full of examples of technological development allowing more man-made output to be produced with less land and labor. Conspicuously absent have been technological improvements designed to conserve on the use of the environment as a waste-sink. Market prices on land and labor have always provided a strong incentive to conserve on these resources. The absence of prices for the use of our atmosphere and waterways, however, made it privately unprofitable to worry about conserving on their use. Marketable pollution rights would remedy this neglect.

Political Pollution

Despite the advantages of a pollution rights approach, the political response to our environmental concerns has been to embrace direct government regulation and controls in the effort to reduce pollution. There are reasons for the political popularity of directly regulating pollution sources that have nothing to do with environmental concerns. In some cases, environmental concerns are simply a convenient vehicle for promoting hidden agendas that can actually result in a reduction in environment quality. It will be helpful in providing a general understanding of such nefarious political practices to examine a deficiency in the political decisionmaking process. This deficiency is closely analogous to the problem that explains excess pollution in private market settings.

Government programs, expenditures, and protections often convey benefits that are largely focused on particular industries, occupation associations, or social groups. Agricultural price supports, import restrictions of shoes, and protecting the Maritime Union with the Jones Act against competition are a few of a large number of examples. Benefiting groups will have a strong motivation to become involved politically for the purpose of protecting and, if possible, expanding their particular program.

These groups will each be organized to one degree or another quite independently of their political activity and will therefore find it relatively easy collectively to confront and influence key political decisionmakers. Of course, these special interest programs will impose costs on the general public in the form of higher taxes and prices. But organizing the general public for the purpose of generating political opposition to these programs will face the same problems encountered by an environmental group attempting to get all those suffering from pollution to contribute toward the purchase of pollution rights. If others are successful in controlling a special interest program, your taxes will be lowered or your benefits raised whether or not you contributed to the effort. So when a program is being considered that benefits the few at the expense of the many, our political representatives can expect to hear from the few but not from the many. The resulting bias in political results is not hard to predict.

We suffer from excessive *environmental* pollution because the private benefits each of us receives from polluting activities are paid for, in large part, by a defenseless public. We suffer from *political* pollution, or excessive government involvement in a whole host of activities, because the various private benefits received from the government programs also are paid for, in large measure, by a defenseless public. Of course, each of us also suffers from the pollution and pays for the government programs of others. Most of us would be willing to reduce our pollution and the programs we favor if everyone else would do the same. Unfortunately, this does not happen, because the political process is flawed for the same reason that the market for a clean environment is flawed: in the absence of private property and exchange, people are not able to communicate their preferences to each other in such a way as to ensure honesty and reciprocity.

Conclusion

Concern over environmental quality is often used as a convenient rationale for the exercise of political power designed to favor the organized interests of the few at the expense of the unorganized interests of the many. This political pollution takes the form of higher prices, less efficient allocation of our resources between different sections of the country, and, if not more rather than less environmental pollution, certainly less pollution abatement than we are paying for. The best way of abating this political pollution, and providing the information and incentives needed seriously to combat environmental pollution, is by increasing our reliance on private property and free market exchange.

Government attempts to reduce pollution are necessarily ill-advised. In the absence of private property rights in key environmental resources, market activity will lead to excessive pollution, and a properly structured government response can protect the environment to the benefit of us all. But caution is advisable before embracing the most obvious government solution to the problem of pollution: granting a government agency (or agencies) the power to regulate and control pollution sources. Political power is exercised in a setting in which the type of communication and consideration that characterizes a properly functioning system of market exchange is largely absent. The consequence is that those who are able to position themselves politically can capture private benefits by imposing cost on others, much the same as polluters can gain private benefits by imposing costs on others. And once political power is created for the purpose of achieving some objective, no matter how noble that objective may be, it is naive in the extreme to imagine that those with political influence will not employ this power for their own narrow purposes.

Fortunately, it is often possible to achieve worthy goals without concentrating enormous power in the hands of a few, by having the government remedy certain market deficiencies. In the case of pollution control, the remedy involves creating and enforcing transferable property rights in the use of the environment as a waste-sink. Once such a pollution rights system is in place, private advantage in polluting activities would require reducing pollution as cheaply as possible and taking the value others place on the environment fully into consideration. Under such a policy, there would be little opportunity for a few politically influential groups to use government for their private benefit at the expense of the general public. The advantage of the pollution rights approach is that it would allow a large number of people an opportunity to influence pollution abatement decisions and would establish the incentives and information necessary for a least-cost response to our environmental concerns. ●

17. The Economic Common Sense of Pollution

Larry E. Ruff

We are going to make very little real progress in solving the problem of pollution until we recognize it for what, primarily, it is: an economic problem, which must be understood in economic terms. Of course, there are *non-economic* aspects of pollution, as there are with all economic problems, but all too often, such secondary matters dominate discussion. Engineers, for example, are certain that pollution will vanish once they find the magic gadget or power source. Politicians keep trying to find the right kind of bureaucracy; and bureaucrats maintain an unending search for the correct set of rules and regulations. Those who are above such vulgar pursuits pin their hopes on a moral regeneration or social revolution, apparently in the belief that saints and socialists have no garbage to dispose of. But as important as technology, politics, law, and ethics are to the pollution question, all such approaches are bound to have disappointing results, for they ignore the primary fact that pollution is an economic problem.

Before developing an economic analysis of pollution, however, it is necessary to dispose of some popular myths.

First, pollution is not new. Spanish explorers landing in the sixteenth century noted that smoke from Indian campfires hung in the air of the Los Angeles basin, trapped by what is now called the inversion layer. Before the first century B.C., the drinking waters of Rome were becoming polluted.

Second, most pollution is not due to affluence, despite the current popularity of this notion. In India, the pollution runs in the streets, and advice against drinking the water in exotic lands is often well taken. Nor can pollution be blamed on the self-seeking activities of greedy capitalists. Once-beautiful rivers and lakes which are now open sewers and cesspools can be found in the Soviet Union as well as in the United States, and some of the world's dirtiest air hangs

Reprinted with permission of the author from: *The Public Interest*, No. 19 (Spring 1970), pp. 69-85. Copyright © 1970 by National Affairs, Inc.

over cities in Eastern Europe, which are neither capitalist nor affluent. In many ways, indeed, it is much more difficult to do anything about pollution in non-capitalist societies. In the Soviet Union, there is no way for the public to become outraged or to exert any pressure, and the polluters and the courts there work for the same people, who often decide that clean air and water, like good clothing, are low on their list of social priorities.

In fact, it seems probable that affluence, technology, and a slow-moving, inefficient democracy will turn out to be the cure more than the cause of pollution. After all, only an affluent, technological society can afford such luxuries as moon trips, three-day weekends, and clean water, although even our society may not be able to afford them all; and only in a democracy can the people hope to have any real influence on the choice among such alternatives.

What *is* new about pollution is what might be called the *problem* of pollution. Many unpleasant phenomena – poverty, genetic defects, hurricanes – have existed forever without being considered problems; they are, or were, considered to be facts of life, like gravity and death, and a mature person simply adjusted to them. Such phenomena become problems only when it begins to appear that something can and should be done about them. It is evident that pollution had advanced to the problem stage. Now the question is what can and should be done?

Most discussions of the pollution problem begin with some starting facts: Did you know that 15,000 tons of filth are dumped into the air of Los Angeles County every day? But by themselves, such facts are meaningless, if only because there is no way to know whether 15,000 tons is a lot or a little. It is much more important for clear thinking about the pollution problem to understand a few economic concepts than to learn a lot of sensational-sounding numbers.

Marginalism

One of the most fundamental economic ideas is that of *marginalism*, which entered economic theory when economists became aware of the differential calculus in the 19th century and used it to formulate economic problems as problems of "maximization." The standard economic problem came to be viewed as that of finding a level of operation of some activity which would maximize the net gain from that activity, where the net gain is the difference between the benefits and the costs of the activity. As the level of activity increases, both benefits and costs will increase; but because of diminishing returns, costs will increase faster than benefits. When a certain level of the activity is reached, any further expansion increases costs more than benefits. At this "optimal" level, "marginal cost" – or the cost of expanding the activity – equals "marginal benefit," of the benefit from expanding the activity. Further expansion would cost more than it is worth, and reduction in the activity would reduce benefits more than it would save costs. The net gain from the activity is said to be maximized at this point.

This principle is so simple that it is almost embarrassing to admit it is the cornerstone of economics. Yet intelligent men often ignore it in discussion of public issues. Educators, for example, often suggest that, if it is better to be literate than illiterate, there is no logical stopping point in supporting education. Or scientists have pointed out that the benefits derived from "science" obviously exceed the costs and then have proceeded to infer that their particular project should be supported. The correct comparison, of course, is between "additional" benefits created by the proposed activity and the "additional" costs incurred.

The application of marginalism to questions or pollution is simple enough conceptually. The difficult part lies in estimating the cost and benefits functions, a question to which I shall return. But several important qualitative points can be made immediately. The first is that the choice facing a rational society is *not* between clean air and dirty air, or between clear water and polluted water, but rather between various *levels* of dirt and pollution. The aim must be to find that level of pollution abatement where the costs of further abatement begin to exceed the benefits.

The second point is that the optimal combination of pollution control methods is going to be a very complex affair. Such steps as demanding a 10 per cent reduction in pollution from all sources, without considering the relative difficulties and costs of the reduction, will certainly be an inefficient approach. Where it is less costly to reduce pollution, we want a greater reduction, to a point where an additional dollar spent on control anywhere yields the same reduction in pollution levels.

Markets, Efficiency, and Equity

A second basic economic concept is the idea — or the ideal — of the self-regulating economic system. Adam Smith illustrated this ideal with the example of bread in London: the uncoordinated, selfish actions of many people — farmer, miller, shipper, baker, grocer — provide bread for the city dweller, without any central control and at the lowest possible cost. Pure self-interest, guided only by the famous "invisible hand" of competition, organizes the economy efficiently.

The logical basis of this rather startling result is that, under certain conditions, competitive prices convey all the information necessary for making the optimal decision. A builder trying to decide whether to use brick or concrete will weigh his requirements and tastes against the prices of the materials. Other users will do the same, with the result that those whose needs and preferences for brick are relatively the strongest will get brick. Further, profit-maximizing producers will weigh relative production costs, reflecting society's productive capabilities, against relative prices, reflecting society's tastes and desires, when deciding how much of each good to produce. The end result is that users get brick and cement in quantities and proportions that reflect their individual tastes and society's production opportunities. No other solution would be better from the standpoint of all the individuals concerned.

This suggests what it is that makes pollution different. The efficiency of competitive markets depends on the identity of *private* costs and *social* costs. As long as the brick-cement producer must compensate somebody for every cost imposed by his production, his profit-maximizing decisions about how much to produce, and how, will also be socially efficient decisions. Thus, if a producer dumps wastes into the air, river, or ocean; if he pays nothing for such dumping; and if the disposed wastes have no noticeable effect on anyone else, living or still unborn; then the private and social costs of disposal are identical and nil, and the producer's private decisions are socially efficient. *But if these wastes do affect others, then the social costs of waste disposal are not zero. Private and social costs diverge, and private profit-maximizing decisions are not socially efficient.* Suppose, for example, that cement production dumps large quantities of dust into the air, which damages neighbors, and that the brick-cement producer pays these neighbors nothing. In the social sense, cement will be over-produced relative to brick and other products because users of the products will make decisions based on market prices which do not reflect true social costs. They will use cement when they should use brick, or when they should not build at all.

This divergence between private and social costs is the fundamental cause of pollution of all types, and it arises in any society where decisions are at all decentralized — which is to say, in any economy of any size which hopes to function at all. Even the socialist manager of the brick-cement plant, told to maximize output given the resources at his disposal, will use the People's Air to dispose of the People's Wastes; to do otherwise would be to violate his instructions. And if instructed to avoid pollution "when possible," he does not know what to do: how can he decide whether more brick or cleaner air is more important for building socialism? The capitalist manager is in exactly the same situation. Without prices to convey the needed information, he does not know what action is in the public interest, and certainly would have no incentive to act correctly even if he did know.

Estimating the Costs of Pollution

Both in theory and practice, the most difficult part of an economic approach to pollution is the measurement of the cost and benefits of its abatement. Only a small fraction of the costs of pollution can be estimated straightforwardly. If, for example, smog reduces the life of automobile tires by 10 per cent, one component of the cost of smog is 10 percent of tire expenditures. It has been estimated that, in a moderately polluted area of New York City, filthy air imposes extra costs for painting, washing, laundry, etc., of $200 per person per year. Such costs must be included in any calculation of the benefits of pollution abatement, and yet they are only a part of the relevant costs — and often a small part. Accordingly it rarely is possible to justify a measure like river pollution control solely on the basis of costs to individuals or firms of treating water because it usually is cheaper to process only the water that is actually used for industrial or municipal purposes, and to ignore the river itself.

The costs of pollution that cannot be measured so easily are often called "intangible" or "noneconomic," although neither term is particularly appropriate. Many of these costs are as tangible as burning eyes or a dead fish, and all such costs are relevant to a valid economic analysis. Let us therefore call these costs "nonpecuniary."

The only real difference between nonpecuniary costs and the other kind lies in the difficulty of estimating them. If pollution in Los Angeles harbor is reducing marine life, this imposes costs on society. The cost of reducing commercial fishing could be estimated directly: it would be the fixed cost of converting men and equipment from fishing to an alternative occupation, plus the difference between what they earned in fishing and what they earn in the new occupation, plus the loss to consumers who must eat chicken instead of fish. But there are other, less straightforward costs: the loss of recreation opportunities for children and sports fishermen and of research facilities for marine biologists, etc. Such costs are obviously difficult to measure and may be very large indeed; but just as surely as they are not zero, so too are they not infinite. Those who call for immediate action and damn the cost, merely because the spiney starfish and furry crab populations are shrinking, are putting an infinite marginal value on these creatures. This strikes a disinterested observer as an overestimate.

The above comments may seem crass and insensitive to those who, like one angry letter-writer to the Los Angeles *Times*, want to ask: "If conservation is not for its own sake, then what in the world *is* it for?" Well, what *is* the purpose of pollution control? Is it for its own sake? Of course not. If we answer that it is to make the air and water clean and quiet, then the question arises: what is the purpose of clean air and water? If the answer is, to please the nature gods, then it must be conceded that all pollution must cease immediately because the cost of angering the gods is presumably infinite. But if the answer is that the purpose of clean air and water is to further human enjoyment of life on this planet, then we are faced with the economists' basic question: given the limited alternatives that a niggardly nature allows, how can we best further human enjoyment of life? And the answer is, by making intelligent marginal decisions on the basis of costs and benefits. Pollution control is for lots of things: breathing comfortably, enjoying mountains, swimming in water, for health, beauty, and the general delectation. But so are many other things, like good food and wine, comfortable housing and fast transportation. The question is not which of these desirable things we should have, but rather what combination is most desirable. To determine such a combination, we must know the rate at which individuals are willing to substitute more of any one desirable thing for less of another desirable thing. Prices are one way of determining those rates.

But if we cannot directly observe market prices for many of the costs of pollution, we must find another way to proceed. One possibility is to infer the costs from other prices, just as we infer the value of an ocean view from real estate prices. In principle, one could estimate the value people put on clean air and beaches by observing how much more they are willing to pay for property in nonpolluted areas. Such information could be obtained; but there is little of it available at present.

Another possible way of estimating the costs of pollution is to ask people how much they would be willing to pay to have pollution reduced. A resident of Pasadena might be willing to pay $100 a year to have smog reduced 10 or 20 per ent. In Barstow, where the marginal cost of smog is much less, a resident might not pay $10 a year to have smog reduced 10 per cent. If we knew how much it was worth to everybody, we could add up these amounts and obtain an estimate of the cost of a marginal amount of pollution. The difficulty, of course, is that there is no way of guaranteeing truthful responses. Your response to the questions, how much is pollution costing *you*, obviously will depend on what you think will be done with this information. If you think you will be compensated for these costs, you will make a generous estimate; if you think that you will be charged for the control in proportion to these costs, you will make a small estimate.

In such cases it becomes very important how the questions are asked. For example, the voters could be asked a question of the form: Would you like to see pollution reduced x per cent if the result is a y per cent increase in the cost of living? Presumably a set of questions of this form could be used to estimate the costs of pollution, including the so-called "unmeasurable" costs. But great care must be taken in formulating the questions. For one thing, if the voters will benefit differentially from the activity, the questions should be asked in a way which reflects this fact. If, for example, the issue is cleaning up a river, residents near the river will be willing to pay more for the cleanup and should have a means of expressing this. Ultimately, some such political procedure probably will be necessary, at least until our more direct measurement techniques are greatly improved.

Let us assume that, somehow, we have made an estimate of the social cost function for pollution levels. We now need an estimate of the benefits of pollution – or, if you prefer, the costs of pollution abatement. So we set the Pollution Control Board (PCB) to work on this task.

The PCB has a staff of engineers and technicians, and they begin working on the obvious question: for each pollution source, how much would it cost to reduce pollution by 10 per cent, 20 per cent, and so on. If the PCB has some economists, they will know that the cost of reducing total pollution by 10 per cent is *not* the total cost of reducing each pollution source by 10 per cent. Rather, they will use the equimarginal principle and find the pattern of control such that an additional dollar spent on control of any pollution source yields the same reduction. This will minimize the cost of achieving any given level of abatement. In this way the PCB can generate a "cost of abatement" function, and the corresponding marginal cost function.

While this procedure seems straightforward enough, the practical difficulties are tremendous. The amount of information needed by the PCB is staggering; to do this job right, the PCB would have to know as much about each plant as the operators of the plant themselves. The cost of gathering these data is obviously prohibitive, and, since marginal principles apply to data collection too, the PCB would have to stop short of complete information, trading off the resulting loss in efficient control against the cost of better information. Of course, just as fast as the PCB obtained the data, a technological change would make it obsolete.

The PCB would have to face a further complication. It would not be correct simply to determine how to control existing pollution sources given their existing locations and production methods. Although this is almost certainly what the PCB would do, the resulting cost functions will overstate the true social cost of control. Muzzling existing plants is only one method of control. Plants can move, or switch to a new process, or even to a new product. Consumers can switch to a less-polluting substitute. There are any number of alternatives, and the poor PCB engineers can never know them all. This could lead to some costly mistakes. For example, the PCB may correctly conclude that the cost of installing effective dust control at the cement plant is very high and hence may allow the pollution to continue, when the best solution is for the cement plant to switch to brick production while a plant in the desert switches from brick to cement. The PCB can never have all this information and therefore is doomed to inefficiency, sometimes an inefficiency of large proportions.

Once cost and benefit functions are known, the PCB should choose a level of abatement that maximizes net gain. This occurs where the marginal cost of further abatement just equals the marginal benefit. If, for example, we could reduce pollution damages by $2 million at a cost of $1 million, we should obviously impose that $1 million cost. But if the damage reduction is only $1/2 million, we should not and in fact should reduce control efforts.

This principle is obvious enough but is often overlooked. One author, for example, has written that the national cost of air pollution is $11 billion a year but that we are spending less than $50 million a year on control; he infers from this that "we could justify a tremendous strengthening of control efforts on purely economic grounds." That *sounds* reasonable, if all you care about are sounds. But what is the logical content of the statement? Does it imply we should spend $11 billion on control just to make things even? Suppose we are spending $11 billion on control and thereby succeeded in reducing pollution costs to $50 million. Would this imply we were spending too *much* on control? Of course not. We must compare the *marginal* decrease in pollution costs to the *marginal* increase in abatement costs.

Difficult Decisions

Once the optimal pollution level is determined, all that is necessary is for the PCB to enforce the pattern of controls which it has determined to be optimal. (Of course, this pattern will not really be the best one, because the PCB will not have all the information it should have.) But now a new problem arises: how should the controls be enforced?

The most direct and widely used method is in many ways the least efficient: direct regulation. The PCB can decide what each polluter must do to reduce pollution and then simply require that action under penalty of law. But this approach has many shortcomings. The polluters have little incentive to install the required devices or to keep them operating properly. Constant inspection is therefore necessary. Once the polluter has complied with the letter of the law, he has no incentive to find better methods of pollution reduction. Direct control of this sort has a long history of inadequacy; the necessary bureaucracies rarely manifest much vigor, imagination, or devotion to the public interest. Still, in some situations there may be no alternative.

A slightly better method of control is for the PCB to set an acceptable level of pollution for each source and let the polluters find the cheapest means of achieving this level. This reduces the amount of information the PCB needs, but not by much. The setting of the acceptable levels becomes a matter for negotiation, political pull, or even graft. As new plants are built and new control methods invented, the limits should be changed; but if they are, the incentive to find new designs and new techniques is reduced.

A third possibility is to subsidize the reduction of pollution, either by subsidizing control equipment or by paying for the reduction of pollution below standard levels. This alternative has all the problems of the above methods, plus the classic shortcoming which plagues agricultural subsidies: the old joke about getting into the not-growing-cotton business is not always so funny.

The PCB will also have to face the related problem of deciding *who* is going to pay the costs of abatement. Ultimately, this is a question of equity or fairness which economics cannot answer; but economics can suggest ways of achieving equity without causing inefficiency. In general, the economist will say: if you think polluter A is deserving of more income at polluter B's expense, then by all means give A some of B's income; but do *not* try to help A by allowing him to pollute freely. For example, suppose A and B each operate plants which produce identical amounts of pollution. Because of different technologies, however, A can reduce his pollution 10 per cent for $100, while B can reduce his pollution 5 percent for $1,000. Suppose your goal is to reduce total pollution 5 per cent. Surely it is obvious that the best (most efficient) way to do this is for A to reduce his pollution 10 per cent while B does nothing. But suppose B is rich and A is poor. Then many would demand that B reduce his pollution 10 per cent while A does nothing because B has a greater "ability to pay." Well, perhaps B does have greater ability to pay, and perhaps it is "fairer" that he pay the costs of pollution control; but if so, B should pay the $100 necessary to reduce A's pollution. To force B to reduce his own pollution 10 per cent is equivalent to taxing B $1,000 and then blowing the $1,000 on an extremely inefficient pollution control method. Put this way, it is obviously a stupid thing to do; but put in terms of B's greater ability to pay, it will get considerable support though it is no less stupid. The more efficient alternative is not always available, in which case it may be acceptable to use the inefficient method. Still, it should not be the responsibility of the pollution authorities to change the distribution of welfare in society; this is the responsibility of higher authorities. The PCB should concentrate on achieving economic efficiency without being grossly unfair in its allocation of costs.

Clearly, the PCB has a big job which it will never be able to handle with any degree of efficiency. Some sort of self-regulating system, like a market, is needed, which will automatically adapt to changes in conditions, provide incentives for development and adoption of improved control methods, reduce the amount of information the PCB must gather and the amount of detailed control it must exercise, and so on. This, by any standard, is a tall order.

Putting a Price on Pollution

And yet there is a very simple way to accomplish all this. *Put a price on pollution.* A price-based control mechanism would differ from an ordinary market transaction system only in that the PCB would set the prices, instead of their being set by demand-supply forces, and that the state would force payment. Under such a system, anyone could emit any amount of pollution so long as he pays the price which the PCB sets to approximate the marginal social cost of pollution. Under this circumstance, private decisions based on self-interest are efficient. If pollution consists of many components, each with its own social cost, there should be different prices for each component. Thus, extremely dangerous materials must have an extremely high price, perhaps stated in terms of "years in jail" rather than "dollars," although a sufficiently high dollar price is essentially the same thing. In principle, the prices should vary with geographical location, season of the year, direction of the wind, and even day of the week, although the cost of too many variations may preclude such fine distinctions.

Once the prices are set, polluters can adjust to them any way they choose. Because they act on self-interest they will reduce their pollution by every means possible up to the point where further reduction would cost more than the price. Because all face the same price for the same type of pollution, the marginal cost of abatement is the same everywhere. If there are economies of scale in pollution control, as in some types of liquid waste treatment, plants can cooperate in establishing joint treatment facilities. In fact, some enterprising individual could buy these wastes from various plants (at negative prices – i.e., they would get paid for carting them off), treat them, and then sell them at a higher price, making a profit in the process.

Obviously, such a scheme does not eliminate the need for the PCB. The board must measure the output of pollution from all sources, collect the fees, and so on. But it does not need to know anything about any plant except its total emission of pollution. It does not control, negotiate, threaten, or grant favors. It does not destroy incentive because development of new control methods will reduce pollution payments.

As a test of this price system of control, let us consider how well it would work when applied to automobile pollution, a problem for which direct control is usually considered the only feasible approach. If the price system can work here, it can work anywhere.

Suppose, then, that a price is put on the emissions of automobiles. Obviously, continuous metering of such emissions is impossible. But it should be easy to determine the average output of pollution for cars of different makes, models, and years, having different types of control devises and using different types of fuel. Through graduated registration fees and fuel taxes, each car owner would be assessed roughly the social cost of his car's pollution, adjusted for whatever control devices he has chosen to install and for his driving habits. If the cost of installing a device, driving a different car, or finding alternative means of transportation is less than the price he must pay to continue his pollution, he will presumably take the necessary steps. But each individual remains free to find the best adjustment to his particular situation. It would be remarkable if everyone decided to install the same devices which some states currently require; and yet that is the effective assumption of such requirements.

Even in the difficult case of auto pollution, the price system has a number of advantages. Why should a person living in the Mojave desert, where pollution has little social cost, take the same pains to reduce air pollution as a person living in Pasadena? Present California law, for example, makes no distinction between such areas; the price system would. And what incentive is there for auto manufacturers to design a less polluting engine? The law says only that they must install a certain device in every car. If GM develops a more efficient engine, the law will eventually be changed to require this engine on all cars, raising costs and reducing sales. But will such development take place? No collusion is needed for manufacturers to decide unanimously that it would be foolish to devote funds to such development. But with a pollution fee paid by the consumer, there is a real advantage for any firm to be first with a better engine, and even a collusive agreement wouldn't last long in the face of such an incentive. The same is true of fuel manufacturers, who now have no real incentive to look for better fuels. Perhaps most important of all, the present situation provides no real way of determining whether it is cheaper to reduce pollution by muzzling cars or industrial plants. The experts say that most smog comes from cars; but *even if true, this does not imply that it is more efficient to control autos rather than other pollution sources.* How can we decide which is more efficient without mountains of information? The answer is, by making drivers and plants pay the same price for the same pollution, and letting self-interest do the job.

In situations where pollution outputs can be measured more or less directly (unlike the automobile pollution case), the price system is clearly superior to direct control. A study of possible control methods in the Delaware estuary, for example, estimated that, compared to a direct control scheme requiring each polluter to reduce his pollution by a fixed percentage, an effluent charge which would achieve the same level of pollution abatement would be only half as costly—a saving of about $150 million. Such a price system would also provide incentive for further improvements, a simple method of handling new plants, and revenue for the control authority.

In general, the price system allocates costs in a manner which is at least superficially fair: those who produce and consume goods which cause pollution, pay the costs. But the superior efficiency in control and apparent fairness are not the only advantages of the price mechanism. Equally important is the case with which it can be put into operation. It is not necessary to have detailed information about all the techniques of pollution reduction, or estimates of all costs and benefits. Nor is it necessary to determine whom to blame or who should pay. All that is needed is a mechanism for estimating, if only roughly at first, the pollution output of all polluters, together with a means of collecting fees. Then we can simply pick a price—any price—for each category of pollution, and we are in business. The initial price should be chosen on the basis of some estimate of its effects but need not be the optimal one. If the resulting reduction in pollution is not "enough," the price can be raised until there is sufficient reduction. A change in technology, number of plants, or whatever, can be accommodated by a change in the price, even without detailed knowledge of all the technological and economic data. Further, once the idea is explained, the price system is much more likely to be politically acceptable than some method of direct control. Paying for a service, such as garbage disposal, is a well-established tradition, and is much less objectionable than having a bureaucrat nosing around and giving arbitrary orders. When businessmen, consumers, and politicians understand the alternatives, the price system will seem very attractive indeed.

Who Sets the Prices?

An important part of this method of control obviously is the mechanism that sets and changes the pollution price. Ideally, the PCB could choose this price on the basis of an estimate of the benefits and costs involved, in effect imitating the impersonal workings of ordinary market forces. But because many of the costs and benefits cannot be measured, a less "objective," more political procedure is needed. This political procedure could take the form of a referendum, in which the PCB would present to the voters alternative schedules of pollution prices, together with the estimated effects of each. There would be a massive propaganda campaign waged by the interested parties, of course. Slogans such as "Vote NO on 12 and Save Your Job," or "Proposition 12 Means Higher Prices, " might be overstatements but would contain some truth, as the individual voter would realize when he considered the suggested increase in gasoline taxes and auto registration fees. But the other side, in true American fashion, would respond by overstating *their* case: "Smog Kills, Yes on 12," or "Stop *Them* From Ruining *Your* Water." It would be up to the PCB to inform the public about the true effects of the alternatives; but ultimately, the voters would make the decision.

It is fashionable in intellectual circles to object to such democratic procedures on the ground that the uncultured masses will not make correct decisions. If this view is based on the fact that the technical and economic arguments are likely to be too complex to be decided by direct referendum, it is certainly a reasonable position; one obvious solution is to set up an elective or appointive board to make the detailed decisions, with the expert board members being ultimately responsible to the voters. But often there is another aspect to the antidemocratic position—a feeling that it is impossible to convince the people of the desirability of some social policy, not because the issues are too complex but purely because their values are "different" and inferior. To put it bluntly: many ardent foes of pollution are not so certain that popular opinion is really behind them, and they therefore prefer a more bureaucratic and less political solution.

The question of who should make decisions for whom, or whose desires should count in a society, is essentially a noneconomic question that an economist cannot answer with authority, whatever his personal views on the matter. The political structures outlined here, when combined with the economic suggestions, can lead to a reasonably efficient solution of the pollution problem in a society where the tastes and values of all men are given some consideration. In such a society, when any nonrepresentative group is in a position to impose its particular evaluation of the costs and benefits, an inefficient situation will result. The swimmer or tidepool enthusiast who wants Los Angeles Harbor converted into a crystal-clear swimming pool, at the expense of all the workers, consumers, and businessmen who use the harbor for commerce and industry, is indistinguishable from the stockholder in Union Oil who wants maximum output from offshore wells, at the expense of everyone in the Santa Barbara area. Both are urging an inefficient use of society's resources; both are trying to get others to subsidize their particular thing—a perfectly normal, if not especially noble, endeavor.

If the democratic principle upon which the above political suggestions are based is rejected, the economist cannot object. He will still suggest the price system as a tool for controlling pollution. With any method of decision—whether popular vote, representative democracy, consultation with the nature gods, or a dictate of the intellectual elite—the price system can simplify control and reduce the amount of information needed for decisions. It provides an efficient, comprehensive, easily understood, adaptable, and reasonably fair way of handling the problem. It is ultimately the only way the problem will be solved. Arbitrary, piecemeal, stop-and-go programs of direct control have not and will not accomplish the job.

Some Objections Aren't an Answer

There are some objections that can be raised against the price system as a tool of pollution policy. Most are either illogical or apply with much greater force to any other method of control.

For example, one could object that what has been suggested here ignores the difficulties caused by fragmented political jurisdictions; but this is true for any method of control. The relevant question is: what method of control makes interjurisdictional cooperation easier and more likely? And the answer is: a price system, for several reasons. First, it is probably easier to get agreement on a simple schedule of pollution prices than on a complex set of detailed regulations. Second, a uniform price schedule would make it more difficult for any member of the "co-operative" group to attract industry from the other areas by promising a more lenient attitude toward pollution. Third, and most important, a price system generates revenues for the control board, which can be distributed to the various political entities. While the allocation of these revenues would involve some vigorous discussion, any alternative methods of control would require the various governments to raise taxes to pay the costs, a much less appealing prospect; in fact, there would be a danger that the pollution prices might be considered a device to generate revenue rather than to reduce pollution, which could lead to an overly-clean, inefficient situation.

Another objection is that the Pollution Control Board might be captured by those it is supposed to control. This danger can be countered by having the board members subject to election or by having the pollution prices set by referendum. With any other control method, the danger of the captive regulator is much greater. A uniform price is easy for the public to understand, unlike obscure technical arguments about boiler temperatures and the costs of electrostatic collectors versus low-sulfur oil from Indonesia; if pollution is too high, the public can demand higher prices, pure and simple. And the price is the same for all plants, with no excuses. With direct control, acceptable pollution levels are negotiated with each plant separately and in private, with approved delays and special permits and other nonsense. The opportunities for using political influence and simple graft are clearly much larger with direct control.

A different type of objection occasionally has been raised against the price system, based essentially on the fear that it will solve the problem. Pollution, after all, is a hot issue with which to assault The Establishment, Capitalism, Human Nature, and Them; any attempt to remove the issue by some minor change in institutions, well within The System, must be resisted by The Movement. From some points of view, of course, this is a perfectly valid objection. But one is hopeful that there still exists a majority more concerned with finding solutions than with creating issues.

'If We Can Go to the Moon, Why . . . etc?'

"If we can go to the moon, why can't we eliminate pollution?" This new, and already trite, rhetorical question invites a rhetorical response: "If physical scientists and engineers approached their tasks with the same kind of wishful thinking and fuzzy moralizing which characterizes much of the pollution discussion, we would never have gotten off the ground." Solving the pollution problem is no easier than going to the moon, and therefore requires a comparable effort in terms of men and resources and the same sort of logical hard-headedness that made Apollo a success. Social scientists, politicians, and journalists who spend their time trying to find someone to blame, searching for a magic device or regulation, or complaining about human nature, will be as helpful in solving the pollution problem as they were in getting us to the moon. The price system outlined here is no magic formula, but it attacks the problem at its roots, and has a real chance of providing a long-term solution. ●

Section FOUR

Governmental Regulation

When those particular incorporations which are now peculiarly called universities were first established, the term of years which it was necessary to study, in order to obtain the degree of master of arts, appears evidently to have been copied from the term of apprenticeship in common trades . . . . so to have studied seven years under a master properly qualified, was necessary to entitle him to become a master, teacher, or doctor (words anciently synonymous) in the

*liberal arts, and to have scholars or apprentices
(words likewise originally synonymous) to study
under him.*

Adam Smith

In codifying the earlier work of the Physiocrats, David Hume and others, Adam Smith outlined a framework for society that creates greater wealth for its members when enterprise is free of restrictions and other restraints on trade. In fact, the concept of free markets espoused in Smith's *Wealth of Nations* was a direct attack on the then ruling mercantilist doctrine that various governmental restraints on trade were necessary to insure economic and political power for the nation state. Through use of anecdotal information, crude mathematics, and mostly sound logical inference, Smith relentlessly argued that a natural order was present that made restraints on trade generally unnecessary, unfair, and inefficient.

Previous sections in this book have presented articles that attempt to explain the natural process that converts private interests to the public good. But apparently no persuasive line of reasoning has been formidable enough to shake the prevailing view that individuals totally free to engage in commerce will eventually in one way or another abuse the system for personal gain. Since it is argued that this abuse comes at the expense of the larger community, many believe the government has a sound basis and even a responsibility to enact or sanction various regulations that prevent individuals from acting in a way that is perceived to be in conflict with the larger community.

The role a benevolent government can play in erecting barriers that serve the public interest has been and continues to be an important topic of economic discourse. Economists have long examined the extent to which externalities, economies of scale, resource constraints or monopolistic markets make it possible for individuals to evade the competitive process and justify in certain situations governmental regulations in the market place.

But reliance on a benevolent government to enact wise and prudent restraints may prove to be foolhardy if the restraints themselves become so pervasive as to undermine the normal workings of a competitive economic system. It might also be the case, as shown in the previous section, that regulations under the guise of protecting the public from an imperfect market economy either knowingly or unknowingly protect and reward special interest groups.

In the first three readings to this section, the authors point to the importance and value of a freely moving price system. The Doti reading discusses the costly consequences to the supply of lendable funds as well as chiminelli seeds if a market-determined price is not paid. Dwight Lee expands the argument by equating price controls with censorship and showing the importance of freely moving prices in communicating information in labor and agricultural markets.

A friend, colleague, and fellow Nobel laureate of Milton Friedman, the eminent economist, George Stigler (1911–), joins him in the third selection to examine the efficacy of non-price rationing of the housing market in 1946. This Friedman-Stigler piece represents one of the first critiques of rent controls in economic literature, a critique as relevant today as it was in 1946.

The final reading in this section from Adam Smith's *Wealth of Nations* presents a forceful argument that restrictions on job entry such as apprenticeship and other occupational licensure laws are often sanctioned by the government. These sanctions largely occur because individuals and organizations work in consort with governments to evade the unremitting pressures of a competitive environment. Smith's point is that such conspiracies with government have costly socio-economic consequences.

In discussing the reasons governments give official sanction to laws protecting special interest groups such as barbers and physicians, Smith perceptively points to the significant political power of a focussed political minority in contrast to the lack of political clout of a generally disinterested political majority. This idea will be an important concept in the next section on "The Proper Role of Government." ●

18. The Price of Chiminelli Seeds and Regulation Q

James L. Doti

In a way, searching for the chiminelli seed was a search for my roots. That thought struck me as my great aunt, Si Annunciata, and I climbed the barren and parched hills of Brienza, Italy, to locate the rare and elusive chiminelli bush, a bush capable of producing a seed of inestimable value to those who know of it.

As we reached the crest of the hill, the incredibly thin and old but still wiry Si Annunciata pointed her gnarled finger to a bush that looked like a diseased tumbleweed. I suddenly realized I was looking for the first time at a chiminelli bush and the seeds that had given me so much sensory delight over the years. After I picked a seed and put it in my mouth, the sudden explosion of flavor unleashed memories of a by-gone day.

● ● ●

It was an important family pow-wow. One could tell by the thoughtful and methodical way the three brothers were shelling their nuts. Their children looked on with obvious pride as the three middle-aged overweight men extracted with surgical precision whole nutmeats from the rock-hard and generally impenetrable Brazil nuts.

"It's too bad the Sox lost that game to the Yankees. If they'd won, they would-a pulled within six games," said Angelo, the youngest of the three brothers.

Angelo's life evolved around the fortunes of the Chicago White Sox, or lack thereof which was generally the case. The fact that the White Sox came in second place behind the Yankees for four consecutive years transformed Angelo's thinking pattern into a series of what-ifs.

Reprinted from *The Freeman*, January, 1990, pp. 4-7, by permission of The Foundation for Economic Education.

Angelo added, "If only Yogi Berra hadn't hit that homer in the ninth . . ."

"Yea, yea, yea," Tony interrupted, "they could've done this, they could've done that, but they never win the big ones. Forget those bums. We have to figure out what to send to the old country."

Tony, the oldest of the three brothers and never one to mince words, had abruptly changed the subject to one of timely importance. It was that time of year for the family to send an annual "care" package to distant relatives in Italy. How much these relatives appreciated the cast off remnants of Italo-American consumers was unclear, but the family regularly received in return a supply of chiminelli seeds, that if used with discretion was good for making a year's supply of an Italian-type pretzel called "biscotti."

It is the chiminelli seed that gives an indescribably rich and sweet flavor to the biscotti. The flavor is so intoxicating that some people have been known to recite poems and sing songs about it. An indication of the seed's value is reflected by the fact that biscotti are not conducive to family sharing; in most homes each family member is given a personal stash to hoard and ration until another batch appears.

The Brienza Connection

The source for the small black seeds that make the biscotti a food fit for the Gods is the ancestral southern Italian village of Brienza, the only area in the world with the proper blend of harsh climate and barren soil that allowed the ugly chiminelli bush not only to survive but to thrive and prosper as well.

The arrival of an annual shipment of chiminelli seeds from Brienza once created quite a stir in Chicago's Little Italy when two FBI agents came to investigate several families regarding their possible involvement in drug trafficking. After each of the agents was given a bag of the chiminelli seed-laden biscotti, the case was closed.

"I have a lot of double-breasted suits I want to get rid of," said Angelo. "What if we send 'em some of those?"

"Yea, Ange, but I can't figure what they use them for. They're farmers for cry'n-out-loud," said Tony.

One of the children fidgeting in his chair suddenly interjected, "Hey, did they like my Slinky that you sent them last year?"

"Anthony, don't butt in when we're talking," said Tony, who then feeling guilty for stifling his son's curiosity, offered Anthony some perfectly shelled Brazil nuts.

Tony continued, "Maybe with the earthquake and all we should send 'em some money."

At the mention of money, the middle brother Rocco, who up to this time had devoted his full attention to a particularly resistant nut, looked up and said, "Just because they have an earthquake means all of a sudden they want our money?"

The possibility of sending money instead of goods was suggested in a recently arrived letter from Brienza that threatened it would be difficult to collect and gather the seeds that year. The contents of the letter also strongly suggested that dollars would go a long way to improving the general lot of life in Brienza, especially after an earthquake virtually levelled half the town. And though the utilitarian value of the goods included in the annual "care" package was not directly questioned, perhaps some dissatisfaction was expressed at the end of the letter when it was asked what one does with a used *Uncle Milton Ant Farm*.

'None of Your Junk'

"What if the earthquake really was as bad as they're saying?" Angelo asked and added, "If we don't send 'em money, maybe we don't get the chiminelli this year."

There was a momentary hush as the brothers contemplated this shocking possibility.

"Sure we'll get 'em," said Rocco. "Wait 'til they see all the baby clothes I'm gonna send."

At that point, Mama, the mother of the three brothers and matriarch of the family, walked in the dining room carrying fruit and biscotti to the table. It was obvious she had been eavesdropping. She said in Italian, "Baby clothes? Those poor people don't even have any babies. Listen, you see these biscotti? If you want any more of them, then we are going to send them money this year and none of your junk."

That pretty much decided things. While up in years and certainly not as active as she used to be, Mama still ruled in most family matters, particularly in those relating to familial relations.

Angelo broke the silence that followed Mama's pronouncement with a loud crack of a Brazil nut and an observation: "You know if the White Sox sweep the series in Boston and the Yankees lose in Detroit. . ."

•   •   •

During the 20th century, the typical response of theFederal Reserve Board (Fed) to inflationary pressures and concomitant distortions in production caused by its own expansionary monetary policies was to sharply reverse course and clamp down on money growth. But because of the long and variable lag before the changes in money growth affected economic activity, the Fed would generally over-compensate for past excesses and, as a result, push the economy into a recession.

Economic cycles were therefore generated by waves of expansionary and contractionary monetary policies on the part of the Fed. These cycles were then exacerbated by government-imposed rigidities of one kind or another that constrained free-market forces and had a tendency to multiply miscues on the part of the Fed and lead to more extreme cyclical activity than otherwise would have occurred. Hence, it was the Fed's disastrous manipulation of the money supply between 1929 and 1932 that precipitated the Great Depression. But other government-imposed market rigidities like the ill-conceived Hawley-Smoot Tariff of 1929 served to significantly aggravate an already desperate situation.

The Repeal of Regulation Q

Perhaps the most important but least recognized change during the deregulatory revolution of the Carter-Reagan years was the repeal of Regulation Q, a regulation that imposed interest rate ceilings on most deposit accounts at financial institutions. The repeal of Regulation Q was mandated in the Depository Institutions Deregulation and Monetary Control Act of 1980 and was carried out during the 1981-84 period by the Depository Institutions Deregulation Committee according to a timetable established by Congress. While the repeal of Regulation Q is sometimes incorrectly lamented today in discussions of the S & L crisis, far more significant is how its repeal has greatly benefited the macroeconomy.

In order for banks and thrifts to have competed effectively for deposits under Regulation Q interest rate ceilings, they found it necessary to give away toasters, crock pots, bun warmers and other nonmonetary goods to induce people to make deposits. But whenever Fed tightening pushed short-term interest rates too far above regulated levels, the various gifts being given out to retain deposits were not valuable enough to prevent an outflow of funds to other investments that were not subject to Regulation Q ceilings. At some point when the spread between market rates and Regulation Q ceilings was wide enough, people would opt for more money in the form of higher interest rates rather than gifts which ultimately turned out to be the stuff upon which future garage sales were born.

The outflow of funds from banks and thrifts, known as disintermediation, had costly economic consequences. Since banks and thrifts were the principal sources of retail credit to the housing industry, the resulting shortage of lendable funds in these institutions led to credit crunch conditions that invariably threw the construction industry into a tailspin. This process would effectively shut down a critical industry that had strong multiplier effects throughout the economy thus making a bad situation only worse. Notice too that the brunt of the resulting downturn would be felt, at least initially, by those industries like housing that were particularly sensitive to the availability of retail credit.

But now that interest-rate caps have been removed, banks and thrifts can compete effectively for deposits. Even if this competitive process pushes interest rates up during times of relative credit scarcity, such a situation is vastly preferable to a credit crunch where deposits in regulated institutions are drained away through financial disintermediation — a process that leads to conditions where lendable funds at those affected banks and thrifts are not readily obtainable even at a high price.

A recent inversion of the yield curve — short-term interest rates now exceed long-term rates — has led to ominous warnings about the economy. These warnings are based on the fact that the U.S. economy invariably moved into recessionary straits soon after such an interest-rate inversion took place. Indeed, the structure of interest rates is a better predictor of construction activity and over-all economic activity than is the level of interest rates.

Freeing capital markets from arbitrary interest-rate caps on bank and thrift deposits, however, has changed all this. The strong negative effect of an inverted yield curve undoubtedly was related to the fact that it served as a proxy for the outflow of funds from banks and thrifts that always occurred to some degree whenever short-term interest rates exceeded long-term rates. This process of financial disintermediation that occurred in the past because people wanted money rather than bun warmers in return for their deposits is not likely to take place in an economic environment where interest rates are allowed to move freely. Hence, the elimination of Regulation Q means that the negative consequences of an inverted yield curve are lessened and, as a result, such an inversion should be significantly discounted as a harbinger of recessionary activity.

The beauty and power of a freely moving price system should be evident here. Freer credit markets tend to lessen the ill effects of erratic Fed monetary policies. A simple change that breathes life into the economy by removing impediments to the free market system mitigates the harmful consequences brought about by knee-jerk reactions of a benevolent but woefully ill-informed Federal Reserve Board.

●   ●   ●

Mama's decision to send money instead of a "care" package turned out to be the right one. The veiled threats made in the letter from Brienza were not just threats. While Mama received her annual supply of chiminelli seeds soon after the family's monetary gift of $200 arrived in Brienza, other Italo-American families with ancestors in Brienza received little or nothing in return for their annual shipment of castoffs.

In fact, one of the families thought there might be a message in having received a Christmas wreath made of the chiminelli bush as a gift instead of the expected chiminelli seeds. Evidently, the earthquake meant that it would take greenbacks rather than trinkets to entice the villagers to scavenge the barren hills of Brienza for the elusive chiminelli seeds.

●   ●   ●

After laboriously gathering a spoonful of seeds from that lone chiminelli bush, Si Annunciata and I climbed down the hill. By the time we reached Si Annunciata's home, perspiration stung my eyes and my clothes clung to me like paper mache. As we entered the centuries old dwelling built with two-foot walls of plaster, stone, and rock, its natural coolness invaded my senses and renewed my spirit.

I pushed several hundred dollars worth of lira into the palm of Si

Annunciata's hand. She quickly deposited the lira in her barely existent bosom. Then she kissed my cheek and brought from the cupboard a large jar full of chiminelli seeds which she tenderly placed in my hands. It was undoubtedly the largest stash of chiminelli seeds I had ever seen. I caressed the jar she had given me as one might caress the Hope diamond and felt proud that I had learned at an early age the market price of chiminelli seeds.

So let Donald Trump buy up casinos, airlines, and skyscrapers; let Queen Helmsley rule over her hotels; and let Rupert Murdoch transform the world's print and electronic media. At that moment I felt I had done something far more significant: I had cornered the market in chiminelli seeds. ●

19. The Price Blackout

Dwight R. Lee

More than any other profession, journalists are aware of the value of open communication and a free flow of information. Certainly no group is more adamant in its condemnation of politically inspired censorship. It is therefore surprising to realize that journalists routinely report sympathetically on a certain kind of political censorship.

The censorship I have in mind is a result of government restraints that block the free flow of price information. In our highly specialized society, market prices communicate crucially important information—to consumers, about product availability; and to producers, about consumers' choices. This price information permits coordination between the plans of consumers and producers that promotes both economic productivity and social harmony.

Government policies that force prices above or below what they would be in a free market thus involve censorship. They violate the right of free expression just as if the government dictated the content of the daily newspaper. And, as with any censorship, such policies impose genuine harm on people, often the very people that supporters of the controls want to help.

Our minimum-wage laws, for example, make it illegal for an unskilled youth to communicate effectively with a potential employer. Many youths would like to tell employers, "I have few skills, and college is out for me. So, if a low wage is all you can manage, I am willing to work for little now, while I have few financial responsibilities, in order to acquire on-the-job experience and training." Without the censorship of minimum-wage legislation, thousands of unemployed youth could be productively preparing for their future in jobs that are now denied them.

Agricultural price supports are another example of this kind of government censorship. It victimizes all consumers, but particularly those whose low income makes hunger a real concern. May a poor family communicate through the marketplace its willingness to buy milk at the lowest price that dairy farmers

Reprinted, with permission, from the October 1985 issue of *REASON* magazine. Copyright 1985 by the Reason Foundation, 2716 Ocean Park Blvd., Suite 1062, Santa Monica, CA 90405.

would be willing to accept? No. That communication is currently illegal in the United States, where milk prices are propped up by the government. Journalists have the opportunity both to strike a blow against censorship and to rally to the cause of the poor. Unfortunately, most journalists see less connection between hunger and price-information censorship than they do between hunger and comments by Ronald Reagan.

Other examples of censorship that journalists seldom recognize as such are rent controls, equal-pay-for-equal-work legislation, tariff duties on imported goods, and still-existing price controls on natural gas. But by censoring market information, these restrictions impair communication that is, in some respects, more important than that protected by freedom of the press.

Journalists could *fill* newspapers with stories of jobless teenagers and write compellingly of the need to expand employment opportunities for our nation's youth. But the effectiveness of this information would be nil in comparison with lower wages, which would serve to tell employers that teenagers are willing to work for less. Similarly, if consumers want access to natural gas or nicer apartments, expressing their demands through uncensored markets will be vastly more effective than writing letters to the editor.

This is not to argue that we should be happy with low wages and high prices. Low wages inform us that productive skills are lacking, and high prices tell us that important products are in short supply. But bad news, whether from the market or elsewhere, is no excuse for suppressing the news.

It may be objected that freedom of price communication discriminates against those with fewer financial resources. But if this is so, then traditional freedom of speech discriminates against those with less savvy or intelligence. Although those who are knowledgeable and articulate have in many respects a great advantage over those who are not, clamping down on the free press is not justified in an effort to protect the ignorant. Nor is denial of freedom in market communication justified in hopes of protecting the poor.

Indeed, censorship would work to the long-run disadvantage of both the ignorant and the poor. Just as free verbal and written expression offer the best hope for developing intellectual skills, so does free market expression offer the best hope for developing economic skills.

We cannot, of course, depend on free-market communication being always honest and accurate. Some firms will have the market power to distort prices in their favor. The unscrupulous will often be able to misrepresent their products to the disadvantage of the unwary. But who is prepared to deny that analogous distortions and misrepresentations often creep into the news, books, magazines, and so on?

Such imperfections can never be eliminated; but they can be moderated and countered by maintaining open communication. The best way to control the harm of misinformation is with the competition of free expression. And this is just as true with information expressed through prices as it is with information expressed through words.

As advocates of freedom in communication, journalists should find government attempts to control prices just as abhorrent as they find government attempts to control the news. Neither has any place in a free society. ●

20. Roofs or Ceilings?
The Current Housing Problem

Milton Friedman and George J. Stigler

I. The Background

The San Francisco earthquake of 18 April, 1906, was followed by great fires which in three days utterly destroyed 3,400 acres of buildings in the heart of the city.

Maj. Gen. Greely, commander of the Federal troops in the area, described the situation in these terms:

> Not a hotel of note or importance was left standing. The great apartment houses had vanished . . . . Two hundred and twenty-five thousand people were . . . homeless.

In addition, the earthquake damaged or destroyed many other homes.

Thus a city of about 400,000 lost more than half of its housing facilities in three days.

Various factors mitigated the acute shortage of housing. Many people temporarily left the city—one estimate is as high as 75,000. Temporary camps and shelters were established and at their peak, in the summer of 1906, cared for about 30,000 people. New construction proceeded rapidly.

However, after the disaster, it was necessary for many months for perhaps one-fifth of the city's former population to be absorbed into the remaining half of the housing facilities. In other words, each remaining house on average had to shelter 40 per cent more people.

Yet when one turns to the *San Francisco Chronicle* of 24 May, 1906—the first available issue after the earthquake—*there is not a single mention of a housing shortage!* The classified advertisements listed 64 offers (some for more than one dwelling) of flats and houses for rent, and 19 of houses for sale, against 5 adver-

Reprinted from *Popular Essays on Current Problems*, Volume 1, Number 2, September, 1946, with permission of The Foundation for Economic Education.

tisements of flats or houses wanted. Then and thereafter a considerable number of all types of accommodation except hotel rooms were offered for rent.

Rationing by rents or chance?

Forty years later another housing shortage descended on San Francisco. This time the shortage was nation-wide. The situation in San Francisco was not the worst in the nation, but because of the migration westward it was worse than average. In 1940, the population of 635,000 had no shortage of housing, in the sense that only 93 percent of the dwelling units were occupied. By 1946 the population had increased by at most a third—about 200,000. Meanwhile the number of dwelling units had increased by at least a fifth.

Therefore, the city was being asked to shelter 10 per cent more people in each dwelling-unit than before the war. One might say that the shortage in 1946 was one-quarter as acute as in 1906, when each remaining dwelling-unit had to shelter 40 per cent more people than before the earthquake.

In 1946, however, the housing shortage did not pass unnoticed by the *Chronicle* or by others. On 8 January the California state legislature was convened and the Governor listed the housing shortage as 'the most critical problem facing California.' During the first five days of the year there were altogether only four advertisements offering houses or apartments for rent, as compared with 64 in one day in May 1906, and nine advertisements offering to exchange quarters in San Francisco for quarters elsewhere. But in 1946 there were 30 advertisements per day by persons wanting to rent houses or apartments, against only five in 1906 after the great disaster. During this same period in 1946, there were about 60 advertisements per day of houses for sale, as against 19 in 1906.

In both 1906 and 1946, San Francisco was faced with the problem that now confronts the entire nation: how can a relatively fixed amount of housing be divided (that is, rationed) among people who wish much more until new construction can fill the gap? In 1906 the rationing was done by higher rents. In 1946, the use of higher rents to ration housing has been made illegal by the imposition of rent ceilings, and the rationing is by chance and favouritism. A third possibility would be for OPA to undertake the rationing.

What are the comparative merits of these three methods?

II. The 1906 Method: Price Rationing

War experience has led many people to think of rationing as equivalent to OPA forms, coupons, and orders.

But this is a superficial view; everything that is not as abundant as air or sunlight must, in a sense, be rationed. That is, whenever people want more of something than can be had for the asking, whether bread, threatre tickets, blankets, or haircuts, there must be some way of determining how it shall be distributed among those who want it.

Our normal peace-time basis of rationing has been the method of the auction sale. If demand for anything increases, competition among buyers tends to

raise its price. The rise in price causes buyers to use the article more sparingly, carefully, and economically, and thereby reduces consumption to the supply.
At the same time, the rise in price encourages producers to expand output.
Similarly, if the demand for any article decreases, the price tends to fall, expanding consumption to the supply and discouraging output.

In 1906 San Francisco used this free-market method to deal with its housing
problems, with a consequent rise of rents. Yet, although rents were higher than
before the earthquake, it is cruel to present-day house seekers to quote a 1906
post-disaster advertisement:

> Six-room house and bath, with 2 additional rooms in basement having
> fire-places, nicely furnished; fine piano; ... $45.

The advantages of rationing by higher rents are clear from our example:

1. In a free market, there is always some housing immediately available
   for rent — at all rent levels.

2. The bidding up of rents forces some people to economise on space.
   *Until there is sufficient new construction, this doubling up is the only
   solution.*

3. The high rents act as a strong stimulus to new construction.

4. No complex, expensive, and expansive machinery is necessary. The
   rationing is conducted quietly and impersonally through the price system.

The full significance of these advantages will be clearer when we have considered the alternatives.

Objections to price rationing

Against these merits, which before the war were scarcely questioned in the
United States, three offsetting objections are now raised.

(a) The first objection is usually stated in this form: 'The rich will get all the
housing, and the poor none.'

This objection is false: *At all times during the acute shortage in 1906 inexpen-
sive flats and houses were available.* What is true is that, under free-market conditions, the better quarters will go to those who pay more, either because they
have larger incomes or more wealth, or because they prefer better housing to,
say, better automobiles.

But this fact has no more relation to the housing problem of today than to
that of 1940. In fact, if inequality of income and wealth among individuals justifies rent controls now, it provided an even stronger reason for such controls

in 1940. The danger, if any, that the rich would get all the housing was even greater then than now.

Each person or family is now using at least as much housing space, on the average, as before the war. Furthermore, the total income of the nation is now distributed more equally among the nation's families than before the war. Therefore, *if rents were freed from legal control and left to seek their own levels, as much housing as was occupied before the war would be distributed more equally than it was then.*

That better quarters go under free-market conditions to those who have larger incomes or more wealth is, if anything, simply a reason for taking long-term measures to reduce the inequality of income and wealth. For those, like us, who would like even more equality than there is at present, not just for housing but for all products, it is surely better to attack directly existing inequalities in income and wealth at their source than to ration each of the hundreds of commodities and services that compose our standard of living. It is the height of folly to permit individuals to receive unequal money-incomes and then to take elaborate and costly measures to prevent them from using their incomes.

(b) The second objection often raised to removing rent controls is that landlords would benefit. Rents would certainly rise, except in the so-called black market; and so would the incomes of landlords. But is this an objection? Some groups will gain under any system of rationing, and it is certainly true that urban residential landlords have benefited less than almost any other large group from the war expansion.

The ultimate solution of the housing shortage must come through new construction. Much of this new construction will be for owner-occupancy. But many persons prefer to or must live in rented properties. Increase or improvement of housing for such persons depends in large part on the construction of new properties to rent. It is an odd way to encourage new rental construction (that is, becoming a landlord) by grudging enterprising builders an attractive return.

(c) The third current objection to a free market in housing is that a rise in rents means an inflation, or leads to one.

But price inflation is a rise of many individual prices, and it is much simpler to attack the threat at its source, which is the increased family income and liquid resources that finance the increased spending on almost everything. Heavy taxation,* governmental economies, and control of the stock of money are the fundamental weapons to fight inflation. Tinkering with millions of individual prices—the rent of house A in San Francisco, the price of steak B in Chicago, the price of suit C in New York — means dealing clumsily and ineffectively with

---

* This may have been true in the USA of 1946. There is increasing doubt whether it is true in the Britain of 1972 if high taxes reduce 'take-home' pay and encourage strong trade unions to demand large increases that monetary expansion enables employers to grant. [Ed.]

the symptoms and results of inflation instead of its real causes.

Yet, it will be said, we are not invoking fiscal and monetary controls, and are not likely to do so, so the removal of rent ceilings *will*, in practice, incite wage and then price increases—the familiar inflationary spiral. We do not dispute that this position is tenable, but is it convincing? To answer, we must, on the one hand, appraise the costs of continued rent control, and, on the other, the probable additional contribution to inflation from a removal of rent controls. We shall discuss the costs of the present system next, and in the conclusion briefly appraise the inflationary threat of higher rents.

The present rationing of houses for sale

The absence of a ceiling on the selling price of housing means that at present homes occupied by their owners are being rationed by the 1906 method—to the highest bidder. The selling price of houses is rising as the large and increasing demand encounters the relatively fixed supply. Consequently, many a landlord is deciding that it is better to sell at the inflated market price than to rent at a fixed ceiling price.

The ceiling on rents, therefore, means that an increasing fraction of all housing is being put on the market for owner-occupation, and that rentals are becoming almost impossible to find, at least at the legal rents. In 1906, when both rents and selling prices were free to rise, the *San Francisco Chronicle* listed three 'houses for sale' for every 10 'houses or apartments for rent.' In 1946, under rent control, about 730 'houses for sale' were listed for every 10 'houses or apartments for rent.'

The free market in houses for sale therefore permits a man who has enough capital to make the down-payment on a house to solve his problem by purchase. Often this means that he must go heavily into debt, and that he puts into the down-payment what he would have preferred to spend in other ways.

Nevertheless, the man who has money will find plenty of houses — and attractive ones at that — to buy. The prices will be high—but that is the reason houses are available. He is likely to end up with less desirable housing, furnishings, and other things than he would like, or than his memories of pre-war prices had led him to hope he might get, but at least he will have a roof over his family.

The methods of rent control used in 1946, therefore, do not avoid one of the chief criticisms directed against rationing by higher rents—that the rich have an advantage in satisfying their housing needs. Indeed, the 1946 methods make this condition worse. By encouraging existing renters to use space freely and compelling many to borrow and buy who would prefer to rent, present methods make the price rise in houses-for-sale larger than it would be if there were no rent controls.

One way to avoid giving persons with capital first claim to an increasing share of housing would be to impose a ceiling on the selling price of houses. This would reduce still further the area of price rationing and correspondingly extend present rent-control methods of rationing rental property. This might be a wise move *if* the present method of rationing rented dwellings were satisfactory.

But what is the situation of the man who wishes to rent?

III. The 1946 Method: Rationing by Chance and Favouritism

The prospective renter is in a position very different from that of the man who is willing to buy. If he can find accommodation, he may pay a 'reasonable,' that is, pre-war rent. But unless he is willing to pay a considerable sum on the side — for 'furniture' or in some other devious manner — he is not likely to find anything to rent.

The legal ceilings on rents are the reason why there are so few places for rent. National money-income has doubled, so that most individuals and families are receiving far higher money-incomes than before the war. They are thus able to pay substantially higher rents than before the war, yet legally they need pay no more; they are therefore trying to get more and better housing.

But not all the millions of persons and families who have thus been trying to spread out since 1940 can succeed, since the supply of housing has increased only about as fast as population. Those who do succeed force others to go without housing. The attempt by the less fortunate and the newcomers to the housing market — returning service men, newly-weds, and people changing homes — to get more housing space than is available and more than they used before the war, leads to the familiar spectacle of a horde of applicants for each vacancy.

Advertisements in the *San Francisco Chronicle* again document the effect of rent ceilings. In 1906, after the earthquake, when rents were free to rise, there was one 'wanted to rent' for every 10 'houses or apartments for rent;' in 1946, there were 375 'wanted for rent' for every 10 'for rent.'

A 'veteran' looks for a house

The *New York Times* for 28 January, 1946, reported the experience of Charles Schwartzman, 'a brisk young man in his early thirties,' recently released from the army. Mr. Schwartzman hunted strenuously for three months,

> riding around in his car looking for a place to live . . . He had covered the city and its environs from Jamaica, Queens, to Larchmont and had registered with virtually every real estate agency. He had advertised in the newspapers and he had answered advertisements. He had visited the New York City Veterans Center at 500 Park Avenue and the American Veterans Committee housing sub-committee; he had spoken to friends, he had pleaded with relatives; he had written to Governor Dewey. The results?
>
> An offer of a sub-standard cold-water flat. An offer of four rooms at Central Park West and 101st Street at a rental of $300 a month provided he was prepared to pay $5,000 for the furniture in the apartment. An offer

of one room in an old brownstone house, repainted but not renovated, at Eighty-eighth Street off Central Park West by a young woman (who was going to Havana) at a rental of $80 a month, provided he buy the furniture for $1,300 and reimburse her for the $100 she had to pay an agent to obtain the "apartment."

And a sub-let offer of two commodious rooms in a West Side hotel at a rental of $75 a month only to find that the hotel owner had taken the suite off the monthly rental list and placed it on the transient list with daily (and higher) rates for each of the rooms.

Who gets the housing?

Rental property is now rationed by various forms of chance and favouritism. First priority goes to the family that rented before the housing shortage and is willing to remain in the same dwelling.

Second priority goes to two classes among recent arrivals: (i) persons willing and able to avoid or evade* rent ceilings, either by some legal device or by paying a cash supplement to the OPA ceiling rent; (ii) friends or relatives of landlords or other persons in charge of renting dwellings.

Prospective tenants not in these favoured classes scramble for any remaining places. Success goes to those who are lucky, have the smallest families, can spend the most time in hunting, are most ingenious in devising schemes to find out about possible vacancies, and are the most desirable tenants.

Last priority is likely to go to the man who must work to support his family and whose wife must care for small children. He and his wife can spend little time looking for the needle in the haystack. And if he should find a place, it may well be refused him because a family with small children is a less desirable tenant than a childless family.

Socio-economic costs of present methods

Practically everyone who does not succeed in buying a house or renting a house or apartment is housed somehow. A few are housed in emergency dwellings — trailer camps, prefabricated emergency housing units, reconverted army camps. Most are housed by doubling-up with relatives or friends, a solution that has serious social disadvantages.

The location of relatives or friends willing and able to provide housing may bear little or no relation to the desired location. In order to live with his family, the husband must sacrifice mobility and take whatever position is available in the locality. If no position or only an inferior one is available there, he may have to separate himself from his family for an unpredictable period to take

---

*   These words have the same meaning as in Britain: tax evasion is the illegal concealment of taxable earnings, tax avoidance the legitimate reduction of taxable income to the minimum. [Ed.]

advantage of job opportunities elsewhere. Yet there is a great social need for mobility (especially at present). The best distribution of population after the war certainly differs from the war-time distribution, and rapid reconversion requires that men be willing and able to change their location.

The spectre of current methods of doubling-up restricts the movement not only of those who double up but also of those who do not. The man who is fortunate enough to have a house or apartment will think twice before moving to another city where he will be one of the disfavoured recent arrivals. One of the most easily predictable costs of moving is likely to be an extended separation from his family while he hunts for housing and they stay where they are or move in on relatives.

The rent ceilings also have important effects in reducing the efficiency with which housing is now being used by those who do not double up. The incentives to economise space are much weaker than before the war, because rents are now lower relatively to average money-incomes. If it did not seem desirable to move to smaller quarters before the war or to take in a lodger, there is no added reason to do so now, except patriotic and humanitarian impulses — or possibly the fear of relatives descending on the extra space!

Indeed, the scarcity resulting from rent ceilings imposes new impediments to the efficient use of housing: a tenant will not often abandon his overly-large apartment to begin the dreary search for more appropriate quarters. And every time a vacancy does occur the landlord is likely to give preference in renting to smaller families or the single.

The removal of rent ceilings would bring about doubling up in an entirely different manner. In a free rental market those people would yield up space who considered the sacrifice of space repaid by the rent received. Doubling-up would be by those who had space to spare and wanted extra income, not, as now, by those who act from a sense of family duty or obligation, regardless of space available or other circumstances. Those who rented space from others would be engaging in a strictly business transaction, and would not feel that they were intruding, accumulating personal obligations, or imposing unfair or unwelcome burdens on benefactors. They would be better able to find rentals in places related to their job opportunities. Workers would regain their mobility, and owners of rental properties their incentive to take in more persons.

IV. The Method of Public Rationing

The defects in our present method of rationing by landlords are obvious and weighty. They are to be expected under private, personal rationing, which is, of course, why OPA assumed the task of rationing meats, fats, canned goods, and sugar during the war instead of letting grocers ration them. Should OPA undertake the task of rationing housing? Those who advocate the rationing of housing by a public agency argue that this would eliminate the discrimination against new arrivals, against families with children, and in favour of families with well-placed friends.

Problems of 'political' rationing

To be fair between owners and renters, however, OPA would have to be able to tell owners that they had excessive space and must either yield up a portion or shift to smaller quarters. One's ear need not be close to the ground to know that it is utterly impracticable from a political viewpoint to order an American family owning its home either to take in a strange family (for free choice would defeat the purpose of rationing) or to move out.

Even if this basic difficulty were surmountable, how could the amount of space that a particular family deserves be determined? At what age do children of different sex require separate rooms? Do invalids need ground-floor dwellings, and who is an invalid? Do persons who work in their own homes (physicians, writers, musicians) require more space? What occupations should be favoured by handy locations, and what families by large gardens? Must a mother-in-law live with the family, or is she entitled to a separate dwelling?

How long would it take an OPA board to answer these questions and to decide what tenants or owners must 'move over' to make room for those who, in the board's opinion, should have it?

The duration of the housing shortage would also be affected. In fairness to both tenants and existing landlords, new construction would also have to be rationed and subjected to rent control. If rents on new dwellings were set considerably higher than on comparable existing dwellings, in order to stimulate new construction, one of the main objectives of rent control and rationing— equal treatment for all — would be sacrificed. On the other hand, if rents on new dwellings were kept the same as rents on existing dwellings, private construction of properties for rent would be small or non-existent.

We may conclude that rationing by a public agency is unlikely to be accepted on a thorough-going basis. Even if applied only to rented dwellings, it would raise stupendous administrative and ethical problems.

V. Conclusions

Rent ceilings, therefore, cause haphazard and arbitrary allocation of space, inefficient use of space, retardation of new construction and indefinite continuance of rent ceilings, or subsidisation of new construction and a future depression in residential building. Formal rationing by public authority would probably make matters worse.

Unless removal of rent ceilings would be a powerful new stimulus to inflation, therefore, there is no important defence for them. In practice, higher rents would have little *direct* inflationary pressure on other goods and services. The extra income received by landlords would be offset by the decrease in the funds available to tenants for the purchase of other goods and services.

The additional inflationary pressure from higher rents would arise *indirectly*; the higher rents would raise the cost of living and thereby provide an excuse for wage rises. In an era of direct governmental intervention in wage-fixing, the existence of this excuse might lead to some wage rises that would not otherwise occur and therefore to some further price rises.

How important would this indirect effect be? Immediately after the removal of ceilings, rents charged to new tenants and some existing tenants without leases would rise substantially. Most existing tenants would experience moderate rises, or, if protected by leases, none at all. Since dwellings enter the rental market only slowly, average rents on all dwellings would rise far less than rents charged to new tenants and the cost of living would rise even less.

As more dwellings entered the rental market, the initial rise in rents charged to new tenants would, in the absence of general inflation, be moderated, although average rents on all dwellings would continue to rise.

After a year or so, average rents might be up by as much as 30 per cent. But even this would mean a rise of only about 5 per cent in the cost of living, since rents account for less than one-fifth of the cost of living. A rise of this magnitude — less than one-half of 1 percent per month in the cost of living — is hardly likely to start a general inflation.

The problem of preventing general inflation should be attacked directly; it cannot be solved by special controls in special areas which may for a time bottle up the basic inflationary pressures but do not remove them. We do not believe, therefore, that rent ceilings are a sufficient defence against inflation to merit even a fraction of the huge social costs they entail.

No solution of the housing problem can benefit everyone; some must be hurt. The essence of the problem is that some people must be compelled or induced to use less housing than they are willing to pay for at present legal rents. Existing methods of rationing housing are forcing a small minority — primarily released veterans and migrating war workers, along with their families, friends and relatives — to bear the chief sacrifice.

Rationing by higher rents would aid this group by inducing many others to use less housing and would, therefore, have the merit of spreading the burden more evenly among the population as a whole. It would hurt more people immediately, *but less severely,* than the existing methods. This is, at one and the same time, the justification for using high rents to ration housing and the chief political obstacle to the removal of rent ceilings.

A final note to the reader; we should like to emphasise as strongly as possible that our objectives are the same as yours — *the most equitable possible distribution of the available supply of housing* and *the speediest possible resumption of new construction.* The rise in rents that would follow the removal of rent control is not a virtue in itself. We have no desire to pay higher rents, to see others forced to pay them, or to see landlords reap windfall profits. Yet we urge the removal of rent ceilings because, in our view, any other solution of the housing problem involves still worse evils. ●

21. Inequalities of Wages and Profit

Adam Smith

The policy of Europe occasions a very important inequality in the whole of the advantages and disadvantages of the different employments of labour and stock, by restraining the competition in some employments to a smaller number than might otherwise be disposed to enter into them.

The exclusive privileges of an incorporated trade necessarily restrains the competition, in the town where it is established, to those who are free of the trade. To have served an apprenticeship in the town, under a master properly qualified, is commonly the necessary requisite for obtaining this freedom. The bye-laws of the corporation regulate sometimes the number of apprentices which any master is allowed to have, and almost always the number of years which each apprentice is obliged to serve. The intention of both regulations is to restrain the competition to a much smaller number than might otherwise be disposed to enter into the trade. The limitation of the number of apprentices restrains it directly. A long term of apprenticeship restrains it more indirectly, but as effectually, by increasing the expence of education.

In Sheffield no master cutler can have more than one apprentice at a time, by a bye-law of the corporation. In Norfolk and Norwich no master weaver can have more than two apprentices, under pain of forfeiting five pounds a month to the king. No master hatter can have more than two apprentices any-where in England, or in the English plantations, under pain of forfeiting five pounds a month, half to the king, and half to him who shall sue in any court of record. Both these regulations, though they have been confirmed by a public law of the kingdom, are evidently dictated by the same corporation spirit which enacted the bye-law of Sheffield. The silk weavers in London had scarce been incorporated a year when they enacted a bye-law, restraining any master from having more than two apprentices at a time. It required a particular act of parliament

Abridged from *The Wealth of Nations*, Modern Library Edition (New York: Random House, 1937), pp. 118-128.

to rescind this bye-law.

Seven years seem anciently to have been, all over Europe, the usual term established for the duration of apprenticeships in the greater part of incorporated trades. All such incorporations were anciently called universities; which indeed is the proper Latin name for any incorporation whatever. The university of smiths, the university of taylors, &c. are expressions which we commonly meet with the old charters of ancient towns. When those particular incorporations which are now peculiarly called universities were first established, the term of years which it was necessary to study, in order to obtain the degree of master of arts, appears evidently to have been copied from the term of apprenticeship in common trades, of which the incorporations were much more ancient. As to have wrought seven years under a master properly qualified, was necessary, in order to entitle any person to become a master, and to have himself apprentices in a common trade; so to have studied seven years under a master properly qualified, was necessary to entitle him to become a master, teacher, or doctor (words anciently synonimous) in the liberal arts, and to have scholars or apprentices (words likewise originally synonimous) to study under him.

The institution of long apprenticeships can give no security that insufficient workmanship shall not frequently be exposed to public sale. When this is done it is generally the effect of fraud, and not of inability; and the longest apprenticeship can give no security against fraud. Quite different regulations are necessary to prevent this abuse. The sterling mark upon plate, and the stamps upon linen and woolen cloth, give the purchaser much greater security than any statute of apprenticeship. He generally looks at these, but never thinks it worth while to enquire whether the workmen had served a seven years apprenticeship.

The institution of long apprenticeships has no tendency to form young people to industry. A journeyman who works by the piece is likely to be industrious, because he derives a benefit from every exertion of his industry. An apprentice is likely to be idle, and almost always is so, because he has no immediate interest to be otherwise. In the inferior employments, the sweets of labour consist altogether in the recompence of labour. They who are soonest in a condition to enjoy the sweets of it, are likely soonest to conceive a relish for it, and to acquire the early habit of industry. A young man naturally conceives an aversion to labour, when for a long time he receives no benefit from it. The boys who are put out apprentices from public charities are generally bound for more than the usual number of years, and they generally turn out very idle and worthless.

Apprenticeships were altogether unknown to the ancients. The reciprocal duties of master and apprentice make a considerable article in every modern code. The Roman law is perfectly silent with regard to them. I know no Greek or Latin work (I might venture, I believe, to assert that there is none) which expresses the idea we now annex to the word Apprentice, a servant bound to work at a particular trade for the benefit of a master, during a term of years, upon condition that the master shall teach him that trade.

Long apprenticeships are altogether unnecessary. The arts, which are much superior to common trades, such as those of making clocks and watches, contain no such mystery as to require a long course of instruction. The first invention of such beautiful machines, indeed, and even that of some of the instruments employed in making them, must, no doubt, have been the work of deep thought and long time, and may justly be considered as among the happiest efforts of human ingenuity. But when both have been fairly invented and are well understood, to explain to any young man, in the completest manner, how to apply the instruments and how to construct the machines, cannot well require more than the lessons of a few weeks: perhaps those of a few days might be sufficient. In the common mechanic trades, those of a few days might certainly be sufficient. The dexterity of hand, indeed, even in common trades, cannot be acquired without much practice and experience. But a young man would practice with much more diligence and attention, if from the beginning he wrought as a journeyman, being paid in proportion to the little work which he could execute, and paying in his turn for the materials which he might sometimes spoil through awkwardness and inexperience. His education would generally in this way be more effectual, and always less tedious and expensive. The master, indeed, would be a loser. He would lose all the wages of the apprentice, which he now saves, for seven years altogether. In the end, perhaps, the apprentice himself would be a loser. In a trade so easily learnt he would have more competitors, and his wages, when he came to be a complete workman, would be much less than at present. The same increase of competition would reduce the profits of the masters as well as the wages of the workmen. The trades, the crafts, the mysteries, would all be losers. But the public would be a gainer, the work of all artificers coming in this way much cheaper to market.

It is to prevent this reduction of price, and consequently of wages and profit, by restraining that free competition which would most certainly occasion it, that all corporations, and the greater part of corporation laws, have been established. In order to erect a corporation, no other authority in ancient times was requisite in many parts of Europe, but that of the town corporate in which it was established. In England, indeed, a charter from the king was likewise necessary. But this prerogative of the crown seems to have been reserved rather for extorting money from the subject, than for the defence of the common liberty against such oppressive monopolies. Upon paying a fine to the king, the charter seems generally to have been readily granted; and when any particular class of artificers or traders thought proper to act as a corporation without a charter, such adulterine guilds, as they were called, were not always disfranchised upon that account, but obliged to fine annually to the king for permission to exercise their usurped privileges. The immediate inspection of all corporations, and of the bye-laws which they might think proper to enact for their own government, belonged to the town corporate in which they were established; and whatever discipline was exercised over them, proceeded commonly, not from the king, but from that greater incorporation of which those subordinate ones were only parts or members.

The government of towns corporate was altogether in the hands of traders and artificers; and it was the manifest interest of every particular class of them, to prevent the market from being overstocked, as they commonly express it, with their own particular species of industry; which is in reality to keep it always understocked. Each class was eager to establish regulations proper for this purpose, and, provided it was allowed to do so, was willing to consent that every other class should do the same. In consequence of such regulations, indeed, each class was obliged to buy the goods they had occasion for from every other within the town, somewhat dearer than they otherwise might have done. But in recompence, they were enabled to sell their own just as much dearer; so that so far it was as broad as long, as they say; and in the dealings of the different classes within the town with one another, none of them were losers by these regulations. But in their dealings with the country they were all great gainers; and in these latter dealings consists the whole trade which supports and enriches every town.

The superiority which the industry of the towns has every-where in Europe over that of the country, is not altogether owing to corporations and corporation laws. It is supported by many other regulations. The high duties upon foreign manufactures and upon all goods imported by alien merchants, all tend to the same purpose. Corporation laws enable the inhabitants of towns to raise their prices, without fearing to be under-sold by the free competition of their own countrymen. Those other regulations secure them equally against that of foreigners. The enhancement of price occasioned by both is every-where finally paid by the landlords, farmers, and labourers of the country, who have seldom opposed the establishment of such monopolies. They have commonly neither inclination nor fitness to enter into combinations; and the clamour and sophistry of merchants and manufacturers easily persuade them that the private interest of a part, and of a subordinate part of the society, is the general interest of the whole. ●

Section FIVE

The Proper Role of Government

The strongest of all arguments against the interference of the public with purely personal conduct, is that when it does interfere, the odds are that it interferes wrongly, and in the wrong place.

John Stuart Mill

Those who favor private enterprise and free markets are commonly viewed as hostile toward government. This view is wrong. Advocates of the market economy recognize that government is essential to the proper functioning of a

163

market based economic system. The specialization and exchange which are the essence of a free market economic order depend on the defense of our borders, the protection of private property, and the adjudication of contractual disputes. These are not functions that can be performed properly without government. In the absence of government the institutional setting necessary for a viable market economy simply could not exist.

The question then is not whether government is necessary, but rather how much government is desirable. No definite answer is possible to this question and reasonable people can, and do, disagree on how big government should be and what functions government should perform. Many feel that government, through its power to tax and spend, can beneficially do more than simply create an environment that is favorable to the productive pursuits of individuals through voluntary exchange and interaction. They can look around and see a host of particular problems that it is conceptually possible for government to alleviate. The existence of these problems is seen as a justification for a large and active government.

Those who place more emphasis on the advantages of the private market and who urge restraint on government don't deny that many problems exist that direct government action could conceivably help solve. The concern is that government power, if extended, will be systematically abused rather than beneficially used. Without tight limits on the exercise of government power, politically influential special interests use government to capture benefits by imposing costs on the general public. The result is concentrated benefits coming at the expense of diffused costs. This motivates those receiving the benefits to use political influence to acquire existing wealth rather than to engage in productive efforts to create new wealth. On balance, less will be accomplished by a big government that attempts to solve particular problems than by a limited government that creates a setting in which people can solve their own problems.

This section contains readings that, from a variety of perspectives, make the case for a limited government. For some the major concern is liberty, for others the creation of wealth. But all of the writers in this section would argue that if government was restricted to its proper role we would have far less government today than we do, and as a result, receive far more benefit from government.

Doti opens this section by relating his experience as a lover of Italian lemonade in Chicago. Much to his regret, his favorite supplier was put out of the Italian lemonade business by the use of government regulation that provided a special privilege to a politically influential interest. In this case, as in so many others, the political process is more responsive to the well connected few than the unorganized many.

In the next selection, Friedman discusses the important, but limited role of government in a free society. The primary function of government is to maintain a framework of private property right and general rules of conduct which allow free people to interact productively with one another. In addition, in the face of natural monopolies and neighborhood effects, government can often play a constructive role through regulation and the provision of certain public goods. But always the concern is with government's tendency to expand beyond acceptable limits and the need is for rigid constraints on the scope of government activity.

The importance of the U.S. Constitution to the economic success of the United States is discussed by Dwight Lee in his article. By imposing limits on government, the U.S. Constitution created a political economy conducive to both freedom and prosperity. Forces are at work constantly, however, to erode the Constitution's effectiveness at constraining the growth of government.

Ayn Rand, while best known for her novels, also wrote on political philosophy. In the selection included here, she discusses both the importance and the threat of government to the survival of men (and women) in a social environment.

In a brief selection by Adam Smith, he limits government to carrying out three primary duties: (1) national defense, (2) maintaining a system of justice, and (3) providing certain public works.

Henry David Thoreau (1817–1862) was a moral philosopher and poet who was concerned with our proper relationship with nature and government. Thoreau's reading is taken from his celebrated essay "On the Duty of Civil Disobedience," an essay that had tremendous influence on Mohandas Gandhi and Martin Luther King in their nonviolent resistance to government oppression. Thoreau's ideal would be a government that did not govern at all, but barring that, he wanted a government better than the one we have. According to Thoreau, the responsibility for improving government lies with the individual who has a moral obligation to withhold support from those government actions with which he or she disapproves.

A selection by John Stuart Mill (1806–1873) closes out this section. Mill's reputation as a political economist is based on his extraordinary skill in codifying the main doctrines of classical liberalism. His *Principles of Political Economy* was the basic source of economic doctrine in the latter 19th Century. In this selection taken from his famous essay "On Liberty," a powerful case is presented for allowing people to do what they want with their time and lives if no one else is affected (except those who insist on being troubled by those who have preferences other than their own). While this may seem to be an unobjectionable position, Mill considers several examples of its violation by government, almost all of which are as relevant today as in Mill's time. ●

22. Italian Lemonade

James L. Doti

The taste of Italian lemonade. . . . How can one describe it? Can't be done! For Italian lemonade to be at its best, it takes more than the right blend of ice, sugars and fruit chunks. And I don't agree with the so-called experts who say it has something to do with perfecting the right ice crystallization techniques.

Surely, these are relevant technical factors, but I think there is more to it than meets the eye or, for that matter, the taste buds. It has something to do with the environment. That's right—slurping on Italian lemonade is an aesthetic experience. I think that is the reason why Italian lemonade in California never tasted as good to me as the Chicago variety.

There is something about the late afternoon on a particularly hot and muggy summer day in Chicago. Just when your body feels most ravaged by the effects of the humidity and your legs feel like they are ready to buckle, the humidity lets up and a faint balmy breeze begins to blow in from Lake Michigan. It was at that moment, I found that Italian lemonade tasted the best. As the cooling flavors of the lemonade invaded the senses, the body's natural rhythm and flow seemed to be restored. It even seemed to help release the grip of the malaise that typically affected Chicagoans during the most severe of summer "scorchers."

No better lemonade could be found than that made by Bella Ciozzia in that part of Chicago known as Little Italy. Not only did all technical aspects of her lemonade rate a perfect "10," but the aesthetic conditions couldn't be better. Little Italy was close enough to the lake to benefit invariably from the soothing effect of the lake breezes. An added bonus was that these breezes also helped push out the fetid odor of the nearby stockyards that hung like a cloud around the area on the hottest of days. Thus, if someone were to ask me what is the epitome of true joy, I would not hesitate: just when the breezes begin to blow on some hot and sticky summer day, true joy is slurping on a Bella Ciozzia Italian lemonade.

Reprinted from *The Freeman*, July, 1984, pp. 416-423, by permission of The Foundation for Economic Education.

I first developed a taste for Bella Ciozzia's Italian lemonade when as a young boy I would spend several weeks visiting my grandmother during summer vacation. Coming from the suburbs, I found Little Italy to be my wonderland, my land of adventure. Nothing I read in "Classic Comic Books" that retold the novels of Alexander Dumas and Robert Louis Stevenson could compare to the real life adventures of Little Italy. The tightly built neighborhood of row houses and scaled-down Victorians with aluminum awnings and permastone siding was such a contrast to the pasteurized environment of suburbia, so too were the idle pleasures of the youth.

When I asked Vito, the son of a friend of my grandmother who was forced to play with me, how he liked the movies "Creature from the Black Lagoon" or Walt Disney's "Peter Pan," he responded with a blank stare. His favorite show was put on by the "Ratman" — a local impresario who used captured vermin to put on a show for all those willing to plunk down a quarter. The show consisted mainly of igniting the unfortunate creatures using what sounded like a variety of rather elaborate stage trappings. The Ratman soon displaced the creature from the black lagoon as the principal heavy in my nightmares.

One might well understand and appreciate then the respite from this world offered me by my daily visits to Bella Ciozzia. My nickel's worth of Italian lemonade bought an inestimable amount of pleasure. A special treat was that Bella Ciozzia allowed me to jiggle her snow-filled glass memento of the 1933 "Century of Progress" Exhibition. Perhaps the most vivid memories of my summertime visits to Little Italy consisted of my slurping an Italian lemonade while watching snow fall on the silhouetted background of the "Century of Progress" skyline.

A Fierce Fighting Spirit

Bella Ciozzia was a soft-spoken, petite, and quite beautiful woman. She earned her name "Bella" because her small nose, blond hair, and blue eyes were roundly admired by the locals. Bella Ciozzia came from a small village in Sicily that was invaded by Nordic traders who evidently had nothing to offer in trade for the goods they received except for some very dominant genes. To this day, everyone who comes from that village has blond hair and blue eyes. But as I was soon to find out, Bella Ciozzia inherited more than her good looks from the Norsemen; she also inherited some of their fierce fighting spirit.

The following summer, probably because of the strange fascination that all children seem to have for the macabre, I inquired about the latest theatrical efforts of the Ratman. Vito glumly responded that the shows had come to an end. It so happened that Bella Ciozzia somehow got wind of the goings-on. Evidently, seeing no socially redeeming merits in the show, Bella Ciozzia interrupted the presentation during a particularly climactic moment, flailing away with a huge Italian rolling pin. The Ratman made a quick and ignominious final exit. So too, as Vito related, did the youthful audience.

From that moment on Bella Ciozzia was my hero. She seemed to represent those of the quiet and meek who say little but when pushed beyond a certain point by some outrage will trigger a mechanism that operates suddenly to release their pent-up emotional energy.

So ten years later when I moved back to Little Italy to attend a nearby university, I was happy to find Bella Ciozzia still scooping out Italian lemonade. But now the calming effect of the lemonade soothed the ravages to my system brought on by "Beowulf" and national income accounting rather than the Ratman. You can well imagine then the consternation I felt when on one balmy Friday afternoon Bella Ciozzia told me the building department came and took her equipment away.

"They tell me I can't sell no more. They say I don't have 20 . . . 222 . . . 280 . . . I don't know—some kind of wire," she said as she shrugged in the characteristic Italian way that roughly translated to, "That's life."

I couldn't understand it; Bella Ciozzia was a neighborhood institution. But being a young student who had just mastered the basic elements of political science, I felt that a wrong had been committed that I could help right.

Take It to Alderman

The person to see was Alderman Tom Cooley, otherwise known as the "General." I was sure that he could help even though everyone in the neighborhood considered him a buffoon and political gladhander. In fact, the General was commonly known in the neighborhood as the *Citrulu* — an Italian term of derision reserved for the more inept of the human species. The locals put up with him, though, and even regularly elected him to his office, in spite of the fact that everyone resented his expecting and getting all the free beer and beef sandwiches his belly could hold at the annual festival of Our Lady of Mt. Carmel. The fact was he controlled all the patronage jobs that were doled out to a few people who were related in some extended and convoluted way to everyone in the neighborhood.

When I walked into the General's office, he sprang out of his chair to shake my hand. The General was animated and lively when we started talking about the people I knew in the neighborhood. But when I began to present an impassioned plea for the gross injustice done to Bella Ciozzia, his eyes glazed. As I continued, his facial expression turned to a look of concern. But the concern was not one of compassion or empathy, it was a look that told me he wasn't listening to a thing I was saying. I was quickly escorted out to meet with the many aides who hovered like flies around his office. All they could do was point to the voluminous stacks containing the city code that specifically pointed to the illegality of Bella Ciozzia's transgressions.

The truth finally came out after meeting with our local precinct captain who said, "Are you crazy . . . going to see the General? That *Citrulu* actually thinks that Bella Ciozzia was closed down because she doesn't have 220 wiring. Ha! The squeeze has already been put on with the higher-ups. Big Jake is building a new house next to Bella Ciozzia's. You think he wants to live next to a lemonade stand? Besides, Bella Ciozzia doesn't need the money; she's living with her daughter."

This was the information I needed. I felt elated as I ran to inform Bella Ciozzia about the seamier side of politics and the real motivation in closing her down. As I ran, I had mental pictures of the General and his aides scurrying in various corners of City Hall being hotly pursued by Bella Ciozzia and her infamous rolling pin.

When I finally got there and told her, Bella Ciozzia gave another one of those shrugs of acceptance. I couldn't believe it. Had the passage of ten years taken away her Nordic fighting spirit?

I don't think so. It was more than that. I think it really involved the fact that Bella Ciozzia, like most of those living in Little Italy, came to this country to escape a land and an economy that was ravaged by an oppressive and corrupt government. Coming to this country, they cherished the freedom and opportunities this new land offered. A little corruption is something these streetwise people understood as a fact of life. Compared to what they had left, it was something they could even accept.

The Tendency of Governments to Expand in Size and Scope

Karl Marx believed he had uncovered an inherent flaw in capitalistic systems when he wrote that exploitation by capitalists will bring about the downfall of capitalistic systems. History has proven Marx wrong. But Marx's use of the Hegelian dialectic could have been directed in a different way to expose a more real danger in capitalistic systems. And that danger relates not to the "unearned surplus" or "subsistence wages" but to the tendency for governments within a capitalistic system to expand in size and scope until they ultimately stifle individual freedom and the inherent efficiency of private markets. Marx's prophecy of doom for capitalism would have been more plausible if he tied its downfall to the exploitation of government and collective decision making rather than capitalists' urge to maximize profits.

A limited government is necessary in a capitalistic system. Adam Smith was specific about the role that government should serve in providing national defense, a judicial system, and other public institutions and works that in the main facilitate the commerce of society.* But Smith was not specific enough; nor could he be. There is no clear line that separates a public from a private good. Thus, those who find operating in the cold, cruel world of the marketplace a less than happy or not very profitable state, have a strong motivation in expanding the role of the government in the free market. This motivation, however, is fairly commonplace. In the end, the free market loses its vitality as economic matters are decided in a tug-of-war fought out among competing interest groups in the halls of government rather than in the arena of the

---

*   *The Wealth of Nations*, The Modern Library Edition, pp. 653-682.

marketplace.

These are the powerful interest groups that have strong incentives to either help make laws or manipulate well-intended laws to their own advantage. The political clout of such groups is evident when one considers that the top spending political action committees (PACs) increased their donations to federal campaigns eighty per cent in 1983 compared to the previous nonelection year of 1981. Recent trends also suggest that spending for the 1984 federal congressional elections will near a half billion dollars of which a large share will be funded by PAC spending.*

The willingness of groups to spend such vast sums is certainly tied to the economic advantages to be gained by a benevolent government. As stated by a representative of the National Association of Realtors: "We give early money to our friends, people who are tried and true. We don't care if a knight in shining armor comes in and runs against him (the incumbent); he's been our knight in shining armor."**

And though the private gains that could occur from this knight come at the cost of a greater loss to society, the gains accrue to an individual or identifiable group while society's loss is spread out thinly among many. As a result, the significant private gains provide a much more powerful incentive to influence government than a less interested individual has in politically opposing such influence. Hence, all groups who find that a system of government coercion will somehow make the uncertainties of the world (profits) less uncertain will continually prod our government until the laws work to their own advantage. And the more laws that exist, the more likely it is for powerful interest groups to bypass normal market forces.

In the case of Bella Ciozzia, someone found it cheaper to use some well-intended building code to close her down rather than use the normal market procedure that would otherwise have been followed — buying her out. It may seem as if the two have the same ultimate impact, but they don't. If a mutually agreed upon price could be reached, that suggests retiring Bella Ciozzia's lemonade scoop would bring about a smaller loss to lemonade consumers than the private gain to the person living in the new residence. But if such a price cannot be agreed upon, the opposite would be true; society would gain more by Bella Ciozzia staying in business. Unfortunately, when government coercion applies, there is no assurance that the efficient market solution will occur.

Someone had a strong private interest in closing Bella Ciozzia's business. And this private interest provides the basis for a much stronger incentive to push the government in a self-serving way than any single Italian lemonade consumer can muster to oppose it. Thus Italian lemonade connoisseurs will likely lose in any political tug-of-war even though in the aggregate or from a social point of

---

*   *The Wall Street Journal*, February 23, 1984, p. 54.
**   *Ibid.*

view, the loss to consumers may be greater than the gain to the person who shut Bella Ciozzia's operation down. In the end, the inefficiency occurs because it is both possible and cheaper to get the building department to close her down rather than buy her out.

Many Similar Incidents

The Bella Ciozzia incident can be retold in countless forms. All you have to do is look at the vast number of laws and regulations that envelop this country. Behind many of these laws, a Bella Ciozzia story is ready to be told. There will be different names, a different location and different motivations, but the theme will be the same: The laws favor a few at the expense of many.

Who are at fault? Are they the General Cooleys of this world? No, they are simply willing dupes. Are they the powerful interest groups that push for self-serving laws? No, they are simply attempting to maximize their private gains — the prime motive force of any economic system. The real fault rests with a people who are not sufficiently vigilant in holding the reins on their government. As John Stuart Mill stated in his classic essay, *On Liberty:*

> Let them be left without a government, every body of Americans is able to improvise one, and to carry on that or any other public business with a sufficient amount of intelligence, order, and decision. This is what every free people ought to be: and a people capable of this is certain to be free; it will never let itself be enslaved by any man or body of men because these are able to seize and pull the reins of the central administration.*

In our recent history, however, we almost seem eager to enslave and shackle ourselves with a heavy chain of laws and taxes. Usually under the guise of helping someone or other or providing for this or that, such laws and taxes may seem justified to a reasonable people. Yet, piling laws and taxes on top of each other ultimately places a heavy burden on society. And this burden becomes more oppressive as laws become agents for dispensing with the normal forces of a free market. We should not quickly forget the greatest danger that John Stuart Mill saw in a rapidly growing government:

> The third and most cogent reason for restricting the interference of government is the great evil of adding unnecessarily to its power. Every function superadded to those already exercised by the government causes its influence over hopes and fears to be more widely diffused, and converts, more and more, the active and ambitious part of the public into hangers-on of the government, or of some party which aims at becoming

---

* *On Liberty*, W. W. Norton & Company, p. 104.

the government.*

Nor should we forget the words of Henry David Thoreau who wrote in a similar vein:

> ... this government never of itself furthered any enterprise, but by the alacrity with which it got out of its way. It does not keep the country free. It does not settle the west. It does not educate. The character inherent in the American people has done all that has been accomplished; and it would have done somewhat more, if the government had not sometimes got in its way.**

●　　　●　　　●

A number of years ago, as I was leaving O'Hare Airport to fly to my new home in California, I caught sight of an article in a local newspaper. It reported that the Chicago City Council was considering a proposal of the Illinois Gasoline Retailers Association to make it illegal to display signs that posted the price of gasoline at local service stations. The rationale was that getting rid of unsightly signs would create a better environment for the city.

Settling back in the airplane, I felt content and happy to escape from a city that allowed such blatant collusion between business and government. But as I started to read a complimentary copy of the *L. A. Times* that the airline had kindly provided, my eyes were drawn to a headline: "State Assembly Considers Limits to Optometrist Advertising."

The airline attendant could only stare when I asked her for an Italian lemonade. ●

---

*　　*On Liberty*, p. 102
**　　*On the Duty of Civil Disobedience*, The Simple Life Press.

23. The Role of Government in a Free Society

Milton Friedman

Government as Rule-Maker and Umpire

It is important to distinguish the day-to-day activities of people from the general customary and legal framework within which these take place. The day-to-day activities are like the actions of the participants in a game when they are playing it; the framework, like the rules of the game they play. And just as a good game requires acceptance by the players both of the rules and of the umpire to interpret and enforce them, so a good society requires that its members agree on the general conditions that will govern relations among them, on some means of arbitrating different interpretations of these conditions, and on some device for enforcing compliance with the generally accepted rules. As in games, so also in society, most of the general conditions are the unintended outcome of custom, accepted unthinkingly. At most, we consider explicitly only minor modifications in them, though the cumulative effect of a series of minor modifications may be a drastic alteration in the character of the game or of the society. In both games and society also, no set of rules can prevail unless most participants most of the time conform to them without external sanctions; unless that is, there is a broad underlying social consensus. But we cannot rely on custom or on this consensus alone to interpret and to enforce the rules; we need an umpire. These then are the basic roles of government in a free society: to provide a means whereby we can modify the rules, to mediate differences among us on the meaning of the rules, and to enforce compliance with the rules on the part of those few who would otherwise not play the game.

The need for government in these respects arises because absolute freedom is impossible. However attractive anarchy may be as a philosophy, it is not feasible in a world of imperfect men. Men's freedoms can conflict, and when they do, one man's freedom must be limited to preserve another's—as a

Abridged from *Capitalism and Freedom*, pp. 22-36, by permission of The University of Chicago Press. Copyright © 1962 by The University of Chicago.

Supreme Court Justice once put it, "My freedom to move my fist must be limited by the proximity of your chin."

The major problem in deciding the appropriate activities of government is how to resolve such conflicts among the freedoms of different individuals. In some cases, the answer is easy. There is little difficulty in attaining near unanimity to the proposition that one man's freedom to murder his neighbor must be sacrificed to preserve the freedom of the other man to live. In other cases, the answer is difficult. In the economic area, a major problem arises in respect of the conflict between freedom to combine and freedom to compete. What meaning is to be attributed to "free" as modifying "enterprise"? In the United States, "free" has been understood to mean that everyone is free to set up an enterprise, which means that existing enterprises are not free to keep out competitors except by selling a better product at the same price or the same product at a lower price. In the continental tradition, on the other hand, the meaning has generally been that enterprises are free to do what they want, including the fixing of prices, division of markets, and the adoption of other techniques to keep out potential competitors. Perhaps the most difficult specific problem in this area arises with respect to combinations among laborers, where the problem of freedom to combine and freedom to compete is particularly acute.

A still more basic economic area in which the answer is both difficult and important is the definition of property rights. The notion of property, as it has developed over centuries and as it is embodied in our legal codes, has become so much a part of us that we tend to take it for granted, and fail to recognize the extent to which just what constitutes property and what rights the ownership of property confers are complex social creations rather than self-evident propositions. Does my having title to land, for example, and my freedom to use my property as I wish, permit me to deny to someone else the right to fly over my land in his airplane? Or does his right to use his airplane take precedence? Or does this depend on how high he flies? Or how much noise he makes? Does voluntary exchange require that he pay me for the privilege of flying over my land? Or that I must pay him to refrain from flying over it? The mere mention of royalties, copyrights, patents; shares of stock in corporations; riparian rights, and the like, may perhaps emphasize the role of generally accepted social rules in the very definition of property. It may suggest also that, in many cases, the existence of a well specified and generally accepted definition of property is far more important than just what the definition is.

Another economic area that raises particularly difficult problems is the monetary system. Government responsibility for the monetary system has long been recognized. It is explicitly provided for in the constitutional provision which gives Congress the power "to coin money, regulate the value thereof, and of foreign coin." There is probably no other area of economic activity with respect to which government action has been so uniformly accepted. This habitual and by now almost unthinking acceptance of governmental responsibility makes thorough understanding of the grounds for such responsibility all the more necessary, since it enhances the danger that the scope of government will spread from activities that are, to those that are not, appropriate in a free society, from providing a monetary framework to determining the allocation of resources among individuals.

In summary, the organization of economic activity through voluntary exchange presumes that we have provided, through government, for the maintenance of law and order to prevent coercion of one individual by another, the enforcement of contracts voluntarily entered into, the definition of the meaning of property rights, the interpretation and enforcement of such rights, and the provision of a monetary framework.

Action Through Government on Grounds of Technical Monopoly and Neighborhood Effects

The role of government just considered is to do something that the market cannot do for itself, namely, to determine, arbitrate, and enforce the rules of the game. We may also want to do through government some things that might conceivably be done through the market but that technical or similar conditions render it difficult to do in that way. These all reduce to cases in which strictly voluntary exchange is either exceedingly costly or practically impossible. There are two general classes of such cases: monopoly and similar market imperfections, and neighborhood effects.

Exchange is truly voluntary only when nearly equivalent alternatives exist. Monopoly implies the absence of alternatives and thereby inhibits effective freedom of exchange. In practice, monopoly frequently, if not generally, arises from government support or from collusive agreements among individuals. With respect to these, the problem is either to avoid governmental fostering of monopoly or to stimulate the effective enforcement of rules such as those embodied in our anti-trust laws. However, monopoly may also arise because it is technically efficient to have a single producer or enterprise. I venture to suggest that such cases are more limited than is supposed but they unquestionably do arise. A simple example is perhaps the provision of telephone services within a community. I shall refer to such cases as "technical" monopoly.

When technical conditions make a monopoly the natural outcome of competitive market forces, there are only three alternatives that seem available: private monopoly, public monopoly, or public regulation. All three are bad so we must choose among evils. Henry Simons, observing public regulation of monopoly in the United States, found the results so distasteful that he concluded public monopoly would be a lesser evil. Walter Eucken, a noted German liberal, observing public monopoly in German railroads, found the results so distasteful that he concluded public regulation would be a lesser evil. Having learned from both, I reluctantly conclude that, if tolerable, private monopoly may be the least of the evils.

If society were static so that the conditions which give rise to a technical monopoly were sure to remain, I would have little confidence in this solution.

In a rapidly changing society, however, the conditions making for technical monopoly frequently change and I suspect that both public regulation and public monopoly are likely to be less responsive to such changes in conditions, to be less readily capable of elimination, than private monopoly.

Railroads in the United States are an excellent example. A large degree of monopoly in railroads was perhaps inevitable on technical grounds in the nineteenth century. This was the justification for the Interstate Commerce Commission. But conditions have changed. The emergence of road and air transport has reduced the monopoly element in railroads to negligible proportions. Yet we have not eliminated the ICC. On the contrary, the ICC, which started out as an agency to protect the public from exploitation by the railroads, has become an agency to protect railroads from competition by trucks and other means of transport, and more recently even to protect existing truck companies from competition by new entrants. Similarly, in England, when the railroads were nationalized, trucking was at first brought into the state monopoly. If railroads had never been subjected to regulation in the United States, it is nearly certain that by now transportation, including railroads, would be a highly competitive industry with little or no remaining monopoly elements.

The choice between the evils of private monopoly, public monopoly, and public regulation cannot, however, be made once and for all, independently of the factual circumstances. If the technical monopoly is of a service or commodity that is regarded as essential and if its monopoly power is sizable, even the short-run effects of private unregulated monopoly may not be tolerable, and either public regulation or ownership may be a lesser evil.

Technical monopoly may on occasion justify a *de facto* public monopoly. It cannot by itself justify a public monopoly achieved by making it illegal for anyone else to compete. For example, there is no way to justify our present public monopoly of the post office. It may be argued that the carrying of mail is a technical monopoly and that a government monopoly is the least of evils. Along these lines, one could perhaps justify a government post office but not the present law, which makes it illegal for anybody else to carry mail. If the delivery of mail is a technical monopoly, no one will be able to succeed in competition with the government. If it is not, there is no reason why the government should be engaged in it. The only way to find out is to leave other people free to enter.

The historical reason why we have a post office monopoly is because the Pony Express did such a good job of carrying the mail across the continent that, when the government introduced transcontinental service, it couldn't compete effectively and lost money. The result was a law making it illegal for anybody else to carry the mail. That is why the Adams Express Company is an investment trust today instead of an operating company. I conjecture that if entry into the mail-carrying business were open to all, there would be a large number of firms entering it and this archaic industry would become revolutionized in short order.

A second general class of cases in which strictly voluntary exchange is impossible arises when actions of individuals have effects on other individuals for which it is not feasible to charge or recompense them. This is the problem of "neighborhood effects." An obvious example is the pollution of a stream. The man who pollutes a stream is in effect forcing others to exchange good water for bad. These others might be willing to make the exchange at a price. But it is not feasible for them, acting individually, to avoid the exchange or to enforce appropriate compensation.

A less obvious example is the provision of highways. In this case, it is technically possible to identify and hence charge individuals for their use of the roads and so to have private operation. However, for general access roads, involving many points of entry and exit, the costs of collection would be extremely high if a charge were to be made for the specific services received by each individual, because of the necessity of establishing toll booths or the equivalent at all entrances. The gasoline tax is a much cheaper method of charging individuals roughly in proportion to their use of the roads. This method, however, is one in which the particular payment cannot be identified closely with the particular use. Hence, it is hardly feasible to have private enterprise provide the service and collect the charge without establishing extensive private monopoly.

These considerations do not apply to long-distance turnpikes with high density of traffic and limited access. For these, the costs of collection are small and in many cases are now being paid, and there are often numerous alternatives, so that there is no serious monopoly problem. Hence, there is every reason why these should be privately owned and operated. If so owned and operated, the enterprise running the highway should receive the gasoline taxes paid on account of travel on it.

Considerations like those I have treated under the heading of neighborhood effects have been used to rationalize almost every conceivable intervention. In many instances, however, this rationalization is special pleading rather than a legitimate application of the concept of neighborhood effects. Neighborhood effects cut both ways. They can be a reason for limiting the activities of government as well as for expanding them. Neighborhood effects impede voluntary exchange because it is difficult to identify the effects on third parties and to measure their magnitude; but this difficulty is present in governmental activity as well. It is hard to know when neighborhood effects are sufficiently large to justify particular costs in overcoming them and even harder to distribute the costs in an appropriate fashion. Consequently, when government engages in activities to overcome neighborhood effects, it will in part introduce an additional set of neighborhood effects by failing to charge or to compensate individuals properly. Whether the original or the new neighborhood effects are the more serious can only be judged by the facts of the individual case, and even then, only very approximately. Furthermore, the use of government to overcome neighborhood effects itself has an extremely important neighborhood effect which is unrelated to the particular occasion for government action. Every act of government intervention limits the area of individual freedom directly and threatens the preservation of freedom indirectly for reasons elaborated in the first chapter.

Our principles offer no hard and fast line how far it is appropriate to use government to accomplish jointly what it is difficult or impossible for us to accomplish separately through strictly voluntary exchange. In any particular case of proposed intervention, we must make up a balance sheet, listing separately the advantages and disadvantages. Our principles tell us what items to put on the one side and what items on the other and they give us some basis for attaching importance to the different items. In particular, we shall always want to enter on the liability side of any proposed government intervention, its neighborhood effect in threatening freedom, and give this effect considerable weight. Just how much weight to give to it, as to other items, depends upon the circumstances. If, for example, existing government intervention is minor, we shall attach a smaller weight to the negative effects of additional government intervention.

Conclusion

A government which maintained law and order, defined property rights, served as a means whereby we could modify property rights and other rules of the economic game, adjudicated disputes about the interpretation of the rules, enforced contracts, promoted competition, provided a monetary framework, engaged in activities to counter technical monopolies and to overcome neighborhood effects widely regarded as sufficiently important to justify government intervention, and which supplemented private charity and the private family in protecting the irresponsible, whether madman or child—such a government would clearly have important functions to perform. The consistent liberal is not an anarchist.

Yet it is also true that such a government would have clearly limited functions and would refrain from a host of activities that are now undertaken by federal and state governments in the United States, and their counterparts in other Western countries. ●

24. The Political Economy of the U. S. Constitution

Dwight R. Lee

No written constitution in history has established a more durable or successful democracy than has the U. S. Constitution. A full appreciation of the Founding Fathers, however, requires an understanding of the economic as well as the political consequences of our Constitution. Every economy is a political economy and the enormous success of the U.S. economy has been as dependent on our political system as on our economic system.

Indeed, many of the problems that currently plague the U.S. economy are the result of our failure to hold on to the political wisdom that guided our Founding Fathers. Economic knowledge is obviously important in the effort to promote economic growth and development. No matter how sound our economic understanding, economic performance will continue to suffer until we once again recognize that political power is a force for progress only when tightly constrained and directed toward limited objectives.

The genesis of the political and economic wisdom of our Founding Fathers is found in the fact that they distrusted government while fully recognizing the necessity of government for a beneficent social order. The cautious embrace the Founders gave government is reflected in their view of democracy as necessary but not sufficient for the proper control of government.

The concerns that led to the colonists' break with Great Britain were very much in the public mind when the Constitutional Convention met in Philadelphia during the summer of 1787. The well known prerevolution rallying cry, "No taxation without representation," reflected a clear understanding of the dangers that accompanied any exercise of government power not answerable to those who are governed. That the government established by the Constitution would be democratic in form was not in doubt. Unchecked democratic rule, however, was anathema to the most thoughtful of the Founding Fathers.

Reprinted from *The Freeman*, February, 1987, pp. 59-69, by permission of The Foundation for Economic Education.

A grievance against English rule rivaling that of "taxation without representation concerned the sovereign authority assumed by the English Parliament in 1767. In that year Parliament decreed that, through its democratically elected members, it had the power to pass or strike down any law it desired. The colonists had brought with them the English political tradition, which dated back at least to the Magna Carta of 1215: the people have certain rights that should be immune to political trespass regardless of momentary desires of a democratic majority. The concern was not only that the colonists were unrepresented in Parliament but, more fundamentally, that Parliament assumed unlimited power to meddle in the private lives of individuals whether represented or not.

Although the Founding Fathers were determined to establish a government that was democratic in the limited sense that political decisions could not ignore citizen input, they had no intention of creating a government that was fully responsive to majority interests. In many ways the Constitution is designed to frustrate the desire of political majorities to work their will through the exercise of government power. The most obvious example of this is the first ten amendments to the Constitution, or the Bill of Rights. These amendments guarantee certain individual freedoms against political infringement regardless of majority will. If, for example, freedom of speech and the press was dependent on majority vote many unpopular but potentially important ideas would never be disseminated. How effectively would a university education expose students to new and controversial ideas if professors had to submit their lectures for majority approval?

Other examples exist of the undemocratic nature of the government set up by the Constitution. There is very little that can be considered democratic about the Supreme Court. Its nine members are appointed for life, and their decision can nullify a law passed by the Congress and supported by the overwhelming majority of the American public. In a five to four decision one member of the court, insulated from the democratic process, can frustrate the political will of a nearly unanimous public. The arrangement whereby the President can reverse the will of the Congress through his veto power is certainly not a very democratic one. Neither is the Senate where the vote cast by a senator from Wyoming carries weight equal to the vote by the senator from California, even though the California senator represents a population fifty times larger than does the Wyoming senator. The senators from the twenty-six least populated states can prevent a bill from clearing Congress, even though it has incontestable popular support in the country at large. Congress is actually less democratic than just indicated once it is recognized that popular bills can be prevented from ever being considered in the full House of Representatives of Senate by a few representatives who serve on key congressional committees.

It is safe to say that the chief concern of the framers of the Constitution was not that of insuring a fully democratic political structure. Instead they were concerned with limiting government power in order to minimize the abuse of majority rule. In the words of R. A. Humphreys, "they [the Founding Fathers] were concerned not to make America safe for democracy, but to make democracy safe for America."*

Prelude to the Constitutional Convention

Fear of the arbitrary power that could be exercised by a strong central government, democratically controlled or otherwise, was evident from the Articles of Confederation. The Articles of Confederation established the "national government" of the thirteen colonies after they declared their independence from England. There is some exaggeration in this use of the term national government, since the Articles did little more than formalize an association (or confederation) of thirteen independent and sovereign states. While the congress created by the Articles of Confederation was free to deliberate on important issues and pass laws, it had no means of enforcing them. The Articles did not even establish an executive branch of government, and congressional resolutions were nothing more than recommendations that the states could honor if they saw fit. The taxes that states were assessed to support the Revolutionary War effort were often ignored, and raising money to outfit and pay the American army was a frustrating business.

Because of the weakness of the national government, the state governments under the Articles of Confederation were strong and often misused their power. Majority coalitions motivated by special interests found it relatively easy to control state legislatures and tramp on the interests of minorities. Questionable banking schemes were promoted by debtors, with legislative assistance, in order to reduce the real value of their debt obligations. States often resorted to the simple expedient of printing money to satisfy their debts. Trade restrictions between the states were commonplace as legislators responded to the interests of organized producers while ignoring the concerns of the general consumers. There was a 1786 meeting in Annapolis, Maryland of the five middle states to discuss ways to reduce trade barriers between the states. At this meeting the call was made for a larger meeting in Philadelphia in the following year to discuss more general problems with the Articles of Confederation. This meeting became the Constitutional Convention.

Achieving Weakness Through Strength

It was the desire of Madison, Hamilton, and other leaders at the Constitutional Convention to replace the government established by the Articles of Confederation with a central government that was more than an association of sovereign states. The new government would have to be strong enough to

---

*   R. A. Humphreys, "The Rule of Law and the American Revolution," *Law Quarterly Review* (1937). Also quoted in F. A. Hayek, *The Constitution of Liberty* (Chicago: University of Chicago Press, 1960), p. 474.

impose some uniformity to financial, commercial, and foreign policy and to establish some general protections for citizens against the power of state governments if the new nation was to be viable and prosperous. In the words of James Madison, we needed a "general government" sufficiently strong to protect "the rights of the minority," which are in jeopardy "in all cases where a majority are united by a common interest or passion."* But this position was not an easy one to defend. Many opponents to a genuine national government saw little merit in the desire to strengthen government power at one level in order to prevent the abuse of government power at another level. Was there any genuine way around this apparent conflict? Many thought not, short of giving up on the hope of a union of all the states. There were those who argued that the expanse and diversity of the thirteen states, much less that of the larger continent, were simply too great to be united under one government without sacrificing the liberty that they had just fought to achieve.**

Madison, however, saw no conflict in strengthening the national government in order to control the abuses of government in general. In his view the best protection against arbitrary government authority was through centers of government power that were in effective competition with one another. The control that one interest group, or faction, could realize through a state government would be largely nullified when political decisions resulted from the interaction of opposing factions within many states. Again quoting Madison,

> The influence of factious leaders may kindle a flame within their particular States but will be unable to spread a general conflagration through the other States. . . . A rage for paper money, for an abolition of debts, for an equal division of property, or for any other improper or wicked project, will be less apt to pervade the whole body of the Union than a particular member of it . . .***

A central government strong enough to unite a large and diverse set of states would weaken, rather than strengthen, the control that government in general could exercise.

To the framers of the Constitution, weakening government in the sense just discussed meant making sure that government was unable to extend itself beyond a relatively limited role in the affairs of individuals. This does not imply, however, impotent government. The referees in a football game, for example, certainly are not the strongest participants on the field and have limited control

---

*   *Records of the Federal Convention of 1787*, Max Ferrand, ed. (New Haven: Yale University Press, 1937) Vol. 1, p. 57 and pp. 134-135.

**   See Herbert J. Storing, *What the Anti-Federalists Were for: The Political Thought of the Opponents of the Constitution* (Chicago: The University of Chicago Press, 1981).

***   Madison in Federalist 10, *The Federalist Papers* (New York: New American Library Edition, 1961).

over specific outcomes in the game. Yet in enforcing the general rules of the game the decisions of the referees are potent indeed. Government, in its role as referee, obviously cannot lack the authority to back up its decisions. In addition to performing its refereeing function, it is also desirable for government to provide certain public goods; goods such as national defense that will not be adequately provided by the private market. Again this is a duty which requires a measure of authority; in this case the authority to impose taxes up to the limit required to provide those public goods which are worth more than they cost.

How to Impose Control?

In granting government the power to do those things government should do, the Founding Fathers knew they were creating a power that had to be carefully controlled. But how could this control be imposed? It could not be imposed by specifying a particular list of government do's and don't's. Such a list would be impossibly detailed and even if it could be drafted it would need to be revised constantly in response to changes in such considerations as population size, age distribution, wealth, and the state of technology. Instead, government has to be controlled by a general set of constitutional rules within which government decisions are made, with specific government outcomes determined through the resulting political process. It was the hope of those at the Constitutional Convention to establish a political process, through constitutional reform, that brought government power into action only when needed to serve the broad interests of the public.

This hope was not based on the naive, though tempting, notion that somehow individuals would ignore their personal advantages and concentrate on the general advantage when making political decisions. While noble motives are seldom completely absent in guiding individual behavior, whether private or public, the Founding Fathers took as a given that most people, most of the time, maintain a healthy regard for their private concerns. The only way to prevent self-seeking people from abusing government power was to structure the rules of the political game in such a way that it would be costly for them to do so. The objective of the framers was to create a government that was powerful enough to do those things that received political approval, but to establish a political process that made it exceedingly difficult to obtain political approval for any action that lacked broad public support.

There were, of course, some powers that the national government was not constitutionally permitted to exercise. The national government was created by the states, and until the Constitution all governmental power resided in the states. Through the Constitution the states relinquished some of their powers to the national government, e.g., the power to impose taxes on the citizens, establish uniform rules of naturalization, raise an army and navy, and declare war. In addition, the states agreed to refrain from exercising certain powers; e.g., the power to coin money, pass laws impairing the obligation of contracts, and pass retroactive laws. Important government powers remained in the states, however, with some of them located in the local governments. Thus the powers that could be exercised by government were limited, and the powers that did exist were diffused over three levels of government. The Constitution further diffused power at the national level by spreading it horizontally over three branches of government, the power of each acting as a check and balance on the power of the others.

The intent of the Founding Fathers was to so fragment government power that it would be extremely difficult for any narrowly motivated faction to gain sufficient control to work its political will. Only those objectives widely shared and consistent with Constitutional limits would be realized through the use of government power. The beauty of the political process established by the Constitution is that it is cumbersome and inefficient. According to Forrest McDonald the process is "So cumbersome and inefficient . . . that the people, however, virtuous or wicked, could not activate it. It could be activated through deals and deceit, through bargains and bribery, through logrolling and lobbying and trickery and trading, the tactics that go with man's baser attributes, most notably his greed and his love of power. And yet, in the broad range and on the average, these private tactics and motivations could operate effectively only when they were compatible with the public good, for they were braked by the massive inertia of society as a whole."* Or, as Clinton Rossiter has said of the Founding Fathers' motives in creating the system of checks and balances, "Liberty rather than authority, protection rather than power, delay rather than efficiency were the concern of these constitution-makers."**

The Economic Success of the Constitution

It is hard to argue with the success of the U.S. Constitution. The history of the United States in the decades after the ratification of the Constitution was one of limited government and individual liberty, major increases in the size of the U.S. in terms of population and geography, and unprecedented growth in economic well-being. With the major exception of (and to a large extent, in spite of) the unfortunate legacy of slavery and the Civil War, millions of diverse people were able to pursue their individual objectives through harmonious and productive interaction with one another. The opportunities created by the process of specialization and exchange made possible by limited and responsible government motivated an outpouring of productive effort that soon transformed a wilderness into one of the most prosperous nations in the world. The role the U.S. Constitution played in this transformation was an important one and can be explained in terms of both negative and positive incentives.

Broadly speaking, there are two ways an individual can acquire wealth: 1)

---

* Forrest McDonald, *E. Pluribus Unum: The Formation of the American Republic 1776-1790* (Indianapolis: Liberty Press, 1979), p. 316.

** Clinton Rossiter, *Seedtime of the Republic: The Origin of the American Tradition of Political Liberty* (New York: Harcourt, Brace and World, 1953), p. 425.

capture existing wealth through nonproductive transfer activities, or 2) create new wealth through productive activities. A major strength of the Constitution is that it established positive incentives for the latter activities and negative incentives for the former.

The most obvious form of nonproductive transfer activity is private theft. The thief simply takes through force or stealth something that belongs to someone else. A primary purpose for establishing government is to outlaw private theft. But the power that government necessarily possesses if it is to enforce laws against private theft is a power that affords individuals or groups the opportunity to benefit through public "theft" (legal transfer activity to phrase it more gently). The more vague and ineffective the limits on government authority, the less difficult it is to acquire legal transfers through political activity, and the larger the number of people who will find this activity offering them the greatest profit opportunity.

While those who are successful at the transfer game can increase their personal wealth, in some cases significantly, it is obvious that the country at large cannot increase its wealth through transfer activity. What one person receives is what another person, or group, loses. No net wealth is created, and for this reason transfer activity is often referred to as a zero-sum game. In fact, it is more accurately described as a negative-sum game. The attempts of some to acquire transfers, and the predictable efforts of others to protect their wealth against transfers, require the use of real resources. These resources could be productively employed creating new wealth rather than wasted in activities that do nothing more than redistribute existing wealth. For every dollar that one person receives from a transfer activity the rest of the community sacrifices more than a dollar.

Incentives to Produce

A major virtue of the U.S. Constitution was that it discouraged people from playing the transfer game. By establishing a governmental apparatus that was very difficult to put in motion for narrowly motivated purposes, the Constitution dampened the incentive to use government as a means of acquiring the wealth of others. This is not to say that the government was not used as a vehicle for transfer in the early days of our Constitutional government. Every political decision results in some redistribution of wealth, and no governmental structure will ever completely insulate the political process against the transfer activities of some.* But the opportunity for personal enrichment through political activity was limited. Most people found that the best way to increase their wealth was through wealth producing activities.

---

*   For a discussion of the use of government to transfer wealth throughout American history, see Jonathan R. T. Hughes, *The Governmental Habit: Economic Controls from Colonial Times to the Present* (New York: Basic Books, 1977).

It was here that the political structure established by the Constitution created positive incentives. Not only did the Constitution establish a climate in which it was difficult to profit from transfer activities, it also created a setting in which productive effort was rewarded. By providing protection against the arbitrary taking of private property (the Fifth Article of the Bill of Rights) people were given assurance that they would not be denied the value generated by their efforts. This provided people with strong incentives to apply themselves and their property diligently. In the words of M. Bruce Johnson, "America was a place where if you were ready to sow, then by God you could reap."*

But the motivation to work hard is not enough for a productive economy. Also needed is information on the objectives toward which effort and resources are best directed, as well as incentives to act on this information. It is the protection of private property that provides the foundation for a system of price communication and market interaction which serves to guide effort and resources into their most valuable employments. To complete this system the concept of private property rights has to be expanded to include the right to transfer one's property to others at terms regulated only by the mutual consent of those who are party to the exchange. The lower the cost of entering into transactions of this type, the more effectively the resulting market prices will allow people to communicate and coordinate with each other to the advantage of all. The U.S. Constitution lowered these transaction costs by reducing government's ability to interfere with mutually acceptable exchanges and by putting the weight of the national government behind the sanctity of the contracts that resulted from these exchanges.

In what has become known as the "contract clause" of the Constitution, the states are forbidden from passing any "law impairing the obligation of contracts. . . ." In the same clause the states are also forbidden from imposing tariff duties on imports or exports (unless absolutely necessary for enforcing inspection laws). In the "commerce clause" the national government was given the power to regulate commerce "among the several states." Though the commerce clause can be interpreted (and indeed has been in recent decades) as providing the central government the authority to substitute political decisions for market decisions over interstate commerce, the U.S. Congress ignored this possibility until it passed the Interstate Commerce Act in 1887. Prior to the Civil War the commerce clause was used instead by the U.S. Supreme Court to rule unconstitutional state laws that attempted to regulate commerce. After 1868 the Supreme Court made use of the doctrine of due process as expressed in the fourteenth amendment to strike down many government attempts to violate the sanctity of contracts through their regulation of such things as prices, working hours, working conditions, and pay.

---

*   M. Bruce Johnson, ed., *Resolving the Housing Crisis: Government Policy, Decontrol, and the Public Interest* (San Francisco: Pacific Institute for Public Research, 1982), p. 3.

In summary, the Constitution created an environment in which private advantage was best served by engaging in productive positive-sum activities. The specialization and exchange facilitated by the Constitutional rules of the game is a system in which individuals can improve their own position only by serving the interests of others. When private property is protected against confiscation, an individual becomes wealthy only by developing skills, creating new products, or innovating better technologies and thereby providing consumers with more attractive options than they would otherwise have. In a truly free enterprise economy, with the minimum government role envisioned by the framers of the Constitution, the rich are the benefactors of the masses, not the exploiters as commonly depicted. Wealth through exploitation becomes possible only when unrestricted government allows negative-sum transfer activity to become more profitable than positive-sum market activity.

Constitutional Erosion and the Rise of Political Piracy

The early success of the Constitution, and the economic system that developed under it, is reflected in the fact that relatively few people felt any urency to worry about politics. Political activity offered little return as there was little chance to exploit others, and little need to prevent from being exploited by others, through political involvement. People could safely get on with their private affairs without having to worry about the machinations and intrigues of politicians and bureaucrats in far-away places. But this very success can, over time, undermine itself as a politically complacent public increases the opportunities for those who are politically involved to engage in political chicanery.

Motivating people to maintain the political vigilance necessary to protect themselves against government is always a difficult task. The individual who becomes involved in political activity incurs a direct cost. By devoting time and resources in attempting to realize political objectives he is sacrificing alternative objectives. The motivation to become politically active will be a compelling one only if the expected political outcome is worth more to the individual than the necessary personal sacrifices. This will typically not be the case when the objective is to prevent government from undermining the market process that it is government's proper role to protect. The benefits that are realized from limited government are general benefits. These benefits accrue to each individual in the community whether or not he personally works to constrain government.

Over the broad range of political issues, then, people quite rationally do not want to get involved. This is not to say, however, that everyone will be apathetic about all political issues. This clearly is not the case, and it is possible to predict the circumstances that will motivate political activism. Often a relatively small number of individuals will receive most of the benefit from a particular political decision, while the community at large bears the cost. Members of such a special interest group will find it relatively easy to organize for the purpose of exerting political influence. The number of people to organize is comparatively small; the group is probably already somewhat organized around a common interest, and the political issues that affect this common interest will be of significant importance to each member of the group.

Of course, the free rider problem exists in all organizational efforts, but the smaller the group and the narrower the objective the easier it is to get everyone to contribute his share. Also, the benefits of effective effort can be so great to particular individuals in the group that they will be motivated to work for the common objective even if some members of the group do free-ride. Not surprisingly then, narrowly focused groups commonly will have the motivation and ability to organize for the purpose of pursuing political objectives.* The result is political piracy in which the politically organized are able to capture ill-gotten gains from the politically unorganized.

The Constitutional limits on government imposed effective restraints on political piracy for many years after the Constitution was ratified. There are undoubtedly many explanations for this. The vast frontier rich in natural resources offered opportunities for wealth creation that, for most people, overwhelmed the opportunities for personal gain through government transfer activity. Also, it can take time for politically effective coalitions to form after the slate has been wiped clean, so to speak, by a social upheaval of the magnitude of first the Revolutionary War and then the Civil War.** Public attitudes were also an important consideration in the control of government.

Much has been written about how the pervasive distrust of government power among the American people shaped the framing of a Constitution that worked to limit government.*** What might be more important is that the Constitution worked to limit government because the public had a healthy distrust of government power. For example, in the 1860s the Baltimore and Ohio railroad had its Harpers Ferry bridge blown up many times by both the Confederate and Union armies, and each time the railroad rebuilt the bridge with its own funds without any attempt to get the government to pick up part of the tab. Or consider the fact that in 1887 President Grover Cleveland vetoed an appropriation of $25,000 for seed corn to assist drought-stricken farmers with the statement, "It is not the duty of government to support the people."**** There is little doubt that Cleveland's view on this matter was in keeping with broad public opinion.

---

*   According to Milton Friedman, "The most potent group in a democracy such as ours is a small minority that has a special interest which it values very highly, for which it is willing to give its vote, regardless of what happens elsewhere, and about which the rest of the community does not care very strongly." See Milton Friedman, "Special Interest and His Law," *Chicago Bar Record* (June 1970).

**   Mancur Olson, *The Rise and Decline of Nations* (New Haven: Yale University Press, 1982).

***   Gordon S. Wood, *The Creation of the American Republic: 1776-1787* (Chapel Hill: The University of North Carolina Press, 1969), especially chapter 1.

**** Quoted in A. Nivens, *Grover Cleveland: A Study in Courage* (New York: Dodd Mead, 1932).

The Constitutional safeguards against government transfer activity unfortunately have lost much of their effectiveness over the years. The western frontier disappeared, and a long period of relative stability in the political order provided time for factions to become entrenched in the political process. Of more direct and crucial importance, however, in the move from productive activity to transfer activity has been the weakening judicial barrier to the use of government to advance special interests. The 1877 Supreme Court decision in *Munn v. Illinois* is often considered to be a watershed case. This decision upheld a lower court ruling that the Illinois state legislature had the authority to determine the rates that could be charged for storing grain. This decision, by sanctioning an expanded role for government in the determination of prices, increased the payoff to political activity relative to market activity and established an important precedent for future increases in that payoff.

In *Chicago, Milwaukee and St. Paul Railroad Co. V. Minnesota*, decided in 1890, the Supreme Court imposed what appeared to be limits on state regulation of economic activity by ruling that such regulation must be reasonable. Unfortunately, this reasonableness doctrine put the effectiveness of judicial restraint on government at the mercy of current fashion in social thought. What is considered unreasonable at one time may be considered quite reasonable at another.* It was unreasonable for the Baltimore and Ohio railroad to consider requesting government funds to repair its Harpers Ferry bridge, destroyed by government forces, during the Civil War. In the 1980s it was considered reasonable for Chrysler Corporation to request and receive a federal government bailout because Chrysler was not competing successfully for the consumer's dollar.

Undermining Constitutional Law

The idea of reasonable regulation significantly undermined the concept of a higher Constitutional law that established protections needed for the long-run viability of a free and productive social order. Once the notion of reasonable regulation stuck its nose into the judicial tent it was just a matter of time before the courts began seeing their task as that of judging particular outcomes rather than overseeing the general rules of the game. Illustrative of this changing emphasis was the legal brief submitted by Louis Brandeis, then an attorney for the state of Oregon, in the 1908 case *Muller v. Oregon*. At issue was the con-

---

* In spite of the two decisions just cited, between 1897 and 1937, the Supreme Court made use of the due process clause of the Fourteenth Amendment to reach decisions that served to protect the market process against political intrusions. See Barnard Siegan, *Economic Liberties and the Constitution* (Chicago: University of Chicago Press, 1981). Unfortunately, this pattern of judicial decisions was not solid enough to prevent these decisions from being ignored or overruled when the political climate and prevailing notions of reasonableness changed.

stitutionality of an Oregon law which regulated the working hours of women. The Brandeis brief contained only a few pages addressing constitutional considerations and well over one hundred pages of social economic data and argumentation attempting to establish the unfortunate consequences of women working long hours. It was a judgment on the reasonableness of a particular outcome, women working long hours, rather than constitutional considerations, which were considered of paramount importance and led to a Supreme Court ruling in favor of Oregon.* When the constitutionality of legislation stands or falls on the "reasonableness" of the particular outcomes it hopes to achieve, opportunities increase for people to increase their wealth through nonproductive political activity.

In the 1911 case *United States v. Grimand,* the Supreme Court handed down a decision that significantly increased the private return to obtaining transfers through political influence. Prior to this decision, the U.S. Congress had increasingly moved toward granting administrative agencies the authority to promulgate specific rules in order to implement the general policy objectives outlined by Congress. In *United States v. Grimand* the high court empowered these administrative rulings with the full force of law. After this decision, the cost of successfully using government authority to transfer wealth decreased significantly as special interest groups seeking preferential treatment could concentrate their influence on a few key members of a particular administrative board or agency. The typical result of this has been the development of symbiotic relationships between bureaucratic agencies and their special interest clients. A special interest group can thrive on the benefits transferred to it by the ruling of a bureaucracy, and the bureaucracy's budget and prestige will depend on a thriving special interest group demanding its services.**

What we have observed over the years is a slow, somewhat erratic, but unmistakable breakdown in the protection the Constitution provides the public against arbitrary government power. Those who want to get on with the task of creating new wealth have much less assurance today than they did in the past

---

*   For a brief but useful discussion of this case see Thomas K. McCraw, *Prophets of Regulation* (Cambridge: The Belknap Press of Harvard University Press, 1984), pp. 87-88.

**   The relationship between the U.S. Department of Agriculture and the farm block is but one of many illustrative examples that could be cited here. It is clear that those employed by the Department of Agriculture strongly support the agricultural price support and subsidy programs that transfer literally billions of dollars from the American consumer and taxpayer to the nation's farmers (most of this transfer goes to the largest and wealthiest farmers; see Bruce L. Gardner, *The Governing of Agriculture* [Lawrence: Regents Press of Kansas, 1981]). It is by expanding these programs that the Department of Agriculture can justify bigger budgets and more employees, something it has been quite successful at doing. In 1920 when the farm population was approximately 31 million, the Department of Agriculture employed 19,500 people. By 1975 the farm population had declined to less than 9 million, but the Department of Agriculture had increased its employment to 121,000 people. This trend toward fewer agricultural workers relative to agricultural bureaucrats has continued into the 1980s.

that significant portions of the wealth they create will not be confiscated by government and transferred to those who have specialized in political influence.

Maintaining constitutional constraints on government transfer activity is a task requiring constant vigilance. Once a breakdown in these constraints begins, it can initiate a destructive dynamic of increasing government transfers that is difficult to control. Any change that makes it easier to obtain transfers through government will motivate some people to redirect their efforts away from productive enterprises and into transfer enterprises. As this is done, those who continue to create new wealth find the payoff from doing so is somewhat diminished as more of this wealth is being taken from them. This further reduction in the relative return to productive activity motivates yet more people to use government power to benefit at the expense of others. Furthermore, the burdens and inefficiencies created by one government program will be used as "justification" for yet additional government programs which will create new burdens and inefficiencies.* This dynamic can lead to what is best characterized as a "transfer society."**

Political Piracy and the Transfer Society

Once we start down the road to the transfer society we can easily find ourselves trapped in a situation almost everyone will disapprove of, but which no one will be willing to change. The analogy of piracy is appropriate here. When all ships are productively employed shipping the goods, a large amount of wealth can be generated. But if sanctions against piracy are eased a few shippers may find it to their personal advantage to stop shipping and start pirating the merchandise being shipped by others, even though this reduces the total wealth available. This piracy by the few will reduce the return the others receive from shipping, and there will be an increase in the number finding the advantage in piracy. Eventually the point may be reached where everyone is sailing the seas looking for the booty that used to be shipped but is no longer. No one is doing well under these circumstances, and indeed, all would be much better off if everyone would return to shipping the goods. Yet who will be willing to return to productive shipping when everyone else is a pirate?

---

* Our Federal farm programs are a perfect example of this process. See Gardner, *Ibid*. Early on, James Madison recognized the possibility of this type of legislative chain reaction. In Federalist 44 Madison states, "that legislative interference, is but the first link of a long chain of repetitions; every subsequent interference being naturally produced by the effects of the preceding."

** For a detailed and compelling analysis of how the breakdown in constitutional limitations on government activity has moved the U.S. away from positive-sum economic activity and toward negative-sum activity, see Terry L. Anderson and Peter J. Hill, *The Birth of a Transfer Society* (Stanford, California: Hoover Institution Press, 1980).

Obviously, we have not yet arrived at the point of being a full-blown transfer society; not everyone has become a political pirate. There are plenty of people who remain productive, and they still receive a measure of protection against the confiscation of the returns to their efforts by the constitutional limitations that remain on government power. But there can be no doubt that these limitations are less effective today than they were in the past. This erosion is in large measure due to a change in the prevailing attitude toward government. The fear of unrestrained government power that guided the Founding Fathers has been largely replaced with the view that discretionary government power is a force for social good. If there is a problem, government supposedly has the obligation and ability to solve it. Such public attitudes have a decisive influence on the effectiveness of constitutional limitations.

Simply writing something down on a document called the Constitution does not by itself make it so. And, because of this fact, Alexis de Tocqueville, writing in the 1830s, predicted that the U.S. Constitution would eventually cease to exercise effective restraint on government. According to Tocqueville, "The government of the Union depends almost entirely upon legal fictions." He continued that it would be difficult to "imagine that it is possible by the aid of legal fictions to prevent men from finding out and employing those means of gratifying their passions which have been left open to them."*

But controlling our passions is what constitutional government is all about. In the absence of government we have the anarchy of the Hobbesian jungle in which those who control their passion for immediate gratification and apply their efforts toward long-run objectives only increase their vulnerability to the predation of those who exercise no control or foresight. Granting government the power to enforce general rules of social interaction is surely a necessary condition if a productive social order is to emerge from a state of anarchy. But without strict constitutional limits on the scope of government activity, the existence of government power will only increase the scope of effective predation. The notion that government can solve all problems becomes a convenient pretense for those who would solve their problems, not in cooperation with others, but at the expense of others. Unlimited government reduces the personal advantage to the productive pursuit of long-run objectives just as surely as does anarchy. In such a case, government is little more than the means of moving from the anarchy of the Hobbesian jungle to the anarchy of the political jungle.

The American experience, however, demonstrates convincingly that with a healthy fear of government power and a realistic understanding of human nature, a constitution can be designed that, over a long period of time, will effectively constrain government to operate within the limits defined by the delicate balance between proper power and prudent restraint. All that is needed

---

*   Quoted in Felix Morley, *Freedom and Federalism*, (Chicago: Regnery, 1959), pp. 138-139.

to restore the U.S. Constitution to its full effectiveness is a return to the political wisdom that guided our Founding Fathers 200 years ago.

Conclusion

The U.S. is a wealthy country today in large part because our Founding Fathers had what can be quite accurately described as a negative attitude toward government. They had little confidence in the ability of government to promote social well-being through the application of government power to achieve particular ends. In their view, the best that government can realistically hope to achieve is the establishment of a social setting in which individuals are free, within the limits of general laws, to productively pursue their own objectives.

This negative view of government contrasts sharply with the dominant view today; the view that government is the problem solver of last resort and has an obligation to provide a solution to any problem not resolved immediately in the private sector. Unfortunately, this positive view of government is less conducive to positive consequences than the negative view of the Founders. According to F. A. Hayek:

> The first [positive view] gives us a sense of unlimited power to realize our wishes, while the second [negative view] leads to the insight that there are limitations to what we can deliberately bring about, and to the recognition that some of our present hopes are delusions. Yet the effect of allowing ourselves to be deluded by the first view has always been that man has actually limited the scope of what he can achieve. For it has always been the recognition of the limits of the possible which has enabled man to make full use of his powers.*

The exercise of government can, without doubt, be used to accomplish particular ends. Neither can it be denied that many of the specific outcomes realized through government programs provide important benefits and advance worthy objectives. But, as is always the case, those accomplishments are only realized at a cost, and the pervasive truth about government accomplishments is that those who benefit from them are seldom those who pay the cost. Indeed, much of the motivation for engaging in political actions is to escape the discipline imposed by the market where individuals are accountable for the cost of their choices.

The escape from market discipline is the inevitable consequence of reducing the constitutional limits on the use of government power. The immediate and visible benefits that are generated by wide-ranging government discretion are paid for by a shift in the incentive structure that, over the long run, will

---

*   Friedrich A. Hayek, *Law, Legislation and Liberty*, Vol. I *Rules and Order* (Chicago: University of Chicago Press, 1973), p. 8.

reduce the amount of good that can be accomplished. More, much more, has been accomplished by the American people because our Founding Fathers had a strong sense of the limits on what can be accomplished by government. ●

25. The Nature of Government

Ayn Rand

A government is an institution that holds the exclusive power to *enforce* certain rules of conduct in a given geographical area.

Do men need such institution — and why?

Since man's mind is his basic tool of survival, his means of gaining knowledge to guide his actions — the basic condition he requires is the freedom to think and to act according to his rational judgment. This does not mean that a man must live alone and that a desert island is the environment best suited to his needs. Men can derive enormous benefits from dealing with one another. A social environment is most conducive to their successful survival — *but only on certain conditions*.

"The two great values to be gained from social existence are: knowledge and trade. Man is the only species that can transmit and expand his store of knowledge from generation to generation; the knowledge potentially available to man is greater than any one man could begin to acquire in his own lifespan; every man gains an incalculable benefit from the knowledge discovered by others. The second great benefit is the division of labour: it enables a man to devote his effort to a particular field of work and to trade with others who specialize in other fields. This form of cooperation allows all men who take part in it to achieve a greater knowledge, skill and productive return on their effort than they could achieve if each had to produce everything he needs, on a desert island or on a self-sustaining farm."

"But these very benefits indicate, delimit and define what kind of men can be of value to one another and in what kind of society: only rational, productive, independent men in a rational, productive, free society." ("The Objectivist Ethics.")

A society that robs an individual of the product of his effort, or enslaves him, or attempts to limit the freedom of his mind, or compels him to act against his own rational judgment — a society that sets up a conflict between its edicts and the requirements of man's nature — is not, strictly speaking, a society, but a mob held together by institutionalized gangrule. Such a society destroys all the values of human coexistence, has no possible justification and represents, not a source of benefits, but the deadliest threat to man's survival. Life on a desert island is safer than and incomparably preferable to existence in Soviet Russia or Nazi Germany.

If men are to live together in a peaceful, productive, rational society and deal with one another to mutual benefit, they must accept the basic social principle without which no moral or civilized society is possible: the principle of individual rights.

To recognize individual rights means to recognize and accept the conditions required by man's nature for his proper survival.

Man's rights can be violated only by the use of physical force. It is only by means of physical force that one man can deprive another of his life, or enslave him, or rob him, or prevent him from pursuing his own goals, or compel him to act against his own rational judgment.

The precondition of a civilized society is the barring of physical force from social relationships — thus establishing the principle that if men wish to deal with one another, they may do so only by means of *reason:* by discussion, persuasion and voluntary, uncoerced agreement.

The necessary consequence of man's right to life is his right to self-defense. In a civilized society, force may be used only in retaliation and only against those who initiate its use. All the reasons which make the initiation of physical force an evil, make the retaliatory use of physical force a moral imperative.

If some "pacifist" society renounced the retaliatory use of force, it would be left helplessly at the mercy of the first thug who decided to be immoral. Such a society would achieve the opposite of its intention: instead of abolishing evil, it would encourage and reward it.

If a society provided no organized protection against force, it would compel every citizen to go about armed, to turn his home into a fortress, to shoot any strangers approaching his door — or to join a protective gang of citizens who would fight other gangs, formed for the same purpose, and thus bring about the degeneration of that society into the chaos of gangrule, i.e., rule by brute force, into perpetual tribal warfare of prehistorical savages.

The use of physical force — even its retaliatory use — cannot be left at the discretion of individual citizens. Peaceful coexistence is impossible if a man has to live under the constant threat of force to be unleashed against him by any of his neighbors at any moment. Whether his neighbors' intentions are good or bad, whether their judgment is rational or irrational, whether they are motivated by a sense of justice or by ignorance or by prejudice or by malice — the use of force against one man cannot be left to the arbitrary decision of another.

Visualize, for example, what would happen if a man missed his wallet, concluded that he had been robbed, broke into every house in the neighborhood to search it, and shot the first man who gave him a dirty look, taking the look to be a proof of guilt.

The retaliatory use of force requires *objective* rules of evidence to establish that a crime has been committed and to *prove* who committed it, as well as objective rules to define punishments and enforcement procedures. Men who attempt to prosecute crimes, without such rules, are a lynch mob. If a society left the retaliatory use of force in the hands of individual citizens, it would degenerate into mob rule, lynch law and an endless series of bloody private feuds or vendettas.

If physical force is to be barred from social relationships, men need an institution charged with the task of protecting their rights under an *objective* code of rules.

This is the task of a government — of a *proper* government — its basic task, is only moral justification and the reason why men do need a government.

A government is the means of placing the retaliatory use of physical force under objective control — i.e., under objectively defined laws.

The fundamental difference between private action and governmental action — a difference thoroughly ignored and evaded today — lies in the fact that a government holds a monopoly on the legal use of physical force. It has to hold such a monopoly, since it is the agent of restraining and combating the use of force; and for that very same reason, its actions have to be rigidly defined, delimited and circumscribed; no touch of whim or caprice should be permitted in its performance; it should be an impersonal robot, with the laws as its only motive power. If a society is to be free, its government has to be controlled.

Under a proper social system, a private individual is legally free to take any action he pleases (so long as he does not violate the rights of others), while a government official is bound by law in his every official act. A private individual may do anything except that which is legally *forbidden*; a government official may do nothing except that which is legally *permitted*.

This is the means of subordinating "might" to "right." This is the American concept of "a government of laws and not of men."

The nature of the laws proper to a free society and the source of its government's authority are both to be derived from the nature and purpose of a proper government. The basic principle of both is indicated in The Declaration of Independence: "to secure these [individual] rights, governments are instituted among men, deriving their just powers from the consent of the governed . . ."

Since the protection of individual rights is the only proper purpose of a government, it is the only proper subject of legislation: all laws must be based on individual rights and aimed at their protection. All laws must be *objective* (and objectively justifiable): men must know clearly, and in advance of taking an action, what the law forbids them to do (and why), what constitutes a crime and what penalty they will incur if they commit it.

The source of the government's authority is "the consent of the governed." This means that the government is not the *ruler* but the servant or *agent* of the citizens; it means that the government as such has no rights except the rights *delegated* to it by the citizens for a specific purpose.

There is only one basic principle to which an individual must consent if he wishes to live in a free, civilized society: the principle of renouncing the use of physical force and delegating to the government his right of physical self-defense, for the purpose of an orderly, objective, legally defined enforcement. Or, to put it another way, he must accept *the separation of force and whim* (any whim, including his own).

Now what happens in case of a disagreement between two men about an undertaking in which both are involved?

In a free society, men are not forced to deal with one another. They do so only by voluntary agreement and, when a time element is involved, by *contract*. If a contract is broken by the arbitrary decision of one man, it may cause a disastrous financial injury to the other — and the victim would have no recourse except to seize the offender's property as compensation. But here again, the use of force cannot be left to the decision of private individuals. And this leads to one of the most important and most complex functions of the government: to the function of an arbiter who settles disputes among men according to objective laws.

Criminals are a small minority in any semicivilized society. But the protection and enforcement of contracts through courts of civil law is the most crucial need of a peaceful society; without such protection, no civilization could be developed or maintained.

Man cannot survive, as animals do, by acting on the range of the immediate moment. Man has to project his goals and achieve them across a span of time; he has to calculate his actions and plan his life long-range. The better a man's mind and the greater his knowledge, the longer the range of his planning. The higher or more complex a civilization, the longer the range of activity it requires — and, therefore, the longer the range of contractual agreements among men, and the more urgent their need of protection for the security of such agreements.

Even a primitive barter society could not function if a man agreed to trade a bushel of potatoes for a basket of eggs and, having received the eggs, refused to deliver the potatoes. Visualize what this sort of whim-directed action would mean in an industrial society where men deliver a billion dollars' worth of goods on credit, or contract to build multimillion-dollar structures, or sign ninety-nine-year leases.

A unilateral breach of contract involves an indirect use of physical force: it consists, in essence, of one man receiving the material values, goods or services of another, then refusing to pay for them and thus keeping them by force (by mere physical possession), not by right — i.e., keeping them without the consent of their owner. Fraud involves a similarly indirect use of force: it consists of obtaining material values without their owner's consent, under false pretenses or false promises. Extortion is another variant of an indirect use of force: it consists of obtaining material values, not in exchange for values, but by the threat of force, violence or injury.

Some of these actions are obviously criminal. Others, such as a unilateral breach of contract, may not be criminally motivated, but may be caused by irresponsibility and irrationality. Still others may be complex issues with some claim to justice on both sides. But whatever the case may be, all such issues have to be made subject to objectively defined laws and have to be resolved by an impartial arbiter, administering the laws, i.e., by a judge (and a jury, when appropriate).

Observe the basic principle governing justice in all these cases: it is the principle that no man may obtain any values from others without the owners' consent — and, as a corollary, that a man's rights may not be left at the mercy of the unilateral decision, the arbitrary choice, the irrationality, *the whim* of another man.

Such, in essence, is the proper purpose of a government: to make social existence possible to men, by protecting the benefits and combating the evils which men can cause to one another.

The proper functions of a government fall into three broad categories, all of them involving the issues of physical force and the protection of men's rights: *the police*, to protect men from criminals — *the armed services*, to protect men from foreign invaders — *the law courts*, to settle disputes among men according to objective laws.

These three categories involve many corollary and derivative issues — and their implementation in practice, in the form of specific legislation, is enormously complex. It belongs to the field of a special science: the philosophy of law. Many errors and many disagreements are possible in the field of implementation, but what is essential here is the principle to be implemented: the principle that the purpose of law and of government is the protection of individual rights.

Today, this principle is forgotten, ignored and evaded. The result is the present state of the world, with mankind's retrogression to the lawlessness of absolutist tyranny, to the primitive savagery of rule by brute force.

In unthinking protest against this trend, some people are raising the question of whether government as such is evil by nature and whether anarchy is the ideal social system. Anarchy, as a political concept, is a naive floating abstraction: for all the reasons discussed above, a society without an organized government would be at the mercy of the first criminal who came along and who would precipitate it into the chaos of gang warfare. But the possibility of human immorality is not the only objection to anarchy: even a society whose every member were fully rational and faultlessly moral, could not function in a state of anarchy; it is the need of *objective* laws and of an arbiter for honest disagreements among men that necessitates the establishment of a government.

The evolution of the concept of "government" has had a long, tortuous history. Some glimmer of the government's proper function seems to have existed in every organized society, manifesting itself in such phenomena as the recognition of some implicit (if often nonexistent) difference between a government and a robber gang—the aura of respect and of moral authority granted to the government as the guardian of "law and order"—the fact that even the most evil types of government found it necessary to maintain some semblance of order and some pretense at justice, if only by routine and tradition, and to claim some sort of moral justification for their power, of a mystical or social nature. Just as the absolute monarchs of France had to invoke "The Divine Right of Kings," so the modern dictators of Soviet Russia have to spend fortunes on propaganda to justify their rule in the eyes of their enslaved subjects.

In mankind's history, the understanding of the government's proper function is a very recent achievement: it is only two hundred years old and it dates from the Founding Fathers of the American Revolution. Not only did they identify the nature and the needs of a free society, but they devised the means to translate it into practice. A free society—like any other human product—cannot be achieved by random means, by mere wishing or by the leaders' "good intentions." A complex legal system, based on *objectively* valid principles, is required to make a society free and *to keep it free* — a system that does not depend on the motives, the moral character or the intentions of any given official, a system that leaves no opportunity, no legal loophole for the development of tyranny.

The American system of checks and balances was just such an achievement. And although certain contradictions in the Constitution did leave a loophole for the growth of statism, the incomparable achievement was the concept of a constitution as a means of limiting and restricting the power of the government.

Today, when a concerted effort is made to obliterate this point, it cannot be repeated too often that the Constitution is a limitation on the government, not on private individuals—that it does not prescribe the conduct of private individuals, only the conduct of the government — that it is not a charter *for* government power, but a charter of the citizens' protection *against* the government.

Now consider the extent of the moral and political inversion in today's prevalent view of government. Instead of being a protector of man's rights, the government is becoming their most dangerous violator; instead of guarding freedom, the government is establishing slavery; instead of protecting men from the initiators of physical force, the government is initiating physical force and coercion in any manner and issue it pleases; instead of serving as the instrument of *objectivity* in human relationships, the government is creating a deadly, subterranean reign of uncertainty and fear, by means of nonobjective laws whose interpretation is left to the arbitrary decisions of random bureaucrats; instead of protecting men from injury by whim, the government is arrogating to itself the power of unlimited whim—so that we are fast approaching the stage of the ultimate inversion: the stage where the government is *free* to do anything it pleases, while the citizens may act only by *permission*; which is the stage of the darkest periods of human history, the stage of rule by brute force.

It has often been remarked that in spite of its material progress, mankind has not achieved any comparable degree of moral progress. That remark is usually followed by some pessimistic conclusion about human nature. It is true that the moral state of mankind is disgracefully low. But if one considers the monstrous moral inversions of the governments (made possible by the altruist-collectivist morality) under which mankind has had to live through most of its history, one begins to wonder how men have managed to preserve even a semblance of civilization, and what indestructible vestige of self-esteem has kept them walking upright on two feet.

One also begins to see more clearly the nature of the political principles that have to be accepted and advocated, as part of the battle for man's intellectual Renaissance. ●

26. Of the Expences of the Sovereign or Commonwealth

Adam Smith

Of the Expence of Defence

The first duty of the sovereign, that of protecting the society from the violence and invasion of other independent societies, can be performed only by means of a military force. But the expence both of preparing this military force in time of peace, and of employing it in time of war, is very different in the different states of society, in the different periods of improvement.

As it is only by means of a well-regulated standing army that a civilized country can be defended; so it is only by means of it, that a barbarous country can be suddenly and tolerably civilized. A standing army establishes, with an irresistible force, the law of the sovereign through the remotest provinces of the empire, and maintains some degree of regular government in countries which could not otherwise admit of any. Whoever examines, with attention, the improvements which Peter the Great introduced into the Russian Empire, will find that they almost all resolve themselves into the establishment of a well-regulated standing army. It is the instrument which executes and maintains all his other regulations. That degree of order and internal peace, which that empire has ever since enjoyed, is altogether owing to the influence of that army.

Men of republican principles have been jealous of a standing army as dangerous to liberty. It certainly is so, wherever the interest of the general and that of the principal officers are not necessarily connected with the support of the constitution of the state. The standing army of Caesar destroyed the Roman republic. The standing army of Cromwell turned the long parliament out of doors. But where the sovereign is himself the general, and the principal nobility and gentry of the country the chief officers of the army; where the military force is placed under command of those who have the greatest interest in the support of the civil authority, because they have themselves the greatest share of that

Abridged from *The Wealth of Nations*, Modern Library Edition (New York: Random House, 1937), pp. 653-681.

authority, a standing army can never be dangerous to liberty. On the contrary, it may in some cases be favourable to liberty. The security which gives to the sovereign renders unnecessary that troublesome jealousy, which, in some modern republics, seems to watch over the minutest actions, and to be at all times ready to disturb the peace of every citizen. Where the security of the magistrate, though supported by the principal people of the country, is endangered by every popular discontent; where a small tumult is capable of bringing about in a few hours a great revolution, the whole authority of government must be employed to suppress and punish every murmur and complaint against it. To a sovereign, on the contrary, who feels himself supported, not only by the natural aristocracy of the country, but by a well-regulated standing army, the rudest, the most groundless, and the most licentious remonstrances can give little disturbance. He can safely pardon or neglect them, and his consciousness of his own superiority naturally disposes him to do so. That degree of liberty which approaches licentiousness can be tolerated only in countries where the sovereign is secured by a well-regulated standing army. It is in such countries only, that the public safety does not require, that the sovereign should be trusted with any discretionary power, for suppressing even the impertinent wantonness of this licentious liberty.

The first duty of the sovereign, therefore, that of defending the society from the violence and injustice of other independent societies, grows gradually more and more expensive, as the society advances in civilization. The military force of the society, which originally cost the sovereign no expence either in time of peace or in time of war, must, in the progress of improvement, first be maintained by him in time of war, and afterwards even in time of peace.

The great change introduced into the art of war by the invention of fire-arms, has enhanced still further both the expence of exercising and disciplining any particular number of soldiers in time of peace, and that of employing them in time of war. Both their arms and their ammunition are become more expensive. A musquet is a more expensive machine that a javelin or a bow and arrows; a cannon or a mortar than a balista or a catapulta. The powder, which is spent in a modern review, is lost irrecoverably, and occasions a very considerable expence. The javelins and arrows which were thrown or shot in an ancient one, could easily be picked up again, and were besides of very little value. The cannon and the mortar are, not only much dearer, but much heavier machines than the balista or catapulta, and require a greater expense, not only to prepare them for the field, but to carry them to it. As the superiority of the modern artillery too, over that of the ancients is very great; it has become much more difficult, and consequently much more expensive, to fortify a town so as to resist even for a few weeks the attack of that superior artillery. In modern times many different causes contribute to render the defence of the society more expensive. The unavoidable effects of the natural progress of improvement have, in this respect, been a good deal enhanced by a great revolution in the art of war, to which a mere accident, the invention of gunpowder, seems to have given occasion.

In modern war the great expence of fire-arms gives an evident advantage to the nation which can best afford that expence; and consequently, to an opulent and civilized, over a poor and barbarous nation. In ancient times the opulent and civilized found it difficult to defend themselves against the poor and barbarous nations. In modern times the poor and barbarous find it difficult to defend themselves against the opulent and civilized. The invention of firearms, an invention which at first sight appears to be so pernicious, is certainly favourable both to the permanency and to the extension of civilization.

Of the Expence of Justice

The second duty of the sovereign, that of protecting, as far as possible, every member of the society from the injustice or oppression of every other member of it, or the duty of establishing an exact administration of justice requires two very different degrees of expence in the different periods of society.

Among nations of hunters, as there is scarce any property, or at least none that exceeds the value of two or three days labour; so there is seldom any established magistrate or any regular administration of justice. Men who have no property can injure one another only in their persons or reputations. But when one man kills, wounds, beats, or defames another, though he to whom the injury is done suffers, he who does it receives no benefit. It is otherwise with the injuries to property. The benefit of the person who does the injury is often equal to the loss of him who suffers it. Envy, malice, or resentment, are the only passions which can prompt one man to injure another in his person or reputation. But the greater part of men are not very frequently under the influence of those passions; and the very worst men are so only occasionally. As their gratification too, how agreeable soever it may be in certain characters, it is not attended with any real or permanent advantage, it is in the greater part of men commonly restrained by prudential considerations. Men may live together in society with some tolerable degree of security, though there is no civil magistrate to protect them from the injustice of those passions. But avarice and ambition in the rich, in the poor the hatred of labour and the love of present ease and enjoyment, are the passions which prompt to invade property, passions much more steady in their operation, and much more universal in their influence. Wherever there is great property, there is great inequality. For one very rich man, there must be at least five hundred poor, and the affluence of the few supposes the indigence of the many. The affluence of the rich excites the indignation of the poor, who are often both driven by want, and prompted by envy, to invade his possessions. It is only under the shelter of the civil magistrate that the owner of that valuable property, which is acquired by the labour of many years, or perhaps of many successive generations, can sleep a single night in security. He is at all times, surrounded by unknown enemies, whom, though he never provoked, he can never appease, and from whose injustice he can be protected only by the powerful arm of the civil magistrate continually held up to chastise it. The acquisition of valuable and extensive property, therefore, necessarily requires the establishment of civil government. Where there is no property, or at least none that exceeds the value of two to three days labour, civil government is not so necessary.

The separation of the judicial from the executive power seems originally to have arisen from the increasing business of the society, in consequence of its increasing improvement. The administration of justice became so laborious and so complicated a duty as to require the undivided attention of the persons to whom it was entrusted. The person entrusted with the executive power, not having leisure to attend to the decision of private causes himself, a deputy was appointed to decide them in his stead. In the progress of the Roman greatness, the consul was too much occupied with the political affairs of the state, to attend to the administration of justice. A praetor, therefore, was appointed to administer it in his stead. In the progress of the European monarchies which were founded upon the ruins of the Roman empire, the sovereigns and the great lords came universally to consider the administration of justice as an office, both too laborious and too ignoble for them to execute in their own persons. They universally, therefore, discharged themselves of it by appointing a deputy, bailiff, or judge.

When the judicial is united to the executive power, it is scarce possible that justice should not frequently be sacrificed to, what is vulgarly called, politics. The persons entrusted with the great interests of the state may, even without any corrupt views, sometimes imagine it necessary to sacrifice to those interests the rights of a private man. But upon the impartial administration of justice depends the liberty of every individual, the sense which he has of his own security. In order to make every individual feel himself perfectly secure in the possession of every right which belongs to him, it is not only necessary that the judicial should be separated from the executive power, but that it should be rendered as much as possible independent of that power. The judge should not be liable to be removed from his office according to the caprice of that power. The regular payment of his salary should not depend upon the good-will, or even upon the good economy of that power.

Of the Expence of public Works and public Institutions

The third and last duty of the sovereign or commonwealth is that of erecting and maintaining those public institutions and those public works, which, though they may be in the highest degree advantageous to a great society, are, however, of such a nature, that the profit could never repay the expence to any individual or small number of individuals, and which it therefore cannot be expected that any individual or small number of individuals should erect or maintain. The performance of this duty requires too very different degrees of expence in the different periods of society.

After the public institutions and public works necessary for the defence of the society, and for the administration of justice, both of which have already been mentioned, the other works and institutions of this kind are chiefly those for facilitating the commerce of the society, and those for promoting the instruction of the people. The institutions for instruction are of two kinds; those for the education of the youth, and those for the instruction of people of all ages. ●

27. On the Duty of Civil Disobedience

Henry David Thoreau

I heartily accept the motto, — "That government is best which governs least;" and I should like to see it acted up to more rapidly and systematically. Carried out, it finally amounts to this, which also I believe, — "That government is best which governs not at all;" and when men are prepared for it, that will be the kind of government which they will have. Government is at best but an expedient; but most governments are usually, and all governments are sometimes, inexpedient. The objections which have been brought against a standing army, and they are many and weighty, and deserve to prevail, may also at last be brought against a standing government. The standing army is only an arm of the standing government. The government itself, which is only the mode which the people have chosen to execute their will, is equally liable to be abused and perverted before the people can act through it. Witness the present Mexican war, the work of comparatively a few individuals using the standing government as their tool; for, in the outset, the people would not have consented to this measure.

This American government, — what is it but a tradition, though a recent one, endeavoring to transmit itself unimpaired to posterity, but each instant losing some of its integrity? It has not the vitality and force of a single living man; for a single man can bend it to his will. It is a sort of wooden gun to the people themselves. But it is not the less necessary for this; for the people must have some complicated machinery or other, and hear its din, to satisfy that idea of government which they have. Governments show thus how successfully men can be imposed on, even impose on themselves, for their own advantage. It is excellent, we must all allow. Yet this government never of itself furthered any enterprise, but by the alacrity with which it got out of its way. *It* does not keep the country free. *It* does not settle the West. *It* does not educate. The charac-

Abridged from *Walden and On the Duty of Civil Disobedience*, Perinnial Classics Edition, (New York: Harper & Row, 1965), pp. 251-271.

ter inherent in the American people has done all that has been accomplished; and it would have done somewhat more, if the government had not sometimes got in its way. For government is an expedient by which men would fain succeed in letting one another alone; and, as has been said, when it is most expedient, the governed are most let alone by it. Trade and commerce, if they were not made of India-rubber, would never manage to bounce over the obstacles which legislators are continually putting in their way; and, if one were to judge these men wholly by the effects of their actions and not partly by their intentions, they would deserve to be classed and punished with those mischievous persons who put obstructions on the railroads.

But, to speak practically and as a citizen, unlike those who call themselves no-government men, I ask for, not at once no government, but *at once* a better government. Let every man make known what kind of government would command his respect, and that will be one step toward obtaining it.

After all, the practical reason why, when the power is once in the hands of the people, a majority are permitted, and for a long period continue, to rule is not because they are most likely to be in the right, nor because this seems fairest to the minority, but because they are physically the strongest. But a government in which the majority rule in all cases cannot be based on justice even as far as men understand it. Can there not be a government in which majorities do not virtually decide right and wrong, but conscience? — in which majorities decide only those questions to which the rule of expediency is applicable? Must the citizen even for a moment, or in the least degree, resign his conscience to the legislator? Why has every man a conscience, then? I think that we should be men first, and subjects afterward. It is not desirable to cultivate a respect for the law, so much as for the right. The only obligation which I have a right to assume is to do at any time what I think right. It is truly enough said, that a corporation has no conscience; but a corporation of conscientious men is a corporation *with* a conscience. Law never made men a whit more just; and, by means of their respect for it, even the well-disposed are daily made agents of injustice. A common and natural result of an undue respect for law is, that you may see a file of soldiers, colonel, captain, corporal, privates, powdermonkeys and all, marching in admirable order over hill and dale to the wars, against their wills, ay, against their common sense and consciences, which makes it very steep marching indeed, and produces a palpitation of the heart. They have no doubt that it is a damnable business in which they are concerned; they are all peaceably inclined. Now, what are they? Men at all? or small movable forts and magazines, at the service of some unscrupulous man in power?

There are thousands who are *in opinion* opposed to slavery and to the war, who yet in effect do nothing to put an end to them; who, esteeming themselves children of Washington and Franklin, sit down with their hands in their pockets, and say that they know not what to do, and do nothing; who even postpone the question of freedom to the question of free-trade, and quietly read the prices-current along with the latest advices from Mexico, after dinner, and it may be, fall asleep over them both. What is the price-current of an honest man and patriot to-day? They hesitate, and they regret, and sometimes they petition; but they do nothing in earnest and with effect. They will wait, well disposed, for others to remedy the evil, but they may no longer have it to regret. At most, they give only a cheap vote, and a feeble countenance and God-speed, to the right, as it goes by them. There are nine hundred and ninety-nine patrons of virtue to one virtuous man. But it is easier to deal with the real possessor of a thing than with the temporary guardian of it.

All voting is a sort of gaming, like checkers or backgammon, with a slight moral tinge to it, a playing with right and wrong, with moral questions; and betting naturally accompanies it. The character of the voters is not staked. I cast my vote, perchance, as I think right; but I am not vitally concerned that right should prevail. I am willing to leave it to the majority. Its obligation, therefore, never exceeds that of expediency. Even voting *for the right* is *doing* nothing for it. It is only expressing to men feebly your desire that it should prevail. A wise man will not leave the right to the mercy of chance, nor wish it to prevail through the power of the majority. There is but little virtue in the action of masses of men. When the majority shall at length vote for the abolition of slavery, it will be because they are indifferent to slavery, or because there is but little slavery left to be abolished by their vote. *They* will then be the only slaves. Only *his* vote can hasten the abolition of slavery who asserts his own freedom by his vote.

Unjust laws exist: shall we be content to obey them, or shall we endeavor to amend them, and obey them until we have succeeded, or shall we transgress them at once? Men generally, under such a government as this, think that they ought to wait until they have persuaded the majority to alter them. They think that, if they should resist, the remedy would be worse than the evil. But it is the fault of the government itself that the remedy *is* worse than the evil. *It* makes it worse. Why is it not more apt to anticipate and provide for reform? Why does it not cherish its wise minority? Why does it cry and resist before it is hurt? Why does it not encourage its citizens to be on the alert to point out its faults, and *do* better than it would have them? Why does it always crucify Christ, and excommunicate Copernicus and Luther, and pronounce Washington and Franklin rebels?

One would think, that a deliberate and practical denial of its authority was the only offense never contemplated by government; else, why has it not assigned its definite, its suitable and proportionate penalty? If a man who has no property refused but once to earn nine shillings for the state, he is put in prison for a period unlimited by any law that I know, and determined only by the discretion of those who placed him there; but if he should steal ninety times nine shillings from the state, he is soon permitted to go at large again.

If the injustice is part of the necessary friction of the machine of government, let it go, let it go: perchance it will wear smooth, — certainly the machine will wear out. It the injustice has a spring, or a pulley, or a rope, or a crank, exclusively for itself, then perhaps you may consider whether the remedy will not be worse than the evil; but if it is of such nature that it requires you to be the agent of injustice to another, then, I say, break the law. Let your life be a counter friction to stop the machine. What I have to do is to see, at any rate, that I do not lend myself to the wrong which I condemn.

As for adopting the ways which the state has provided for remedying the evil, I know not of such ways. They take too much time, and a man's life will be gone. I have other affairs to attend to. I came into this world, not chiefly to make this a good place to live in, but to live in it, be it good or bad. A man has not everything to do, but something; and because he cannot do *everything*, it is not necessary that he should do *something* wrong. It is not my business to be petitioning the Governor or the Legislature any more than it is theirs to petition me; and if they should not hear my petition, what should I do then? But in this case the state has provided no way: its very Constitution is the evil. This may seem to be harsh and stubborn and unconciliatory; but it is to treat with the utmost kindness and consideration the only spirit that can appreciate or deserves it. So is all change for the better, like birth and death, which convulse the body.

I do not hesitate to say, that those who call themselves Abolitionists should at once effectually withdraw their support, both in person and property, from the government of Massachusetts and not wait till they constitute a majority of one, before they suffer the right to prevail through them. I think that it is enough if they have God on their side, without waiting for that other one. Moreover, any man more right than his neighbors constitutes a majority of one already.

Under a government which imprisons any unjustly, the true place for a just man is also a prison. The proper place today, the only place which Massachusetts has provided for her free and less desponding spirits, is in her prisons, to be put out and locked out of the state by her own act, as they have already put themselves out by their principles. It is there that the fugitive slave, and the Mexican prisoner on parole, and the Indian come to plead the wrongs of his race should find them; on that separate, but more free and honorable ground, where the State places those who are not *with* her, but *against* her, — the only house in a slave State in which a free man can abide with honor. If any think that their influence would be lost there, and their voices no longer afflict the ear of the State, that they would not be as an enemy within its walls, they do not know by how much truth is stronger than error, nor how much more eloquently and effectively he can combat injustice who has experienced a little in his own person. Cast your whole vote, not a strip of paper merely, but your whole influence. A minority is powerless while it conforms to the majority; it is not even a minority then; but it is irresistible when it clogs by its whole weight. If the alternative is to keep all just men in prison, or give up war and slavery, the State will not hesitate which to choose. If a thousand men were not to pay their tax-bills this year, that would not be a violent and bloody measure, as it would be to pay them, and enable the State to commit violence and shed innocent blood. This is, in fact, the definition of a peaceable revolution, if any such is possible.

Thus the State never intentionally confronts a man's sense, intellectual or moral, but only his body, his senses. It is not armed with superior wit or honesty, but with superior physical strength. I was not born to be forced. I will breathe after my own fashion. Let us see who is the strongest. What force has a multitude? They only can force me who obey a higher law than I. They force me to become like themselves. I do not hear of *men* being *forced* to live this way or that by masses of men. What sort of life were that to live? When I meet a government which says to me, "Your money or your life," why should I be in haste to give it my money? It may be in a great strait, and not know what to do: I cannot help that. It must help itself; do as I do. It is not worth the while to snivel about it. I am not responsible for the successful working of the machinery of society. I am not the son of the engineer. I perceive that, when an acorn and a chestnut fall side by side, the one does not remain inert to make way for the other, but both obey their own laws, and spring and grow and flourish as best they can, till one, perchance, overshadows and destroys the other. If a plant cannot live according to its nature, it dies; and so a man.

The authority of government, even such as I am willing to submit to, — for I will cheerfully obey those who know and can do better than I, and in many things even those who neither know nor can do so well, — is still an impure one: to be strictly just, it must have the sanction and consent of the governed. It can have no pure right over my person and property but what I concede to it. The progress from an absolute to a limited monarchy, from a limited monarchy to a democracy, is a progress toward a true respect for the individual. Even the Chinese philosopher was wise enough to regard the individual as the basis of the empire. Is a democracy, such as we know it, the last improvement possible in government? Is it not possible to take a step further towards recognizing and organizing the rights of man? There will never be a really free and enlightened State until the State comes to recognize the individual as a higher and independent power, from which all its own power and authority are derived, and treats him accordingly. I please myself with imagining a State at last which can afford to be just to all men, and to treat the individual with respect as a neighbor; which even would not think it consistent with its own repose if a few were to live aloof from it, not meddling with it, nor embraced by it, who fulfilled all the duties of neighbors and fellow-men. A State which bore this kind of fruit, and suffered it to drop off as fast as it ripened, would prepare the way for a still more perfect and glorious State, which also I have imagined, but not yet anywhere seen. ●

28. Of the Limits to the Authority of Society Over the Individual

John Stuart Mill

What, then, is the rightful limit to the sovereignty of the individual over himself? Where does the authority of society begin? How much of human life should be assigned to individuality, and how much to society?

Each will receive its proper share, if each has that which more particularly concerns it. To individuality should belong the part of life in which it is chiefly the individual that is interested; to society, the part which chiefly interests society.

Though society is not founded on a contract, and though no good purpose is answered by inventing a contract in order to deduce social obligations from it, every one who receives the protection of society owes a return for the benefit, and the fact of living in society renders it indispensable that each should be bound to observe a certain line of conduct towards the rest. This conduct consists, first, in not injuring the interests of one another; or rather certain interests, which, either by express legal provision or by tacit understanding, ought to be considered as rights; and secondly, in each person's bearing his share (to be fixed on some equitable principle) of the labors and sacrifices incurred for defending the society or its members from injury and molestation. These conditions society is justified in enforcing, at all costs to those who endeavor to withhold fulfillment. Nor is this all that society may do. The acts of an individual may be hurtful to others, or wanting in due consideration for their welfare, without going the length of violating any of their constituted rights. The offender may then be justly punished by opinion, though not by law. As soon as any part of a person's conduct affects prejudicially the interests of others, society has jurisdiction over it, and the question whether the general welfare will or will not be promoted by interfering with it, becomes open to discussion. But there is no room for entertaining any such question when a person's con-

Abridged from *On Liberty*, Harvard Classics Edition (New York: P. F. Collier & Son, 1909), pp. 281-301.

duct affects the interests of no persons besides himself, or needs not affect them unless they like (all the persons concerned being of full age, and the ordinary amount of understanding). In all such cases there should be perfect freedom, legal and social, to do the action and stand the consequences.

It would be a great misunderstanding of this doctrine, to suppose that it is one of selfish indifference, which pretends that human beings have no business with each other's conduct in life, and that they should not concern themselves about the well-doing or well-being of one another, unless their own interest is involved. Instead of any diminution, there is need of a great increase of disinterested exertion to promote the good of others. But disinterested benevolence can find other instruments to persuade people to do their good, than whips and scourges, either of the literal or the metaphorical sort. I am the last person to undervalue the self-regarding virtues; they are only second in importance, if even second, to the social. It is equally the business of education to cultivate both. But even education works by conviction and persuasion as well as by compulsion, and it is by the former only that, when the period of education is past, the self-regarding virtues should be inculcated. Human beings owe to each other help to distinguish the better from the worse, and encouragement to choose the former and avoid the latter. They should be forever stimulating each other to increased exercise of their higher faculties, and increased direction of their feelings and aims toward wise instead of foolish, elevating instead of degrading, objects and contemplations. But neither one person, nor any number of persons, is warranted in saying to another human creature of ripe years, that he shall not do with his life for his own benefit what he chooses to do with it. He is the person most interested in his own well-being, the interest which any other person, except in cases of strong personal attachment, can have in it, is trifling, compared with that which he himself has; the interest which society has in him individually (except as to his conduct to others) is fractional, and altogether indirect: while, with respect to his own feelings and circumstances, the most ordinary man or woman has means of knowledge immeasurably surpassing those that can be possessed by any one else. The interference of society to overrule his judgment and purposes in what only regards himself, must be grounded on general presumptions; which may be altogether wrong, and even if right, are as likely as not to be misapplied to individual cases, by persons no better acquainted with the circumstances of such cases than those are who look at them merely from without. In this department, therefore, of human affairs, individuality has its proper field of action. In the conduct of human beings towards one another, it is necessary that general rules should for the most part be observed, in order that people may know what they have to expect; but in each person's own concerns, his individual spontaneity is entitled to free exercise. Considerations to aid his judgment, exhortations to strengthen his will, may be offered to him, even obtruded on him, by others; but he, himself, is the final judge. All errors which he is likely to commit against advice and warning, are far outweighted by the evil of allowing others to constrain him to what they deem his good.

But the strongest of all the arguments against the interference of the public with purely personal conduct, is that when it does interfere, the odds are that it interferes wrongly, and in the wrong place. On questions of social morality, of duty to others, the opinion of the public, that is, of an overruling majority, though often wrong, is likely to be still oftener right; because on such questions they are only required to judge of their own interests; of the manner in which some mode of conduct, if allowed to be practiced, would affect themselves. But the opinion of a similar majority, imposed as a law on the minority, on questions of self-regarding conduct, is quite as likely to be wrong as right; for in these cases public opinion means, at the best, some people's opinion of what is good or bad for other people; while very often it does not even mean that; the public, with the most perfect indifference, passing over the pleasure of convenience of those whose conduct they censure, and considering only their own preference. There are many who consider as an injury to themselves any conduct which they have a distaste for, and resent it as an outrage to their feelings; as a religious bigot, when charged with disregarding the religious feelings of others, has been known to retort that they disregard his feelings, by persisting in their abominable worship or creed. But there is no parity between the feeling of a person for his own opinion, and the feeling of another who is offended at his holding it; no more than between the desire of a thief to take a purse, and the desire of the right owner to keep it. And a person's taste is as much his own peculiar concern as his opinion of his purse. It is easy for any one to imagine an ideal public, which leaves the freedom and choice of individuals in all uncertain matters undisturbed, and only requires them to abstain from modes of conduct which universal experience has condemned. But where has there been seen a public which set any such limit to its censorship.

Wherever the Puritans have been sufficiently powerful, as in New England, and in Great Britain at the time of the Commonwealth, they have endeavored, with considerable success, to put down all public, and nearly all private, amusements: especially music, dancing, public games, or other assemblages for purposes of diversion, and the theater. There are still in this country large bodies of persons by whose notions of morality and religion these recreations are condemned; and those persons belonging chiefly to the middle class, who are the ascendant power in the present social and political condition of the kingdom, it is by no means impossible that persons of these sentiments may at some time or other command a majority in Parliament. How will the remaining portion of the community like to have the amusements that shall be permitted to them regulated by the religious and moral sentiments of the stricter Calvinists and Methodists? Would they not, with considerable peremptoriness, desire these intrusively pious members of society to mind their own business? This is precisely what should be said to every government and every public, who have the pretension that no person shall enjoy any pleasure which they think wrong. But if the principle of the pretension be admitted, no one can reasonably object to its being acted on in the sense of the majority, or other preponderating power in the country; and all persons must be ready to conform to the idea of a Christian commonwealth, as understood by the early settlers in New England, if a religious profession similar to theirs should ever succeed in regaining its lost ground, as religions supposed to be declining have so often been known to do.

To imagine another contingency, perhaps more likely to be realized than the one last mentioned. There is confessedly a strong tendency in the modern world towards a democratic constitution of society, accompanied or not by popular political institutions. It is affirmed that in the country where this tendency is most completely realized—where both society and the government are most democratic—the United States—the feeling of the majority, to whom any appearance of a more showy or costly style of living than they can hope to rival is disagreeable, operates as a tolerably effectual sumptuary law, and that in many parts of the Union it is really difficult for a person possessing a very large income, to find any mode of spending it, which will not incur popular disapprobation. Though such statements as these are doubtless much exaggerated as a representation of existing facts, the state of things they describe is not only a conceivable and possible, but a probable result of democratic feeling, combined with the notion that the public has a right to a veto on the manner in which individuals shall spend their incomes. We have only further to suppose a considerable diffusion of Socialist opinions, and it may become infamous in the eyes of the majority to possess more property than some very small amount, or any income not earned by manual labor. Opinions similar in principle to these, already prevail widely among the artisan class, and weigh oppressively on those who are amenable to the opinion chiefly of that class, namely, its own members. It is known that the bad workmen who form the majority of the operatives in many branches of industry, are decidedly of opinion that bad workmen ought to receive the same wages as good, and that no one ought to be allowed, through piecework or otherwise, to earn by superior skill or industry more than others can without it. And they employ a moral police, which occasionally becomes a physical one, to deter skillful workmen from receiving, and employers from giving, a larger remuneration for a more useful service. If the public have any jurisdiction over private concerns, I cannot see that these people are in fault, or that any individual's particular public can be blamed for asserting the same authority over his individual conduct, which the general public asserts over people in general.

But, without dwelling upon supposititious cases, there are, in our own day, gross usurpations upon the liberty of private life actually practiced, and still greater ones threatened with some expectation of success, and opinions proposed which assert an unlimited right in the public not only to prohibit by law everything which it thinks wrong, but in order to get at what it thinks wrong, to prohibit any number of things which it admits to be innocent.

Under the name of preventing intemperance, the people of one English colony, and of nearly half the United States, have been interdicted by law from making any use whatever of fermented drinks, except for medical purposes: for prohibition of their sale is in fact, as it is intended to be, prohibition of their use. And though the impracticability of executing the law has caused its repeal in several of the States which had adopted it, including the one from which it derives its name, an attempt has notwithstanding been commenced, and is prosecuted with considerable zeal by many of the professed philanthropists, to agitate for a similar law in this country. The association, or "Alliance" as it terms itself, which has been formed for this purpose, has acquired some notoriety through the publicity given to a correspondence between its Secretary and one of the very few English public men who hold that a politician's opinions ought to be founded on principles. Lord Stanley's share in this correspondence is calculated to strengthen the hopes already built on him, by those who know how rare such qualities as are manifested in some of his public appearances, unhappily are among those who figure in political life. The organ of the Alliance, who should "deeply deplore the recognition of any principle which could be wrested to justify bigotry and persecution," undertakes to point out the "broad and impassable barrier" which divides such principles from those of the association. "All matters relating to thought, opinion, conscience, appear to me," he says, "to be without the sphere of legislation; all pertaining to social act, habit, relation, subject only to a discretionary power vested in the State itself, and not in the individual, to be within it." No mention is made of a third class, different from either of these, viz., acts and habits which are not social but individual; although it is to this class, surely, that the act of drinking fermented liquors belongs. Selling fermented liquors, however, is trading, and trading is a social act. But the infringement complained of is not on the liberty of the seller, but on that of the buyer and consumer; since the State might just as well forbid him to drink wine, as purposely make it impossible for him to obtain it. The Secretary, however, says, "I claim, as a citizen, a right to legislate whenever my social rights are invaded by the social act of another." And now for the definition of these "social rights." "If anything invades my social rights, certainly the traffic in strong drink does. It destroys my primary right of security, by constantly creating and stimulating social disorder. It invades my right of equality, by deriving a profit from the creation of a misery I am taxed to support. It impedes my right to free moral and intellectual development, by surrounding my path with dangers, and by weakening and demoralizing society, from which I have a right to claim mutual aid and intercourse." A theory of "social rights," the like of which probably never before found its way into distinct language: being nothing short of this — that it is the absolute social right of every individual, that every other individual shall act in every respect exactly as he ought; that whosoever fails thereof in the smallest particular, violates my social right, and entitles me to demand from the legislature the removal of the grievance. So monstrous a principle is far more dangerous than any single interference with liberty; there is no violation of liberty which it would not justify, it acknowledges no right to any freedom whatever, except perhaps to that of holding opinions in secret, without ever disclosing them; for, the moment an opinion which I consider noxious passes any one's lips, it invades all the "social rights" attributed to me by the Alliance. The doctrine ascribes to all mankind a vested interest in each other's moral, intellectual, and even physical perfection, to be defined by each claimant according to his own standard.

Another important example of illegitimate interference with the rightful liberty of the individual, not simply threatened, but long since carried into triumphant effect, is Sabbatarian legislation. Without doubt, abstinence on one day in the week, so far as the exigencies of life permit, from the usual daily occupation, though in no respect religiously binding on any except Jews, is a highly beneficial custom. And inasmuch as this custom cannot be observed without a general consent to that effect among the industrious classes, therefore, in so far as some persons by working may impose the same necessity on others, it may be allowable and right that the law should guarantee to each, the observance by others of the custom, by suspending the greater operations of industry on a particular day. But this justification, grounded on the direct interest which others have in each individual's observance of the practice, does not apply to the self-chosen occupations in which a person may think fit to employ his leisure; nor does it hold good, in the smallest degree, for legal restrictions on amusements. It is true that the amusement of some is the day's work of others; but the pleasure, not to say the useful recreation, of many, is worth the labor of a few, provided the occupation is freely chosen, and can be freely resigned. The operatives are perfectly right in thinking that if all worked on Sunday, seven days' work would have to be given for six days' wages: but so long as the great mass of employments are suspended, the small number who for the enjoyment of others must still work, obtain a proportional increase of earnings; and they are not obliged to follow those occupations, if they prefer leisure to emolument. If a further remedy is sought, it might be found in the establishment by custom of a holiday on some other day of the week for those particular classes of persons. The only ground, therefore, on which restrictions on Sunday amusements can be defended, must be that they are religiously wrong; a motive of legislation which never can be too earnestly protested against. *Deorum injuriae Diis curae.* It remains to be proved that society or any of its officers holds a commission from on high to avenge any supposed offense to Omnipotence, which is not also a wrong to our fellow creatures. The notion that it is one man's duty that another should be religious, was the foundation of all the religious persecutions ever perpetrated, and if admitted, would fully justify them. Though the feeling which breaks out in the repeated attempts to stop railway traveling on Sunday, in the resistance to the opening of Museums, and the like, has not the cruelty of the old persecutors, the state of mind indicated by it is fundamentally the same. It is a determination not to tolerate others in doing what is permitted by their religion, because it is not permitted by the persecutor's religion. It is a belief that God not only abominates the act of the misbeliever, but will not hold us guiltless if we leave him unmolested.

I cannot refrain from adding to these examples of the little account commonly made of human liberty, the language of downright persecution which breaks out from the press of this country, whenever it feels called on to notice the remarkable phenomenon of Mormonism. Much might be said on the unexpected and instructive fact, that an alleged new revelation, and a religion, founded on it, the product of palpable imposture, not even supported by the *prestige* of extraordinary qualities in its founder, is believed by hundreds of thousands, and has been made the foundation of a society, in the age of newspapers, railways, and the electronic telegraph. What here concerns us is, that this religion, like other and better religions, has its martyrs; that its prophet and founder was, for his teaching, put to death by a mob; that others of its adherents lost their lives by the same lawless violence; that they were forcibly expelled, in a body, from the country in which they first grew up; while, now that they have been chased into a solitary recess in the midst of a desert, many in this country openly declare that it would be right (only that it is not convenient) to send an expedition against them, and compel them by force to conform to the opinions of other people. The article of the Mormonite doctrine which is the chief provocative to the antipathy which thus breaks through the ordinary restrains of religious tolerance, is its sanction of polygamy; which, though permitted to Mahomedans, and Hindoos, and Chinese, seems to excite unquenchable animosity when practiced by persons who speak English, and profess to be a kind of Christians. No one has a deeper disapprobation than I have of this Mormon institution; both for other reasons, and because, far from being in any way countenanced by the principle of liberty, it is a direct infraction of that principle, being a mere riveting of the chains of one half of the community, and an emancipation of the other form reciprocity of obligation towards them. Still, it must be remembered that this relation is as much voluntary on the part of the women concerned in it, and who may be deemed the sufferers by it, as is the case with any other form of the marriage institution; and however surprising this fact may appear, it has its explanation in the common ideas and customs of the world, which teaching women to think marriage the one thing needful, make it intelligible that many a woman should prefer being one of several wives, to not being a wife at all. Other countries are not asked to recognize such unions, or release any portion of their inhabitants from their own laws on the score of Mormonite opinions. But when the dissentients have conceded to the hostile sentiments of others, far more than could justly be demanded; when they have left the countries to which their doctrines were unacceptable, and established themselves in a remote corner of the earth, which they have been the first to render habitable to human beings; it is difficult to see on what principles but those of tyranny they can be prevented from living there under what laws they please, provided they commit no aggression on other nations, and allow perfect freedom of departure to those who are dissatisfied with their ways. A recent writer, in some respects of considerable merit, proposes (to use his own words) not a crusade, but a *civilizade*, against this polygamous community, to put an end to what seems to him a retrograde step in civilization. It also appears so to me, but I am not aware that any community has a right to force another to be civilized. So long as the sufferers by the bad law do not invoke assistance from other communities, I cannot admit that persons entirely unconnected with them ought to step in and require that a condition of things with which all who are directly interested appear to be satisfied, should be put an end to because it is a scandal to persons some thousands of miles distant, who have no part or concern in it. Let them send missionaries, if they please, to preach against it; and let them, by any fair means (of which silencing the teachers is not one), oppose the progress of similar doctrines among their own people. If civilization has got the better of barbarism when barbarism had the world to itself, it is too much to profess to be afraid lest barbarism, after having been fairly got under, should revive and conquer civilization. A civilization that can thus succumb to its vanquished enemy must first have become so degenerate, that neither its appointed priests and teachers, nor anybody else, has the capacity, or will take the trouble, to stand up for it. If this be so, the sooner such a civilization receives notice to quit, the better. It can only go on from bad to worse, until destroyed and regenerated (like the Western Empire) by energetic barbarians. ●

Section SIX

Scarcity, Conflict, and Social Cooperation

The question is commonly thought of as one in which A inflicts harm on B and what has to be decided is: how should we restrain A? But this is wrong. We are dealing with a problem of reciprocal nature. To avoid the harm to B would inflict harm on A. The real question that has to be decided is: should A be allowed to harm B or should B be allowed to harm A?

R. H. Coase

The one constant in all economic systems is scarcity. Regardless of how efficient an economic system is at producing wealth, it remains true that people will want more than is available. No one will have as much as they would like, and everyone will experience frustration as they see resources which they could be using wisely being put to what they see as frivolous uses by others. Therefore, in all economic systems the potential for social conflict is high.

However, while scarcity generates the potential for social conflict, it also generates the need for social cooperation.

Competition is commonly identified with conflict and seen as the antithesis of cooperation. Fortunately, this is not the case. Competition is inevitable in our world of scarcity, but under the appropriate rules, and proper respect for those rules, competition becomes a force for social cooperation. Cooperation is a necessary ingredient into a productive economy and the most effective cooperation of this type is the cooperation that emerges from competition within the rules of the private enterprise system.

With the rules of private property and voluntary exchange, both the information and incentives exist for people to cooperate with others by taking their concerns into consideration. With private property and exchange, prices materialize that inform market participants of the relative value others place on goods and services and the cost of providing them. Those who are best able to respond to the information contained in market prices have a strong profit motivation to do so. In a market setting, one best furthers his or her aims, no matter what they are, by appealing to the concerns of others and seeking out areas of mutual interest.

In this section the emphasis is on the potential for social conflict and the potential for social cooperation to emerge out of the exchanges that take place under the rule of private property.

People will naturally cooperate with each other through exchange in the marketplace. This cooperation occurs in response to market prices that motivate suppliers to make products available in quantities equal to the amount consumers desire. The urge that people have to cooperate in this way through the market is sufficiently strong that this cooperation persists even when the government makes it illegal by imposing legal restrictions on prices. Doti's story of a loan shark and his customers in Little Italy illustrates the tendency for cooperative behavior to persist in spite of government efforts to suppress it. Lee follows up by contrasting the cooperation that is motivated through market competition with the conflict that is the natural consequence of political competition.

James M. Buchanan (1919–), the winner of the 1986 Nobel Prize in Economics, considers different attitudes people have toward one another, toward the rules of acceptable conduct, and how the degree of social cooperation is affected by these attitudes. The United States and Japan are compared and contrasted within the general framework developed.

The final selection of this section is taken from a classic article by Ronald

Coase (1910–) who was born in England but who has lived in the United States since the 1950s and has taught at the University of Virginia and the University of Chicago. Coase provided a new and important perspective on a problem which has long concerned economists: the problem of neighborhood or spillover effects that arise when the actions of one individual or firm adversely affects others. Coase's insight was that this problem was primarily one of transaction costs; the costs of getting the concerned parties together, of reaching agreement, and enforcing the terms of that agreement. In cases where transaction costs are low, Coase argued that cooperative behavior would generate efficient outcomes and these outcomes would be independent of the initial assignment of rights.

George Stigler recently recalled in his biography, *Memoirs of an Unregulated Economist*, the meeting in 1960 of twenty economists from the University of Chicago where Ronald Coast first presented his then heretical ideas:

> Ronald asked us also to believe a second proposition about this world without transaction costs: Whatever the assignment of legal liability for damages, or whatever the assignment of legal rights of ownership, the assignments would have no effect upon the way economic resources would be used! We strongly objected to this heresy. Milton Friedman did most of the talking, as usual. He also did most of the thinking, as usual. In the course of two hours of argument the vote went from twenty against and one for Coase to twenty-one for Coase. What an exhilarating event!* •

---

* From *Memoirs of an Unregulated Economist*, by George Stigler. Copyright © 1989 by Basic Books, Inc. Reprinted by permission of Basic Books, Inc., Publishers, New York.

29. Commare N'Ciuzza and the Loan Shark

James L. Doti

I had just purchased an Italian lemonade and was contentedly licking a chunk of lemon peel embedded in the ice as I walked across the intersection of Aberdeen and Taylor. Just then, two black sedans screeched around the corner, and I froze in my tracks as I heard the nerve-shattering sound of guns being fired. The next moment I felt I was being dragged and pulled by someone whose powerful hands were firmly gripped around my shoulder. Several minutes later I was pleased to find I was sitting in the kitchen of the woman who had done the dragging and pulling — Commare N'Ciuzza.

Almost a year earlier I had met and befriended Commare N'Ciuzza. At the time I was a student at a new university that was built on a large portion of an old neighborhood known as Little Italy. This neighborhood had once served as the melting pot for newly immigrating Italians to Chicago. Those who still lived in the small portion of neighborhood that survived the university's construction looked upon the few students who lived there with a mingling of fear and suspicion. It was only after people noticed my special friendship with Commare N'Ciuzza that I was allowed to take part in the many neighborhood rituals.

One of these rituals included my being allowed to enter the hallowed doors of the Italo-American Lodge Hall (Post #28). The Lodge Hall consisted of a motley assortment of kitchen chairs arranged around an old rattan coffee table that held back issues of the *Fra Noi* newspaper. The stark interior, however, belied the heated exchanges that generally involved the relative merits (usually demerits) of the Chicago White Sox and Chicago Cubs. In another important ritual, I felt proud to be invited on Friday nights to join families on their front porches to engage in lively conversations that typically involved comparing the vocal range of Mario Lanza with the old maestro Enrico Caruso.

With the sound of gunfire still ringing in my ears, I sensed the strong taste of

---

Reprinted from *The Freeman*, August, 1983, pp. 495-501, by permission of The Foundation for Economic Education.

Commare N'Ciuzza's homemade Italian wine on my lips and realized that she was maternally treating my shock in the best way she knew how.

"Mangia, Mangia!" she commanded as she brought cookies to the table.

The sight of the familiar "S"-shaped cookies which are intended for winedunking calmed my nerves. So, too, did the bountiful supply of food that was accumulating on the table as a result of the rapid-fire trips that Commare N'Ciuzza was making to and from the refrigerator. That is, rapid-fire for someone whose large slippered feet never left the ground but slid along the floor.

Commare N'Ciuzza was a large woman. I first saw her on my way home from school when she would invariably be sitting with her head out the window and her bosom supported by the windowsill. As a result of her husband's passing ten years earlier, she was still wearing the familiar black Sicilian mourning dress that I noticed adorned many of the older women in the neighborhood. Our friendship was slow to develop. But from the moment she discovered that my mother came from her hometown in Sicily, she decided it was her calling in life to protect and watch over me. With Commare N'Ciuzza, as with most Italians, that meant making sure I was always well fed. In fact, everyone in the neighborhood called her "Commare" (Godmother) because of her strong maternal instincts.

"Mangia, mangia!" she continued to command as I slowly dunked the "S"-shaped cookies into the wine.

Big Jake

When she noticed my still frozen white countenance, she said, "Figgiu mio, don't be scared. That's only Big Jake and his boys. They come to collect their money."

She went on to explain that Big Jake, the local loan shark, had recently loaned money to a family that everyone in the neighborhood for reasons I never fully understood called gypsies. She shrugged in a characteristic Italian way as she said, "They buy a car, but they don't pay so Big Jake comes to scare them."

When I begin to deride Commare N'Ciuzza for accepting the likes of Big Jake as a normal part of the neighborhood, she interrupted me before I could complete my harangue.

"Don't say bad things about Big Jake. He's a good man. I always light a candle for him on Sundays."

The high regard that Commare N'Ciuzza evidently held for Big Jake aroused my interest. When I began to ask her more direct questions about her association with him I noticed she looked over me in silence, obviously pleased with the interest she had succeeded in arousing.

"Mangia, Mangia!" she continued as her latest sortie to the refrigerator resulted in an unfamiliar eggplant dish being set in front of me.

When I asked her, pleadingly, to get on with the story, I half-expected to hear a story that would prove beyond all doubt the noble intentions of Big Jake. Her story, however, did little to romanticize him.

It all happened thirty years earlier during the worst part of the Great Depression. Commare N'Ciuzza, her husband Tony, and their five children were renting a small apartment. But when Commare N'Ciuzza's three year old son urinated on one of the landlord's pepper plants, a fierce battle ensued and the upshot was that Commare N'Ciuzza and her family were ordered to leave.

With Tony out of a job and Commare N'Ciuzza just able to make ends meet with her work as a seamstress, the family had no place to go. But with a loan from Big Jake, they were able to buy a house.

When I asked her how she was able to make payments to Big Jake, she replied, "We rent a bedroom in my house to a boarder, and my Tony found work. We paid off Big Jake in ten years."

When I asked why she didn't go to a bank for the money, she smiled at my naiveté and said, "Figgiu mio, you think the banks are gonna give money when my Tony has no job. They don't even give money to my brother-in-law, Salvatore, and he works for the city."

But could she accept the shooting—the unrelenting pressure that must have sent chills through the hearts of people who just could not pay? When I put this question to her, she could only shrug and remind me that I had stopped eating.

Commare N'Ciuzza was bringing more food to the table as I got up to leave. The only strategy that worked at this point was to leave as quickly as possible. As I turned to thank her, I heard her mutter something in Italian about how the youth of today were all too thin and undernourished.

On the way home I was startled to see the head of the "gypsy" clan, Rocco, happily engaged in washing his newly purchased used '58 DeSoto. When I asked him if everything was OK, he smiled and said, "Sure, I forget to pay, but Big Jake reminded me. I pay him, and now he's happy."

When I asked him how he was going to continue making the payments, he said having a car would make it possible for him to drive to work in the suburbs where his brother-in-law had just bought a pizza parlor.

I tried to question him further about his dealings with Big Jake, but it was difficult to get his attention away from the DeSoto. As he worked feverishly on polishing a large strip of chrome, I noticed the proud and satisfied look on his face that so distinguishes a new car purchaser from the rest of humanity. Not wishing to disturb him from his euphoria, I quickly walked away. As I left, I noticed he was happily applying a Brillo pad to the three-inch whitewalls that adorned his tires.

Principles of Economics

As with other goods, the price of loanable funds is determined by supply and demand. A simple analysis of the supply and demand of loanable funds in a free market, however, offers no economic rationale for the illegal operations practiced by Big Jake. When interest rates are allowed to reach their natural levels, the demand and supply of loanable funds will be equal. Of course, higher interest rates will be necessary for those loans that involve greater risk— otherwise, loanable funds will not be supplied to high-risk borrowers.

Thus, we should not expect to see a single determined market rate of interest but, rather, a variety of interest rates that depend on the specific circumstances and, in particular, on the risks associated with various loans. This description of capital markets, however, suggests that high-risk loan candidates like a Commare N'Ciuzza or Rocco would be able to obtain legal loans in the free market if they were willing to pay the market-determined price. What, then, explains the existence of illegal loan operations?

By and large, the Big Jakes of this world are created as a result of governmental policies that take the form of usury laws (ceilings on the maximum interest rate that can be legally charged). Such laws serve to cut off the supply of loanable funds to high risk borrowers by making it legally impossible to compensate lenders for the added risks they assume when granting such loans.

Contempt for lenders in general and in particular for lenders-of-last-resort has long historical tradition. This is evidenced by the fact that usury laws have been enacted throughout most of recorded history. The rationale for such laws can be found in many scholarly works, including the writings of Aristotle, Thomas Aquinas, and the Bible.

Protestations against "lending at usury" are even found in the unlikeliest place of all — *The Wealth of Nations*. Adam Smith contradicts his basic belief in the efficacy of the free market when he states:

In countries where interest is permitted, the law, in order to prevent the extortion of usury, generally fixes the highest rate which can be taken without incurring a penalty. . . . The legal rate, it is to be observed, though it ought to be somewhat above, ought not to be much above the lowest market rate. If the legal rate of interest in Great Britain, for example, was fixed so high as eight or ten per cent, the greater part of the money which was to be lent, would be lent to prodigals and projectors, who alone would be willing to give this high interest. Sober people, who will give for the use of money no more than a part of what they are likely to make by the use of it, would not venture into the competition. A great part of the capital of the country would thus be kept out of the hands which were most likely to make a profitable and advantageous use of it, and thrown into those which were most likely to waste and destroy it. Where the legal rate of interest, on the contrary, is fixed but at a very little above the lowest market rate, sober people are universally preferred, as borrowers, to prodigals and projectors. The person who lends money gets nearly as much interest from the former as he dares to take from the latter, and his money is much safer in the hands of the one set of people, than in those of the other. A great part of the capital of the country is thus thrown into the hands in which it is most likely to be employed with advantage.*

But setting the maximum interest rate that can be charged to "very little above the lowest market rate" would preclude the granting of loans to those individuals and businesses that entail a greater degree of risk. Rather than preventing the lending of capital to "prodigals and projectors," usury laws would prevent or, at least, make it legally difficult to lend to high-risk borrowers – generally low-income individuals.

Laws against the Poor

Even though the most noble intentions may be behind the existence of usury laws, their impact is to take away alternatives and eliminate legal options that lower-income individuals can use to succeed in the marketplace. How can people be better off when such legal alternatives are taken away?

Perhaps Commare N'Ciuzza was able to understand this in observing life outside her kitchen window. I tend to think, though, that it was her good common sense and the practical impact that such laws have on the most disadvantaged that allowed her to understand something that has eluded even the greatest of scholars.

The impact of usury laws cuts far deeper than discriminating against the poor and disadvantaged. This is something even Commare N'Ciuzza did not fully understand. The fact that illegal loan markets develop in free markets to get around the restrictive impact of usury laws does not mean that an efficient market solution is achieved in spite of the existence of usury laws. Illegal loans are unenforceable in our courts, and since more expensive and morally intolerable methods of enforcement are applied, Big Jake's interest rates are higher than would have occurred if market-determined rates were allowed.

Adam Smith seemed to sense this in the following statement:

In some countries the interest of money has been prohibited by law. But as something can every-where be made by the use of money, something ought everywhere to be paid for the use of it. This regulation, instead of preventing, has been found from experience to increase the evil of usury; the debtor being obliged to pay, not only for the use of the money, but for the risk which his creditor runs by accepting a compensation for that use. He is obliged, if one may say so, to insure his creditor from the penalties of usury. . . . If this legal rate should be fixed below the lowest market rate, the effects of this fixation must be nearly the same as those of a total prohibition of interest. The creditor will not lend his money for

*   Adam Smith, *The Wealth of Nations*, Modern Library Edition (New York: Random House, 1937, pp. 339-40.

less than the use of it is worth, and the debtor must pay him for the risk which he runs by accepting the full value of that use. If it is fixed precisely at the lowest market price, it ruins with honest people, who respect the laws of their country, the credit of all those who cannot give the very best security, and obliges them to have recourse to exorbitant usurers.*

Thus, the gun-toting tactics of Big Jake that Commare N'Ciuzza could only shrug over result from laws that place a ceiling on the legal interest rate that can be charged. Big Jake had no legal recourse in enforcing his contract. As a result, the most abhorrent aspects of loan-sharking — the tactics that caused my momentary fright on Aberdeen Street — take place because of laws that make market-determined interest rates illegal.

● ● ●

Several years ago I returned to Little Italy. Commare N'Ciuzza was gone, of course, and even her home was replaced by a new residence that took on a Spanish motif but had a strange contemporary look about it. The bespectacled professor who answered the door of the residence had never heard of Commare N'Ciuzza.

Even the Lodge Hall was taken over by a new "greenbelt" park. As far as I could figure, a statue of Garibaldi stood on the spot where lodge members spent countless hours arguing sports trivia.

Asking around, I found that the Lodge Hall had been moved to a room in the newly constructed Senior Citizens' Center. When I got there, I found a brightly painted and spaciously furnished room with the latest issues of *Time, Newsweek,* and the *Chicago Tribune,* but no *Fra Noi.* I also noticed that no one was there.

On my way out of the building I heard an elderly man ask his companion, "Did your son-in-law get good rate from Big Jake?"

"No, he went to First Savings Bank and did better."

Well, at least Big Jake is still around. But now even Big Jake has competition. ●

---

*   Smith, p. 339.

30. The Political Economy of Social Conflict, or Malice in Plunderland

Dwight R. Lee

Individuals are intent on increasing their wealth for a variety of purposes, yet available wealth is always limited and must be allocated among opposing uses and users. The resulting competition leads inevitably to conflicts and animosities as people see many of their goals and aspirations frustrated, at least partially, by the greed of others. A legitimate function of government is to establish an environment that moderates social discord and directs our energies into efforts more productive than wrath, indignation, and belligerence.

An obvious way to contain social conflict is for government to establish the "rules-of-the-game" in such a way that productive, wealth-increasing activities are encouraged. This requires the enforcement of property rights over productive resources, with the judicial system making it difficult for any person to gain by plundering the wealth of another. Under the incentives established by these rules, individuals will engage in those productive activities that not only serve their personal interests, but, as an unintended consequence, increase the wealth of the entire community.

Creating Malice by Rewarding Virtue

No matter how much wealth the economy produces, it will never be regarded as enough. There will always be individuals, both rich and poor, who genuinely feel they have been short-changed. Indeed, are there any who do not desire more resources? Individuals feel strongly that they, or the causes they espouse, deserve more and could effectively use more, and they will often see opportunities to get more through political action. Those who have a comparative advantage in exerting political influence will find it personally profitable to

Abridged from International Institute for Economic Research (IIER), Original Paper 36, February, 1982, by permission of IIER.

engage in the production of political outcomes that favor their interests at the expense of others.

Of course, political advantages are seldom secured by blatant appeals to self-interest. Effectiveness in the political arena requires that private advantage be disguised behind the rhetoric of social justice and virtue. Political interests that are most adept at depicting as fair those policies they favor, and as unfair those they oppose, will have a major advantage in the competition for political influence.

The result is political competition that pits one view of fairness and justice and equity against another. Issues tend to become conflicts over principles — philosophic, aesthetic, even theologic — that must be decided categorically, with little sentiment for compromise on either side. This tendency for political decisions to become clashes between opposing moral imperatives is strengthened by the desire of political interests to motivate active support for their positions. The connection between political action and reward is a tenuous one. People do not become politically exercised over the prospect of a small increase in some commonplace advantage. Noble causes and strong emotions fuel the political process, so the greatest political mileage is achieved by those whose arguments minimize the acceptability of compromise.

With little hope for cooperation between competing interests, there is limited opportunity for both sides of a political issue to gain. Typically, the interest that prevails in the political arena does so at the expense of other interests. In fact, stripped of the rhetoric that rationalizes political action, one finds that the opportunity to use government power to transfer wealth from one group to another motivates much political activity.

Not surprisingly, the political process contains enormous potential for generating malice and ill will between various segments of society. Having perceived that the best way to achieve certain goals is by politicizing the issues, people find their interests furthered by identifying them with a moral imperative — an advantage that greatly strengthens the natural tendency to equate personal advantage with social justice. Emotions are inflamed as opposing sides seek political advantage in exaggerating the benefits associated with the "correct" decision and the dire consequences certain to follow the "wrong" decision. When a decision is made, the losers feel, not simply disappointment and frustration, but a righteous indignation that associates evil with those who prevailed and the process that allowed them to do so.

The process can degenerate easily into a malicious exercise in which the major preoccupation becomes that of inflicting harm and ridicule on the enemy. War, the most blatant example of plunder through government, seldom rewards even the winning combatant with spoils sufficient to pay for the victory. Although the original motivation for war is often conquest and plunder, it is self-righteous hatred that typically prolongs the conflict.

Harmony Through Market Exchange

The conflicts engendered by scarcity and associated with political decisions will never be completely eliminated, but much of the divisiveness generated by political decisionmaking is unnecessary and could be replaced by a spirit of mutual accommodation.

How? The solution would require nothing more radical than reducing government responsibility in areas that would be better handled by the incentives of private property and market exchange. Success in market exchange does not require moral posturing or battling for inviolate principles; it does require broadening the range for compromise and coordination through a willingness to sacrifice incremental quantities of one thing in return for incremental qualities of another. In a market setting, one best furthers his aims, no matter what they are, by appealing to the concerns of others and seeking out areas of mutual interest.

The harmony generated by the market process is easily appreciated when the divisiveness that characterizes public land use decisions is contrasted with the spirit of accommodation and resolution that surrounds similar decisions on the use of privately owned wilderness land.

The Audubon Society, a group whose position on the preservation versus development issue is well-known, owns large tracts of land which it maintains as wildlife preserves. The largest of these is the 26,800-acre Rainey Wildlife Sanctuary in Vermilion Parish, Louisiana. Like most land, the Rainey Sanctuary can be put to several valuable uses. For one thing, it is the natural habitat of a large variety of birds and other wildlife. Of course, the Audubon Society places a high value on maintaining such habitats, but the Rainey Sanctuary also contains deposits of natural gas that the major energy companies find commercially attractive.

If the Rainey Sanctuary were owned by the federal government, this situation would find the Audubon Society and the oil industry natural enemies, with each side confronting the other from an unyielding position. However, the incentives provided by private ownership have enabled the Audubon Society and several oil companies to work out a cooperative agreement allowing drilling for natural gas to take place in parts of the Rainey Sanctuary.*

This cooperative attitude is explained by the simple fact that, under private ownership, each side is best able to advance its interests by accommodating the interests of the other. If the Rainey Sanctuary were publicly owned, restricting its use to a wildlife preserve would cost the Audubon Society nothing; the cost would be imposed on those who value the Rainey land for alternative uses. But

---

*   For a more detailed discussion of how the Audubon Society and the oil industry have worked out a mutually acceptable arrangement over the use of the Rainey Sanctuary, see John Baden and Richard Stroup, "Saving the Wilderness: A Radical Proposal," *Reason*, July 1981, pp. 28-36.

the situation is far different with Audubon Society membership. If alternative uses of the land are prevented, the Audubon Society itself is foregoing the value others place on, and are willing to pay for, these alternative uses. Giving up these potential revenues means fewer opportunities to establish additional wildlife sanctuaries, or to further other ends valued by the Audubon Society. Members of the Audubon Society therefore have a strong incentive to work cooperatively with the oil companies.

Similarly, the oil companies now see their advantage served by taking into consideration the concerns of the Audubon Society. An oil company is more likely to obtain the right to recover energy resources from the Rainey Sanctuary on favorable terms by demonstrating a commitment to respect wildlife and other natural features of the sanctuary. The result is a cooperative and harmonious relationship that has served the interests of the Audubon Society, the oil companies, and the energy consuming public.

This kind of productive cooperation could replace the counterproductive divisiveness that now characterizes federal land use by continuing a national policy of the 1800s, a policy that did much to promote economic growth and social tranquility in this country. That policy was the systematic transfer of land from public to private ownership. Over 33 percent of United States land is still owned by the federal government. Even if much of this land were simply given away to the private sector, government revenues would probably increase, since taxes paid by private owners productively employing the land would exceed the income that public lands generate. Also, even if the transferred land were given entirely to preservationist groups such as the Audubon Society, the Sierra Club, Friends of the Earth, and the National Rifle Association, the position of potential developers would surely be no worse than it is now. An oil or timber company, for example, would almost certainly find economic exchange with the Sierra Club more profitable than political combat.

Giving away federal land would certainly generate acrimonious political competition among different interest groups for their "fair" share. This is but another example of the type of social strife that always accompanies government allocation. But this temporary conflict would be a small price to pay for the elimination of persistent conflict over federal land.

Other Unnecessary Conflicts

The socially disruptive conflict over federal land is just one example of the unnecessary strife caused by the substitution of government control for market exchange.

No Consensus on the Census. Increasingly, government programs redistribute wealth among different areas of the country on the basis of population changes, demographic structure, racial mix, and other such considerations. As a result, the U.S. Census Bureau has become embroiled in a growing number of political battles. Despite the fact that the 1980 census is, according to most demographers, the most complete count ever, big city mayors and ethic leaders have bitterly denounced its accuracy. In a law suit won recently by the city of Detroit, the Census Bureau was ordered to inflate its official count of blacks and Hispanics. Other law suits have been filed, and some judges have even threatened the bureau's director, Vincent Barabba, with jail.

When the Census becomes an instrument of political plunder, it must be expected that it will become also the source of conflict and animosity.

Conflict over the Census will never be completely eliminated. There will always be political decisions which affect wealth positions and which legitimately need to be decided on the basis of Census data. But clearly government has generated unnecessary dissension over the Census through direct involvement in activities that would be carried out both more harmoniously and efficiently by the private sector. Public employment and urban renewal are two examples of programs that have ineffectively substituted government solutions for market solutions while increasing the role of the Census in the political transfer of wealth. Not only would reducing (better yet, eliminating) programs of this type increase the likelihood of real solutions to specific problems, but would also allow the Bureau of the Census to get on with its important work with a minimum of conflict.

Conflict over Education. As the federal government has become more involved in financing and controlling public education, government choice has increasingly replaced parental choice in educational decisions. Parents are required to send their children to a school (which may or may not be a neighborhood school) decided upon by the government or pay twice for education by sending their children to a private school. The public schools have a largely captive clientele, and thus have little motivation to respond to the diversity of educational preferences represented in a community.

Not surprisingly, single interest groups have found public schools to be tempting vehicles for imposing their strongly held views on others. Such groups, of course, encounter hostile reactions from those with equally strong, but opposing, views. With limited choice over where their children attend school, parents who, for example, strongly favor or oppose sex education in school, often find political combat the most effective approach in gaining their objective. Having turned our public schools into battlegrounds for contentious issues such as sex education, racial balance, creation versus evolution, and censorship of books, it is little wonder that all available evidence indicates that education is being neglected.

Controversy over education would be substantially reduced if individual choice were allowed to replace government choice through a policy of education vouchers, or tax credits. Parents could, under such a policy, select directly the type of school they think best for their children. In response to the incentives that vouchers would provide, schools with diverse approaches and philosophies would become available. Parents could not only exercise a wide variety of legitimate educational preferences, but they could do so without conflicting with the preferences of others.

The Old Against the Young. As a final example of governmentally inspired conflict, consider the problems of Social Security. The controversy that currently surrounds Social Security, and that is sure to intensify in the future, is rooted in political expediency. Soon after the Social Security Act was passed in 1935, the labor force paying into the program was growing rapidly while the number of retired recipients was small. With the Social Security coffers swelling, the political temptation to expand benefits without increasing taxes was impossible to resist. In 1939, benefits were increased as the Social Security Act was amended to become a nonfunded pay-as-we-go program, with current retirement payments being financed by current taxpayers. Instead of a retirement plan in which benefits were tied directly to contributions, Social Security became another transfer program with benefits determined by the political ability of one group to impose costs on another group.

The social conflict inherent in the post-1939 Social Security program lay dormant until recently. For years, economic growth and the demographic mix allowed benefits to be expanded without painful increases in the tax burden. This is no longer the case. Sluggish economic growth in the 1970s, coupled with a rapid increase in the retirement-age population, has placed the interests of older citizens in direct opposition to the interests of the working population.

This conflict will intensify as it becomes impossible to save the Social Security System without significant tax increases and/or benefit reductions. A program inspired by concern for the elderly, but structured in response to political incentives, will pit younger against older persons and create a social division of major significance.

The solvency of the Social Security System could have been insured, and the divisiveness now surrounding it prevented, if a direct tie between individual benefits and individual contributions had been continued. Whether such a vested retirement program can ever be established and maintained by government is debatable. We do know such programs can be efficiently supplied by private insurance companies; indeed, they are the only type provided by private companies. If individuals had been allowed to provide for their own retirement through private plans, the current and growing conflict between the old and the young would never have arisen. Indeed, quite the opposite of conflict would have prevailed. Under private plans, higher retirement benefits to the old would mean higher take-home pay for the young, as higher current retirement benefits could have resulted only from higher past savings and investment, which translate into greater current labor productivity.

The initial justification for the mandatory Social Security program was based on the dubious contention that people would not voluntarily provide for their own retirement. Accepting this judgment, however, still provides no reason for the requirement that individuals purchase their retirement plan from the government. Participation in a social security system could have been required and at the same time have remained private. All that would now be needed to move us quickly toward the privatization of social security would be the elimination of the requirement that the obligatory retirement plan be purchased from the government. Unfortunately, the failure of the existing program, a failure evidenced by the huge indebtedness that has built up, makes this choice politically unrealistic. Given the opportunity, new entrants into the labor force would overwhelmingly opt out of the system because its viability is uncertain. This, of course, would guarantee the demise of Social Security as a self-financing system. As is often the case with flawed government programs, the political viability of the Social Security System is explained by its failure, not its success.

Conclusion

Maintaining a cohesive social order is not an easy task. Indeed, as long as scarcity exists, social conflict will be a consequence of competition for the limited means of achieving our unlimited ends. Although competition is inevitable, noncooperation and contention are not. Depending on how things of value are rationed among competing uses and users, our persistent desire for more can motivate either cooperative or noncooperative behavior. It is in this regard that we derive the significant advantage from market rationing. Market exchange establishes a positive-sum environment that not only allows mutual gains, but rewards those who expand the scope for cooperative interaction by increasing the opportunities to realize these gains.

Unfortunately, this source of social cooperation is subject to constant erosion as special interest groups find it to their short-run advantage to replace market allocation with political allocation. The power vested in government to perform its legitimate functions can easily be used by politically influential groups to capture gains at the expense of others. When zero-sum political plunder replaces positive-sum market exchange, the stage is set for malice in plunderland. •

31. Moral Community, Moral Order, or Moral Anarchy

James Buchanan

I. Introduction*

I shall discuss the 'ties that bind' persons with each other in society and the instruments and attitudes that may break those ties that exist. I am concerned with the ways that persons act and feel towards one another. For this reason, I have inserted the adjective 'moral' before each of the nouns in my title. 'Community, Order, or Anarchy', standing alone, would not convey my desired emphasis on personal interaction. To forestall misunderstanding at the outset, however, I should note that there is no explicitly moral content in the chapter, if the word 'moral' is interpreted in some normative sense.

My diagnosis of American society is informed by the notion that we are living during a period of erosion of the 'social capital' that provides the basic framework for our culture, our economy, and our polity — a framework within which the 'free society' in the classically liberal ideal perhaps came closest to realization in all of history. My efforts have been directed at trying to identify and to isolate the failures and breakdowns in institutions that are responsible for this erosion. **

---

*   This chapter was initially published as *The Abbot Memorial Lecture No. 17* by Colorado College, Colorado Springs, Colorado, 1981. The lecture itself was presented on 6 May 1981. I am indebted to Professor Timothy Fuller and to Colorado College for Permission to reprint the lecture, substantially without change.

**   For earlier works that provide some indication of the development of the ideas presented in this chapter, *see: The Limits of Liberty* (Chicago: University of Chicago Press, 1975); 'Markets, States, and the Extent of Morals', *American Economic Review*, 68 (May 1978), 364-8; 'Moral Community and Moral Order: The Intensive and Extensive Limits of Interaction', in *Ethics and Animals*, ed. Harlan Miller and W. Williams (Clifton, N.J.: Humana Press, 1983), pp. 95-102; 'A Governable Country', in *Japan Speaks*, 1981 (Osaka, Japan: Suntory Foundation, 1981) III, pp. 1-12.

My discussion here will be exclusively conducted in terms of the three abstract models or forms of interaction listed in my title: (I) moral community, (II) moral order, and (III) moral anarchy. Any society may be described empirically as embodying some mix among these three forms or elements. A society is held together by some combination of moral community and moral order. Its cohesion is reduced by the extent to which moral anarchy exists among its members. The precise mix among the three forms or elements will therefore determine the observed 'orderliness' of any society, along with the degree of governmental coercion reflected in the pattern that is observed to exist. The need for governance as well as the difficulty of governing are directly related to the mix among the three elements.

II. Moral Community

I shall commence by defining the three abstract models or forms of interaction. A *moral community* exists among a set of persons to the extent that individual members of the group identify with a collective unit, a community, rather than conceive themselves to be independent, isolated individuals. In one sense, of course, moral community always exists. No person is totally autonomous, and no one really thinks exclusively of himself as a solitary unit of consciousness. Each person will to some extent identify with some community (or communities) whether this be with the nuclear family, the extended family, the clan or tribe, a set of locational, ethic, racial, or religious cohorts, the trade union, the business firm, the social class, or, finally, with the nation-state. Most persons will identify simultaneously and with varying degrees of loyalties with several communities of varying sizes, types and sources of valuation. The set of communities and the value or loyalty weights assigned to the members of the set will of course differ from person to person. I suggest, however, that it is possible to characterize different societies in terms of the relative importance of *moral community* as an element of social cohesion among persons within those societies. It is possible to classify societies as more or less communitarian (collectivistic) — as less or more individualistic.

III. Moral Order

A *moral order* exists when participants in social interaction treat each other as moral reciprocals, but do so without any sense of shared loyalties to a group or community. Each person treats other persons with moral indifference, but at the same time respects their equal freedoms with his own. Mutual respect, which is an alternative way of stating the relationship here, does not require moral community in any sense of personal identification with a collectivity or community. Each person thinks about and acts towards other persons as if they are autonomous individuals, independently of whom they might be in terms of some group or community classification scheme. In a moral order it is possible for a person to deal with other persons who are not members of his own community if both persons have agreed, explicitly or implicitly, to abide by the behavioral precepts required for reciprocal trust and confidence.

The emergence of the abstract rules of behaviour describing moral order had the effect of expanding dramatically the range of possible interpersonal dealings. Once rules embodying reciprocal trust came to be established, it was no longer necessary that both parties to a contract identify themselves with the same moral community of shared values and loyalties. There was no longer any requirement that trading partners claim membership in the same kinship group.* Under the rules of a moral order it is conceptually possible for a genuinely autonomous individual to remain a viable entity, whereas no such existence would be possible in a structure characterized solely by moral community.

I suggest that different societies may be classified in terms of the relative importance of the rules of moral order in describing the observed relationships among the persons within each society. These rules may either supplement the sense of moral community as a source of social cohesion where the latter exists, or these rules may substitute for moral community to the extent of rendering it unnecessary.

IV. Moral Anarchy

Moral anarchy exists in a society (if it can remain a society) when individuals do not consider other persons to be within their moral communities and when they do not accept the minimal requirements for behaviour in a moral order. In moral anarchy, each person treats other persons exclusively as means to further his own ends or objectives. He does not consider other persons to be his fellows (brothers) in some community of shared purpose (as would be the case in moral community), or to be deserving of reciprocal mutual respect and trust as autonomous individuals (as would be the case in moral order).

In a real sense, moral anarchy becomes the negation of both moral community and moral order. It is a setting within which persons violate the basic Kantian moral precept that human beings are to be treated as ends not as means. It is perhaps more difficult to conceptualize moral anarchy as a general model of human interaction than the two alternative models already discussed. Moral anarchy seems somehow less descriptive of the behaviour that we observe around us. For my purposes, however, I want to employ the model in the same way as the others. I suggest that it is possible to classify different societies in terms of the relative significance of moral anarchy in describing the attitudes and behaviour of their members, one to another.

---

*   F. A. Hayek has stressed the emergence of these abstract rules of behaviour through some process of cultural evolution, rules that man does not and cannot understand and which run counter to those instinctual bases of behaviour which find their sources in the primitive sense of moral community. *See* F. A. Hayek, *Law, Legislation, and Liberty*, Vol. III, *The Political Order of a Free People* (Chicago: The University of Chicago Press, 1979), especially 'Epilogue', pp. 153-76.

V. Implications for Social Stability and Governability: Moral Anarchy

I shall now employ the three basic models or elements of interaction in order to discuss problems of social viability and, indirectly, problems of governability in a society. It will be useful to take extreme examples in which one of the three models is primarily descriptive rather than some undefined mix among the three. It will also be useful to change the order of discussion from that which was used in defining the three elements. I shall first take up moral anarchy, then moral order, and, finally, moral community.

Consider first, then, a setting in which many persons behave as moral anarchists. In this setting, life for the individual is 'poore, nasty, brutish, and short', to employ the colorful language of Thomas Hobbes. Men who neither feel a sense of community with others nor respect others as individuals in their own right, must be ruled. Individuals will sacrifice their liberties to the coercive sovereign government that can effectively ensure order and personal security. But those persons who act on behalf of the sovereign government may also be moral anarchists. There would seem to be no reason to anticipate that persons who secure powers of governance would be less likely to behave as moral anarchists than their fellows; indeed, the opposite conclusion seems the more plausible here. Social stability is purchased by individuals at the price of a coercive state regime. Repressive government may emerge as a necessary condition in a society with many moral anarchists.

VI. Implications for Social Stability and Governability: Moral Order

In sharp contrast with the setting discussed above, now consider a setting where many persons adhere to the precepts and behavioural rules of a moral order. Each individual treats other persons as deserving of mutual respect and tolerance, even though there exists no necessary sense of belonging to a community or collectivity of shared values and loyalties. In this setting, individuals may be secure in their persons and property; social stability may exist, and the needs for governance may be minimized. Correspondingly, the liberties of individuals are maximized.

In the extreme case where, literally, all persons behave in accordance with the rules of moral order, there would be no need for government at all. 'Orderly anarchy' would be produced by the universalized adherence to rules of mutual respect among persons. In a more plausibly realistic setting, where most but not necessarily all persons are expected to follow the precepts of moral order, government, as such, may be restricted to a minimal, night-watchman or protective state role.* The government need only protect personal and property rights

---

*   The term 'minimal state' is used by Robert Nozick in his *Anarchy, State and Utopia* (New York: Basic Books, 1974). I used the term 'protective state' in my *The Limits of Liberty* (Chicago: The University of Chicago Press, 1975). The nineteenth-century writers often used the term 'night-watchman state'.

and enforce contracts among persons. In more general terms, the government may be limited to enforcing the laws. It need not do more. In one sense there is no need for 'governing' as such.

VII. Implications for Social Stability and Governability: Moral Community

I have relegated moral community to third position here because this model is much the more difficult of the three to discuss in terms of the implications for overall social stability and for the needs for governance. The difficulties arise because of the many possible moral communities that may exist within a single society simultaneously, communities that may carry with them quite differing implications for the viability of social order. At one limit, if all persons should identify with the community that is coincident in membership with the inclusive political unit, the nation-state, the implications are relatively straightforward. In such a setting as this, all persons act as if they share the same objectives, as members of the national collectivity, including those persons who act on behalf of the government. Vis-a-vis other nations, this model of society might be a source of nationalistic adventure. Or, to put the same point in a different perspective, when the national unit is threatened by external enemies, the sense of national community is more likely to emerge as a real force. Since all persons tend to share the same objectives, governance becomes easy. Persons 'obey' the sovereign because they feel themselves to be part of the larger unit; conversely, the sovereign also behaves as persons would have it behave. Persons, ruled or rulers, do not behave towards each other as separate interacting individuals. They do not really consider themselves to be autonomous units.

At the other limit there may exist no sense of moral community, no shared values, over the whole membership of the inclusive political unit, the nation-state, while at the same time all or substantially all persons may express and act upon loyalties to collective units, subnationally classified. Persons may identify with specific communities (ethnic, racial, religious, regional, occupational, employment, class, etc.) while sensing no identification with or loyalty to the national unit. This sort of society will have some of the characteristics of that which contains only moral anarchists. The difference here is that the relevant entities are themselves collectives rather than individuals. Persons may in this society exhibit sharply divergent behaviour patterns as between treatment of members of the relevant community and persons who do not qualify for membership. Social conflict will tend to emerge between the relevant communities or between persons who are members of differing communities. Because of the prevalence of such conflicts, there will be a need for governance, and possibly by a coercive sovereign. Without such force, the Hobbesian war of each against all may apply to the separate collectivities rather than to individuals.

VIII. Moral Community, Moral Order and the Range and Scope for Governmental Action

In this section I shall compare the two forces for potential social cohesion, moral community and moral order, in terms of the specific implications for the range and scope for governmental actions. I shall largely ignore the considerations raised in section VII concerning the existence of moral communities of subnational memberships. I shall restrict discussion to the sense of moral community that exists among all members of a polity. As noted, in such a setting persons share the same national objectives and need not be 'directed', as such, by the state. In a moral order, as noted above, persons further their own objectives within a legal framework that requires no active interference by government.

As we part from the idealizations of these two models, however, and as we allow for a potential threat of moral anarchy in each case, important differences emerge. The necessary conditions required for the maintenance of tolerably effective social stability are considerably more constrained in moral order than in moral community. The difference to be emphasized here lies in that between the individualized basis of any effective moral order and the non-individualistic or collectivist basis of any effective moral community. In the former, individuals are bound together in adherence to a set of abstract rules or laws which are fundamentally impersonal and which are grounded in the generalized recognition that all persons are cooperating moral equals. The moral requirements placed on persons in such an order are minimal. The individual need not feel himself to be part of some inclusive collectivity. He need not exhibit feelings of benevolence or altruism towards any other persons, whether these be his neighbours or strangers. On the other hand, if he is expected to abide by the minimal behavioural precepts for such an order, to refrain from lapsing into the role of moral anarchist, he must think that the framework rules of the legal-political order are themselves 'fair' in the sense that all persons are effectively required to play by the same rules.

In an effective moral order, a government that discriminates among persons in its treatment, that violates elementary precepts for fairness in dealing with separate individuals, will immediately face resentment and must ultimately expect rebellion. This predicted reaction follows from the very autonomy of individuals; each person remains a person and as such can claim entitlement to uniform treatment by those who administer the law. There exists no overriding 'community interest' within which individual interests are subsumed.

This setting may be contrasted with one properly described as moral community coincident in membership with the national political unit. Here government may discriminate among persons without necessarily generating negative feedbacks in citizen discontent provided only that the discrimination is justified, explained, or legitimized in terms of the wider interest of the inclusive national community, an interest that exists by definition of the community, as such, and which is, also by definition, shared by everyone. Since the individual person in such a setting thinks of himself as a member of the community rather than as an individual, he will more readily acquiesce in what would seem overtly unfair treatment under a moral order. In the setting best described as moral community, therefore, the whole set of issues involving 'justice' or 'fairness' in governmental dealings with separate persons does not arise with nearly the same degree of intensity as they do in a moral order. It follows that government in a society described by national moral community will possess a wider range of options in taking actions than would government operating within a comparable moral order.

The range and scope for governmental action is more limited in a society that locates its source of social cohesion largely in moral order rather than moral community. At the same time, however, such a society (one based on moral order) can allow for greater flexibility and change in the attitudes and behaviour of its individual members. As noted, in an effective moral order, individuals need not share common purposes; they need only respect each other as individuals. From this it follows that individual attitudes and behaviour may be widely varying and may accordingly change within wide limits, still within the minimal requirement for productive interpersonal interchanges. Individuals are free to select their own private purposes in this setting, a freedom that is necessarily absent in moral community.

The range and scope for governmental action is more extensive in a society that locates its sources of social cohesion in moral community rather than in adherence to the rules of moral order. On the other hand, the society largely held together by moral community is necessarily more vulnerable to shifts in the attitudes and the behaviour patterns that might reflect individual departures from the shared purposes of the community. Persons are tied, one to another, by their common identification with the collective, with their shared sense of nationhood, race, class, or ideology. The loss of this identification may involve an unavoidable plunge into moral anarchy. Persons are not free to 'do their own thing', within limits, as they might be in a society organized on the principles of moral order, principles that are mutually acknowledged to generate general benefits to all adherents.

IX. The United States in the 1980s

To this point my discussion has been confined to a generalized analysis of the three abstract models or forms of social interaction: moral community, moral order, and moral anarchy. Any historically observed society will embody elements of each one of these models. Nonetheless, the mix may vary significantly among separate societies, and these differences may be important. In the next two sections I shall apply the analysis to real-world societies. In this section I shall discuss the United States in the 1980s in terms of the three models of interaction. In section X, I shall briefly discuss modern Japan for purposes of comparison and contrast with the United States.

In the United States of the 1980s there is little moral community that extends to the limits of the inclusive national unit, the nation-state, as such, and which embodies the central instrument of the polity, the federal government in all of its arms and agencies. There is relatively little sense of shared purpose among the 230 million persons in the nation. Individuals tend instead to relate to and to identify with communities larger than themselves and their immediate families, but these communities tend to be of subnational sizes of membership, both geographically and numerically. The central government, therefore, is unable to call upon or to exploit a strong sense of genuine 'national interest' or 'national purpose', although, of course, such an 'interest' might be called into being in the face of a demonstrated and well-understood external threat. Further, and importantly, those persons who themselves serve as 'governors' possess little sense of 'national interest', and they are not seen to possess such interest by those who are 'governed'. Those persons in positions of political power, like their cohorts who are outside governmental office, identify with various subnational groupings, if indeed they adhere to moral community at all in any relevant way.

The United States, as a single society, does not depend primarily or critically on the presence of national moral community among its citizens. By historical tradition, the society has been made viable because its citizens have adhered behaviourally to the precepts of a moral order. There has existed a tradition of respect for adherence to the rule of law, for general rules, for promise-keeping, for honesty in trading even of the most complex types. Voluntary adherence to the rules and regulations laid down by government remains widespread, including the voluntary payment of income taxes. With relatively few exceptions, government has not needed to become repressive.

For several decades, however, our moral order has been in the process of erosion. Larger and larger numbers of persons seem to become moral anarchists; they seem to be losing a sense of mutual respect one for another along with any feeling of obligation to abide by generalizable rules and codes of conduct. To the extent that such erosion continues and/or accelerates, the internal social stability of the United States must deteriorate. If confronted with this apparent breakdown in the internal cohesion of the social structure, more and more persons who are not themselves moral anarchists will turn to the arms and agencies of government for more direct protection than seems to be currently provided. The problem is explicitly exemplified in observed increases, in criminal activity, which must, after some time lag, result in an increase in governmental coercion on all persons, the lawful and the unlawful alike. The voluntary limits on behaviour that have worked in the past but which now seem to fail must be replaced by governmentally imposed restrictions. Government necessarily will move towards repression in the society as moral anarchy becomes more and more descriptive of the relationships among persons.

Government itself is partially responsible for the erosion of the traditional moral order in America. As the national government sought to take on a more the presence or presumed presence of some 'national interest', it has been unable to find moral support in the communitarian sense discussed above. Those who have promoted the extension of government's role under the folly that some national interest exists have, perhaps unwittingly, aided in the breakdown of effective moral order. As laws and regulations have multiplied, competing group interests have been promoted. And persons selected for governmental office have exploited their positions to advance their own private interests under the guise of non-existent 'national purpose'. Observing this, citizens have become more disillusioned with governmental processes and are more and more attracted to assume roles as moral anarchists. Confronted with a government that imposes rules that seem to command little or no respect, individuals quite naturally come to question other long-standing rules that have traditionally solicited voluntary adherence. Restoration of moral order, or even a stop to the erosion process, requires a roll-back of governmental intrusions into the lives of citizens, while, at the same time, the growth in moral anarchy suggests, for the reasons noted above, an expanded governmental role in maintaining social stability.

Somewhat paradoxically, as our traditional moral order loses its ability to ensure social stability, the United States becomes increasingly ungovernable even while the share of resources commanded politically continues to increase and as governmental interferences with the lives of ordinary citizens expand.

X. Japan: Comparison and Contrast

I shall now discuss modern Japanese society for purposes of drawing comparisons and contrasts with the United States. I do this not because I claim any expert knowledge of Japan and its people but because my initial reflections on the subject matter of this chapter were prompted by an assignment to examine the 'governability' of the Japanese.

There is widespread agreement, both among modern Japanese themselves and among external observers, that there is a relatively strong sense of identification of persons with moral communities beyond themselves, or, in terms of my three models, that Japan is clearly less individualistic and more communitarian than the United States. Disputes may arise concerning the relative importance of national and localized moral communities in modern Japan. To a degree, of course, the communitarian sense is limited to subnational groups and notably to the employing firms. But, nonetheless, for many reasons, it remains evident that there does also exist a relevant national moral community. The Japanese, as Japanese, share a set of values that affects their behaviour as individuals. There is genuine meaning in the term 'Japan, Incorporated'.

As I have noted, this relationship between the individual and his fellow citizens in the inclusive national community allows the Japanese government greater freedom in the formulation and administration of laws and regulations than would be the case in a society more critically dependent on moral order. However, and also for the reasons discussed above, the continuing stability of the society may be dependent on the maintenance of the shared loyalties that now exist. From this it seems to follow that Japan may possibly be more vulnerable to shifts in attitudes and behaviour patterns on the part of individuals and groups who somehow lose their identification with the nation. If such identification should be lost, such individuals may lapse directly into roles of moral anarchists.

If this scenario should unfold, there might exist no apparent means through which Japan could recapture its sense of national moral community short of possible international adventure. If my diagnosis is at all suggestive here, the question that emerges is whether or not a nation like the Japanese, faced with a possible erosion in their shared sense of moral community, could adopt essentially Western notions of moral order before moral anarchy assumes predominant importance and generates a breakdown in social structure. Can the Japanese citizen, circa the year 2000 or 2050, who may have lost his identity with the nation as a community, as an entity that commands his loyalty and respect, can he come to understand, appreciate, and live by the behavioural precepts of moral order, precepts that require him to grant fellow citizens mutual respect as moral equivalents and which give him criteria for evaluating governmental rules in some personal and non-communitarian way? Can Japanese governments, in their own right, keep within the limits of power that will allow a functioning moral order to evolve, and, further, can Japanese governments hold this stance as Western nations, themselves, are observed to sink further into the collectively dominated moral anarchy that now seems their fate?

XI. Prospects for Constructive Reform

F. A. Hayek has stressed that modern man's behavioural instincts are those that characterize what I have here called moral community and which evolved over the ages in essentially tribal settings. He suggests that Western man very slowly evolved patterns of adherence to abstract rules that he does not understand, the rules of moral order, and which really run counter to his instinctual proclivities.* Professor Hayek's response to the first question posed for the Japanese society above would presumably be negative. The behavioural rules of effective moral order cannot be 'laid on', cultural evolution cannot be directed. I am somewhat less evolutionist and more constructivist than Hayek, but my concern here is not primarily with what the Japanese society may face in future decades. My concern is with the prospects for constructive reform in the social order of the United States, and I should stress that reform need not depend exclusively on changes in rules for behaviour.

I have suggested that those who have promoted the extension of Western national governments have done so in their failure to recognize that the moral order, described as voluntary adherence to abstract rules of behaviour, carries

---

*   See Hayek, *op. cit.*

implications for the reach of governance. Accordingly, these governments have been allowed to grow far beyond the limits that might sustain and reinforce effective moral order, while, at the same time, they have failed to generate effective moral community as a replacement force that might in turn legitimate such extended governance. Indeed, the moral anarchists among us have used the instruments of governance to subvert both moral community and moral order as necessary to advance their own ends.

Even in the 1980s, however, relatively few Americans are moral anarchists; most Americans continue to treat their fellows with mutual respect and abide by the rules of moral order. Most Americans also maintain a limited sense of moral community, a sense that could be maximally exploited with appropriate devolution and decentralization of governmental authority. Constructive reform is possible provided that the institutions of social order are so modified as to make them consistent with the *empirical realities* of modern man as he is rather than man as the naive reformers of decades past have hoped he might become.

Institutional and constitutional reforms are not equivalent to behavioural reforms, and they need not depend critically on changing 'man's nature'. In economists' terminology, institutional-constitutional change operates upon the constraints within which persons maximize their own utilities; such change does not require that there be major shifts in the utility functions themselves. ●

32. The Problem of Social Cost

R. H. Coase

I. The Problem to Be Examined*

This paper is concerned with those actions of business firms which have harmful effects on others. The standard example is that of a factory the smoke from which has harmful effects on those occupying neighbouring properties. The economic analysis of such a situation has usually proceeded in terms of a divergence between the private and social product of the factory, in which economists have largely followed the treatment of Pigou in *The Economics of Welfare*. The conclusions to which this kind of analysis seems to have led most economists is that it would be desirable to make the owner of the factory liable for the damage caused to those injured by the smoke, or alternatively, to place a tax on the factory owner varying with the amount of smoke produced and equivalent money in terms to the damage it would cause, of finally, to exclude the factory from residential districts (and presumably from other areas in which the emission of smoke would have harmful effects on others). It is my contention that the suggested courses or action are inappropriate, in that they lead to results which are not necessarily, or even usually, desirable.

II. The Reciprocal Nature of the Problem

The traditional approach has tended to obscure the nature of the choice that has to be made. The question is commonly thought of as one in which A inflicts

---

*   This article, although concerned with a technical problem of economic analysis, arose out of the study of the Political Economy of Broadcasting which I am now conducting. The argument of the present article was implicit in a previous article dealing with the problem of allocating radio and television frequencies (The Federal Communications Commission, J. Law & Econ. [1959]) but comments which I have received seemed to suggest that it would be desirable to deal with the question in a more explicit way and without reference to the original problem of the solution of which the analysis was developed.

Abridged from *The Journal of Law and Economics*, Volume II, October, 1960, pp. 1-18, by permission of The University of Chicago Press. Copyright © 1960 by The University of Chicago.

harm on B and what has to be decided is: how should we restrain A? But this is wrong. We are dealing with a problem of reciprocal nature. To avoid the harm to B would inflict harm on A. The real question that has to be decided is: should A be allowed to harm B or should B be allowed to harm A? The problem is to avoid the more serious harm. I instanced in my previous article* the case of a confectioner the noise and vibrations from whose machinery disturbed a doctor in his work. To avoid harming the doctor would inflict harm on the confectioner. The problem posed by this case was essentially whether it was worth while, as a result of restricting the methods of production which could be used by the confectioner, to secure more doctoring at the cost of a reduced supply of confectionery products. Another example is afforded by the problem of straying cattle which destroy crops on neighbouring land. If it is inevitable that some cattle will stray, an increase in the supply of meat can only be obtained at the expense of a decrease in the supply of crops. The nature of the choice is clear: meat or crops. What answer should be given is, of course, not clear unless we know the value of what is obtained as well as the value of what is sacrificed to obtain it. To give another example, Professor George J. Stigler instances the contamination of a stream.** If we assume that the harmful effect of the pollution is that it kills the fish, the question to be decided is: is the value of the fish lost greater or less than the value of the product which the contamination of the stream makes possible. It goes almost without saying that this problem has to be looked at in total *and* at the margin.

III. The Pricing System with Liability for Damage

I propose to start my analysis by examining a case in which most economists would presumably agree that the problem would be solved in a completely satisfactory manner: when the damaging business has to pay for all damage caused *and* the pricing system works smoothly (strictly this means that the operation of a pricing system is without cost).

A good example of the problem under discussion is afforded by the case of straying cattle which destroy crops on neighboring land. Let us suppose that a farmer and a cattle-raiser are operating on neighboring properties. Let us further suppose that, without any fencing between the properties, an increase in the size of the cattle-raiser's herd increases the total damage to the farmer's crops. What happens to the marginal damage as the size of the herd increases is another matter. This depends on whether the cattle tend to follow one another or to roam side by side, on whether they tend to be more or less restless as the herd increases and on other similar factors. For my immediate purpose, it is immaterial what assumption is made about marginal damage as the size of the herd increases.

---

*   Coase, The Federal Communications Commission, 2 J. Law & Econ. 26-27 (1959).
**   G. J. Stigler, The Theory of Price 105 (1952).

To simplify the argument, I propose to use an arithmetical example. I shall assume that the annual cost of fencing the farmer's property is $9 and that the price of the crop is $1 per ton. Also, I assume that the relation between the number of cattle in the herd and the annual crop loss is as follows:

Number in Herd (Steers)	Annual Crop Loss (Tons)	Crop Loss per Additional Steer (Tons)
1	1	1
2	3	2
3	6	3
4	10	4

Given that the cattle-raiser is liable for the damage caused, the additional annual cost imposed on the cattle-raiser if he increased his herd from, say, 2 to 3 steers is $3 and in deciding on the size of the herd, he will take this into account along with his other costs. That is, he will not increase the size of the herd unless the value of the additional meat produced (assuming that the cattle-raiser slaughters the cattle), is greater than the additional costs that this will entail, including the value of the additional crops destroyed. Of course, if, by the employment of dogs, herdsmen, aeroplanes, mobile radio and other means, the amount of damage can be reduced, these means will be adopted when their cost is less than the value of the crop which they prevent being lost. Given that the annual cost of fencing is $9, the cattle-raiser who wished to have a herd with 4 steers or more would pay for fencing to be erected and maintained, assuming that other means of attaining the same end would not do so more cheaply. When the fence is erected, the marginal cost due to the liability for damage becomes zero, except to the extent that an increase in the size of the herd necessitates a stronger and therefore more expensive fence because more steers are liable to lean against it at the same time. But, of course, if may be cheaper for the cattle-raiser not to fence and to pay for the damaged crops, as in my arithmetical example, with 3 or fewer steers.

It might be thought that the fact that the cattle-raiser would pay for all crops damaged would lead the farmer to increase his planting if a cattle-raiser came to occupy the neighbouring property. But this is not so. If the crop was previously sold in conditions of perfect competition, marginal cost was equal to price for the amount of planting undertaken and any expansion would have reduced the profits of the farmer. In the new situation, the existence of crop damage would mean that the farmer would sell less on the open market but his receipts for a given production would remain the same, since the cattle-raiser would pay the market price for any crop damaged. Of course, if cattle-raising commonly involved the destruction of crops, the coming into existence of a cattle-raising industry might raise the price of the crops involved and farmers would then extend their planting. But I wish to confine my attention to the individual farmer.

I have said that the occupation of a neighbouring property by a cattle-raiser would not cause the amount of production, or perhaps more exactly the amount of planting, by the farmer to increase. In fact, if the cattle-raising has any effect, it will be to decrease the amount of planting. The reason for this is that, for any given tract of land, if the value of the crop damaged is so great that the receipts from the sale of the undamaged crop are less than the total costs of cultivating that tract of land, it will be profitable for the farmer and the cattle-raiser to make a bargain whereby that tract of land is left uncultivated. This can be made clear by means of an arithmetical example. Assume initially that the value of the crop obtained from cultivating a given tract of land is $12 and that the cost incurred in cultivating this tract of land is $10, the net gain from cultivating the land being $2. I assume for purposes of simplicity that the farmer owns the land. Now assume that the cattle-raiser starts operations on the neighbouring property and that the value of the crops damaged is $1. In this case $11 is obtained by the farmer from sale on the market and $1 is obtained from the cattle-raiser for damage suffered and the net gain remains $2. Now suppose that the cattle-raiser finds it profitable to increase the size of his herd, even though the amount of damage rises to $3; which means that the value of the additional meat production is greater than the additional costs, including the additional $2 payment for damage. But the total payment for damage is now $3. The net gain to the farmer from cultivating the land is still $2. The cattle-raiser would be better off if the farmer would agree not to cultivate his land for any payment less than $3. The farmer would be agreeable to not cultivating the land for any payment greater than $2. There is clearly room for a mutually satisfactory bargain which would lead to the abandonment of cultivation.* But the same argument applies not only to the whole tract cultivated by the farmer but also to any subdivision of it. Suppose, for example, that the cattle have a well-defined route, say, to a brook or to a shady area. In these circumstances, the amount of damage to the crop along the route may well be great and if so, it could be that the farmer and the cattle-raiser would find it profitable to make a bargain whereby the farmer would agree not to cultivate this strip of land.

---

* The argument in the text has proceeded on the assumption that the alternative to cultivation of the crop is abandonment of cultivation altogether. But this need not be so. There may be crops which are less liable to damage by cattle but which would not be as profitable as the crop grown in the absence of damage. Thus, if the cultivation of a new crop would yield a return to the farmer of $1 instead of $2, and the size of the herd which would cause $3 damage with the old crop would cause $1 damage with the new crop, it would be profitable to the cattle-raiser to pay any sum less than $2 to induce the farmer to change his crop (since this would reduce damage liability from $3 to $1) and it would be profitable for the farmer to do so if the amount received was more than $1 (the reduction in his return caused by switching crops). In fact, there would be room for a mutually satisfactory bargain in all cases in which a change of crop would reduce the amount of damage by more than it reduces the value of the crop (excluding damage) - in all cases, that is, in which a change in the crop cultivated would lead to an increase in the value of production.

But this raises a further possibility. Suppose that there is such a well-defined route. Suppose further that the value of the crop that would be obtained by cultivating this strip of land is $10 but that the cost of cultivation is $11. In the absence of the cattle-raiser, the land would not be cultivated. However, given the presence of the cattle-raiser, it could well be that if the strip was cultivated, the whole crop would be destroyed by the cattle. In which case, the cattle-raiser would be forced to pay $10 to the farmer. It is true that the farmer would lose $1. But the cattle-raiser would lose $10. Clearly this is a situation which is not likely to last indefinitely since neither party would want this to happen. The aim of the farmer would be to induce the cattle-raiser to make a payment in return for an agreement to leave this land uncultivated. The farmer would not be able to obtain a payment greater than the cost of fencing off this piece of land nor so high as to lead the cattle-raiser to abandon the use of the neighbouring property. What payment would in fact be made would depend on the shrewdness of the farmer and the cattle-raiser as bargainers. But as the payment would not be so high as to cause the cattle-raiser to abandon this location and as it would not vary with the size of the herd, such an agreement would not affect the allocation of resources but would merely alter the distribution of income and wealth as between the cattle-raiser and the farmer.

I think it is clear that if the cattle-raiser is liable for damage caused and the pricing system works smoothly, the reduction in the value of production elsewhere will be taken into account in computing the additional cost involved in increasing the size of the herd. This cost will be weighed against the value of the additional meat production and, given perfect competition in the cattle industry, the allocation of resources in cattle-raising will be optimal. What needs to be emphasized is that the fall in the value of production elsewhere which would be taken into account in the costs of the cattle-raiser may well be less than the damage which the cattle would cause to the crops in the ordinary course of events. This is because it is possible, as a result of market transactions, to discontinue cultivation of the land. This is desirable in all cases in which the damage that the cattle would cause, and for which the cattle-raiser would be willing to pay, exceeds the amount which the farmer would pay for the use of the land. In conditions of perfect competition, the amount which the farmer would pay for the use of the land is equal to the difference between the value of the total production when the factors are employed on this land and the value of the additional product yielded in their next best use (which would be what the farmer would have to pay for the factors). If damage exceeds the amount the farmer would pay for the use of the land, the value of the additional product of the factors employed elsewhere would exceed the value of the total product in this use after damage is taken into account. It follows that it would be desirable to abandon cultivation of the land and to release the factors employed for production elsewhere. A procedure which merely provided for payment for damage to the crop caused by the cattle but which did not allow for the possibility of cultivation being discontinued would result in too small an employment of factors of production in cattle-raising and too large an employment of factors in cultivation of the crop. But given the possibility of market transactions, a situation in which damage to crops exceeded the rent of the land would not endure. Whether the cattle-raiser pays the farmer to leave the land uncultivated or himself rents the land by paying the land-owner an amount slightly greater than the farmer would pay (if the farmer was himself renting the land), the final result would be the same and would maximize the value of production. Even when the farmer is induced to plant crops which it would not be profitable to cultivate for sale on the market, this will be a purely short-term phenomenon and may be expected to lead to an agreement under which the planting will cease. The cattle-raiser will remain in that location and the marginal cost of meat production will be the same as before, thus having no long-run effect on the allocation of resources.

IV. The Pricing System with No Liability for Damage

I now turn to the case in which, although the pricing system is assumed to work smoothly (that is, costlessly), the damaging business is not liable for any of the damage which it causes. This business does not have to make a payment to those damaged by its actions. I propose to show that the allocation of resources will be the same in this case as it was when the damaging business was liable for damage caused. As I showed in the previous case that the allocation of resources was optimal, it will not be necessary to repeat this part of the argument.

I return to the case of the farmer and the cattle-raiser. The farmer would suffer increased damage to his crop as the size of the herd increased. Suppose that the size of the cattle-raiser's herd is 3 steers (and that this is the size of the herd that would be maintained if crop damage was not taken into account. Then the farmer would be willing to pay up to $3 if the cattle raiser would reduce his herd to 2 steers, up to $5 if the herd were reduced to 1 steer and would pay up to $6 if cattle-raising was abandoned. The cattle-raiser would therefore receive $3 from the farmer if he kept 2 steers instead of 3. This $3 foregone is therefore part of the cost incurred in keeping the third steer. Whether the $3 is a payment which the cattle-raiser has to make if he adds the third steer to his herd (which it would be if the cattle-raiser was liable to the farmer for damage caused to the crop) or whether it is a sum of money which he would have received if he did not keep a third steer (which it would be if the cattle-raiser was not liable to the farmer for damage caused to the crop) does not affect the final result. In both cases $3 is part of the cost of adding a third steer, to be included along with the other costs. If the increase in the value of production in cattle-raising through increasing the size of the herd from 2 to 3 is greater than the additional costs that have to be incurred (including the $3 damage to crops), the size of the herd will be increased. Otherwise, it will not. The size of the herd will be the same whether the cattle-raiser is liable for damage caused to the crop or not.

It may be argued that the assumed starting point — a herd of 3 steers — was arbitrary. And this is true. But the farmer would not wish to pay to avoid crop damage which the cattle-raiser would not be able to cause. For example, the maximum annual payment which the farmer could be induced to pay could not exceed $9, the annual cost of fencing. And the farmer would only be willing to pay this sum if it did not reduce his earnings to a level that would cause him to abandon cultivation of this particular tract of land. Furthermore, the farmer would only be willing to pay this amount if he believed that, in the absence of any payment by him, the size of the herd maintained by the cattle-raiser would be 4 or more steers. Let us assume that this is the case. Then the farmer would be willing to pay up to $3 if the cattle raiser would reduce his herd to 3 steers, up to $6 if the herd were reduced to 2 steers, up to $8 if one steer only were kept and up to $9 if cattle-raising were abandoned. It will be noticed that the change in the starting point has not altered the amount which would accrue to the cattle-raiser if he reduced the size of his herd by any given amount. It is still true that the cattle-raiser could receive an additional $3 from the farmer if he agreed to reduce his herd from 3 steers to 2 and that the $3 represents the value of the crop that would be destroyed by adding the third steer to the herd. Although a different belief on the part of the farmer (whether justified or not) about the size of the herd that the cattle-raiser would maintain in the absence of payments from him may affect the total payment he can be induced to pay, it is not true that this different belief would have any effect on the size of the herd that the cattle-raiser will actually keep. This will be the same as it would be if the cattle-raiser had to pay for damage caused by his cattle, since a receipt foregone of a given amount is the equivalent of a payment in the same amount.

It might be thought that it would pay the cattle-raiser to increase his herd above the size that he would wish to maintain once a bargain had been made, in order to induce the farmer to make a larger total payment. And this may be true. It is similar in nature to the action of the farmer (when the cattle-raiser was liable for damage) in cultivating land on which, as a result of an agreement with the cattle-raiser, planting would subsequently be abandoned (including land which would not be cultivated at all in the absence of cattle-raising). But such manoeuvres are preliminaries to an agreement and do not affect the long-run equilibrium position, which is the same whether or not the cattle-raiser is held responsible for the crop damage brought about by his cattle.

It is necessary to know whether the damaging business is liable or not for damage caused since without the establishment of this initial delimitation of rights there can be no market transactions to transfer and recombine them. But the ultimate result (which maximises the value of production) is independent of the legal position if the pricing system is assumed to work without cost.

V. The Cost of Market Transactions Taken into Account

The argument has proceeded up to this point on the assumption that there were no costs involved in carrying out market transactions. This is, of course, a very unrealistic assumption. In order to carry out a market transaction it is necessary to discover who it is that one wishes to deal with, to inform people that one wishes to deal and on what terms, to conduct negotiations leading up to a bargain, to draw up the contract, to undertake the inspection needed to make sure that the terms of the contract are being observed, and so on. These operations are often extremely costly, sufficiently costly at any rate to prevent many transactions that would be carried out in a world in which the pricing system worked without cost.

In earlier sections, when dealing with the problem of the rearrangement of legal rights through the market, it was argued that such a rearrangement would be made through the market whenever this would lead to an increase in the value of production. But this assumed costless market transactions. Once the costs of carrying out market transactions are taken into account it is clear that such a rearrangement of rights will only be undertaken when the increase in the value of production consequent upon the rearrangement is greater than the costs which would be involved in bringing it about. When it is less, the granting of an injunction (or the knowledge that it would be granted) or the liability to pay damages may result in an activity being discontinued (or may prevent its being started) which would be undertaken if market transactions were costless. In these conditions the initial delimitation of legal rights does have an effect on the efficiency with which the economic system operates. One arrangement of rights may bring about a greater value of production than any other. But unless this is the arrangement of rights established by the legal system, the costs of reaching the same result by altering and combining rights through the market may be so great that this optimal arrangement of rights, and the greater value of production which it would bring, may never be achieved.

It is clear that an alternative form of economic organisation which could achieve the same result at less cost than would be incurred by using the market would enable the value of production to be raised. As I explained many years ago, the firm represents such an alternative to organising production through market transactions.* Within the firm individual bargains between the various cooperating factors of production are eliminated and for a market transaction is substituted an administrative decision. The rearrangement of production then takes place without the need for bargains between the owners of the factors of production. A landowner who has control of a large tract of land may devote his land to various uses taking into account the effect that the interrelations of the various activities will have on the net return of the land, thus rendering unnecessary bargains between those undertaking the various activities. Owners of a large building or of several adjoining properties in a given area may act in much the same way. In effect, using our earlier terminology, the firm

---

* See Coase, The Nature of the Firm, 4 *Economica*, New Series, 385 (1937). Reprinted in Readings in Price Theory, 331 (1952).

would acquire the legal rights of all the parties and the rearrangement of activities would not follow on a rearrangement of rights by contract, but as a result of an administrative decision as to how the rights should be used.

It does not, of course, follow that the administrative costs of organising a transaction through a firm are inevitably less than the costs of the market transactions which are superseded. But where contracts are peculiarly difficult to draw up and an attempt to describe what the parties have agreed to do or not to do (e.g. the amount and kind of a smell or noise that they may make or will not make) would necessitate a lengthy and highly involved document, and, where, as is probable, a long-term contract would be desirable;* it would be hardly surprising if the emergence of a firm or the extension of the activities of an existing firm was not the solution adopted on many occasions to deal with the problem of harmful effects. This solution would be adopted whenever the administrative costs of the firm were less than the costs of the market transactions that it supersedes and the gains which would result from the rearrangement of activities greater than the firm's costs of organizing them. I do not need to examine in great detail the character of this solution since I have explained what is involved in my earlier article.

But the firm is not the only possible answer to this problem. The administrative costs of organising transactions within the firm may also be high, and particularly so when many diverse activities are brought within the control of a single organisation. In the standard case of a smoke nuisance, which may affect a vast number of people engaged in a wide variety of activities, the administrative costs might well be so high as to make any attempt to deal with the problem within the confines of a single firm impossible. An alternative solution is direct Government regulation. Instead of instituting a legal system of rights which can be modified by transactions on the market, the government may impose regulations which state what people must or must not do and which have to be obeyed. Thus, the government (by statute or perhaps more likely through an administrative agency) may, to deal with the problem of smoke nuisance, decree that certain methods of production should or should not be used (e.g. that smoke preventing devices should be installed or that coal or oil should not be burned) or may confine certain types of business to certain districts (zoning regulations).

The government is, in a sense, a super-firm (but of a very special kind) since it is able to influence the use of factors of production by administrative decision. But the ordinary firm is subject to checks in its operations because of the competition of other firms, which might administer the same activities at lower cost and also because there is always the alternative of market transactions as against organisation within the firm if the administrative costs become too great. If the government is able, if it wishes, to avoid the market altogether, which a firm can never do. The firm has to make market agreements with the owners of the fac-

---

*   For reasons explained in my earlier article, see Readings in Price Theory, n. 14 at 337.

tors of production that it uses. Just as the government can conscript or seize property, so it can decree that factors of production should only be used in such-and-such a way. Such authoritarian methods save a lot of trouble (for those doing the organising). Furthermore, the government has at its disposal the police and the other law enforcement agencies to make sure that its regulations are carried out.

It is clear that the government has powers which might enable it to get some things done at a lower cost than could a private organisation (or at any rate one without special government powers). But the governmental administrative machine is not itself costless. It can, in fact, on occasion be extremely costly. Furthermore, there is no reason to suppose that the restrictive and zoning regulations, made by a fallible administration subject to political pressures and operating without any competitive check, will necessarily always be those which increase the efficiency with which the economic system operates. Furthermore, such general regulations which must apply to a wide variety of cases will be enforced in some cases in which they are clearly inappropriate. From these considerations it follows that direct governmental regulation will not necessarily give better results than leaving the problem to be solved by the market or the firm. But equally there is no reason why, on occasion, such governmental administrative regulation should not lead to an improvement in economic efficiency. This would seem particularly likely when, as is normally the case with the smoke nuisance, a large number of people are involved and in which therefore the costs of handling the problem through the market or the firm may be high.

There is, of course, a further alternative, which is to do nothing about the problem at all. And given that the costs involved in solving the problem by regulations issued by the governmental administrative machine will often be heavy (particularly if the costs are interpreted to include all the consequences which follow from the Government engaging in this kind of activity), it will no doubt be commonly the case that the gain which would come from regulating the actions which give rise to the harmful effects will be less than the costs involved in Government regulation. ●

The Distribution of Income

The exorbitant rewards of players, opera-singers, opera-dancers, & c. are founded upon those two principles: the rarity and beauty of the talents, and the discredit of employing them in this manner.

Adam Smith

The most persistent criticism of the private enterprise system is that it generates an unfair distribution of income. It is widely believed that market competition has impoverished a significant segment of the population and that government has a responsibility to alter the market distribution of income in favor of the poor.

There is no denying that market competition results in an unequal distribution of income. Two things are worth considering, however. First, an unequal distribution of income is a necessary result of a system that effectively motivates the production of wealth. In a pure private enterprise system each person's economic well-being depends on how well one uses one's talents and resources to improve the well-being of others. If government redistributes income so that people are rewarded independently of their economic contributions, their economic contributions will diminish and less wealth will be available in general.

The productivity costs of government redistribution programs are not, by themselves, a compelling argument against these programs. We may be willing to suffer from less output in order to increase the income of the less fortunate. This brings us to the second consideration. There is a great deal of evidence indicating that government transfer programs have done little, if anything, to help the poor. A sizable percentage of gross national product is transferred through government programs each year, but most of it is transferred to organized interest groups whose members are seldom poor. Just as in the market place, it takes skill, resourcefulness, and organization to compete successfully in the political arena. Those who are poor because they are not able to compete successfully in the market are not likely to be able to compete effectively for government transfers.

This raises the serious possibility that, on balance, government transfer programs have not only reduced economic productivity, but reduced the well-being of the poor in the process. If, as evidence indicates, government transfers have reduced the size of the economic pie without providing the poor a larger percentage of that pie, then these transfers have made the poor absolutely worse off.

This section features articles on the distribution of income, how it is determined in a market economy, and why government attempts to alter it are likely to be unsuccessful.

The parallels between market competition and political competition are developed by Lee in the first selection. These parallels and a great deal of evidence suggest that increasing political control over the income distribution has done little, if anything, to reduce income inequality. Yet poverty programs can become politically entrenched for the very reason that they have failed to help the poor.

Milton Friedman and his wife Rose address the issue of income distribution in a selection from their bestselling book, *Free to Choose.* Perfect equality, either in terms of opportunity or outcome, is impossible regardless of the economic system. But attempts to impose more equality by usurping the freedom of the market with the coercion of government result in less equality and less freedom.

Charles Murray became the object of both applause and criticism in the mid 1980s when he published the book, *Losing Ground,* in which he argued that the poor have been victimized by government programs designed to reduce poverty. In this selection, which is excerpted from this book, Murray considers the difficulty of helping people in poverty without reducing the motivation for them to take the action necessary to escape poverty, or reducing the motivation for people to stay out of poverty.

A piece by Gordon Tullock (1922–) follows. Tullock, a pioneer in the field of public choice, describes the economic analysis of the political process. He explains why the democratic process will not necessarily transfer income from the rich to the poor, at least not very efficiently. Tullock closes his discussion with an explanation of why people prefer to express their charitable feelings through voting for public philanthropy rather than giving to private charity.

The final selection by Adam Smith considers the factors that determine the wage difference between occupations in the market place. Having read the previous readings in this section, a reasonable conclusion is that these market determined differences in wages have an effect on the distribution of income that is not likely to be much affected by government action. ●

33. The Politics of Poverty and the Poverty of Politics

Dwight R. Lee

[T]he poor [may] deserve more, but if the government tries to provide more, it will not do anyone any good.

*Nathan Glazer**

Introduction

The notion that we have to depend on government to assist the poor has acquired the status of revealed truth. Even those who acknowledge the unparalleled success of market economies at creating wealth are uneasy about, if not outright hostile to, the market distribution of this wealth. There can be no denying that some people will be left behind by market competition. Indeed, the very success of the market at creating wealth comes from the fact that it constantly threatens people with poverty; and when consumers signal with their thumbs down, the threat is carried out without mercy.

But even if it is assumed that the market fails to generate a distribution of income that most people find satisfactory, does this justify government programs to promote a more acceptable income distribution? The answer depends crucially on whether or not there are reasons for believing that such government programs will improve matters. If, for example, government welfare programs impose a heavy burden on economic productivity, yet are incapable of changing the distribution of income in a more acceptable direction, then the "failure" of the market with regards to income distribution would provide no justification for government intervention in the market process.

The importance of comparing realistically the income distribution conse-

*   "Reagan's Social Policy — A Review," The Public Interest (Spring 1984): 94.

Abridged from *The Cato Journal*, Volume 5, Number 1, Spring/Summer, 1985, by permission of The Cato Institute.

quences of the market process with those of the political process may seem obvious. But in fact, such a comparison is seldom made. The market process is seen to be driven by competition between self-seeking individuals who are unconcerned about the impact of their decisions on the overall distribution of income. Income inequality is correctly judged to be endemic to the market process. On the other hand, the political process is seen to be driven by concern for broad social objectives. The prime motivation for government transfer programs is assumed to be to help the poor and reduce income inequality. If these programs fail in what they were set up to accomplish, the problem is seldom seen to be anything inherent in the political process that spawned the programs.

The evidence is strong that government transfer programs have failed. The U.S. Bureau of the Census announced in August, 1984 that 35.3 million people, or 15.2 percent of the population, were living in poverty. This is a startling statistic given the enormous amounts the government is spending on social welfare programs. Though it is difficult to pin down the total welfare bill with precision, it has been estimated that it came to over $403 billion in 1982.* This amounts to $11,730 per officially designated poor person, or $46,920 for each poor family of four.

But predictably, the blame for this blatant failure seldom cuts to the fundamentals of the problem: a realistic assessment of the political process. At the partisan level, the blame is placed on insufficient funds for these programs, with the Reagan budget "cut backs" being singled out for special criticism. Although funding was reduced for some poverty programs during the early years of the Reagan administration, overall spending for poverty programs continued upward during the 1980s. More important, since 1973 there has been a persistent increase in the number of poor as measured by the Bureau of the Census. An explanation of the existing level of poverty, given the amounts being spent to eliminate it, requires something more sophisticated than an attack on the Reagan administration for being insensitive. The seriousness with which this attack is made, and widely accepted as justified, reflects the reluctance to subject the political process behind transfer programs to the same critical examination to which the market process is subjected.

Even those most critical of the government welfare programs seldom see the problems as inextricably tied to the political process. Favorite targets are fraud and corruption that should be rooted out with tighter controls over existing programs. Others see the solution coming from reforming existing programs;

---

* This figure comes from Jonathan Hobbs, "Welfare Need and Welfare Spending," Heritage Foundation Backgrounder, Washington, D.C., 13 October 1982, and includes only the welfare component of Social Security payments.

such as reducing reliance on in-kind transfers with more aid being provided in the form of cash payments.* But such calls for reform have been made for decades, and they have always been rendered politically impotent. In any event, welfare fraud can account for only a small amount of the costs of our welfare industry. And given the outpouring of scholarly articles on the poverty question, it is difficult to argue that the failures of our poverty programs can be reversed with yet more advice on desirable reforms.

It is not, then, the purpose of this paper to suggest welfare reform. Rather, an effort will be made to explain why poverty has been, and will continue to be, amazingly immune to political measures to alleviate it. In order to accomplish this, we will subject the political process to the same type of analytical scrutiny which economists have always applied to the market process. This means incorporating the same motivational assumption into our political analysis as is incorporated into standard economic analysis: namely, that individuals are motivated predominantly, though not solely, by considerations of self-interest.** Proceeding with this self-interest assumption, we will be led to the conclusion that political activity is not likely to significantly alter the distribution of income away from that which results from market activity. Furthermore, this theoretically arrived at conclusion is shown to be empirically supported.

The Distribution of Income

Based on the evidence that exists, it appears that the impact of the huge growth in transfer programs has been rather minor. In a study of the distribution of income and wealth in the United States Reynolds and Smolensky concluded that, when the net benefits of all government programs were added to the incomes U.S. households received from labor and capital, there was no significant change in the distribution of income between 1950 and 1970. For example, according to their study, those households in the lowest 20 percent of the income distribution received 6.4 percent of national net income in 1950 and 6.7 percent in 1970. At the other end of the distribution, the percentage of net income going to those households in the top 20 percent declined slightly from 39.9 in 1950 to 39.1 in 1970.***

Given the increase in transfer expenditures that occurred over this period of time this is a rather startling result, but one quite consistent with our analysis of the political incentives that create and are created by government transfer

---

*   See Hobbs, "Welfare Need." Also for a list of suggested reforms in our approach to social welfare spending, see John C. Goodman, "Poverty and Welfare" in *To Promote Prosperity: U.S. Domestic Policy in the Mid-1980s*, ed. John Moore (Stanford, Calif.: Hoover Institution Press, 1984).

**   Even if one chooses to quibble with this assumption, no one can argue persuasively that objectivity is served by applying it to the market process but not to the political process.

***   Morgan Reynolds and Eugene Smolensky, "Distribution of Income and Wealth: The Fading Effect of Government on Inequality," *Challenge* (July/August 1978): 32-37.

programs. In providing their own explanation for the impotency of these transfer programs Reynolds and Smolensky state:

> The very scale of government spending programs today mitigate
> against augmenting their capacity to redistribute net income. . . . Even if
> a democratic government initially directed additional benefits and costs
> "efficiently" toward an identifiable group, it would find efficiency hard to
> preserve. With such large sums at stake, more players find it worthwhile
> to compete for a larger share of the benefits and a smaller share of the
> taxes.*

More recent studies of the distribution of income have reached conclusions
similar to those of Reynolds and Smolensky. For example, evidence cited in an
extensive review of the literature on the affect of U.S. income transfer programs,
indicated that over the period 1965 to about 1978 the "income inequality has
remained relatively constant."**

It should be pointed out that some studies indicate that government transfer
programs have resulted in an income distribution that is significantly more equal
than it would otherwise be.*** The general approach of these studies involves
comparing the post-transfer distribution of income with the counterfactual
income that would have existed in the absence of government transfers. Unfortunately, estimating "what would have been" is extremely difficult and typically the comparison is between the income distribution with government transfers
and the income distribution that results when these transfers are eliminated.
But obviously this overstates the effect of the transfers. As previously discussed,
the response to the availability of public transfers has been a reduction in private
charity and the substitution, on the part of the poor, of transfer income for
earned income. To simply eliminate the effect of transfer programs after people
have, over a number of years, adjusted their behavior to them yields income estimates for the poor that are lower than the income they would have received,
either from private charity or earnings, had the public transfers never been available. Studies, such as the one by Reynolds and Smolensky, which look at the
income distribution, as it actually is, over time and find that it has not changed
appreciably in response to large increases in government transfer programs,
speak more accurately to the question of how effective these programs have
been than do studies which see the income of the poor increasing a dollar for
every transfer dollar received.

In discussing the income distribution we have been talking about the effect

---

*   *Ibid.*, p. 36.
**   See Sheldon Danziger, Robert Haveman, and Robert Plotnick, "How Income Transfer
        Programs Affect Work, Saving, and the Income Distribution: A Critical Review," *Journal of
        Economic Literature* 19 (September 1981), p. 978.
***   These studies are discussed in Danziger et al., pp. 1006-15.

of government transfer programs on the *relative* income of the poor, as opposed to the absolute income. If, as the evidence seems to indicate, massive transfer expenditures have not increased the relative income of the poor, then it is surely the case that these expenditures have decreased the absolute income of the poor. The taxes necessary to finance transfer payments reduce the private returns to labor, to savings, and to investment, and to wealth producing activity in general. Therefore these taxes create wealth-reducing distortions in the economy. Similarly, the payment of transfers typically reduces the incentive of recipients to engage in productive activities. A large number of empirical studies have been made in the attempt to estimate the size of the negative productivity effects of taxes and transfers. Not surprisingly these estimates vary, with some studies finding large negative effects and others finding much smaller effects.* But no one has seriously argued that the effect of taxes and transfers on economic productivity is neutral or positive. And even if the huge increase in transfer programs over recent decades, and the huge increase in taxes necessary to finance them, have had only a slightly negative effect on national income, these programs have still made the poor absolutely worse off if they have left the distribution of national income unchanged. If the negative impact of taxes and transfers on productivity is as large as many believe to be the case, then the poor could be left absolutely worse off even if their relative income has been increased by government transfer programs.

None of this is to deny that transfer programs can, and indeed do, benefit particular groups, including the poor, in the short-run. But these short-run benefits come at the expense of long-run reductions in the general economic welfare that harm the poor as well as the nonpoor. But it is the short-run consequences of transfer programs that dominate myopic political considerations, not the long-run consequences. Furthermore, the eroding effectiveness of government transfer programs not only fails to discourage politicians from embracing these programs but has the perverse effect of actually increasing the political support they receive.

The Political Success of Economic Failure

In order to understand the political success of economic failure in the case of transfer programs, it is useful to consider the argument most commonly used by those who believe these programs have been successful in helping the poor. This argument relies on statistics which indicate that if the anti-poverty programs were eliminated the percentage of the population falling below the official poverty line would increase dramatically. For example, figures for 1982, published by the Congressional Research Service (CRS), indicate that in the

---

*   Many of these studies are discussed in Danziger *et al.*

absence of government support programs the poverty rate would have gone from 8.8 percent to 24 percent. Also according to calculations by the CRS, the elimination of government programs would result in 14 to 16 million elderly people, between 55 and 60 percent of the elderly population, living in poverty.*

Little thought is required to recognize this argument forms a dubious basis for heralding the success of government transfer programs. If these programs had never come into existence it is inconceivable that one-fourth of the entire population, or over one-half of the elderly, would be living in poverty. With the data indicating that the increase in social welfare programs have had little impact on the income distribution, the rate of relative poverty in the counterfactual world with no history of government transfers would be little different than that which is actually observed with these transfers. The argument that the elimination of transfer programs would result in high rates of poverty points to the failure of these programs, not their success. The programs are doing little to reduce the poverty rate below what it would be in the long run without them, but they are doing a lot to discourage independence and encourage dependence. This is hardly a testimony to the success of these programs. It is, however, the reason these transfer programs are so resilient politically.

Even if transfer recipients would have been better off in the absence of transfer programs, having accommodated to these programs they would experience genuine suffering in the short run if the programs were suddenly scaled back or eliminated. Welfare recipients cannot develop instantly the skills and earning potential needed to replace welfare income. From the perspective of individuals who have failed to develop productive skills, who have had children they cannot themselves support, or who have absorbed an attitude of dependency from their surroundings, the short run may extend over an extensive period of time. Certainly, we are talking about a period of time that extends well beyond the time horizon of the political process. The political pressures that would be brought to bear on any serious attempt to curtail transfer programs, whether they are targeted to the poor or otherwise, would obscure the long-run benefits that would result from such a curtailment. Once the political process starts down the transfer path it is no easy task to turn back, even after it has been determined to be the wrong path.

Instead of reversing direction and reducing transfer payments, the political process will more likely be pushing in the opposite direction. The failure of transfer programs will not be seen to be inherent in the politics of these programs. Instead, continuing poverty will be seen as justification for an expansion of existing transfer programs and/or the establishment of additional programs. This view is reinforced by political myopia. Measured poverty can be temporarily reduced by another infusion of government transfer payments, and

---

*   These figures are cited by Spencer Rich in his article, "The Skeptics Are Wrong: Anti-Poverty Programs Do Work," *Washington Post*, 6 May 1984, p. F1.

near-term political gains are available to politicians who are able to take credit for such a reduction in poverty. Of course, over the long run the expansion in transfer programs will fail to reduce relative poverty, and will likely increase absolute poverty. But with the future consequences of political action being discounted as heavily as they are, these future failures will be largely ignored.

The further the political process travels down the path of ever larger transfer programs, the more difficult it will be to reverse course. As more people respond to the expansion of transfer programs by becoming dependent on them, the short-run political cost of scaling these programs back becomes greater. The greater the failure of social welfare programs, as measured by the dependence they create, the more successful they will be, as measured by political viability.

Conclusion

Not only are an increasing number of poor people in the country caught in a trap of welfare dependency, we as a society are also snared in a welfare trap. Having created a dependent subculture we cannot, indeed should not, suddenly cut these people off. To do so would be to practice an extreme form of political deception and cruelty.

But we can at least be realistic in assessing the effectiveness of government welfare programs. It is surely not very useful to continue with the pretense that these programs have been successful when, in fact, they have been failures. At the very minimum, we should recognize the folly of attempting to overcome the failures of existing programs by further expansions in these programs.

Yet if we continue to trust in politics as usual, it is almost certain that transfer programs will continue to grow and proliferate. Electing the "right" politicians, urging "sensible" reforms, or swings in the public attitude may temporarily slow this growth on occasion, but ever present political incentives will always be pushing toward expansion. And the only natural barrier to this expansion is economic stagnation and decay.

The best, possibly the only, hope for halting the destructive excesses of ever increasing transfer programs is through a collective realization that we all suffer, rich and poor alike, when the government is free to hand out benefits to every group which is prepared to organize politically around some narrow interest. Overriding the myopic pressures of ordinary politics with some type of constitutional cap on the percentage of our national income that government can spend would be a beneficial result of this realization. That constitutional amendments of this type are being discussed and considered seriously today is an encouraging sign.

Of course, many will argue that any arbitrary constraint on government will hurt the poor. But this is simply not true. To recommend limiting government expenditures is not to lack compassion and concern for the poor. Quite the contrary. Once one faces up to how the political process actually works, as opposed to how we might ideally wish it worked, it is realized that both compassion and common sense will be served by constraining the size and scope of government. ●

34. Created Equal

Milton and Rose Friedman

Equality of Opportunity

Literal equality of opportunity—in the sense of "identity"—is impossible. One child is born blind, another with sight. One child has parents deeply concerned about his welfare who provide a background of culture and understanding; another has dissolute, improvident parents. One child is born in the United States, another in India, or China, or Russia. They clearly do not have identical opportunities open to them at birth, and there is no way that their opportunities can be made identical

Like personal equality, equality of opportunity is not to be interpreted literally. Its real meaning is perhaps best expressed by the French expression dating from the French Revolution: *Une carrière ouverte aux les talents* — a career open to the talents. No arbitrary obstacles should prevent people from achieving those positions for which their talents fit them and which their values lead them to seek. Not birth, nationality, color, religion, sex, nor any other irrelevant characteristic should determine the opportunities that are open to a person — only his abilities.

Equality of Outcome

That different concept, equality of outcome, has been gaining ground in his century. It first affected government policy in Great Britain and on the European continent. Over the past half-century it has increasingly affected government policy in the United States as well. In some intellectual circles the desirability of equality of outcome has become an article of religious faith: everyone should finish the race at the same time. As the Dodo said in *Alice in Wonderland*, "*Everybody* has won, and *all* must have prizes."

For this concept, as for the other two, "equal" is not to be interpreted literally as "identical." No one really maintains that everyone, regardless of age or sex or other physical qualities, should have identical rations of each separate item

Excerpts abridged from *Free to Choose*, copyright © 1980 by Milton and Rose Friedman, reprinted by permission of Harcourt Brace Jovanovich, Inc.

of food, clothing, and so on. The goal is rather "fairness," a much vaguer notion—indeed, one that is difficult, if not impossible, to define precisely. "Fair shares for all" is the modern slogan that has replaced Karl Marx's, "To each according to his needs, from each according to his ability."

This concept of equality differs radically from the other two. Government measures that promote personal equality or equality of opportunity enhance liberty; government measures to achieve "fair shares for all" reduce liberty. If what people get is to be determined by "fairness," who is to decide what is "fair"? As a chorus of voices asked the Dodo, "But who is to give the prizes?" "Fairness" is not an objectively determined concept once it departs from identity. "Fairness," like "needs," is in the eye of the beholder. If all are to have "fair shares," someone or some group of people must decide what shares are fair—and they must be able to impose their decisions on others, taking from those who have more than their "fair" share and giving to those who have less. Are those who make and impose such decisions equal to those for whom they decide? Are we not in George Orwell's *Animal Farm*, where "all animals are equal, but some animals are more equal than others?"

In addition, if what people get is determined by "fairness" and not by what they produce, where are the "prizes" to come from? What incentive is there to work and produce? How is it to be decided who is to be the doctor, who the lawyer, who the garbage collector, who the street sweeper? What assures that people will accept the roles assigned to them and perform those roles in accordance with their abilities? Clearly, only force or the threat of force will do.

Much of the moral fervor behind the drive for equality of outcome comes from the widespread belief that it is not fair that some children should have a great advantage over others simply because they happen to have wealthy parents. Of course it is not fair. However, unfairness can take many forms. It can take the form of the inheritance of property—bonds and stocks, houses, factories; it can also take the form of the inheritance of talent—musical ability, strength, mathematical genius. The inheritance of property can be interfered with more readily than the inheritance of talent. But from an ethical point of view, is there any difference between the two? Yet many people resent the inheritance of property but not the inheritance of talent.

Life is not fair. It is tempting to believe that government can rectify what nature has spawned. But it is also important to recognize how much we benefit from the very unfairness we deplore.

It is certainly not fair that Muhammad Ali should be able to earn millions of dollars in one night. But wouldn't it have been even more unfair to the people who enjoyed watching him if, in the pursuit of some abstract ideal of equality, Muhammad Ali had not been permitted to earn more for one night's fight—or for each day spent in preparing for a fight—than the lowest man on the totem pole could get for a day's unskilled work on the docks? It might have been possible to do that, but the result would have been to deny people the opportunity to watch Muhammad Ali. We doubt very much that he would have been willing to undergo the arduous regimen of training that preceded his fights, or to subject himself to the kind of fights he has had, if he were limited to the pay of an unskilled dockworker.

The system under which people make their own choices—and bear most of the consequences of their decisions—is the system that has prevailed for most of our history. It is the system that gave the Henry Fords, the Thomas Alva Edisons, the George Eastmans, the John D. Rockefellers, the James Cash Penneys the incentive to transform our society over the past two centuries. It is the system that gave other people an incentive to furnish venture capital to finance the risky enterprises that those ambitious inventors and captains of industry undertook. Of course, there were many losers along the way—probably more losers than winners. We don't remember their names. But for the most part they went in with their eyes open. They knew they were taking chances. And win or lose, society as a whole benefited from their willingness to take a chance.

The fortunes that this system produced came overwhelmingly from developing new products or services, or of distributing them widely. The resulting addition to the wealth of the community as a whole, to the well-being of the masses of the people, amounted to many times the wealth accumulated by the innovators. Henry Ford acquired a great fortune. The country acquired a cheap and reliable means of transportation and the techniques of mass production. Moreover, in many cases the private fortunes were largely devoted in the end to the benefit of society. The Rockefeller, Ford, and Carnegie foundations are only the most prominent of the numerous private benefactions which are so outstanding a consequence of the operation of a system that corresponded to "equality of opportunity" and "liberty" as these terms were understood until recently.

Consequences of Egalitarian Policies

In shaping our own policy, we can learn from the experience of Western countries with which we share a common intellectual and cultural background, and from which we derive many of our values. Perhaps the most instructive example is Great Britain, which led the way in the nineteenth century toward implementing equality of opportunity and in the twentieth toward implementing equality of outcome.

Since the end of World War II, British domestic policy has been dominated by the search for greater equality of outcome. Measure after measure has been adopted designed to take from the rich and give to the poor. Taxes were raised on income until they reached a top rate of 98 percent on property income and 83 percent on "earned" income, and were supplemented by ever heavier taxes on inheritances. State-provided medical, housing, and other welfare services were greatly expanded, along with payments to the unemployed and the aged. Unfortunately, the results have been very different from those that were intended by the people who were quite properly offended by the class structure that dominated Britain for centuries. There has been a vast redistribution of wealth, but the end result is not an equitable distribution.

Instead, new classes of privileged have been created to replace or supplement the old: the bureaucrats, secure in their jobs, protected against inflation both when they work and when they retire; the trade unions that profess to represent the most downtrodden workers but in fact consist of the highest paid laborers in the land—the aristocrats of the labor movement; and the new millionaires—people who have been cleverest at finding ways around the laws, the rules, the regulations that have poured from Parliament and the bureaucracy, who have found ways to avoid paying taxes on their income and to get their wealth overseas beyond the grasp of the tax collectors. A vast reshuffling of income and wealth, yes; greater equity, hardly.

The drive for equality in Britain failed, not because the wrong measures were adopted—though some no doubt were; not because they were badly administered—though some no doubt were; not because the wrong people administered them—though no doubt some did. The drive for equality failed for a much more fundamental reason. It went against one of the most basic instincts of all human beings. In the words of Adam Smith, "The uniform, constant, and the uninterrupted effort of every man to better his condition*—and, one may add, the condition of his children and his children's children." Smith, of course, meant by "condition" not merely material well-being, though certainly that was one component. He had a much broader concept in mind, one that included all of the values by which men judge their success—in particular the kind of social values that gave rise to the outpouring of philanthropic activities in the nineteenth century.

When the law interferes with people's pursuit of their own values, they will try to find a way around. They will evade the law, they will break the law, or they will leave the country. Few of us believe in a moral code that justifies forcing people to give up much of what they produce to finance payments to persons they do not know for purposes they may not approve of. When the law contradicts what most people regard as moral and proper, they will break the law—whether the law is enacted in the name of a noble ideal such as equality or in the naked interest of one group at the expense of another. Only fear of punishment, not a sense of justice and morality, will lead people to obey the law.

Capitalism and Equality

Everywhere in the world there are gross inequities of income and wealth. They offend most of us. Few can fail to be moved by the contrast between the luxury enjoyed by some and the grinding poverty suffered by others.

In the past century a myth has grown up that free market capitalism—equality of opportunity as we have interpreted that term—increases such inequalities, that it is a system under which the rich exploit the poor.

---

*   *Wealth of Nations*, vol. I, p. 325 (Book II, Chap. III.).

Nothing could be further from the truth. Wherever the free market has been permitted to operate, wherever anything approaching equality of opportunity has existed, the ordinary man has been able to attain levels of living never dreamed of before. Nowhere is the gap between rich and poor wider, nowhere are the rich richer and the poor poorer, than in those societies that do not permit the free market to operate. That is true of feudal societies like medieval Europe, India before independence, and much of modern South America, where inherited status determines position. It is equally true of centrally planned societies, like Russia or China or India since independence, where access to government determines position. It is true even where central planning was introduced, as in all three of these countries, in the name of equality.

Russia is a country of two nations: a small privileged upper class of bureaucrats, Communist party officials, technicians; and a great mass of people living little better than their great-grandparents did. The upper class has access to special shops, schools, and luxuries of all kind; the masses are condemned to enjoy little more than the basic necessities. We remember asking a tourist guide in Moscow the cost of a large automobile that we saw and being told, "Oh, those aren't for sale; they're only for the Politburo." Several recent books by American journalists document in great detail the contrast between the privileged life of the upper classes and the poverty of the masses.* Even on a simpler level, it is noteworthy that the average wage of a foreman is a larger multiple of the average wage of an ordinary worker in a Russian factory than in a factory in the United States – and no doubt he deserves it. After all, an American foreman only has to worry about being fired; a Russian foreman also has to worry about being shot.

Conclusion

A society that puts equality – in the sense of equality of outcome – ahead of freedom will end up with neither equality nor freedom. The use of force to achieve equality will destroy freedom, and the force, introduced for good purposes, will end up in the hands of people who use it to promote their own interests.

On the other hand, a society that puts freedom first will, as a happy by-product, end up with both greater freedom and greater equality. Though a by-product of freedom, greater equality is not an accident. A free society releases the energies and abilities of people to pursue their own objectives. It prevents some people from arbitrarily suppressing others. It does not prevent some people from achieving positions of privilege, but so long as freedom is maintained, it prevents those positions of privilege from becoming institutionalized; they are subject to continued attack by other able, ambitious people. Freedom means diversity but also mobility. It preserves the opportunity for today's disad-

---

*   See Smith, *The Russians*, and Kaiser, *Russia: The People and the Power*.

vantaged to become tomorrow's privileged and, in the process, enables almost everyone, from top to bottom, to enjoy a fuller and richer life. ●

35. The Constraints on Helping

Charles Murray

A Thought Experiment

To illustrate the general problem we are about to approach, let me pose a problem in the form that Einstein used to call a "thought experiment." Whereas Einstein used the device to imagine such things as the view from the head of a column of light, we will use it for the more pedestrian purpose of imagining the view from the office of a middle-echelon bureaucrat. Our task: to think through how to structure a specific government social action program so that it might reasonably be expected to accomplish net good.

The experiment calls for us to put ourselves in the role of a government planner who must implement a new piece of legislation, The Comprehensive Anti-Smoking Act. The Act has several provisions common to the genre. It establishes a federal agency to coordinate the federal government's activities relating to the goal of less smoking. A large anti-smoking advertising campaign is planned. Federal matching funds are provided for school systems that teach courses on the perils of smoking.

In addition to these initiatives, the legislation provides for direct, concrete incentives for people to quit smoking. A billion dollars will be appropriated annually for the indefinite future, to be used for cash rewards to persons who quit. We are in charge of designing this effort, with complete freedom to specify whatever rules we wish, provided they are consistent with constitutional rights. After five years an evaluation will be conducted to determine whether the number of cigarettes consumed and the number of smokers have been reduced by the program.

The challenge in this experiment is to use the $1 billion in a way that (in our own best estimate) will meet this test. My proposition is that we cannot do so: that any program we design will either (1) have no effect on smoking or (2) actually *increase* smoking. I maintain that we are helpless to use the billion dollars to achieve our goal.

Designing the Program

The heart of the problem is designing a reward that will induce smokers to quit — and will not induce others to begin smoking, continue smoking, or increase their smoking to become eligible to receive the reward. Let us work through one scenario to illustrate the nature of the conundrum.

Three sets of choices will decisively affect the success or failure of the program: choices about

- the size of the reward,
- conditions for receiving the reward, and
- eligibility to participate in the program.

What is a first approximation of a program that has a good chance of working?

Choosing the size of the reward. We know from the outset that the reward cannot be small. No one will quit smoking for pocket change, other than those who were going to quit anyway. On the other hand, the theoretical power of a cash reward is plausible — almost everyone would become and remain a non-smoker in return for a million dollars. We settle on the sum of $10,000 as a reward that is an extremely powerful inducement to large numbers of persons.*

Conditions for receiving the reward. We seek a middle ground between conditions that maximize the likelihood that a person has permanently quit smoking and conditions that make the reward so difficult to win that few will bother. Thus, for example, we reject plans that would spread the reward over several years. Eventually we decide to require that a person must remain smoke-free for one year. We make the award a one-time prize, so that people have no incentive to recommence smoking to qualify for another $10,000. A repayment scheme is added: People who begin smoking again will have to give up their award.

Eligibility to participate. The intent of the program is to appeal to the heavy smoker whose health is most at risk. On the other hand, it would defeat our purpose to limit eligibility too severely — to persons, for example, who have smoked three packs a day for twenty years — because in so doing we would disqualify many people in the vulnerable group of moderate smokers who are likely to become heavy, lifelong smokers unless something is done. The compromise solution we reach is to require that a person have smoked at least one pack a day for five years.

Now let us consider the results.

---

*   Other types of rewards (a trip to Jamaica, or a full college scholarship for one's first-born, for example) do not seem to change the nature of the calculation, nor does the payment schedule associated with the reward.

After One Year

We think ahead a year, and are pleased. The $10,000 reward has substantial effects on the people who are eligible for the program on day one – that is, persons who have smoked at least a pack a day for five years at the time the experiment begins. The effect is not unfailing; not everyone quits smoking to get the reward; and we must assume that not everyone who stops for a year is able to avoid a relapse. Some cheating occurs despite our precautions. But some people quit smoking permanently as a direct result of the program.

We recognize, of course, that we achieve the effect inefficiently. Thousands of persons in the target population quit smoking every year even in the absence of a monetary reward. Under the program, they collect money for doing what they would have done anyway. But the problem posed in our thought experiment says nothing about being efficient; the problem is only to create a program that reduces net smoking.

After Two Years

We think ahead two years, and are disturbed. For now comes time to examine the effects of the program on people who have been smoking a pack a day but for a period of less than five years when the program begins.

Everyone who would have quit after four years and eleven months continues to smoke for another month. These cigarettes represent an increase in smoking that must be subtracted from the gross reduction in smoking created by the program. *Almost* everyone who would otherwise have quit during any point in the fifth year continues to smoke until the five-year requirement has been met. Or, to put it more generally: We find that for all persons who have been smoking less than the required period of time, the program provides a payment to continue. For the person who has been smoking for exactly four years, the payment is $10,000 in return for smoking for one more year. Given that the smoking habit has its own attractions, the payment is exceedingly effective. In fact, we notice an unfortunate imbalance: For the person who has already smoked for five years (our target population), the inducement of $10,000 to quit must fight against the attractions of smoking and is not always adequate to achieve the desired result. For the smoker who has not reached this limit, the inducement to continue smoking is reinforced by those very attractions. Thus the effective power of $10,000 to induce continued smoking for one year in the one population is much greater than its power to induce cessation of smoking for one year in the other.

To this point, we have been concerned only with those who were already smoking at the pack-a-day level. Now we consider the effects of the program on smokers who had been smoking less than that amount. We find that a significant number of smokers increase their consumption to a pack a day, for the same reason. (Everyone who smokes nineteen cigarettes a day increases to twenty, almost everyone who smokes eighteen cigarettes a day increases to twenty, and so on.) This effect is strongest among those persons who think they "should" quit but who doubt their ability to quit without help. For them — through a process of plausible but destructive logic — it seems that the best way to do what they think they want to do (to quit smoking) is to smoke more.

Among those who are nonsmokers, the effects are entirely negative. A considerable number of teenagers who were wavering between starting or not starting to smoke decide in favor of smoking — they can enjoy smoking now, and then give it up when they qualify for the reward.

After Five Years

When we think ahead five years, we note a final logical by-product of the program. Quitting the habit after five years of smoking a pack a day is generally more difficult than quitting sooner and after lesser levels of smoking. Many people who try to stop when the fifth year is ended find that the $10,000 is no longer a sufficient inducement, though it may have seemed to them a few years earlier that it should be. The rules of the program have made heavy smokers out of people who would have remained light smokers and thereby have induced a certain number of people not only to smoke more and longer until they became eligible for the $10,000 but to become impervious to the effects of the reward once they do become eligible.

What is the net outcome? If 90 percent of the population had been smoking for five years when the program began, we might still argue that the program would show a net reduction in smoking. But only about 15 percent of the adult population smokes a pack a day or more.* Let us estimate that a third of this number have been smoking at that rate for more than five years. If so, our plan has the potential for reducing smoking among five percent of the adult population and the potential for increasing smoking among 95 percent of the adult population. It is exceedingly difficult to attach numbers to the considerations we have just reviewed without coming to the conclusion that the program as specified would have the net effect of increasing both the number of cigarettes consumed and the number of smokers.

Back to Square One

When we reconsider the three parameters and try to select a combination that meets the challenge, the nature of their interdependence becomes clear. Suppose, for example, that we require a smoking history of at least ten years, and thereby, as intended, reduce the number of persons who are drawn into smoking just because of the reward. But such a step makes no difference in the calculations of those who have already been smoking more than five years (they are, in effect, operating under the logic of a five-year eligibility rule). Among those who have smoked less than five years, the change in the eligibility require-

---

*   *SAUS 81,* table 202.

ment has two counterproductive effects. First, persons who have smoked less than five years constitute a large proportion of smokers that the program should be reaching—younger, with more to gain from quitting. By extending the requirement to ten years, the program has been made irrelevant to many of them. For those who do think that far ahead, the effects will tend to be harmful, inducing a sense that there will be time to quit—and profit to be made—at a later point in their lives. Thus lengthening the eligibility period to ten years does not help; it makes matters worse.

As we ponder ways out of this bind, it becomes clear that the most dramatic reductions in smoking occur among persons who quit the soonest—a person who quits smoking at age sixty-five saves only a few years' worth of smoking, whereas a person who quits at twenty saves decades. Why not focus our efforts among the very young. Even granting the tendency of the award to encourage smoking so as to qualify, perhaps this will be more than counterbalanced by the very long periods of "savings" that will result from each success. So we target the program at youth (perhaps by installing an age-eligibility criterion—the specific method makes no difference). But the results are even more disastrous. The qualification criteria must be loose, because only a tiny fraction of the teenaged smokers we want to reach have had time to smoke very long. The result, when combined with a significant reward for quitting, is that the inducement effect is overpowering. Even teenagers who have no desire to smoke at all find it worth inculcating the habit for a year (or whatever our time limit is reduced to). Once started, only a proportion of those who smoked *only* because the program existed and who fully intended to quit are actually able to quit. The age effect backfires: While it is true that inducing a youngster to quit (who otherwise would not have quit) saves decades of smoking, it is equally true that inducing a youngster to start costs decades of smoking, and we produce far more of the latter than the former.

Laws of Social Programs

At first glance, the smoking example seems most apt for a certain type of social program, the one that seeks to change behavior from X to Y—what might be called "remedial" social programs. It seems less analogous, if not altogether irrelevant, to programs such as AFDC that simply provide an allowance without (through the allowance itself) trying to stimulate change. But in fact it applies to transfer programs of all types. In all cases, the transfer is legitimized by the recipient's being in a certain condition (whether smoking or poverty) that the government would prefer the recipient not be in. The burden of the smoking example is not that we failed to reduce smoking—to achieve the desired behavioral change—but that we increased the number of people who end up in the undesired condition. This charge applies to transfers in general.

The reasons why are not idiosyncratic. Let me suggest some characteristics we observed in the thought experiment that occur so widely and for such embedded reasons that they suggest laws. That is, no matter how ingenious the

[handwritten margin note: how about a program rewarding 20 & below who never smoked with never smoke $ a reward?]

design of a social transfer program may be, we cannot — in a free society — design programs that escape their influence. Together, they account for much of the impasse we observe in the anti-smoking example and point to some important principles for designing social programs that work.

1. *The Law of Imperfect Selection.* Any objective rule that defines eligibility for a social transfer program will irrationally exclude some persons.

It can always be demonstrated that some persons who are excluded from the Food Stamps program are in greater need than some persons who receive Food Stamps. It can always be demonstrated that someone who is technically ineligible for Medicaid really "ought" to be receiving it, given the intent of the legislation.

These inequities, which are observed everywhere, are not the fault of inept writers of eligibility rules, but an inescapable outcome of the task of rule-writing. Eligibility rules must convert the concept of "true need" into objectified elements. The rules constructed from these bits and pieces are necessarily subject to what Herbert Costner has called "epistemic error" — the inevitable gap between quantified measures and the concept they are intended to capture.* We have no way of defining "truly needy" precisely — not those who truly need to stop smoking, nor those truly in need of college scholarships or subsidized loans or disability insurance. Any criterion we specify will inevitably include a range of people, some of whom are unequivocally the people we intended to help, others of whom are less so, and still others of whom meet the letter of the eligibility requirement but are much less needy than some persons who do not.

Social welfare policy in earlier times tended to deal with this problem by erring in the direction of exclusion — better to deny help to some truly needy persons than to let a few slackers slip through. Such attitudes depended, however, on the assumption that the greater good was being served. Moral precepts had to be upheld. Whenever a person was inappropriately given help, it was bad for the recipient (undermining his character) and a bad example to the community at large.

When that assumption is weakened or dispensed with altogether, it follows naturally that the Law of Imperfect Selection leads to programs with constantly broadening target populations. If persons are not to blame for their plight, no real harm is done by giving them help they do not fully "need." No moral cost is incurred by permitting some undeserving into the program. A moral cost *is* incurred by excluding a deserving person. No one has a scalpel sharp enough to excise only the undeserving. Therefore it is not just a matter of political expedience to add a new layer to the eligible population rather than to subtract one (though that is often a factor in the actual decision-making process). It is also

---

*   Herbert Costner, "Theory, Deducation, and Rules of Correspondence," in Hubert M. Blalock, Jr., ed., *Casual Models in the Social Sciences* (Chicago: Aldine Atherton, 1971), 299-319.

the morally correct thing to do, given the premises of the argument.

2. *The Law of Unintended Rewards.* Any social transfer increases the net value of being in the condition that prompted the transfer.

A deficiency is observed — too little money, too little food, too little academic achievement — and a social transfer program tries to fill the gap — with a welfare payment, Food Stamps, a compensatory education program. An unwanted behavior is observed — drug addition, crime, unemployability — and the program tries to change that behavior to some other, better behavior — though a drug rehabilitation program, psychotherapy, vocational training. In each case, the program, however unintentionally, *must* be constructed in such a way that it increases the net value of being in the condition that it seeks to change — either by increasing the rewards or by reducing the penalties.

For some people in some circumstances, it is absurd to think in terms of "net value," because they so clearly have no choice at all about the fix they are in or because the net value is still less desirable than virtually any alternative. Paraplegics receiving Medicaid cannot easily be seen as "rewarded" for becoming paraplegics by the existence of free medical care. Poor children in Head Start cannot be seen as rewarded for being poor. Persons who are in the unwanted condition *completely involuntarily* are not affected by the existence of the reward.

But the number of such pure examples is very small. Let us return to the case of the middle-aged worker who loses his job, wants desperately to work, but can find nothing. He receives Unemployment Insurance, hating every penny of it. He would seem to be "completely involuntarily" in his situation and his search for a job unaffected by the existence of Unemployment Insurance. In fact, however, his behavior (unless he is peculiarly irrational) *is* affected by the existence of the Unemployment Insurance. For example, the cushion provided by Unemployment Insurance may lead him to refuse to take a job that requires him to move to another town, whereas he would take the job and uproot his home if he were more desperate. Most people (including me) are glad that his behavior is so affected, that he does not have to leave the home and friends of a lifetime, that he can wait for a job opening nearby. But he is not "completely involuntarily" unemployed in such a case, and the reason he is not is that the Unemployment Insurance has made the condition of unemployment more tolerable.

Our paraplegic anchors one end of the continuum labeled "Degree of Voluntarism in the Conditions that Social Policy Seeks to Change or Make Less Painful," and our unemployed worker is only slightly to one side of him — but he is to one side, not in the same place. The apparent unattractiveness of most of the conditions that social policy seeks to change must not obscure the continuum involved. No one chooses to be a paraplegic, and perhaps no one chooses to be a heroin addict. But the distinction remains: very few heroin addicts developed their addiction by being tied down and forcibly injected with heroin. They may not have chosen to become addicts, but they *did* choose initially to take heroin.

Let us consider the implications in terms of the archetypical social program for helping the chronic unemployed escape their condition, the job-training program.

Imagine that a program is begun that has the most basic and benign inducement of all, the chance to learn a marketable skill. It is open to everybody. By opening it to all, we have circumvented (for the time being) the Law of Unintended Rewards. All may obtain the training, no matter what their job history, so no unintended reward is being given for the condition of chronic unemployment.

On assessing the results, we observe that the ones who enter the program, stick with it, and learn a skill include very few of the hardcore unemployed whom we most wanted to help. The typical "success" stories from our training program are persons with a history of steady employment who wanted to upgrade their earning power. This is admirable. But what about the hardcore unemployed? A considerable number entered the program, but almost all of them dropped out or failed to get jobs once they left. Only a small proportion used the training opportunity as we had hoped. The problem of the hardcore unemployed remains essentially unchanged.

We may continue to circumvent the Law of Unintended Rewards. All we need do is continue the job-training program unchanged. It will still be there, still available to all who want to enroll, but we will do nothing to entice participation. Our theory (should we adopt this stance) is that, as time goes on, we will continue to help at least a few of the hardcore unemployed who are in effect skimmed from the top of the pool. We may even hope that the number skimmed from the top will be larger than the number who enter the pool, so that, given enough time, the population of hardcore unemployed will diminish. But this strategy is a gradualist one and relies on the assumption that other conditions in society are not creating more hardcore unemployed than the program is skimming off.

The alternative is to do something to get more of the hardcore unemployed into the program, and to improve the content so that more of them profit from the training. And once this alternative is taken, the program planner is caught in the trap of unintended rewards. Because we cannot "draft" people into the program or otherwise coerce their participation, our only alternative is to make it more attractive by changing the rules a bit.

Suppose, for example, we find that the reason many did not profit from the earlier program was that they got fired from (or quit) their new jobs within a few days of getting them, and that the reason they did so had to do with the job-readiness program. The ex-trainee was late getting to work, the boss complained, the ex-trainee reacted angrily and was fired. We observe this to be a common pattern. We know the problem is not that the ex-trainee is lazy or unmotivated, but that he has never been socialized into the discipline of the workplace. He needs more time, more help, more patience than other workers until he develops the needed work habits. Suppose that we try to compensate —

for example, by placing our trainees with employers who are being subsidized to hire such persons. The employer accepts lower productivity and other problems in return for a payment to do so (such plans have been tried frequently, with mixed results). Given identical work at identical pay, the ex-trainee is being rewarded for his "credential" of hardcore unemployment. He can get away with behavior that an ordinary worker cannot get away with.

May we still assume that the program is making progress in preparing its trainees for the real-world marketplace? Will the hardcore unemployed modify their unreliable behavior? What will be the effect on morale and self-esteem among those trainees who were succeeding in the program before the change of rules? It is tempting to conclude that the program has already ceased to function effectively for anyone anymore, that the change in rules has done more harm than good. But my proposition is for the moment a more restricted one: The reward for unproductive behavior (both past and present) now exists.

What of the case of a drug addict who is chronically unemployed because (let us assume) of the addiction? It might seem that the unintended reward in such a case is innocuous; it consists of measures to relieve the addict of his addiction, measures for which the nonaddict will have no need or use. If we were dealing with an involuntary disability—our paraplegic again—the argument would be valid. But in the case of drug addiction (or any other behavior that has its rewards), a painless cure generally increases the attractiveness of the behavior. Imagine, for example, a pill that instantly and painlessly relieved dependence on heroin, and the subsequent effects on heroin use.

Thus we are faced with the problem we observed in the thought experiment. The program that seeks to change behavior must offer an inducement that unavoidably either adds to the attraction of, or reduces the penalties of engaging in, the behavior in question. The best-known example in real life is the thirty-and-a-third rule for AFDC recipients. It becomes more advantageous financially to hold a job than not to hold a job (the intended inducement for AFDC recipients to work), but it also becomes more advantageous to be on AFDC (the unintended reward to nonrecipients).

We are now ready to tackle the question of when a social program can reasonably be expected to accomplish net good and when it can reasonably be expected to produce net harm. Again let us think in terms of a continuum. All social programs, I have argued, provide an unintended reward for being in the condition that the program is trying to change or make more tolerable. But some of these unintended rewards are so small that they are of little practical importance. Why then can we not simply bring a bit of care to the design of such programs, making sure that the unintended reward is *always* small? The reason we are not free to do so lies in the third law of social programs:

3. *The Law of Net Harm.* The less likely it is that the unwanted behavior will change voluntarily, the more likely it is that a program to induce change will cause net harm.

A social program that seeks to change behavior must do two things. It must induce participation by the persons who are to benefit, as described under the Law of Unintended Rewards. Then it must actually produce the desired change in behavior. It must succeed, and success depends crucially on one factor above all others: the price that the participant is willing to pay.

The more that the individual is willing to accept whatever needs to be done in order to achieve the desired state of affairs, the broader the discretion of the program designers. Thus, expensive health resorts can withhold food from their guests, hospitals can demand that their interns work inhuman schedules, and elite volunteer units in the armed forces can ask their trainees to take risks in training exercises that seem (to the rest of us) suicidal. Such programs need offer no inducement at all except the "thing in itself" that is the *raison d'être* of the program — a shapelier body, a career as a physician, membership in the elite military unit. Similarly, the drug addict who is prepared to sign over to a program a great deal of control over his own behavior may very well be successful — witness the sometimes impressive success rates of private treatment clinics.

The smaller the price that the participant is willing to pay, the greater the constraints on program design. It makes no difference to an official running a training program for the hardcore unemployed that (for example) the Marine Corps can instill exemplary work habits in recruits who come to the Corps no more "job-ready" than the recruits to the job-training program. If the training program tried for one day to use the techniques that the Marine Corps uses, it would lose its participants. Boot camp was not part of the bargain the job trainees struck with the government when they signed on. Instead, the training program must not only induce persons to join the program (which may be fairly easy). It must also induce them to stay in the program, induce them to cooperate with its curriculum, and induce them, finally to adopt major changes in outlook, habits, and assumptions. The program content must be almost entirely carrot.

There is nothing morally reprehensible in approaches that are constrained to use only positive inducements. The objections are practical.

First, it is guaranteed that success rates will be very low. The technology of changing human behavior depends heavily on the use of negative reinforcement in conjunction with positive reinforcement. The more deeply ingrained the behavior to be changed and the more attractions it holds for the person whose behavior is involved, the more important it is that the program have both a full tool kit available to it *and* the participant's willingness to go along with whatever is required. The Marine Corps has both these assets. Social programs to deal with the hardcore unemployed, teenaged mothers, delinquents, and addicts seldom do.

Second, as inducements become large — as they must, if the program is dealing with the most intractable problems — the more attractive they become to people who were not in need of help in the first place. We do not yet know how large they must finally become. We do know from experience, however, that quite generous experimental programs have provided extensive counseling, training, guaranteed jobs, and other supports—and failed.* We can only guess at what would be enough—perhaps a matter of years of full-time residential training, followed by guaranteed jobs at double or triple the minimum wage; we do not know. Whatever they are, however, consider their effects on the people not in the program. At this point, it appears that any program that would succeed in helping large numbers of the hardcore unemployed will make hardcore unemployment a highly desirable state to be in.

The conditions that combine to produce net harm are somewhat different in the theoretical and the practical cases, but they come to the same thing. Theoretically, any program that mounts an intervention with sufficient rewards to sustain participation and an effective result will generate so much of the unwanted behavior (in order become eligible for the program's rewards) that the net effect will be to increase the incidence of the unwanted behavior. In practice, the programs that deal with the most intractable behavior problems have included a package of rewards large enough to induce participation, but not large enough to produce the desired result.

My conclusion is that social programs in a democratic society tend to produce net harm in dealing with the most difficult problems. They will inherently tend to have enough of an inducement to produce bad behavior and not enough of a solution to stimulate good behavior; and the more difficult the problem, the more likely it is that this relationship will prevail. The lesson is not that we can do no good at all, but that we must pick our shots. ●

---

*   Probably the most extreme available example is the $82 million "Supported Work" summarized in Board of Directors, Manpower Demonstration Research Corporation. Its findings are summarized in Board of Directors, Manpower Demonstration Research Corporation, *Summary and Findings of the National Supported Work Demonstration* (Cambridge, Mass.: Ballinger, 1980). The hardcore unemployed who volunteered for the program were provided with intensive orientation *and* nonjob supports *and* a subsidized job (generally for twelve months). The evaluation claimed modest success (in terms of the cost-benefit ratio over the long term) for two of the groups, AFDC mothers and ex-addicts; it did not claim success for the other two groups (ex-offenders and youth). These results had to be based, unfortunately, on those persons who could still be found under the program. Despite intensive efforts by the evaluators to track down members of the samples, continuous follow-up information after eighteen months could be obtained for only 48 percent of the AFDC sample, 16 percent of the ex-addict sample, 28 percent of the ex-offender sample, and 35 percent of the youth sample (computed from table 3-1, 47). This raises the serious problem of what is called "sample attrition bias;" for example, it is highly unlikely that the 16 percent of the ex-addicts who could be found were representative of the sample as a whole in their job behavior. The report does not address this issue. The more salient point is that, even taking the conclusions at face value, the program, providing an unprecedented level of support, did not make a substantial dent in the behavior of the hardcore unemployed. We do not yet know what level of intervention would do the job. Even at the levels of support provided by the Supported Work program, the unintended reward is quite tangible and large. See Ken Auletta, *The Underclass* (New York: Random House, 1982), for an absorbing narrative account of the people and the program.

36. The Charity of the Uncharitable

Gordon Tullock

Leaving aside for a moment any further discussion of the empirical facts about redistribution, let us turn to what has been done in the way of more formal theory of redistribution in a democracy.* The first of these in point of time is the argument of Anthony Downs that democracy will always lead to transfer of income from the wealthy to the poor. Indeed, he regards this as a major justification of democracy. We may contrast this with Benjamin Ward's view that redistribution in democracy would be essentially indeterminate.** Finally, there is the view expressed in *The Calculus of Consent* (J. M. Buchanan and G. Tullock) that the nature of the voting process in democracy is such that real resources will be transferred away from the rich, although it is not specified who will receive them. It will surprise no one that I espouse the Buchanan and Tullock view, but the Ward model will be used to supplement it by indicating that the actual output of the political process is not predetermined.***

The essence of the difference between the Downs model and the Ward model is simply that Downs implicitly assumes that redistribution must take place along a one-dimensional continuum in which people are arranged from the poorest to the wealthiest. At first glance, there would seem to be no obvious reason why the bottom 51 percent of the population, using their majority to take

---

* This paper is entirely concerned with redistribution in democracies because this is the area where our knowledge of politics is best. I should not like to leave the implication that I am convinced that redistribution operates better in despotisms.

** Note that Ward actually demonstrates that there would be cyclical majority in all such cases. Since the process must stop, however, and in observed reality *does* stop at some point, the statement that he proved indeterminancy of the process is not an unjust summary.

*** The two models may be reconciled by use of the apparatus presented by G. Tullock, "A Simple Algebraic Logrolling Model," *Amer. Econ. Rev.*, June, 1970, *60*, 419-26.

Abridged from *The Western Economic Journal*, December, 1971, pp. 379-392, by permission of the Western Economic Association.

money from the wealthy, would be more likely than the top 51 percent using their majority to take money from the poor. Indeed, the 2 percent of the population lying at the middle line would be the determining factor in such a choice, and hence we might anticipate that money would come from both ends to the middle.

In practice, of course, the wealthy have more money, and hence can be subject to heavier taxes. Thus the cost of admitting a wealthy person into a coalition, which proposes to transfer money away from the 49 percent of the population not members, is higher than the cost of permitting the entry of a poor person.

If the dominant coalition is likely to be made up of the bottom 51 percent of the population, this tells us nothing very much about how that coalition will divide the spoils. Further, it is obvious that this coalition must contain a good many persons who are not poor by any ordinary definition. If we accept the bottom 10 percent of the population as poor, then they make up only 20 percent of this coalition of the bottom 51 percent. If we are more generous and count 20 percent of the population as poor, then they make up 40 percent. Clearly, this minority cannot dominate the coalition. If they received more per head than the other members of the coalition, they would do so because the lower middle class was generous.

Turning to formal bargaining theory, it is obvious that any transfer mechanism must provide at least as much for the top portion of those bottom 51 percent coalition as for anyone else in the coalition because if it does not, the 49 percent who are not members can very readily purchase the top 2 percent for a coalition that transfers a small amount from the top income groups to this small 2 percent group and to no one else. Indeed, such a coalition might take the entire transfer out of the bottom part of the population instead of out of the top. The reasoning so far would indicate that the people toward the top of the bottom 51 percent might receive much more than the people at the lower end. The only restriction on a delivery of the bulk of the resources transferred from the wealthy to the upper end of the bottom coalition (other than charitable instincts on the part of the members of the upper end) would seem to be the possibility that the wealthy would attempt a coalition with the very poor.

If we look at the real world, we do see some signs of such coalition attempts. Among those persons who argue that all transfers should be strictly limited to the very poor by way of a stringent means test, it is likely that wealthy persons predominate. This is, of course, sensible from even a selfish standpoint. They could arrange to give to the present-day poor considerably more money than the poor are now receiving, in return for a coalition in which transfers to people in the upper part of the bottom 51 percent are terminated, and make a neat profit. This particular coalition has so far foundered largely because of miscalculations by the poor. The poor realize that the interests of the wealthy are clearly not congruent with their interests, but they do not realize that the interests of people between the twentieth and the fifty-first percentile of the income distribution are also not identical with theirs. They therefore tend to favor a coalition with the second group rather than the former.

The situation is interesting, and we may pause briefly to examine it by way of a three-person model. Suppose we have wealthy Mr. *A*, middle-class Mr. *B*, and poor Mr. *C*. *B* and *C* form a coalition for the purpose of extracting money from Mr. *A*, and let us begin by assuming that their money is to be equally divided between them. Suppose, further, that Mr. *C*'s income is $1,000 per year before transfer, Mr. *B*'s is $2,000 per year, and Mr. *A*'s is $3,000 per year. Clearly, if the amount of transfer were somehow externally fixed at $500 but Mr. *A* were permitted to decide how it was to be allocated, he would give all of it to Mr. *C*.* He would reason that not until Mr. *C*'s income had risen to $2,000 per year was it sensible to supplement Mr. *B*'s income. Mr. *B* receives his payment simply because he wants it, not because there is any charitable motive involved on the part of anyone.

Under the circumstances, it is clear that Mr. *A* would be willing to enter into a coalition with Mr. *C* under which a transfer of $300 was made from *A* to *C* and none was made to *B*. This would be to the advantage of Mr. *C*, and it seems likely that only the generally bad information and low I.Q. and/or motivation which we observe among the poor prevents such coalitions. Indeed, it is possible the poor would do better if they depended entirely on the charitable motives of the wealthy. It might be that Mr. *A*, if left entirely to himself, would be willing to give Mr. *C* more than $250, although he objects to spending $500 for $250 apiece to *B* and *C*. Most persons, after all, are to some extent charitable and it may well be that the very poor would do better than at present if they depended on the charity of the wealthy.

For example, an organization of society in which all transfers were made by a special electorate composed of persons in the top 10 percent of the income stream who tax themselves for the purpose of benefiting other persons might lead to larger transfers to the genuinely poor than they now receive. Certainly, if we fixed the total amount of transfer away from the upper income groups at its present level but gave them complete discretion as to how it was to be spent, they would spend far more of it on the very poor.

So far, however, we have unrealistically assumed that transfers must be made between different income groups along a unidimensional continuum. If we look at the real world, we observe that the bulk of the transfers are made to groups

---

* Such a situation might be made available to taxpayers by allowing them to "earmark" on their income tax returns a portion of their tax for alternative transfer programs.

not defined by income. Farmers, college students, owners of oil wells, owners of private aircraft, older people regardless of their income, and, in all probability, the intellectual class are the major recipients of transfers, even though the bulk of the members of these groups are by no means poor.*

If we accept the real world situation as being one in which transfers are made to organized groups and these organized groups receive their transfers largely in terms of their political power (which seems to be a correct statement about the real world), there is no reason why we should anticipate that the poor would do particularly well. For one thing, they are hard to organize. Thus, the very large transfers that we do observe in the world are essentially demonstrations of the Ward Proof, supplemented by the Buchanan-Tullock logrolling process, which only rather accidentally benefit the bottom 10 to 15 percent of the population. For the reasons given above, we would anticipate that the top income groups would do rather badly from these transfers, and indeed they do. The Lampman study shows a transfer away from the upper income brackets of about 13 percent of their income. The beneficiaries of these transfers, however, we would anticipate would not be particularly concentrated among the poor and, indeed, granted their general political ineptness, one might expect that they would do rather badly, which is what we observe in the real world.

A somewhat cursory examination would seem to indicate that the actual percentage of income derived from wealthy people in democracies is an inverse function of the ease with which they can migrate. Very small countries, such as Switzerland, Sweden, and Luxembourg, make no serious effort to collect taxes on the wealthy which are even as large in percentage terms as those they collect from the rest of the population. Medium-sized countries, like England, Germany, France, and Italy, are in a better position for taxing the wealthy, and the United States is able to implement substantial *effective* progression in top income brackets. In no case, so far as I know, is the actual amount of progression in the taxes collected as high as the progression in the tax tables, but it is nevertheless real in the larger countries.

When we turn to expenditures, a quite different picture emerges. Any individual's vote is worth as much as any other individual's vote in getting expenditures. Indeed, the wealthy, well-informed person who is capable of making sizable campaign expenditures may well be able to receive a considerably larger portion of the total tax collections than is someone without these advantages.**

---

*   The inclusion of intellectuals is essentially a subjective guess, based on general knowledge. It seems to be likely that the principal beneficiaries of those changes in our society that originated with the New Deal have been the intellectuals who, through their control of both the educational process and the media, have been able to divert very large resources into their own pockets. So far as I know, however, there is no statistical evidence for or against this point of view.

**   B. Frey, "Why Do High Income People Participate More in Politics," *Public Choice*, Fall 1971, *11*, pp. 101-5.

If we subtract tax payments from receipts, we would anticipate some negative amount to turn up from a wealthy person and perhaps, although not certainly, a positive amount for the rest of the population. The reason the second sum is not necessarily positive is because of certain intrinsic inefficiencies in the transfer system. It is to be expected that expenditures that actually cost more than the net total benefit will be made.* Under the circumstances, it is possible that, although the rich are injured, the rest of the population make very small or negative profits.

Thus, to repeat, we would anticipate that in democracy there would be some transfer of money away from the wealthy, but there is no obvious reason that this transfer would go to the poor. If we look at the real world, we do find this pattern. This pattern is, however, a relatively minor part of the redistribution of income as seen in the modern state. Economists frequently point out that confiscation of *all* the income of the wealthy in a typical modern state would pay only a tiny part of the routine expenditures of the existing government. On the other hand, there can be no doubt whatsoever that massive redistributions of income do occur by way of the political process. These redistributions, however, are not in the main transfers of funds from the wealthy to the poor, but transfers of funds among the middle-class. The bulk of these transfers come from people who lie between the twentieth and the ninetieth percentile of income, and the bulk of them go to the same income classes. This is, of course, the area with the largest taxable capacity, and also the area where political power is concentrated in a democracy.

These transfers do not meet any egalitarian criteria. Basically they are transfers from groups of people who, for one reason or another, are not politically powerful to people who are. Always and everywhere in democracies, the farmers do very well. As a matter of practical fact, the United States probably wastes fewer resources in supporting its farm program than almost any other Western country. This may surprise Americans, accustomed to our massively inefficient method of transferring money to some people who are, on the whole, about as well-off as the people from whom the transfers come; but examination of what is done in the Common Market will convince them very quickly that Americans are fortunate in this respect.

The farm program is not the only example; the Social Security Administration transfers money from the young to the old, regardless of income. Indeed, in this particular case, the very poor are badly damaged by the institution. Due to the method in which the taxes to pay for Social Security are collected, the poor pay a very substantial part of their tiny wages to the Social Security Administration. If, however, they are very poor, i.e., require public assistance when they are old, then the local authorities will subtract their Social Security payment from the amount they receive. The result from their standpoint is that

---

*   W. A. Niskanen, *Bureaucracy and Representative Government*. Chicago 1971.

they pay taxes, but receive no net benefit. This must lead to a significant transfer of resources away from the very poor.

The urban renewal project is another obvious, even scandalous, example of the type of redistribution we observe, and another major example is, of course, the subsidized public education system. The latter is particularly obvious as a redistribution to the well-off at the university level. In general, students who can get into a university, particularly those who can get scholarships, have enough natural talent so that they enter the university with a lifetime income well above average. At the expense of the taxpayer, they are then given an even higher lifetime expected income. But even if we turn to lower-level schools, somewhat the same problem exists. To begin with, these are clearly transfers from those in society who do not have children to those who do — to say nothing, of course, of the transfer to the children themselves.

Secondly, however, it is fairly certain that the payoff to education, even at the elementary level, is greatly varying, depending on both the inherited genes and the home environment. Thus, the return in real terms to education is vastly higher to the person who both has the natural talent and the background to have a good income all his life than to the person whose natural talent and background are such that he probably will be poor. We would, if we were interested in relatively egalitarian measures, make direct payments to these two parties which could then be invested in a manner that would be most suitable in each case. By compelling the transfer to be taken in a form that is of maximum benefit to people who are going to be well-off anyway and of minimum benefit to people who are going to be poor, we make the average citizen richer and the poor poorer.

These examples are merely a small part of a wide universe. It is clear that in most democracies the poor receive relatively minor transfers — in any realistic sense — from society, although *not* zero transfers. Although very large amounts of money are redistributed by government action, the bulk of this redistribution is composed of transfers back and forth within the middle income brackets. It is obvious why these transfers occur. Obtaining such a transfer is a rational investment of resources, and people do put their resources into it. The only thing which is in any sense astonishing about this phenomenon is that it is so little noted. Almost all standard discussion of redistribution imply that it is normally from the rich to the poor. Some such redistribution does indeed go on, but it is a trivial phenomenon compared to the redistribution within the middle class. I find the concentration of discussion of redistribution upon the very minor phenomenon of redistribution from the wealthy to the poor and the general ignoring of the major phenomenon — redistribution back and forth within the middle income groups in terms of political organization — most remarkable.

This remarkable concentration on the minor part of this activity and ignoring of the major part requires, I feel, some explanation. Unfortunately, the only explanation I can offer is basically psychological. It will be outlined below, but

I should begin by apologizing to the reader for introducing a nonrigorous discussion of personal psychology, instead of something more satisfying.

We must begin by talking a little bit about a well-tested psychological phenomenon: "reduction of cognitive dissonance." It is well established that individuals' perception of the world is, to some extent, affected by a subconscious desire to reduce internal dissonance. Thus, an individual will, without any dishonesty, believe that certain activities which are in accord with motive A are also in accord with motive B, even if objectively they are not. The reason for this is that he does not wish to admit, even to himself, that he is disregarding motive B. Needless to say, this phenomenon occurs only when motive A and motive B would, in objective terms, lead to different actions and where the individual in fact regards motive A as more important than motive B.

Most of us have been trained in such a way that we are presented with a problem of this nature. All of us from the time we were small have been told that it is our duty to be charitable, to help the poor, and to do various other good acts. On the other hand, most of us have strong selfish drives. Clearly the injunction that if a man takes your coat, you should give him your cloak also, is not descriptive of the ordinary behavior of most human beings. It is, however, descriptive of what they say. Indeed, if we observe our colleagues in the university, we shall find that their expressed opinions are largely in accord with the ethically-given drive toward "loving thy neighbor" and "giving all you own to the poor." If we look at their actual behavior on the other hand, it turns out that they make few sacrifices for the poor.

It is clear, then, that they find these two drives — spending your own income yourself and helping the poor — in conflict, and that this should cause some internal tension. I should say, perhaps, that in my classes I commonly tell my students that if they really want to help the poor what they should do is get two jobs, work as hard as they possibly can, and then give all their income except that minimum amount that they need to stay alive to the inhabitants of India. They normally object to this pattern of behavior, but are normally not willing to admit that the reason they object is simply that they do not *really* feel that charitable.*

Indeed, if I ask my students or my faculty colleagues how much they personally give to the poor, it often turns out to be a small amount — in many cases zero. They very commonly explain their attitude by saying that they prefer governmental charitable activity. They seldom give any explanation as to why

---

*   I should say that in general the farther to the left the individual student, the more incoherent
he becomes in dealing with this particular problem. It is not that the people on the right are
willing to admit that they act selfishly, but simply that they are much less embarrassed by the
question than the members of the New Left. Being less embarrassed, they are less likely to
sputter.

they should use the government channel for this activity and, in particular, never turn to the perfectly genuine externality arguments that do exist for this purpose.* They sometimes allege, however, that it is more efficient for them to vote for charity that to make a charitable contribution themselves because this brings in other people's money, too.

Suppose that it is suggested that I give $100 to the poor. Suppose further that this proposal is in the form of two options. Option 1 is that I take $100 out of my pocket and give it to some charity. Option 2 is that we vote on whether I should be taxed $100 for the purpose of making this charitable payment. The cost to me of making the direct payment is $100. The cost to me of voting for the tax, however, is $100 discounted by my estimate of the influence my vote will have on the outcome. Granted the constituency is 100,000 or more, the discounted cost to me of voting for this special tax on myself is vanishingly small. Thus, if I feel just a little bit charitable, I would not make the $100 payment but I would vote for the tax. I would make this vote in full awareness of the fact that many other persons are also voting on the same issue and that my vote will make very little difference in the outcome. Thus the cost to me of casting my vote is small. Putting it differently, the act that I am called upon to perform in voting is very low cost, even though it refers to a $100 gift; the private gift is high cost. Under the circumstances, one would predict that I would be more likely to vote for charitable activity than to undertake it myself.

Here, also, our phenomenon of reduction of cognitive dissonance comes in. If I am possessed both of selfish desires to spend my own money and a feeling that I must be charitable, I am wise to vote charitably and act selfishly. I should also tend, in discussion, to put much greater weight upon the importance of my vote than is actually justified, and to resent people who tell me that the vote makes almost no difference. At this point, the rationale for the ethical rule that private charity is bad and that all redistribution should be public becomes apparent. It provides a rationalization for "ethical" behavior in urging government redistribution while actually making almost no sacrifice. It permits one to have the best of both worlds.

Some further implications can be drawn from this phenomenon. As the size of the constituency in which I am voting increases, the likelihood that my vote will have any effect on the outcome decreases. Consider my paying $100 to charity, voting on a tax of $100 to be levied on me by my local government for charitable purposes, voting on a similar tax for similar purposes for the state government, and finally voting on a similar tax for similar purposes by the national government. Clearly, the cost to me is monotonically decreasing through this set. I would be more likely to vote for the tax by the national government than for the state government, for the tax by the state government than for

---

*   For a statement of these reasons by a man who cannot possibly be accused of socialism, see
    Milton Friedman, *Capitalism and Freedom*. Chicago 1962.

the local government, and more likely to vote for the tax by the local government than to make the direct payment myself. It is quite possible that this phenomenon explains the tendency to transfer charitable activity from local governments toward the national government. Looked at from the standpoint of the voter, he can obtain the satisfaction of "behaving charitably" in a national election much cheaper than he can in the local election. ●

37. Inequalities Arising from the Nature of the Employments Themselves

Adam Smith

The whole of the advantages and disadvantages of the different employments of labour and stock must, in the same neighbourhood, be either perfectly equal or continually tending to equality. If in the same neighbourhood, there was any employment evidently either more or less advantageous than the rest, so many people would crowd into it in the one case, and so many would desert it in the other, that its advantages would soon return to the level of other employments. This at least would be the case in a society where things were left to follow their natural course, where there was perfect liberty, and where every man was perfectly free both to chuse what occupation he thought proper, and to change it as often as he thought proper. Every man's interest would prompt him to seek the advantageous, and to shun the disadvantageous employment.

The five following are the principal circumstances which, so far as I have been able to observe, make up for a small pecuniary gain in some employments, and counter-balance a great one in others: first, the agreeableness or disagreeableness of the employments themselves; secondly, the easiness and cheapness, or the difficulty and expense of learning them; thirdly, the constancy or inconstancy of employment in them; fourthly, the small or great trust which must be reposed in those who exercise them; and fifthly, the probability or improbability of success in them.

First, The wages of labour vary with the ease or hardship, the cleanliness or dirtiness, the honourableness or dishonourableness of the employment. Thus in most places, take the year round, a journeyman taylor earns less than a journeyman weaver. His work is much easier. A journeyman weaver earns less than a journeyman smith. His work is not always easier, but it is much cleanlier. A

Abridged from *The Wealth of Nations*, Modern Library Edition (New York: Random House, 1937), pp. 99-110.

journeyman blacksmith, though an artificer, seldom earns so much in twelve hours as a collier, who is only a labourer, does in eight. His work is not quite so dirty, is less dangerous and is carried on in day-light, and above ground. Honour makes a great part of the reward of all honourable professions. In point of pecuniary gain, all things considered, they are generally under-recompensed, as I shall endeavour to show by and by. Disgrace has the contrary effect. The trade of a butcher is a brutal and an odious business; but it is in most places more profitable than the greater part of common trades. The most detestable of all employments, that of public executioner, is, in proportion to the quantity of work done, better paid than any common trade whatever.

Hunting and fishing, the most important employments of mankind in the rude state of society, become in its advanced state their most agreeable amusements, and they pursue for pleasure what they once followed from necessity. In the advanced state of society, therefore, they are all very poor people who follow as a trade, what other people pursue as a pastime. Fishermen have been so since the time of Theocritus. A poacher is every-where a very poor man in Great Britain. In countries where the rigour of the law suffers no poachers, the licensed hunter is not in a much better condition. The natural taste for those employments makes more people follow them than can live comfortably by them, and the produce of their labour, in proportion to its quantity, comes always too cheap to market to afford anything but the most scanty subsistence to the labourers.

Disagreeableness and disgrace affect the profits of stock in the same manner as the wages of labour. The keeper of an inn or tavern, who is never master of his own house, and who is exposed to the brutality of every drunkard, exercises neither a very agreeable nor a very credible business. But there is scarce any common trade in which a small stock yields so great a profit.

Secondly, The wages of labour vary with the easiness and cheapness, or the difficulty and expence of learning the business.

When any expensive machine is erected, the extraordinary work to be performed by it before it is worn out, it must be expected will replace the capital laid out upon it, with at least the ordinary profits. A man educated at the expence of much labour and time to any of those employments which require extraordinary dexterity and skill, may be compared to one of those expensive machines. The work which he learns to perform, it must be expected, over and above the usual wages of common labour, will replace to him the whole expence of his education, with at least the ordinary profits of an equally valuable capital. It must do this too in a reasonable time, regard being had to the very uncertain duration of human life, in the same manner as to the more certain duration of the machine.

The difference between the wages of skilled labour and those of common labour, is founded upon this principle.

Thirdly, The wages of labour in different occupations vary with the constancy or inconstancy of employment.

Employment is much more constant in some trades than in others. In the greater part of manufacturers, a journeyman may be pretty sure of employment almost every day in the year that he is able to work. A mason or bricklayer, on the contrary, can work neither in hard frost nor in foul weather, and his employment at all other times depends upon the occasional calls of his customers. He is liable, in consequence, to be frequently without any. What he earns, therefore, while he is employed, must not only maintain him while he is idle, but make him some compensation for those anxious and desponding moments which the thought of so precarious a situation must sometimes occasion. Where the computed earnings of the greater part of manufacturers, accordingly, are nearly upon a level with the day wages of common labourers, those of masons and bricklayers are generally from one half more to double those wages. Where common labourers earn four and five shillings a week, masons and bricklayers frequently earn seven and eight; where the former earn six, the latter often earn nine and ten, and where the former earn nine and ten, as in London, the latter commonly earn fifteen and eighteen. No species of skilled labour, however, seems more easy to learn than that of masons and bricklayers. Chairmen in London, during the summer season, are said sometimes to be employed as bricklayers. The high wages of those workmen, therefore, are not so much the recompence of their skill, as the compensation for the inconstancy of their employment

A house carpenter seems to exercise rather a nicer and more ingenious trade than a mason. In most places, however, for it is not universally so, his day-wages are somewhat lower. His employment, though it depends much, does not depend so entirely upon the occasional calls of his customers; and it is not liable to be interrupted by the weather.

When the trades which generally afford constant employment, happen in a particular place not to do so, the wages of the workmen always rise a good deal above their ordinary proportion to those of common labour. In London almost all journeymen artificers are liable to be called upon and dismissed by their masters from day to day, and from week to week, in the same manner as day-labourers in other places. The lowest order of artificers, journeymen taylors, accordingly, earn their half a crown a day, though eighteen pence may be reckoned the wages of common labour. In small towns and country villages, the wages of journeymen taylors frequently scarce equal those of common labour; but in London they are often many weeks without employment, particularly during the summer.

When the inconstancy of employment is combined with the hardship, disagreeableness, and dirtiness of the work, it sometimes raises the wages of the most common labour above those of the most skilful artificers. A collier working by the piece is supposed, at Newcastle, to earn commonly about double, and in many parts of Scotland about three times the wages of common labour. His high wages arise altogether from the hardship, disagreeableness, and dirtiness of his work. His employment may, upon most occasions, be as constant as he pleases. The coal-heavers in London exercise a trade which in hardship, dirtiness, and disagreeableness, almost equals that of colliers; and from the unavoidable irregularity in the arrivals of coal-ships, the employment of the greater part of them is necessarily very inconstant. If colliers, therefore, commonly earn double and triple the wages of common labour, it ought not to seem unreasonable that coal-heavers should sometimes earn four and five times those wages. In the enquiry made into their condition a few years ago, it was found that at the rate at which they were then paid, they could earn from six to ten shillings a day. Six shillings are about four times the wages of common labour in London, and in every particular trade, the lowest common earnings may always be considered as those of the far greater number. How extravagant soever those earnings may appear, if they were more than sufficient to compensate all the disagreeable circumstances of the business, there would soon be so great a number of competitors as, in a trade which has no exclusive privilege, would quickly reduce them to a lower rate.

Fourthly, The wages of labour vary according to the small or great trust which must be reposed in the workmen.

The wages of goldsmiths and jewellers are every-where superior to those of many other workmen, not only of equal, but of much superior ingenuity; on account of the precious materials with which they are intrusted.

We trust our health to the physician; our fortune and sometimes our life and reputation to the lawyer and attorney. Such confidence could not safely be reposed in people of a very mean or low condition. Their reward must be such, therefore, as may give them that rank in the society which so important a trust requires. The long time and the great expence which must be laid out in their education, when combined with this circumstance, necessarily enhance still further the price of their labour.

Fifthly, The wages of labour in different employments vary according to the probability or improbability of success in them.

The probability that any particular person shall ever be qualified for the employment to which he is educated, is very different in different occupations. In the greater part of mechanic trades, success is almost certain; but very uncertain in the liberal professions. Put your son apprentice to a shoemaker, there is little doubt of his learning to make a pair of shoes: But send him to study the law, it is at least twenty to one if ever he makes such proficiency as will enable him to live by the business. In a perfectly fair lottery, those who draw the prizes ought to gain all that is lost by those who draw the blanks. In a profession where twenty fail for one that succeeds, that one ought to gain all that should have been gained by the unsuccessful twenty. The counsellor at law who, perhaps, at near forty years of age, begins to make something by his profession, ought to receive the retribution, not only of his own so tedious and expensive education, but of that of more than twenty others who are never likely to make any thing by it. How extravagant soever the fees of counsellors at law may sometimes appear, their real retribution is never equal to this. Compute in any particular place, what is likely to be annually gained, and what is likely to be annually spent, by all the different workmen in any common trade, such as that of shoemakers or weavers, and you will find that the former sum will generally exceed the latter. But make the same computation with regard to all the counsellors and students of law, in all the different inns of court, and you will find that their annual gains bear but a very small proportion to their annual expence, even though you rate the former as high, and the latter as low, as can well be done. The lottery of the law, therefore, is very far from being a perfectly fair lottery; and that, as well as many other liberal and honourable professions, is, in point of pecuniary gain, evidently under-recompenced.

Those professions keep their level, however, with other occupations, and, notwithstanding these discouragements, all the most generous and liberal spirits are eager to crowd into them. Two different causes contribute to recommend them. First, the desire of the reputation which attends up in superior excellence in any of them; and, secondly, the natural confidence which every man has more or less, not only in his own abilities, but in his own good fortune.

To excel in any profession, in which but few arrive at mediocrity, is the most decisive mark of what is called genius or superior talents. The public admiration which attends upon such distinguished abilities, makes always a part of their reward; a greater or smaller in proportion as it is higher or lower in degree. It makes a considerable part of that reward in the profession of physic; a still greater perhaps in that of law; in poetry and philosophy it makes almost the whole.

There are some very agreeable and beautiful talents of which the possession commands a certain sort of admiration; but of which the exercise for the sake of gain is considered, whether from reason or prejudice, as a sort of public prostitution. The pecuniary recompence, therefore, of those who exercise them in this manner, must be sufficient, not only to pay for the time, labour, and expence of acquiring the talents, but for the discredit which attends the employment of them as the means of subsistence. The exorbitant rewards of players, opera-singers, opera-dancers, &c. are founded upon those two principles; the rarity and beauty of the talents, and the discredit of employing them in this manner. It seems absurd at first sight that we should despise their persons, and yet reward their talents with the most profuse liberality. While we do the one, however, we must of necessity do the other. Should the public opinion or prejudice ever alter with regard to such occupations, their pecuniary recompence would quickly diminish. More people would apply to them, and the competition would quickly reduce the price of their labour. Such talents, though far from being common, are by no means so rare as is imagined. Many people possess them in great perfection, who disdain to make this use of them; and many more are capable of acquiring them, if any thing could be made honourably by them.

The over-weening conceit which the greater part of men have of their own abilities, is an ancient evil remarked by the philosophers and moralists of all ages. Their absurd presumption in their own good fortune, has been less taken notice of. It is, however, if possible, still more universal. There is no man living who, when in tolerable health and spirits, has not some share of it. The chance of gain is by every man more or less over-valued, and the chance of loss is by most men under-valued, and by scarce any man, who is in tolerable health and spirits, valued more than it is worth.

That the chance of gain is naturally over-valued, we may learn from the universal success of lotteries. The world neither ever saw, nor will ever see, a perfectly fair lottery; or one in which the whole gain compensated the whole loss; because the undertaker could make nothing by it. In the state lotteries the tickets are really not worth the price which is paid by the original subscribers, and yet commonly sell in the market for twenty, thirty, and sometimes forty per-cent advance. The vain hope of gaining some of the great prizes is the sole cause of this demand. The soberest people scarce look upon it as a folly to pay a small sum for the chance of gaining ten or twenty thousand pounds; though they know that even that small sum is perhaps twenty or thirty per cent, more than the chance is worth. In a lottery in which no prize exceeded twenty pounds, though in other respects it approached much nearer to a perfectly fair one than the common state lotteries, there would not be the same demand for tickets. In order to have a better chance for some of the great prizes, some people pur-chase several tickets, and others, small shares in a still greater number. There is not, however, a more certain proposition in mathematics, than that the more tickets you adventure upon, the more likely you are to be a loser. Adventure upon all the tickets in the lottery, and you lose for certain; and the greater the number of your tickets the nearer you approach to this certainty.

That the chance of loss is frequently undervalued, and scarce ever valued more than it is worth, we may learn from the very moderate profit of insurers. In order to make insurance, either from fire or sea-risk, a trade at all, the com-mon premium must be sufficient to compensate the common losses, to pay the expence of management, and to afford such a profit as might have been drawn from an equal capital employed in any common trade. The person who pays no more than this, evidently pays no more than the real value of the risk, or the lowest price at which he can reasonably expect to insure it. But though many people have made a little money by insurance, very few have made a great for-tune; and from this consideration alone, it seems evident enough, that the ordi-nary balance of profit and loss is not more advantageous in this, than in other common trades by which so many people make fortunes. Moderate, however, as the premium of insurance commonly is, many people despise the risk too much to care to pay it. Taking the whole kingdom at an average, nineteen houses in twenty, or rather perhaps, ninety-nine in a hundred, are not insured from fire. Sea risk is more alarming to the greater part of people, and the proportion of ships insured to those not insured is much greater. Many sail, however, at all seasons, and even in time of war, without any insurance. This may sometimes perhaps be done without any imprudence. When a great company, or even a great merchant, has twenty or thirty ships at sea, they may, as it were, insure one another. The premium saved upon them all, may more than compensate such losses as they are likely to meet with in the common course of chances. The neglect of insurance upon shipping, however, in the same manner as upon houses, is, in most cases, the effect of no such nice calculation, but of mere thoughtless rashness and presumptuous contempt of the risk.

The contempt of risk and the presumptuous hope of success, are in no period of life more active than at the age at which young people chuse their professions. How little the fear of misfortune is then capable of balancing the hope of good luck, appears still more evidently in the readiness of the common people to enlist as soldiers, or to go to sea, than in the eagerness of those of better fashion to enter into what are called the liberal professions.

What a common soldier may lose is obvious enough. Without regarding the danger, however, young volunteers never enlist so readily as at the beginning of a new war; and though they have scarce any chance of preferment, they figure to themselves, in their youthful fancies, a thousand occasions of acquiring honour and distinction which never occur. These romantic hopes make the whole price of their blood. Their pay is less than that of common labourers, and in actual service their fatigues are much greater.

The lottery of the sea is not altogether so disadvantageous as that of the army. The son of a creditable labourer or artificer may frequently go to sea with his father's consent; but if he enlists as a soldier, it is always without it. Other people see some chance of his making something by the one trade: nobody but himself sees any of his making any thing by the other. The great admiral is less the object of public admiration than the great general, and the highest success in the sea service promises a less brilliant fortune and reputation than equal success in the land. The same difference runs through all the inferior degrees of preferment in both. By the rules of precedency a captain in the navy ranks with a colonel in the army: but he does not rank with him in the common estimation. As the great prizes in the lottery are less, the smaller ones must be more numerous. Common sailors, therefore, more frequently get some fortune and preferment than common soldiers; and the hope of those prizes is what principally recommends the trade. Though their skill and dexterity are much superior to that of almost any artificers, and though their whole life is one continual scene of hardship and danger, yet for all this dexterity and skill, for all those hardships and dangers, while they remain in the condition of common sailors, they receive scarce any other recompence but the pleasure of exercising the one and or surmounting the other. Their wages are not greater than those of common labourers at the port which regulates the rate of seamen's wages. As they are continually going from port to port, the monthly pay of those who sail from all the different ports of Great Britain, is more nearly upon a level than that of any other workmen in those different places; and the rate of the port to and from which the greatest number sail, that is the port of London, regulates that of all the rest. At London the wages of the greater part of the different classes of workmen are about double those of the same classes at Edinburgh. But the sailors who sail from the port of London seldom earn above three or four shillings a month more than those who sail from the port of Leith, and the difference is frequently not so great. In time of peace, and in the merchant service, the London price is from a guinea to about seven-and-twenty shillings the calendar month. A common labourer in London, at the rate of nine or ten shillings a week, may earn in the calendar month from forty to five-and-forty shillings. The sailor, indeed, over and above his pay, is supplied with provisions. Their value, however, may not perhaps always exceed the difference between his pay and that of the common labourer; and though it sometimes should, the excess will not be clear gain to the sailor, because he cannot share it with his wife and family, whom he must maintain out of his wages at home.

The dangers and hair-breadth escapes of a life of adventures, instead of disheartening young people, seem frequently to recommend a trade to them. A tender mother, among the inferior ranks of people, is often afraid to send her son to school at a sea-port town, lest the sight of the ships and the conversation and adventures of the sailors should entice him to go to sea. The distant prospect of hazards, from which we can hope to extricate ourselves by courage and address, is not disagreeable to us, and does not raise the wages of labour in any employment. It is otherwise with those in which courage and address can be of no avail. In trades which are known to be very unwholesome, the wages of labour are always remarkably high. Unwholesomeness is a species of disagreeableness, and its effects upon the wages of labour are to be ranked under that general head. ●

Section EIGHT

International Trade

To produce the wine in Portugal might require only the labour of 80 men for one year, and to produce the cloth in the same country might require the labour of 90 men for the same time. It would therefore be advantageous for her to export wine in exchange for cloth. This exchange might even take place notwithstanding that the commodity imported by Portugal could be produced there with less labour than in England.

David Ricardo

The law of comparative advantage, developed in the early 1800s by the great economist David Ricardo (1772–1823), states that there are gains from trade even when one participant in the trade is absolutely more efficient in producing all goods — as long as there are relative differences in the opportunity costs of production. Since relative differences in production costs surely exist between exchanging parties, Ricardo was able to rigorously show the benefits that accrue to all participants in the trading process. This view was in direct contrast to the mercantilist belief that there are winners and losers in a trade and one party inevitably bests another.

A corollary to the Ricardian view that trade is naturally good and to be encouraged is that barriers to free trade such as tariffs, quotas, and other regulations should be eliminated. Unlike the mercantilist view that suggested a nation state needs to be protected from harmful trade, classical liberals such as Ricardo, David Hume, Adam Smith, and others felt free trade would result in the greatest good for all.

The benefits of free trade are readily acknowledged for trade that occurs within a nation. Indeed, the success of the U.S. Constitution as compared to the earlier Articles of Confederation was in large part due to the Constitution's adherence to free trade principles that broke down government-imposed trade barriers between states. Yet, while free trade among exchanging parties within a nation is a right generally protected by a nation's laws, free trade among nations rarely exists.

The divergence in policy regarding inter and intra nation trade policies seems even more puzzling in light of the great abundance of economic analysis from Ricardo to the present that in the main shows clear and significant gains from free trade among nations. This difference between mainstream economic and political policy forms the grist of most of the articles in this section.

The authors in this section argue that barriers to free trade represent another attempt on the part of special interest groups to evade competitive market pressures. By limiting the number of market participants through the use of trade barriers officially sanctioned by law, these special interest groups stand to benefit at the expense of the larger community. But since the benefits are concentrated on a few while the greater costs are spread thinly among many, the political clout of the few is often telling.

James Doti introduces this section with an anecdote about a grandmother who finds her niche without benefit of protective trade policies. Marc Levinson follows with a persuasive rebuttal of the common view that "dumping" cheap foreign products on local markets hurts U.S. commerce.

In a second selection included in this book from their powerful *Free to Choose*, Milton and Rose Friedman present a compelling analysis of the economic and political arguments for free international trade.

The French economist, Frédéric Bastiat (1801–50), follows with his famous satire, the "Candlemakers' Petition." This satirical petition which represents a classic example of Bastiat's skill as a writer and popularisor of economic theories pushes the arguments in favor of tariffs to the extreme in order to vividly show the vacuous nature of those arguments.

Unlike Bastiat who espoused a rather dogmatic and unrelenting belief in the doctrine of *laissez-faire*, Adam Smith's broadmindedness would often lead him to veer from "gospel." This characteristic is exemplified by the Smith piece included in this section that outlines the cases in which it may be desirable to place restrictions on international trade.

David Ricardo, the son of a Sephardic Jewish family, was disinherited after marrying the daughter of a Quaker family and changing his religion from Orthodox Judaism to Unitarianism. He overcame his disinherited status by becoming a stockbroker and banker and was so successful in these pursuits that he probably became the wealthiest economist who ever lived. Retiring from business at the age of 30, he spent the rest of his life studying and writing in the field of political economy. As an ardent follower and intellectual descendant of Adam Smith, Ricardo made many significant contributions to economic thought. But his most valuable and lasting contribution to economics surely was his original and important discovery of the law of comparative advantage. This law was the genesis of economists' fervent belief in free trade — a belief that continues to this day. In addition, the law of comparative advantage represents a formidable buttress in arguments espousing the efficacy of the market system. While all students of economics learn about the law of comparative advantage, this reading gives one the opportunity to read it in the original.

Perhaps it is fitting to include in this book of readings with another essay by Frédéric Bastiat. This great writer of the 19th Century brought the credo of laissez-faire to the people. His original and inventive prose remains biting to this day. In this concluding piece, Bastiat vividly identifies the gainers and losers of protectionist trade policies. ●

38. Ravioli and the Economics of Trade

James L. Doti

Memories are formed more by discontinuities than continuities in our lives. Because of this, I think, the only Christmas I remember well is a Christmas celebrated away from home, a Christmas spent in Little Italy, a Christmas memory whose edges take on more clarity over the passage of time.

December 24, 1955 — Christmas Eve Day

My dog Blackie and I look out of a frosted window that separates the crisp Chicago winter morning from the comforting warmth of Grandma's flat. My parents, brothers, aunts, uncles, and cousins will join us tomorrow for a traditional family Christmas celebration, but for now my dog and I are here to keep Grandma company. I don't mind since Grandma and I are tight — a special closeness that comes more easily when one is the youngest of a hoard of grandchildren.

Her wizened face is dark, almost swarthy. She wears spectacles with thin silver rims and all manner of long, old-fashioned dresses with shawls, usually black. Her diminutiveness emphasizes the kindly countenance of her face. Many years of dough-kneading have given her strong muscles, but she is old now and often short of breath.

She speaks with a thick, Italian accent and I with a speech impediment that renders my English barely intelligible. Yet, we have no problem communicating; our communicating does not necessarily require the spoken word. We work with silent efficiency in packing the last of the ravioli that we will bring to market. As I gather the now-dried ravioli which are spread throughout the flat, I savor the rich and sweet aroma of fresh basil.

A chilled wind hits our faces as we pack the last cartons of ravioli on the two decrepit *Red Flyer* wagons we use for transport. But Grandma has bundled me

Reprinted from *The Freeman*, December, 1986, pp. 444-449, by permission of The Foundation for Economic Education.

up, and I am dressed in galoshes, so except for my face which feels the harsh wind, the rest of me is sweaty and uncomfortably hot.

We pull our wagons past Laflin Street and Ashland Blvd., and we make it to Halsted Avenue which will lead us to our destination — South Water Market. Tall buildings and narrow alleys cut sharp angles and make deep shadows. The vibrant and festive street life which envelopes the area during summer months is absent now. Table-top Christmas trees seen in several sooty windows and cheap Woolworth's Christmas wreaths hanging on heavily painted sea grey-green doors fail dismally in conveying any Christmas cheer. Perhaps because the neighborhood is unfamiliar but perhaps too because of its lifelessness, my dog, in contrast to his usual bounding ways, trails closely behind me, tail low. As our expeditionary force of three makes slow and steady progress towards our destination, I fantasize I am Captain Scott heading towards the South Pole.

When we arrive, our hopes are dashed in much the same way I suspect Captain Scott's were when he found that the Norwegian interloper, Roald Amundsen, had beaten him. No one occupies the office Grandma usually frequents. We wander through various warehouses and loading bays trailing our wagons and wondering why we are alone. Finally, a familiar face is found, a gruff man with an inflated sense of self-importance who is accustomed to beshawled old ladies with thick accents and *Red Flyer* wagons. Hardly looking up from a newspaper he is reading, he exposes prodigious gaps in his cigar-stained teeth when he tells Grandma, "We ain't buyin' anymore raviolese from youse ladies. We're importin' em in frozen from Italy. We can get 'em a lot cheaper dat way." Grandma's protestations fall on deaf ears. The man whose jawline had long ago disappeared into one of his chins rises from his chair while making a lifting gesture with both arms and says, "Listen lady, I gotta make a living too."

As we leave the building with our still heavily-laden wagons we encounter a bitter wind laced with sleet. Sleet, a cruel mixture of snow and icy rain, stings our faces as we head home. We are preoccupied with our disappointment when a bus veers toward us and comes to a screeching halt just by the curb where we stand. The shrill sound of brakes and a fountain of slush sprayed by the huge wheels paralyzes my grandma and me, but Blackie bolts. I turn and see him rounding a corner at breakneck speed. We desperately follow but lose sight of him.

Lost! Lost! My dog Blackie is lost.

Tears mingle with the sleet on my face as we venture further into an unknown neighborhood. Grandma pleads with me to abandon the search, but I don't give up until she bodily drags me off. Even though I know down deep that Blackie must be hopelessly lost, I fight, scream, and cry. It is only when I see the look on Grandma's face that I realize we too are lost. My attention now turns from dog-saving to people-saving.

As dusk settles upon us the cold turns colder and the sleet turns icier. Like captain Scott and his men on their ill-fated trip back to base camp, our movement is painfully slow and misdirected as we trudge in circles over previously covered ground. Several children, seemingly oblivious to the cold, throw snowballs at each other in a dangerously boisterous way. Grandma is too proud to ask anyone for directions. When I, risking the ridicule that usually accompanies my speech, do ask and get us back on track, I feel for the first time in my life the exuberance that comes when one sheds the weakness of youth and assumes some measure of responsibility and control. I fantasize that my decision to ask a stranger for directions is one of life-saving importance and is a heroic act that is witnessed, cheered, and applauded by many.

It is not long before we see the familiar spires of Our Lady of Pompeii Church. As we enter the sturdy and old church where my parents were married and my oldest brother was baptized, the redolence of incense and burning candles invades our senses. The church feels peopled and full. Sisters of Mercy in their glory bustle down marble aisles while arranging alter cloths and poinsettia plants. The delicious warmth of the church comforts us. Grandma prays for economic survival; I pray for Blackie's survival. Before we leave, Grandma fumbles in her purse and gives me a few coins to leave in the poor box.

A block from home, we give the unsold and now surplus ravioli to Miss Amberg, the beloved director of Madonna Center, the settlement house where my parents first met. As we pull our now empty wagons over that last block, our slow and spiritless walk conveys Grandma's woe at failing in the marketplace, my woe at losing a dog. In contrast to the quick movements down the steps when we loaded the wagons, Grandma now negotiates the steps with resigned fatigue as she brings both of her high-laced shoes together on each level before proceeding to the next step.

At the doorway, a scratching sound from within the flat is heard. Blackie! He jumps and slobbers on me when we open the door. A note is on the kitchen table.

Dear Ma,

When we came to bring you your Christmas present, we found Blackie yapping to get inside. The Christmas present in the back room is from all of us. See you tomorrow.

Your Loving Children

In the back room, an enclosed porch that serves as Grandma's knitting room, rests a state-of-the-art swivel model mahogany RCA Victor black and white 21-inch television set wrapped in a large red bow.

Later that evening while watching the Christmas episode of *The Honeymooners* on the new RCA set, I stuff pretzel-shaped biscotti in my mouth and wash it all down with cream soda. Blackie snuggles near me beside a clanging radiator.

Grandma looks outside. She hears carollers below the window from Madonna Center singing songs of Christmas celebration, celebrating her and her ravioli. She smiles a distant smile, but her eyes do not reflect contentment; they reflect apprehension. With that special sense of knowing that children sometimes feel but do not fully understand, I see a troubled woman, a woman oblivious to the joyful presence of Blackie, the RCA console, the biscotti, the cream soda, and the carollers' songs of celebration.

She has no real monetary worries to speak of. Her children are all financially well-off and will gladly provide for her. But she is a fiercely independent woman. It is an independence that she may have been born with but more likely developed in the hard and brutal struggle it takes to leave one's native land, one's relatives, and one's traditions in order to emigrate to a new and strange land.

It was an emigration that allowed her to take her only possessions—her children and her values: respecting others and taking pride in one's work. She would use these values in a free land not merely to survive but to help her and her family live a fuller and more spirited life. They were strong values that she imbued in her children and her children's children.

But now she looked out the window with apprehension. A heartless process in this free land, a process she did not understand, had taken away her sole means of independence and dealt her a cruel blow. She failed in the marketplace and with a fierce sense of price, this was something she could not accept.

● ● ●

The solution to my grandmother's difficulty would be simple today: form a strong political action committee and lobby for a stiff tariff on Italian ravioli. If such a course of action seems improbable consider the fact that the National Pasta Association (NPA) recently convinced the White House to slap a stiff retaliatory tariff of 40 percent on European pasta without egg and a 25 percent tariff on pasta with egg. The retaliation was aimed at the European Economic Community (EEC) for a tariff it had imposed not on U. S. pasta but on U.S. citrus products. Evidently, the EEC was convinced by the European citrus industry that it needed protection.

Meanwhile, the NPA is lobbying to protect its tariff. Corby Kummer, in *The Atlantic Monthly* states:

As soon as the tariff went into effect, it (NPA) mailed promotional literature (accompanied by packages of domestic pasta) to congressmen telling them to remember that American pasta must be protected. Before the tariff was imposed, the NPA predicted that, unchecked, Italian pasta could claim a 20 percent market share by 1988 to 1989—something extremely unlikely, given that it had only a 4.5 percent market share at the time. *

Although the pasta tariff and most other restrictions on trade are intended to protect domestic industries, as with most well-intended governmental policies, the ultimate impact is quite different. The reason for this is straight forward: Tariffs and other restrictive policies reduce the overall benefits to be derived from trade. A corollary to this is that protected industries in the long-run generally fare poorly when they are not fully subjected to the harsh realities of a competitive environment.

Almost all economists agree that free trade is better than protectionism. What is it that is so unmistakably good about free trade that has done the impossible — namely, get economists to agree with each other?

We can be very analytical about it and show the net benefits of trade by describing the theory of comparative advantage. Adam Smith was far too interesting a writer to get bogged down with such analytics. David Ricardo, however, had no such compunction. Ricardo rigorously showed that two nations will benefit from trade even when one of the nations is absolutely more efficient in the production of all goods.

We need not be so analytical. Actually the benefits of free trade are simple to understand within the context of a free enterprise system. Our economic system is based on greed. Of course, this is not so bad as it sounds. Thankfully, almost everyone is a profit maximizing individual and competition among many profit maximizers assures that prices are kept low and that goods and services are being produced that people demand.

How does free trade enter into this? Free trade simply allows more profit-maximizing producers to get in on the action and helps insure that the competitive process functions more efficiently. Looking at a concrete example, consider the impact of the 1980 automobile import quotas. Is it so surprising that U.S. automobile prices increased 50 percent from 1980 to 1985 when overall consumer prices increased at half that rate or that automobile profits increased over 80 percent to $10 billion over that time period? Such a result is not surprising. It is a typical short-run outcome of protectionist policies.

If the case is so open and shut in favor of free trade, why do we erect barriers? The answer to this question, I believe, is that vocal private interest groups stand to gain much in the short-run by pushing for self-serving laws. Unfortunately, the political strength of a vocal minority is often more politically potent than that of a more disinterested majority. Case in point: As a result of steel quotas, the share of steel imports is projected to drop from 30 percent to 18 percent of the U.S. market. Presumably, some domestic jobs in the steel industry will be saved in the short-run. But how many jobs will be lost in count-

---

*   *The Atlantic Monthly*, July, 1976, p. 41.

less other industries as a result of having to pay a higher price for steel? The steel industry recognizes the short-run private gains accruing to it because of restrictive trade policies; the costs of such policies are spread too thinly and across too many industries to ferment such opposition. The fact that the individual gains from trade regulations are swamped by the costs, however, should be clear. As F. Kenneth Iverson writes in *The Wall Street Journal:*

> The cost to consumers is staggering. The trigger price mechanism under President Carter cost consumers an estimated $1 billion per year for more than three years and saved, temporarily, some 12,000 steelworking jobs. That's more than $80,000 per year per job, much more than the jobs paid.
>
> But the delay in modernization and the cost to consumers are only two parts of the picture. The greatest hazard is the destruction protectionism causes to U. S. manufacturers for whom steel is a significant part of their costs. Because the American steel industry is sheltered, world prices on some steel items are $100 to $200 a ton lower than in the U.S. This enables foreign manufacturers or American companies that move abroad to undersell domestic manufacturers. Automotive parts, oil rigs, farm implements, appliances, railroad parts and numerous other products are examples of domestic products suffering under this handicap. In 1979 the imports of these downstream steel products were estimated at five million tons. In 1985 they reached an estimated 15 million tons.
>
> One steel analyst has projected that the increased imports of such products will cause a decrease in the domestic steel market of more than 1% a year. As this occurs, our steel industry will have to shrink even further. How ironic that protectionism will accomplish the very thing it is supposed to prevent.*

Adam Smith understood all this as long ago as 1776:

> Each nation has been made to look with an invidious eye upon the prosperity of all the nations with which it trades, and to consider their gain as its own loss. . .
>
> That it was the spirit of monopoly which originally both invented and propagated this doctrine, cannot be doubted; and they who first taught it were by no means such fools as they who believed it. In every country it always is and must be the interest of the great body of the people to buy whatever they want of those who sell it cheapest. The proposition is so very manifest, that it seems ridiculous to take any pains to prove it; nor could it ever have been called in question, had not the interested sophistry

---

* *The Wall Street Journal*, August 21, 1986, p. 22.

of merchants and manufacturers confounded the common sense of mankind. Their interest is, in this respect, directly opposite to that of the great body of people. As it is the interest of the freemen of a corporation to hinder the rest of the inhabitants from employing any workmen but themselves, so it is the interest of the merchants and manufacturers of every country to secure to themselves the monopoly of the home market. Hence in Great Britain, and in most other European countries, the extraordinary duties upon almost all goods imported by alien merchants. Hence the high duties and prohibitions upon all those foreign manufacturers which can come into competition with our own.*

In commenting on the discovery of America, Adam Smith also states:

It is not by the importation of gold and silver that the discovery of America has enriched Europe. . . By opening a new and inexhaustible market to all the commodities of Europe, it gave occasion to new divisions of labour and improvements of art, which, in the narrow circle of the ancient commerce, could never have taken place for want of a market to take off the greater part of their produce. The productive powers of labour were improved, and its produce increased in all the different countries of Europe, and together with it the real revenue and wealth of the inhabitants.**

Nor should it be supposed that restrictive trade policies provide long-run benefits to the protected industries. Notice that the benefits alluded to in the above examples were couched in terms of *short-run* benefits. Without the unbridled powers of competition present to give correct signals to an enterprise, protected industries will soon become dead industries.

After years of protectionism, the steel industry is ailing, and there are no immediate signs of turnaround. Indeed, the current question is whether a viable steel industry will exist in the U.S. ten years from now. Even in the case of the pasta tariff, the volume of pasta imports into the U.S. is as high as it was before the imposition of the tariff.

The fact that restrictive trade policies offer no long-run protection to beleaguered industries is even more obvious in a world of multinational enterprise. An interesting case-in-point is offered by Marc Levinson, a senior editor at *Dun's Business Month* who writes:

International Salt Company, based in Clark Summit, Pennsylvania, charged last year that dumped Canadian rock salt endangered the welfare of U.S. salt companies and of some 1,600 American workers. A Commerce Department

---

*   The *Wealth of Nations*, Modern Library Edition, 1937, pp. 460-61.
**   *Ibid*. pp. 415-16.

investigation found that the salt was indeed being sold in the United States at less than its Canadian price. Low profits for U.S. salt producers in 1983, when dumping was alleged to have occurred, seemed to make International Salt's case even stronger.

But there was a twist to this other wise mundane matter. The "U.S. company" claiming injury, International Salt, is owned by a company based in Holland. The villain alleged to be doing most of the dumping was none other than Morton Salt Company of Chicago, the largest producer of rock salt in the United States as well as a major importer. Was Morton dumping Canadian salt to injure itself? Should America's dumping laws protect a foreign film against imports by a U.S. firm? In January, the ITC ruled that the domestic salt industry's problems in 1983 were due to a warm winter, not to dumping.*

The automobile, steel, salt, pasta, and all other industries do not need protection from free trade. Neither did my grandmother.

• • •

March 19, 1956 — St. Joseph's Day

I withdraw a spoonful, no more — no less, of ricotta filling and almost simultaneously place the filling onto a rolled sheet of dough. Grandma rolls another sheet of dough out of her newest capital investment, a deluxe Rolletti pasta-making machine. She ritualistically places the smooth and elastic sheet of dough onto the sheet containing twenty dollops of ricotta filling.

The final step is the most satisfying and certainly my favorite part. A newly purchased ravioli cutter allows me to cut and seal the ravioli pockets at the same time. The satisfaction of seeing the clean serrated edges left by the cutter is not unlike the sense of satisfaction one feels when correctly tieing a complex knot.

The efficiency in ravioli production brought about by the recently acquired capital equipment ($14.78), allows Grandma to make 500 ravioli in the same amount of time it took to make 100 ravioli several months ago. Moreover, she charges a lower price to compete with the frozen Italian produce and still makes it all worthwhile.

Grandma may not even have to worry about the inferior Italian product much longer. It turns out that the frozen patties have a tendency to break apart in the cooking process leaving a large quantity of naked ricotta balls and trails of pasta remnants looking like discarded rags floating in a pot of boiling water. Even those ravioli that survive the cooking process are mushy — not the requisite al dente.

She smiles at me while I take the tray full of ravioli to the bedroom to dry. I suddenly realize the sense of pride and satisfaction one must feel when inge-

---

*   "Down in the Import Dumps," *Across the Board*, April, 1983, p. 57.

nuity and hard work bring success in the marketplace.

Grandma beat the market, and that smile on her face told me she knew it. ●

39. Down in the Import Dumps

Marc Levinson

For the U.S. candle industry, 1984 turned out to be a difficult year. China, a new player in the candle game, had aggressively conquered 25 percent of the U.S. market, and the 90 American candlemaking companies didn't like what they saw. Imports from China, they claimed, had grown by 3,700 percent in just five years, and were selling for less than a fourth of what it cost to make them. Like increasing numbers of their fellow capitalists, the candle-makers knew where to turn for help. In September 1985, the National Candle Association filed petitions with the United States Government, charging the Chinese with dumping.

As industry after industry has been battered by imports, dumping — the below-cost sale of goods made abroad — has emerged as an ever louder complaint of U.S. manufacturers. Although some economists doubt that such a thing as dumping even occurs, American business has beaten a path to the doors of the Commerce Department and the International Trade Commission in search of relief. The number of dumping complaints filed with the ITC jumped from 75 in 1983 to 119 in 1985. In every case, a company or group of companies located in the United States is asking the Government to impose an extra tariff on imported goods to help protect it against low-cost foreign competition.

In common speech, the term "dumping" is often misused. Subsidized foreign steel, fake "designer" dresses, and textile shipments mislabeled to circumvent quotas are indeed unfair trade practices, but they have nothing to do with the anti-dumping laws. Those laws cover the relatively few cases in which individual foreign companies sell a product in the United States for less than their costs or for less than they sell it at home. Such below-cost sales are hardly the reason that the U.S. trade deficit reached a record $149 billion last year. "Given the strong dollar many companies have enjoyed in exporting to the United States," says Paula Stern, the ITC chairwoman, "they've got a lot more competitive advantages going for them than dumping."

Reprinted from *Across the Board*, April, 1986, pp. 52-58, by permission of The Conference Board, Inc.

For some U.S. industries, however, dumping may make the difference between life and death. Last June, Micron Technology Inc., a Boise, Idaho, maker of semiconductors, filed a complaint charging that Japanese electronics firms were dumping 64-kilobyte dynamic random-access memory chips in the United States. The Department of Commerce has tentatively agreed, finding that one Japanese firm, Mitsubishi Electric Company, was selling chips in the United States at barely half its own cost of production. Says Larry Grant, Micron Technology's vice president and general counsel, "You have to let them know they cannot ravage our markets. That's why we turned to the anti-dumping statute. The alternative was to do nothing, and let them steal the cookies out of the cookie jar."

Similarly, the beleaguered steel industry has brought dumping complaints by the score. Already this year, Federal agencies have investigated alleged dumping of steel pipes from Thailand, offshore oil platform equipment from Japan, nails from Yugoslavia, and iron construction castings from Brazil, Canada, India, and China. "I don't think there's any question that [dumping] is a major problem in steel," says Robert E. Lighthizer, a Washington trade lawyer who until 1985 handled steel negotiations for the Office of the United States Trade Representative. In steel, Lighthizer says, dumping is encouraged by the fact that many of the world's steel producers receive heavy government subsidies. "A company or an industry that is heavily subsidized in a foreign market is more likely to dump," he asserts.

The steel and semiconductor industries may indeed be ailing, but dumping may not be the cause. "I think there's a lot of reasons the U.S. guys haven't made it," says Lane Mason, senior industry analyst with Dataquest Inc., a computer market-research firm. "You can shake your finger at the Japanese, but part of this is their own doing. In '85, everyone had grandiose expectations about what the market was going to do. It didn't materialize, and their collective behavior drove prices down." Economist Robert W. Crandall, a senior fellow at the Brookings Institution in Washington who has closely studied the steel industry, says the same is true in steel. "The dumping issue is largely irrelevant to the problems of the steel industry," he says. "What is important is that the domestic companies and the foreign companies all made the same error, assuming that steel consumption would continue to grow in the 1970s and 1980s. That led to overcapacity and overproduction, and this facilitated the charge of dumping. What dumping is is the fall of prices in competitive markets."

The act of dumping is not illegal. A foreign company can sell its goods in the United States for whatever price it chooses. But under the General Agreement of Tariffs and Trade, the 90-nation treaty governing trade in manufactured goods, any country can take action against certain "unfair" practices of others. When a complaint is filed, the Commerce Department determines whether a foreign manufacturer is selling goods in the United States below their "fair value." Meanwhile, the ITC tries to decide whether an American industry is being injured or might be injured as a result. If both questions are answered in the affirmative, the importer must pay an extra duty equal to the amount of dumping determined to have occurred. This "antidumping duty" remains until another investigation finds that the dumping has ceased.

That seems simple enough. Enforcing the law, however, is a different matter altogether. The economics of dumping are far from simple. In fact, a company found guilty of dumping may not actually be doing anything unfair.

Take, for example, the case of ABC Widget Corporation, which makes widgets in a small South American country. In order to repay its foreign bank loans, ABC lengthens its production runs to turn out widgets for export. Since the company's domestic sales already cover the cost of maintaining the factory, ABC's profits increase so long as the price of its exported widgets is greater than the extra cost involved in making them. Thus, ABC's widgets may sell for less abroad than they do at home. Although these foreign sales may truly be profitable, under U.S. law, the company is dumping. To compete fairly here, ABC Widget must charge more than it charges at home.

But even if its U.S. price is higher than the price at the factory, ABC Widget is not home free. An American competitor can still complain that the U.S. price is below the company's actual costs of production, transportation, and customs duties. In that case, Commerce Department investigators will comb the company's accounting system to determine what its production cost is. Since ABC's main widget factory also produces a dozen other goods, the investigators must decide what share of operating costs and mortgage payments to attribute to widget production. To that, they tack on 10 percent for administrative costs, and then they build in an 8 percent profit margin, even if ABC Widget's U.S. competitors are generating no profits at all. Divide that total by the number of widgets produced and you've got ABC's per-widget cost. If ABC charges less, it may have to pay an anti-dumping duty.

ABC's American competitors, however, *do* charge less: Since they plan to keep their factory open anyway, they can increase their profits at any price above the extra cost of making more widgets. In fact, in a competitive economy, this marginal price is the price firms *should* charge. "In a period of slack demand," says John Jackson, professor of law at the University of Michigan and a former U.S. trade official, "a firm is rational in charging anything above its short-term variable costs. It has to pay its fixed costs anyway. So you have lost the economic advantage that accrues from the willingness to sell above short-term variable cost. The consumer is losing."

The difficulties don't end there. Even estimating the foreign company's input costs raises troublesome issues. For example, in some countries petroleum producers "flare off" natural gas uncovered in oil drilling. "There's no price," points out C. Michael Aho, director of the trade program at the Council on Foreign Relations. "So if instead of flaring it off, they sell it as petrochemicals, should we take action?" Such thorny issues make an "objective" assessment of production a fantasy. "Trying to determine what it costs to produce anything is almost impossible," contends Robert Crandall. "A politically adroit Commerce Department can come up with any costs it wants if it hires the right guy."

Although claims of dumping may provide relief for troubled companies — and fees for Washington's growing corps of trade lawyers — the economic case against dumping is hotly disputed. Many economists argue that dumping is actually a good thing for the American economy. If goods are dumped, that means their price in the United States is less than it would be otherwise. American consumers are getting a bargain. "If you deny yourselves this cheap product, you lose the gains from trade," says Gary Clyde Hufbauer, an economist at Georgetown University. Charging different prices in different markets is a normal aspect of a competitive economic system, Hufbauer says.

The standard rejoinder is that dumping is only a temporary benefit. Once foreign competitors have knocked the U.S. industry flat, they will monopolize the market and put the screws to American consumers. This fear of "strategic dumping" raises worries among nationalistic politicians in many countries that foreigners will establish monopolies in their markets. "I have certainly developed the impression that strategic dumping has occurred in certain areas," says Alan F. Holmer, the general counsel to the Office of the U.S. Trade Representative and formerly the Commerce Department official in charge of dumping cases. Holmer cites steel and semiconductors as two areas where such strategic conduct may be a factor.

But the path from dumping to monopolization is far from direct. For one thing, the dumper has to be a monopoly. Otherwise, this argument assumes that a group of foreign companies will agree to take losses in the United States until all competing American firms fail, after which they can carve up the U.S. market. "It is highly unlikely that a cartel could, over a sustained period of time, behave in this fashion," contends Lawrence J. White, a New York University economics professor who served as chief economist in the antitrust division of the Justice Department in 1982 and 1983. Until the American firms fail, White says, each of the foreign firms would like the others to take the lion's share of the losses from below-cost sales, and after the American firms collapse the foreigners would be tempted to compete with one another for market share. "You would need a phenomenal amount of coordination for this [joint dumping] to occur," White says.

Even if it did somehow occur, it's not enough to drive the U.S. firms out. If it's easy to go back into the business, new companies can enter every time the foreigners try to jack up prices. This is a key issue in semiconductors, with some experts arguing that if U.S. makers are driven from the market for 64K and 256K chips now, they won't be able to maintain the research and development base needed to compete in the more powerful one-megabit chips of the future. The truth of that argument is hard to gauge, but White is skeptical. "General Motors and IBM and AT&T have the bucks to get into this game," he says. "We are not talking about mom-and-pop grocery stores that, if times get tough, get driven out of business and don't come back.

Many businessmen and politicians, however, view dumping, particularly by

Japan, as just one aspect of a broader strategy to target certain industries in which Japanese companies seek to dominate world production. In 1985, for example, Motorola Corporation successfully pursued dumping claims against Japanese makers of mobile cellular telephones. The Japanese Government, Motorola claimed, had encouraged Japanese firms to drive it from the nascent cellular phone industry.

Semiconductors demonstrate dumping allegations at their most complex. The average price of 64K and 256K chips has plummeted in the face of worldwide overcapacity. Demand for 64K chips, used mainly in less powerful computers, actually declined in 1985's weak computer market. American manufacturers, such as Micron Technology and Texas Instruments, have struggled, while Intel, once a major player in the business, abandoned production of 256K RAM chips altogether in 1985. American manufacturers blame the Japanese, who have conquered almost two thirds of the $1.5 billion U.S. market for 64K chips and three quarters of the smaller 256K market. Last fall, under political pressure to deal with a record trade deficit, President Reagan directed the Commerce Department to consider whether Japanese electronics manufacturers were dumping 256K chips on the U.S. market. In March, the department ruled tentatively that they were, and proposed to assess anti-dumping duties ranging from 20 percent for Hitachi to 109 percent for NEC and Mitsubishi.

Micron Technology's Larry Grant admits that the Japanese didn't cause his industry's overcapacity with falling prices, but says they made a bad situation worse by cutting their prices below cost. In the fierce competitive battle that ensued, the price of 256K chips dropped from $14 in January 1985 to $1.50 last fall, while the price of 64K chips fell from $2.30 to 55 cents. The huge Japanese electronics firms, including Mitsubishi, Hitachi, and Nippon Electronic Company, could subsidize chip manufacturing with profits from other electronic products. Most of the American chip-makers, except for IBM and AT&T, the industry giants, simply lacked deep enough pockets to play the Japanese game.

The industry contends that far more than short-term profit is at stake. Steve Sparks, a marketing official for Motorola, told the International Trade Commission that his company had almost been forced out of the business of producing random-access memories. "If the market conditions caused by the Japanese dumping do not change soon, it is unlikely that we will be able to reenter in the future," he said.

"As we move to more complex components with more memory, we have to be better at it," says Larry Grant. "You only gain that experience by participating in the industry. It was not hard to enter into 16K chip manufacture, and was a little bit harder to get into 64K chips. As we move further down the process, it will become even harder to enter the one-megabit RAM [1,000K] market without any previous experience. The ability to make a 64K dynamic RAM well is going to be reflected in your experience in making others."

Dataquest's Mason, while acknowledging that dumping may have hurt U.S. chip manufacturers, says the industry itself is responsible for the bulk of its problems. One U.S. company after another had difficulty getting its 64K chips into production in the 1980-82 period, he recalls. Furthermore, "They weren't prepared when the 64K market shifted and it was time to move on to the 256K."

Mason is not convinced that anti-dumping duties on either type of chip will make the industry vibrant again. "Even without duties, it is possible for a manufacturer to enter the market and be successful," he says. "Whether they will is a question in my mind." In other industries, Mason notes, trade restraints have generated profits to use in diversification, not in reinvestment. In semiconductors, he says, "I'm not convinced the U.S. guys really want to get back in there and slug it out."

So far, the chip-makers have won half a loaf. On 64K chips, the Commerce Department has imposed anti-dumping duties far smaller than Micron Technology requested, an indication that the department believed that dumping was not the only reason for the low Japanese prices. The mere announcement of the preliminary dumping findings last fall changed minds in Tokyo, causing Japanese manufacturers to raise U.S. chip prices and cut back their production plans for 1986. On 256K chips, the Commerce Department's preliminary finding in March will provide temporary relief, but may turn out to be a hollow victory. The market for 64K chips is already in decline, and the 256K chip is likely to give way to the next generation, with one million characters of memory, within a few years. The ruling in March applied to 256K chips *and above*, but any attempt to apply it to the one-megabit chips of the future is certain to be tested in the courts.

The much publicized semiconductor cases stand in sharp contrast to the obscure issues that are usually investigated amid dumping charges. Typically, the cases involve small industries with relatively few employees, and the problem is more likely to stem from the aggressive export efforts of newly industrializing countries than the targeting plans of Japan. When not analyzing steel and semiconductors, the ITC has spent its time considering whether shipments of natural-bristle paintbrush heads from the People's Republic of China, castor oil from Brazil, and porcelain-on-steel cookware from Mexico have caused material injury to American producers. It's not always clear that the national interest is at stake. Nor is there any attempt to weigh the jobs and profits lost to dumped imports against the jobs and profits those imports create. By law, there are no trade-offs to consider in a dumping case.

This leads to many dumping cases that don't seem to have much merit. One case filed in 1984 claimed that companies in Italy were dumping stackable metal chairs on the American market; never mind that the stackable metal chair industry did not even exist in the United States until 1982, that it employed only 184 workers, or that U.S. manufacturers had increased production by 66 percent and capacity by even more between 1982 and 1984. How many jobs exist in importing, distributing, or selling the popular Italian patio chairs nobody knows. The Commerce Department found that the chairs had indeed been dumped, but after almost a year of investigation the ITC ruled that imports weren't the cause of the industry's problems. Like many legal actions, however, a case such as this can help the complaining firm even if it loses, since its foreign competitors must pay heavy legal costs, post an expensive bond, and operate in a business environment of great uncertainty until the matter is resolved.

In a world of multinational enterprise, things can become even more convoluted. Take, for example, the case of rock salt, a product most Americans think of only when they strew it on icy steps and walkways in the winter.

International Salt Company, based in Clark Summit, Pennsylvania, charged last year that dumped Canadian rock salt endangered the welfare of U.S. salt companies and of some 1,600 American workers. A Commerce Department investigation found that the salt was indeed being sold in the United States at less than its Canadian price. Low profits for U.S. salt producers in 1983, when dumping was alleged to have occurred, seemed to make International Salt's case even stronger.

But there was a twist to this otherwise mundane matter. The "U.S. company" claiming injury, International Salt, is owned by a company based in Holland. The villain alleged to be doing most of the dumping was none other than Morton Salt Company of Chicago, the largest producer of rock salt in the United States as well as a major importer. Was Morton dumping Canadian salt to injure itself? Should America's dumping laws protect a foreign firm against imports by a U.S. firm? These questions remain unresolved. In January, the ITC ruled that the domestic salt industry's problems in 1983 were due to a warm winter, not to dumping.

In none of these cases does the U.S. Government have discretion. If the Commerce Department finds that no dumping has occurred, or if the ITC fails to identify dumping as a source of injury, unhappy manufacturers can take the Government to court. If Commerce or the ITC does impose anti-dumping duties, the Administration has no power to reject or modify that decision. That lack of flexibility strengthens the hand of U.S. trade negotiators, but it also gives import-sensitive industries tremendous power over trade negotiations. In negotiating reductions of certain steel imports, for example, Robert Lighthizer was limited by the domestic industry's ability to reject any settlement and pursue its quest for extra duties on foreign steel. "I had discretion," he says. "All I had to do was get the permission of the industry. That's how I put together the steel deals. An awful lot of deals are put together that way."

That, many trade analysts say, is precisely what is wrong with the law. Quotas on imports, such as those established by consent of the steel industry, are far worse than import duties because they limit import competition and guarantee a market for the domestic product, regardless of its price. Duties, by contrast, raise the price of foreign products, but still force domestic producers to compete for the market.

"The main problem in the anti-dumping and countervailing-duty laws is not rock salt, it's carbon steel," contends Georgetown's Gary Hufbauer. "In these big cases, the remedy is totally perverted, so the case becomes a springboard for a cartel or some kind of restriction that's far worse than countervailing duties." Says Robert E. Baldwin, professor of international economics at the University of Wisconsin, Madison: "I would like the ITC to consider the national interest. The ITC should discuss the effect on the total economy, on consumers, users, foreign-policy interests."

American industry has had trouble winning dumping cases ever since the Anti-Dumping Act was passed in 1921. In response, Congress has repeatedly tightened the law to make cases easier to win. In 1974, it loosened the definition of dumping to include sales below average cost as well as sales below the home market price. In 1979, it transferred investigating authority from the Treasury to the Commerce Department, which has traditionally been more sympathetic to businesses' cries for relief. Since 1984, the law has allowed an industry that can't prove injury from any one country's imports to show that dumped imports from several small producers, added together, are the source of its problems.

Perhaps the most troublesome recent change in the law, though, requires the ITC to examine whether dumping threatens material injury to a U.S. industry in the future. "Those threat things are so hard to define that in general I would be skeptical about the feasibility of implementing that," says Robert Baldwin. "You just can't foresee the future." The difficulty is so daunting that even the ITC has avoided basing decisions on that clause. "We are supposed to be making our decisions based on economics," complains Paula Stern. "We're not supposed to be looking at just theoretical or speculative threats."

Now, as election-year outrage over trade deficits settles in on the Potomac, Congress is once again seeking to tighten the laws against allegedly unfair trade practices. When legislators cannot win protection for their favored industries directly – President Reagan vetoed a bill last December to restrict imports of shoes, apparel, and textiles – they will seek to win indirectly, by making it easier for constituents to have their foreign competitors penalized for playing unfairly. Already, Senator Charles E. Grassley of Iowa, unable to get the Administration to clamp down on Canadian pork imports, has proposed tightening the law so that producers of raw agricultural products and of processed foods would be treated as one industry. Thus, if dumped pork were found to be injuring Iowa meat processors, antidumping duties would be placed not just on pork, but also on pigs, so importers could not shift from one commodity to the other.

The Administration, meanwhile, may well seek to expand the law into the murky area of "upstream dumping." If, for example, an Argentine company dumps steel wire in Canada, and a Canadian company turns that wire into barbed wire fencing for sale in the United States, U.S. trade authorities are powerless to keep the Canadians from underselling their U.S. counterparts. The situation, however, will be difficult to remedy: U.S. action against the Canadian firm would be a violation of international trade agreements, and the Argentines would have no reason to cooperate with a U.S. inquiry into their costs of production. In addition, American intervention in such a matter would be sure to raise hackles in Canada.

The most complex problem with the dumping laws, though, is one that Congress is unlikely to consider. In an increasingly internationalized economy, the distinction between American and foreign products is rapidly blurring. Can the U.S. semiconductor industry honestly claim to be injured by Japanese imports when many of the components it uses come from Japan? Does a manufacturer who buys cheap Brazilian steel and rolls it into pipes have the right to complain about imports of Brazilian pipes? When the ITC studies whether dumping has injured an American industry, are companies that import parts and assemble them in California to be considered along with companies that manufacture all their parts in Cleveland? On these issues, the well-defined world of trade law just doesn't fit with the way America does business. "We have just become extraordinarily internationalized," says Paula Stern. "It is possible that our laws, which are based on certain assumptions as to what the 'U.S. industry' is, don't address the reality of the marketplace." ●

40. The Tyranny of Controls

Milton & Rose Friedman

In discussing tariffs and other restrictions on international trade in his *Wealth of Nations*, Adam Smith wrote:

> What is prudence in the conduct of every private family, can scarce be folly in that of a great kingdom. If a foreign country can supply us with a commodity cheaper than we ourselves can make it, better buy it of them with some part of the produce of our own industry, employed in a way in which we have some advantage.... In every country, it is and must be the interest of the great body of the people to buy whatever they want of those who sell it cheapest. The proposition is so very manifest, that it seems ridiculous to take any pains to prove it; nor could it ever have been called in question, had not the interested sophistry of merchants and manufacturers confounded the common sense of mankind. Their interest is, in this respect, directly opposite to that of the great body of the people.*

These words are as true today as they were then. In domestic as well as foreign trade, it is in the interest of "the great body of the people" to buy from the cheapest source and sell to the dearest. Yet "interested sophistry" has led to a bewildering proliferation of restrictions on what we may buy and sell, from whom we may buy and to whom we may sell and on what terms, whom we may employ and whom we may work for, where we may live, and what we may eat and drink.

Adam Smith pointed to "the interested sophistry of merchants and manufacturers." They may have been the chief culprits in his day. Today they have much company. Indeed, there is hardly one of us who is not engaged in "interested sophistry" in one area or another. In Pogo's immortal words, "We have met the

---

* *Wealth of Nations*, vol. I, pp. 422 and 458.

enemy and they is us." We rail against "special interests" except when the "special interest" happens to be our own. Each of us knows that what is good for him is good for the country—so *our* "special interest" is different. The end result is a maze of restraints and restrictions that makes almost all of us worse off than we would be if they were all eliminated. We lose far more from measures that serve other "special interests" than we gain from measures that serve our "special interest."

The clearest example is in international trade. The gains to some producers from tariffs and other restrictions are more than offset by the loss to other producers and especially to consumers in general. Free trade would not only promote our material welfare, it would also foster peace and harmony among nations and spur domestic competition.

Controls on foreign trade extend to domestic trade. They become intertwined with every aspect of economic activity. Such controls have often been defended, particularly for underdeveloped countries, as essential to provide development and progress. A comparison of the experience of Japan after the Meiji Restoration in 1867 and of India after independence in 1947 tests this view. It suggests, as do other examples, that free trade at home and abroad is the best way that a poor country can promote the well-being of its citizens.

The economic controls that have proliferated in the United States in recent decades have not only restricted our freedom to use our economic resources, they have also affected our freedom of speech, of press, and of religion.

International Trade

It is often said that bad economic policy reflects disagreement among the experts; that if all economists gave the same advice, economic policy would be good. Economists often do disagree, but that has not been true with respect to international trade. Ever since Adam Smith there has been virtual unanimity among economists, whatever their ideological position on other issues, that international free trade is in the best interest of the trading countries and of the world. Yet tariffs have been the rule. The only major exceptions are nearly a century of free trade in Great Britain after the repeal of the Corn Laws in 1846, thirty years of free trade in Japan after the Meiji Restoration, and free trade in Hong Kong today. The United States had tariffs throughout the nineteenth century and they were raised still higher in the twentieth century, especially by the Smoot-Hawley tariff bill of 1930, which some scholars regard as partly responsible for the severity of the subsequent depression. Tariffs have since been reduced by repeated international agreements, but they remain high, probably higher than in the nineteenth century, though the vast changes in the kinds of items entering international trade make a precise comparison impossible.

Today, as always, there is much support for tariffs—euphemistically labeled "protection," a good label for a bad cause. Producers of steel and steelworkers' unions press for restrictions on steel imports from Japan. Producers of TV sets and their workers lobby for "voluntary agreements" to limit imports of TV sets or components from Japan, Taiwan, or Hong Kong. Producers of textiles, shoes, cattle, sugar—they and myriad others complain about "unfair" competition from abroad and demand that government do something to "protect" them. Of course, no group makes its claim on the basis of naked self-interest. Every group speaks of the "general interest," of the need to preserve jobs or to promote national security. The need to strengthen the dollar vis-à-vis the mark or the yen has more recently joined the traditional rationalizations for restrictions on imports.

The Economic Case for Free Trade

One voice that is hardly ever raised is the consumer's. So-called consumer special interest groups have proliferated in recent years. But you will search the news media, or the records of congressional hearings in vain, to find any record of their launching a concentrated attack on tariffs or other restrictions on imports, even though consumers are major victims of such measures. The self-styled consumer advocates have other concerns.

The individual consumer's voice is drowned out in the cacophony of the "interested sophistry of merchants and manufacturers" and their employees. The result is a serious distortion of the issue. For example, the supporters of tariffs treat it as self-evident that the creation of jobs is a desirable end, in and of itself, regardless of what the persons employed do. That is clearly wrong. If all we want are jobs, we can create any number—for example, have people dig holes and then fill them up again, or perform other useless tasks. Work is sometimes its own reward. Mostly, however, it is the price we pay to get the things we want. Our real objective is not just jobs but productive jobs—jobs that will mean more goods and services to consume.

Another fallacy seldom contradicted is that exports are good, imports bad. The truth is very different. We cannot eat, wear, or enjoy the goods we send abroad. We eat bananas from Central America, wear Italian shoes, drive German automobiles, and enjoy programs we see on our Japanese TV sets. Our gain from foreign trade is what we import. Exports are the price we pay to get imports. As Adam Smith saw so clearly, the citizens of a nation benefit from getting as large a volume of imports as possible in return for its exports, or equivalently, from exporting as little as possible to pay for its imports.

The misleading terminology we use reflects these erroneous ideas. "Protection" really means exploiting the consumer. A "favorable balance of trade" really means exporting more than we import, sending abroad goods of greater total value than the goods we get from abroad. In your private household, you would surely prefer to pay less for more rather than the other way around, yet that would be termed an "unfavorable balance of payments" in foreign trade.

The argument in favor of tariffs has the greatest emotional appeal to the public at large is the alleged need to protect the high standard of living of American workers from the "unfair" competition of workers in Japan or Korea or Hong Kong who are willing to work for a much lower wage. What is wrong with this argument? Don't we want to protect the high standard of living of our people?

The fallacy in this argument is the loose use of the terms "high" wage and "low" wage. What do high and low wages mean? American workers are paid in dollars; Japanese workers are paid in yen. How do we compare wages in dollars and wages in yen? How many yen equal a dollar? What determines that exchange rate?

Consider an extreme case. Suppose that, to begin with, 360 yen equal a dollar. At this exchange rate, the actual rate of exchange for many years, suppose that the Japanese can produce and sell everything for fewer dollars than we can in the United States—TV sets, automobiles, steel, and even soybeans, wheat, milk, and ice cream. If we had free international trade, we would try to buy all our goods from Japan. This would seem to be the extreme horror story of the kind depicted by defenders of tariffs—we would be flooded with Japanese goods and could sell them nothing.

Before throwing up your hands in horror, carry the analysis one step further. How would we pay the Japanese? We would offer them dollar bills. What would they do with the dollar bills? We have assumed that at 360 yen to the dollar everything is cheaper in Japan, so there is nothing in the U.S. market that they would want to buy. If the Japanese exporters were willing to burn or bury the dollar bills, that would be wonderful for us. We would get all kinds of goods for green pieces of paper that we can produce in great abundance and very cheaply. We would have the most marvelous export industry conceivable.

Of course, the Japanese would not in fact sell us useful goods in order to get useless pieces of paper to bury or burn. Like us, they want to get something real in return for their work. If all goods were cheaper in Japan than in the United States at 360 yen to the dollar, the exporters would try to get rid of their dollars, would try to sell them for 360 yen to the dollar in order to buy the cheaper Japanese goods. But who would be willing to buy the dollars? What is true for the Japanese exporter is true for everyone in Japan. No one will be willing to give 360 yen in exchange for one dollar if 360 yen will buy more of everything in Japan than one dollar will buy in the United States. The exporters, on discovering that no one will buy their dollars at 360 yen, will offer to take fewer yen for a dollar. The price of the dollar in terms of yen will go down—to 300 yen for a dollar, or 250 yen, or 200 yen. Put the other way around, it will take more and more dollars to buy a given number of Japanese yen. Japanese goods are priced in yen so their price in dollars will go up. Conversely, U.S. goods are priced in dollars, so the more dollars the Japanese get for a given number of yen, the cheaper U.S. goods become to the Japanese in terms of yen.

The price of the dollar in terms of yen would fall until, on the average, the dollar value of goods that the Japanese buy from the United States roughly equaled the dollar value of goods that the United States buys from Japan. At that price everybody who wanted to buy yen for dollars would find someone who was willing to sell him yen for dollars.

The actual situation is, of course, more complicated than this hypothetical example. Many nations, and not merely the United States and Japan, are engaged in trade, and the trade often takes roundabout directions. The Japanese may spend some of the dollars they earn in Brazil, the Brazilians in turn may spend those dollars in Germany, and the Germans in the United States, and so on in endless complexity. However, the principle is the same. People, in whatever country, want dollars primarily to buy useful items, not to hoard.

Another complication is that dollars and yen are used not only to buy goods and services from other countries but also to invest and make gifts. Throughout the nineteenth century the United States had a balance of payments deficit almost every year — an "unfavorable" balance of trade that was good for everyone. Foreigners wanted to invest capital in the United States. The British, for example, were producing goods and sending them to us in return for pieces of paper — not dollar bills, but bonds promising to pay back a sum of money at a later time plus interest. The British were willing to send us their goods because they regarded those bonds as a good investment. On the average, they were right. They received a higher return on their savings than was available in any other way. We, in turn, benefited by foreign investment that enabled us to develop more rapidly than we could have developed if we had been forced to rely solely on our own savings.

In the twentieth century the situation was reversed. U.S. citizens found that they could get a higher return on their capital by investing abroad than they could at home. As a result the United States sent goods abroad in return for evidence of debt — bonds and the like. After World War II, the U.S. government made gifts abroad in the form of the Marshall Plan and other foreign aid programs. We sent goods and services abroad as an expression of our beliefs that we were thereby contributing to a more peaceful world. These government gifts supplemented private gifts — from charitable groups, churches supporting missionaries, individuals contributing to the support of relatives abroad, and so on.

None of these complications alters the conclusion suggested by the hypothetical extreme case. In the real world, as well as in that hypothetical world, there can be no balance of payments problem so long as the price of the dollar in terms of the yen or the mark or the franc is determined in a free market by voluntary transactions. It is simply not true that high-wage American workers are, as a group, threatened by "unfair" competition from low-wage foreign workers. Of course, particular workers may be harmed if a new or improved product is developed abroad, or if foreign producers become able to produce such products more cheaply. But that is no different from the effect on a particular group of workers of other American firms' developing new or improved products or discovering how to produce at lower costs. That is simply market competition in practice, the major source of the high standard of life of the American worker. If we want to benefit from a vital, dynamic, innovative economic system, we must accept the need for mobility and adjustment. It may be desirable to ease these adjustments, and we have adopted many arrangements, such as unemployment insurance, to do so, but we should try to achieve that objective without destroying the flexibility of the system—that would be to kill the goose that has been laying the golden eggs. In any event, whatever we do should be evenhanded with respect to foreign and domestic trade.

What determines the items it pays us to import and to export? An American worker is currently more productive than a Japanese worker. It is hard to determine just how much more productive—estimates differ. But suppose he is one and a half times as productive. Then, on average, the American's wages would buy about one and a half times as much as a Japanese worker's wages. It is wasteful to use American workers to do anything at which they are less than one and a half times as efficient as their Japanese counterparts. In the economic jargon coined more than 150 years ago, that is the *principle of comparative advantage*. Even if we were more efficient than the Japanese at producing everything, it would not pay us to produce anything. We should concentrate on doing those things we do best, those things where our superiority is the greatest.

As a homely illustration, should a lawyer who can type twice as fast as his secretary fire the secretary and do his own typing? If the lawyer is twice as good a typist but five times as good a lawyer as his secretary, both he and his secretary are better off if he practices law and the secretary types letters.

Another source of "unfair competition" is said to be subsidies by foreign governments to their producers that enable them to sell in the United States below cost. Suppose a foreign government gives such subsidies, as no doubt some do. Who is hurt and who benefits? To pay for the subsidies the foreign government must tax its citizens. They are the ones who pay for the subsidies. U.S. consumers benefit. They get cheap TV sets or automobiles or whatever it is that is subsidized. Should we complain about such a program of reverse foreign aid? Was it noble of the United States to send goods and services as gifts to other countries in the form of Marshall Plan aid, or later, foreign aid, but ignoble for foreign countries to send us gifts in the indirect form of goods and services sold to us below cost? The citizens of the foreign government might well complain. They must suffer a lower standard of living for the benefit of American consumers and of some of their fellow citizens who own or work in the industries that are subsidized. No doubt, if such subsidies are introduced suddenly or erratically, that will adversely affect owners and workers in U.S. industries producing the same products. However, that is one of the ordinary risks of doing business. Enterprises never complain about unusual or accidental events that confer windfall gains. The free enterprise system is a *profit* and *loss* system. As already noted, any measures to ease the adjustment to sudden changes should be applied evenhandedly to domestic and foreign trade.

In any event, disturbances are likely to be temporary. Suppose that, for whatever reason, Japan decided to subsidize steel very heavily. If no additional tariffs or quotas were imposed, imports of steel into the United States would go up sharply. That would drive down the price of steel in the United States and force steel producers to cut their output, causing unemployment in the steel industry. On the other hand, products made of steel could be purchased more cheaply. Buyers of such products would have extra money to spend on other things. The demand for other items would go up, as would employment in enterprises producing those items. Of course, it would take time to absorb the now unemployed steelworkers. However, to balance that effect, workers in other industries who had been unemployed would find jobs available. There need be no net loss of employment, and there would be a gain in output because workers no longer needed to produce steel would be available to produce something else.

The same fallacy of looking at only one side of the issue is present when tariffs are urged in order to add to employment. If tariffs are imposed on, say, textiles, that will add to output and employment in the domestic textile industry. However, foreign producers who no longer can sell their textiles in the United States earn fewer dollars. They will have less to spend in the United States. Exports will go down to balance decreased imports. Employment will go up in the textile industry, down in the export industries. And the shift of employment to less productive uses will reduce total output.

The national security argument that a thriving domestic steel industry, for example, is needed for defense has no better basis. National defense needs take only a small fraction of total steel used in the United States. And it is inconceivable that complete free trade in steel would destroy the U.S. steel industry. The advantages of being close to sources of supply and fuel and to the market would guarantee a relatively large domestic steel industry. Indeed, the need to meet foreign competition, rather than being sheltered behind governmental barriers, might very well produce a stronger and more efficient steel industry than we have today.

Suppose the improbable did happen. Suppose it did prove cheaper to buy *all* our steel abroad. There are alternative ways to provide for national security. We could stockpile steel. That is easy, since steel takes relatively little space and is not perishable. We could maintain some steel plants in mothballs, the way we maintain ships, to go into production in case of need. No doubt there are still other alternatives. Before a steel company decides to build a new plant, it investigates alternative ways of doing so, alternative locations, in order to choose the most efficient and economical. Yet in all its pleas for subsidies on national security grounds, the steel industry has never presented cost estimates for alternative ways of providing national security. Until they do, we can be sure the national security argument is a rationalization of industry self-interest, not a valid reason for the subsidies.

No doubt the executives of the steel industry and of the steel labor unions are sincere when they adduce national security arguments. Sincerity is a much overrated virtue. We are all capable of persuading ourselves that what is good for us is good for the country. We should not complain about steel producers making such arguments, but about letting ourselves be taken in by them.

What about the argument that we must defend the dollar, that we must keep it from falling in value in terms of other currencies — the Japanese yen, the German mark, or the Swiss franc? That is a wholly artificial problem. If foreign exchange rates are determined in a free market, they will settle at whatever level will clear the market. The resulting price of the dollar in terms of the yen, say, may temporarily fall below the level justified by the cost in dollars and yen respectively of American and Japanese goods. If so, it will give persons who recognize that situation an incentive to buy dollars and hold them for a while in order to make a profit when the price goes up. By lowering the price in yen of American exports to Japanese, it will stimulate American exports; by raising the price in dollars of Japanese goods, it will discourage imports from Japan. These developments will increase the demand for dollars and so correct the initially low price. The price of the dollar, if determined freely, serves the same function as all other prices. It transmits information and provides an incentive to act on that information because it affects the incomes that participants in the market receive.

Why then all the furor about the "weakness" of the dollar? Why the repeated foreign exchange crises? The proximate reason is because foreign exchange rates have not been determined in a free market. Government central banks have intervened on a grand scale in order to influence the price of their currencies. In the process they have lost vast sums of their citizens' money (for the United States close to $2 billion from 1973 to early 1979). Even more important, they have prevented this important set of prices from performing its proper function. They have not been able to prevent the basic underlying economic forces from ultimately having their effect on exchange rates, but have been able to maintain artificial exchange rates for substantial intervals. The effect has been to prevent gradual adjustment to the underlying forces. Small disturbances have accumulated into large ones, and ultimately there has been a major foreign exchange "crisis."

Why have governments intervened in foreign exchange markets? Because foreign exchange rates reflect internal policies. The U.S. dollar has been weak compared to the Japanese yen, the German mark, and the Swiss franc primarily because inflation has been much higher in the United States than in the other countries. Inflation meant that the dollar was able to buy less and less at home. Should we be surprised that it has also been able to buy less abroad? Or that Japanese or Germans or Swiss should not be willing to exchange as many of their own currency units for a dollar? But governments, like the rest of us, go to great lengths to try to conceal or offset the undesirable consequences of their own policies. A government that inflates is therefore led to try to manipulate the foreign exchange rate. When it fails, it blames internal inflation on the decline in the exchange rate, instead of acknowledging that cause and effect run the other way.

In all the voluminous literature of the past several centuries on free trade and protectionism, only three arguments have ever been advanced in favor of tariffs that even in principle may have some validity.

First is the national security argument already mentioned. Although that argument is more often a rationalization for particular tariffs than a valid reason for them, it cannot be denied that on occasion it might justify the maintenance of otherwise uneconomical productive facilities. To go beyond this statement of possibility and establish in a specific case that a tariff or other trade restriction is justified in order to promote national security, it would be necessary to compare the cost of achieving the specific security objective in alternative ways and establish at least a *prima facie* case that a tariff is the least costly way. Such cost comparisons are seldom made in practice.

The second is the "infant industry" argument advanced, for example, by Alexander Hamilton in his *Report on Manufactures*. There is, it is said, a potential industry which, if once established and assisted during its growing pains, could compete on equal terms in the world market. A temporary tariff is said to be justified in order to shelter the potential industry in its infancy and enable it to grow to maturity, when it can stand on its own feet. Even if the industry could compete successfully once established, that does not of itself justify an initial tariff. It is worthwhile for consumers to subsidize the industry initially— which is what they in effect do by levying a tariff— only if they will subsequently get back at least that subsidy in some other way, through prices later lower than the world price, or through some other advantages of having the industry. But in that case, is a subsidy needed? Will it then not pay the original entrants into the industry to suffer initial losses in the expectation of being able to recoup them later? After all, most firms experience losses in their early years, when they are getting established. That is true if they enter a new industry or if they enter an existing one. Perhaps there may be some special reason why the original entrants cannot recoup their initial losses even though it be worthwhile for the community at large to make the initial investment. But surely the presumption is the other way.

The infant industry argument is a smoke screen. The so-called infants never grow up. Once imposed, tariffs are seldom eliminated. Moreover, the argument is seldom used on behalf of true unborn infants that might conceivably be born and survive if given temporary protection. They have no spokesmen. It is used to justify tariffs for rather aged infants that can mount political pressure.

The third argument for tariffs that cannot be dismissed out of hand is the "beggar-thy-neighbor" argument. A country that is a major producer of a product, or that can join with a small number of other producers that together control a major share of production, may be able to take advantage of its monopoly position by raising the price of the product (the OPEC cartel is the obvious current example). Instead of raising the price directly, the country can do so indirectly by imposing an export tax on the product — an export tariff. The benefit to itself will be less than the cost to others, but from the national point of view, there can be a gain. Similarly, a country that is the primary purchaser of a product — in economic jargon, has monopsony power — may be able to benefit by driving a hard bargain with the sellers and imposing an unduly low price on them. One way to do so is to impose a tariff on the import of the product. The net return to the seller is the price less the tariff, which is why this can be equivalent to buying at a lower price. In effect, the tariff is paid by the foreigners (we can think of no actual example). In practice this nationalistic approach is highly likely to promote retaliation by other countries. In addition, as for the infant industry argument, the actual political pressures tend to produce tariff structures that do not in fact take advantage of any monopoly or monopsony positions.

A fourth argument, one that was made by Alexander Hamilton and continues to be repeated down to the present, is that free trade would be fine if all other countries practiced free trade but that so long as they do not, the United States cannot afford to. This argument has no validity whatsoever, either in principle or in practice. Other countries that impose restrictions on international trade do hurt us. But they also hurt themselves. Aside from the three cases just considered, if we impose restrictions in turn, we simply add to the harm to ourselves and also harm them as well. Competition in masochism and sadism is hardly a prescription for sensible international economic policy! Far from leading to a reduction in restrictions by other countries, this kind of retaliatory action simply leads to further restrictions.

We are a great nation, the leader of the free world. It ill behooves us to require Hong Kong and Taiwan to impose export quotas on textiles to "protect" our textile industry at the expense of U.S. consumers and of Chinese workers in Hong Kong and Taiwan. We speak glowingly of the virtues of free trade, while we use our political and economic power to induce Japan to restrict exports of steel and TV sets. We should move unilaterally to free trade, not instantaneously, but over a period of, say, five years, at a pace announced in advance.

Few measures that we could take would do more to promote the cause of freedom at home and abroad than complete free trade. Instead of making grants to foreign governments in the name of economic aid — thereby promoting socialism — while at the same time imposing restrictions on the products they produce — thereby hindering free enterprise — we could assume a consistent and principled stance. We could say to the rest of the world: we believe in freedom and intend to practice it. We cannot force you to be free. But we can offer full cooperation on equal terms to all. Our market is open to you without tariffs or other restrictions. Sell here what you can and wish to. Buy whatever you can and wish to. In that way cooperation among individuals can be worldwide and free.

The Political Case for Free Trade

Interdependence is a pervasive characteristic of the modern world: in the economic sphere proper, between one set of prices and another, between one industry and another, between one country and another; in the broader society, between economic activity and cultural, social, and charitable activities; in the organization of society, between economic arrangements and political arrangements, between economic freedom and political freedom.

In the international sphere as well, economic arrangements are intertwined with political arrangements. International free trade fosters harmonious relations among nations that differ in culture and institutions just as free trade at home fosters harmonious relations among individuals who differ in beliefs, attitudes, and interests.

In a free trade world, as in a free economy in any one country, transactions take place among private entities — individuals, business enterprises, charitable organizations. The terms at which any transaction takes place are agreed on by all the parties to that transaction. The transaction will not take place unless all parties believe they will benefit from it. As a result, the interests of the various parties are harmonized. Cooperation, not conflict, is the rule.

When governments intervene, the situation is very different. Within a country, enterprises seek subsidies from their government, either directly or in the form of tariffs or other restrictions on trade. They will seek to evade economic pressures from competitors that threaten their profitability or their very existence by resorting to political pressure to impose costs on others. Intervention by one government in behalf of local enterprises leads enterprises in other countries to seek the aid of their own government to counteract the measures taken by the foreign government. Private disputes become the occasion for disputes between governments. Every trade negotiation becomes a political matter. High government officials jet around the world to trade conferences. Frictions develop. Many citizens of every country are disappointed at the outcome and end up feeling they got the short end of the stick. Conflict, not cooperation, is the rule.

The century from Waterloo to the First World War offers a striking example of the beneficial effects of free trade on the relations among nations. Britain was the leading nation of the world, and during the whole of that century it had nearly complete free trade. Other nations, particularly Western nations, including the United States, adopted a similar policy, if in somewhat diluted form. People were in the main free to buy and sell goods from and to anyone, wherever he lived, whether in the same or a different country, at whatever terms were mutually agreeable. Perhaps even more surprising to us today, people were free to travel all over Europe and much of the rest of the world without a passport and without repeated customs inspection. They were free to emigrate and in much of the world, particularly the United States, free to enter and become residents and citizens.

As a result, the century from Waterloo to the First World war was one of the most peaceful in human history among Western nations, marred only by some minor wars — the Crimean War and the Franco-Prussian Wars are the most memorable — and, of course, a major civil war within the United States, which itself was a result of the major respect — slavery — in which the United States departed from economic and political freedom.

In the modern world, tariffs and similar restrictions on trade have been one source of friction among nations. But a far more troublesome source has been the far-reaching intervention of the state into the economy in such collectivist states as Hitler's Germany, Mussolini's Italy, and Franco's Spain, and especially the communist countries, from Russia and its satellites to China. Tariffs and similar restrictions distort the signals transmitted by the price system, but at least they leave individuals free to respond to those distorted signals. The collectivist countries have introduced much farther-reaching command elements.

Completely private transactions are impossible between citizens of a largely market economy and of a collectivist state. One side is necessarily represented by government officials. Political considerations are unavoidable, but friction would be minimized if the governments of market economies permitted their citizens the maximum possible leeway to make their own deals with collectivist governments. Trying to use trade as a political weapon or political measures as a means to increase trade with collectivist countries only makes the inevitable political frictions even worse.

Free International Trade and Internal Competition

The extent of competition at home is closely related to international trade arrangements. A public outcry against "trusts" and "monopolies" in the late nineteenth century led to the establishment of the Interstate Commerce Commission and the adoption of the Sherman Anti-Trust Law, later supplemented by many other legislative actions to promote competition. These measures have had very mixed effects. They have contributed in some ways to increased competition, but in others they have had perverse effects.

But no such measure, even if it lived up to every expectation of its sponsors, could do as much to assure effective competition as the elimination of all barriers to international trade. The existence of only three major automobile producers in the United States — and one of those on the verge of bankruptcy — does raise a threat of monopoly pricing. But let the automobile producers *of the world* compete with General Motors, Ford, and Chrysler for the custom of the American buyer, and the specter of monopoly pricing disappears.

So it is throughout. A monopoly can seldom be established within a country without overt and covert government assistance in the form of a tariff or some other device. It is close to impossible to do so on a world scale. The De Beers diamond monopoly is the only one we know of that appears to have succeeded. We know of no other that has been able to exist for long without the direct assistance of governments — the OPEC cartel and earlier rubber and coffee cartels being perhaps the most prominent examples. And most such government-sponsored cartels have not lasted long. They have broken down under the pressure of international competition — a fate that we believe awaits OPEC as well. In a world of free trade, international cartels would disappear even more quickly. Even in a world of trade restrictions, the United States, by free trade, unilateral if necessary, could come close to eliminating any danger of significant internal monopolies. ●

41. Candlemakers' Petition

Frédéric Bastiat

Petition of the manufacturers of candles, wax-lights, lamps, candle-sticks, street lamps, snuffers, extinguishers, and of the producers of oil, tallow, resin, alcohol, and, generally, of everything connected with lighting.

To Messieurs the Members of the Chamber of Deputies

Gentlemen, — You are on the right road. You reject abstract theories, and have little consideration for cheapness and plenty. Your chief care is the interest of the producer. You desire to protect him from foreign competition, and reserve the *national market* for *national industry*.

We are about to offer you an admirable opportunity of applying your — what shall we call it? — your theory? No; nothing is more deceptive than theory — your doctrine? your system? your principle? But you dislike doctrines, you abhor systems, and as for principles you deny that there are any in social economy. We shall say, then, your practice — your practice without theory and without principle.

We are suffering from the intolerable competition of a foreign rival, placed, it would seem, in a condition so far superior to ours for the production of light that he absolutely *inundates* our *national market* with it at a price fabulously reduced. The moment he shows himself our trade leaves us — all consumers apply to him; and a branch of native industry, having countless ramifications, is all at once rendered completely stagnant. This rival, who is no other than the sun, wages war to the knife against us, and we suspect that he has been raised up by *perfidious Albion* (good policy as times go); inasmuch as he displays towards that haughty island a circumspection with which he dispenses in our case.

What we pray for is, that it may please you to pass a law ordering the shutting up of all windows, skylights, dormer-windows, outside and inside shutters,

Reprinted from *Fallacies of Protection*, translated by Patrick James Stirling, LL.D., F.R.S.E., pp. 60-65, published for the Cobden Club by Cassell and Company, Ltd.

curtains, blinds, bull's-eyes; in a word, of all openings, holes, chinks, clefts, and fissures, by or through which the light of the sun has been in use to enter houses, to the prejudice of the meritorious manufactures with which we flatter ourselves we have accommodated our country—a country which, in gratitude, ought not to abandon us now to a strife so unequal.

We trust, Gentlemen, that you will not regard this our request as a satire, or refuse it without at least previously hearing the reasons which we have to urge in its support.

And, first, if you shut up as much as possible all access to natural light, and create a demand for artificial light, which of our French manufacturers will not be encouraged by it?

If more tallow is consumed, then there must be more oxen and sheep; and, consequently, we shall behold the multiplication of meadows, meat, wool, hides, and, above all, manure, which is the basis and foundation of all agricultural wealth.

If more oil is consumed, then we shall have an extended cultivation of the poppy, of the olive, and of rape. These rich and exhausting plants will come at the right time to enable us to avail ourselves of the increased fertility which the rearing of additional cattle will impart to our lands.

Our heaths will be covered with resinous trees. Numerous swarms of bees will, on the mountains, gather perfumed treasures, now wasting their fragrance on the desert air, like the flowers from which they emanate. No branch of agriculture but will then exhibit a cheering development.

The same remark applies to navigation. Thousands of vessels will proceed to the whale fishery; and, in a short time, we shall possess a navy capable of maintaining the honour of France, and gratifying the patriotic aspirations of your petitioners, the undersigned candlemakers and others.

But what shall we say of the manufacture of *articles de Paris?* Henceforth you will behold gildings, bronzes, crystals, in candlesticks, in lamps, in lustres, in candelabra, shining forth, in spacious warerooms, compared with which those of the present day can be regarded but as mere shops.

No poor *resinier* from his heights on the seacoast, no coalminer from the depth of his sable gallery, but will rejoice in higher wages and increased prosperity.

Only have the goodness to reflect, Gentlemen, and you will be convinced that there is, perhaps, no Frenchman, from the wealthy coalmaster to the humblest vendor of lucifer matches, whose lot will not be ameliorated by the success of this our petition.

We foresee your objections, Gentlemen, but we know that you can oppose to us none but such as you have picked up from the effete works of the partisans of Free Trade. We defy you to utter a single word against us which will not instantly rebound against yourselves and your entire policy.

You will tell us that, if we gain by the protection which we seek, the country will lose by it, because the consumer must bear the loss.

We answer:

You have ceased to have any right to invoke the interest of the consumer; for, whenever his interest is found opposed to that of the producer, you sacrifice the former. You have done so for the purpose of *encouraging labour and increasing employment*. For the same reason you should do so again.

You have yourselves obviated this objection. When you are told that the consumer is interested in the free importation of iron, coal, corn, textile fabrics — yes, you reply, but the producer is interested in their exclusion. Well, be it so; if consumers are interested in the free admission of natural light, the producers of artificial light are equally interested in its prohibition.

But, again, you may say that the producer and consumer are identical. If the manufacturer gain by protection, he will make the agriculturist also a gainer; and if agriculture prosper, it will open a vent to manufactures. Very well; if you confer upon us the monopoly of furnishing light during the day, first of all we shall purchase quantities of tallow, coals, oils, resinous substances, wax, alcohol — besides silver, iron, bronze, crystal — to carry on our manufactures; and then we, and those who furnish us with such commodities, having become rich will consume a great deal, and impart prosperity to all the other branches of our national industry.

If you urge that the light of the sun is a gratuitous gift of nature, and that to reject such gifts is to reject wealth itself under pretence of encouraging the means of acquiring it, we would caution you against giving a death-blow to your own policy. Remember that hitherto you have always repelled foreign products, *because* they approximate more nearly than home products to the character of gratuitous gifts. To comply with the exactions of other monopolists, you have only *half a motive;* and to repulse us simply because we stand on a stronger vantage-ground than others would be to adopt the equation $+ x + = -$; in other words, it would be to heap *absurdity* upon *absurdity*.

Nature and human labour co-operate in various proportions (depending on countries and climates) in the production of commodities. The part which nature executes is always gratuitous; it is the part executed by human labour which constitutes value, and is paid for.

If a Lisbon orange sells for half the price of a Paris orange, it is because natural, and consequently gratuitous, heat does for the one what artificial, and therefore expensive, heat must do for the other.

When an orange comes to us from Portugal, we may conclude that it is furnished in part gratuitously, in part for an onerous consideration; in other words, it comes to us at *half-price* as compared with those of Paris.

Now, it is precisely the *gratuitous half* (pardon the word) which we contend should be excluded. You say, How can national labour sustain competition with foreign labour, when the former has all the work to do, and the latter only does one-half, the sun supplying the remainder? But if this *half*, being *gratuitous*, determines you to exclude competition, how should the *whole*, being *gratuitous*, induce you to admit competition? If you were consistent, you would, while excluding as hurtful to native industry what is half gratuitous, exclude *a fortiori* and with double zeal, that which is altogether gratuitous.

Once more, when products such as coal, iron, corn, or textile fabrics are sent us from abroad, and we can acquire them with less labour than if we made them ourselves, the difference is a free gift conferred upon us. The gift is more or less considerable in proportion as the difference is more or less great. It amounts to a quarter, a half, or three-quarters of the value of the product, when the foreigner only asks us for three-fourths, a half, or a quarter of the price we should otherwise pay. It is as perfect and complete as it can be, when the donor (like the sun in furnishing us with light) asks us for nothing. The question, and we ask it formally, is this: Do you desire for our country the benefit of gratuitous consumption, or the pretended advantages of onerous production? Make your choice, but be logical; for as long as you exclude, as you do, coal, iron, corn, foreign fabrics, *in proportion* as their price approximates to *zero*, what inconsistency it would be to admit the light of the sun, the price of which is already at *zero* during the entire day! ●

42. Restraints on Particular Imports

Adam Smith

There seem, however, to be two cases in which it will generally be advantageous to lay some burden upon foreign, for the encouragement of domestic industry.

The first is, when some particular sort of industry is necessary for the defence of the country. The defence of Great Britain, for example, depends very much upon the number of its sailors and shipping. The act of navigation, therefore, very properly endeavours to give the sailors and shipping of Great Britain the monopoly of the trade of their own country, in some cases, by absolute prohibitions, and in others by heavy burdens upon the shipping of foreign countries.

The act of navigation is not favourable to foreign commerce, or to the growth of that opulence which can arise from it. The interest of a nation in its commercial relations to foreign nations is, like that of a merchant with regard to the different people with whom he deals, to buy as cheap and to sell as dear as possible. But it will be most likely to buy cheap, when by the most perfect freedom of trade it encourages all nations to bring to it the goods which it has occasion to purchase; and, for the same reason, it will be most likely to sell dear, when its markets are thus filled with the greatest number of buyers. The act of navigation, it is true, lays no burden upon foreign ships that come to export the produce of British industry. Even the ancient aliens duty, which used to be paid upon all goods exported as well as imported, has, by several subsequent acts, been taken off from the greater part of the articles of exportation. But if foreigners, either by prohibitions or high duties, are hindered from coming to sell, they cannot always afford to come to buy; because coming without a cargo, they must lose the freight from their own country to Great Britain. By diminishing the number of sellers, therefore, we necessarily diminish that of buyers, and are thus

Abridged from *The Wealth of Nations*, Modern Library Edition (New York: Random House, 1937), pp. 431-439 and 455-460.

likely not only to buy foreign goods dearer, but to sell our own cheaper, than if there was a more perfect freedom of trade. As defence, however, is of much more importance than opulence, the act of navigation is, perhaps, the wisest of all the commercial regulations of England.

The second case, in which it will generally be advantageous to lay some burden upon foreign for the encouragement of domestic industry, is, when some tax is imposed at home upon the produce of the latter. In this case, it seems reasonable that an equal tax should be imposed upon the like produce of the former. This would not give the monopoly of the home market to domestic industry, nor turn towards a particular employment a greater share of the stock and labour of the country, than what would naturally go to it. It would only hinder any part of what would go to it from being turned away by the tax, into a less natural direction, and would leave the competition between foreign and domestic industry, after the tax, as nearly as possible upon the same footing as before it. In Great Britain, when any such tax is laid upon the produce of domestic industry, it is usual at the same time, in order to stop the clamorous complaints of our merchants and manufacturers, that they will be undersold at home, to lay a much heavier duty upon the importation of all foreign goods of the same kind.

As there are two cases in which it will generally be advantageous to lay some burden upon foreign, for the encouragement of domestic industry; so there are two others in which it may sometimes be a matter of deliberation; in the one, how far it is proper to continue the free importation of certain foreign goods; and in the other, how far, or in what manner, it may be proper to restore that free importation after it has been for some time interrupted.

The case in which it may sometimes be a matter of deliberation how far it is proper to continue the free importation of certain foreign goods, is, when some foreign nation restrains by high duties or prohibitions the importation of some of our manufactures into their country. Revenge in this case naturally dictates retaliation, and that we should impose the like duties and prohibitions upon the importation of some or all of their manufactures into ours. Nations accordingly seldom fail to retaliate in this manner. The French have been particularly forward to favour their own manufactures by restraining the importation of such foreign goods as could come into competition with them. In this consisted a great part of the policy of Mr. Colbert, who, notwithstanding his great abilities, seems in this case to have been imposed upon by the sophistry of merchants and manufacturers, who are always demanding a monopoly against their countrymen. It is at present the opinion of the most intelligent men in France that his operations of this kind have not been beneficial to his country. That minister, by the tariff of 1667, imposed very high duties upon a great number of foreign manufactures. Upon his refusing to moderate them in favour of the Dutch, they in 1671 prohibited the importation of the wines, brandies and manufactures of France. The war of 1672 seems to have been in part occasioned by this commercial dispute. The peace of Nimeguen put an end to it in 1678, by moderating some of those duties in favour of the Dutch, who in consequence took off their prohibition. It was about the same time that the French and English began mutually to oppress each other's industry, by the like duties and prohibitions, of which the French, however, seem to have set the first example. The spirit of hostility which has subsisted between the two nations ever since, has hitherto hindered them from being moderated on either side. In 1697 the English prohibited the importation of bonelace, the manufacture of Flanders. The government of that country, at that time under the dominion of Spain, prohibited in return the importation of English woollens. In 1700, the prohibition of importing bonelace into England, was taken off upon condition that the importation of English woollens into Flanders should be put on the same footing as before.

There may be good policy in retaliations of this kind, when there is a probability that they will procure the repeal of the high duties or prohibitions complained of. The recovery of a great foreign market will generally more than compensate the transitory inconveniency of paying dearer during a short time for some sorts of goods. To judge whether such retaliations are likely to produce such an effect, does not, perhaps, belong so much to the science of a legislator, whose deliberations ought to be governed by general principles which are always the same, as to the skill of that insidious and crafty animal, vulgarly called a statesman or politician, whose councils are directed by the momentary fluctuations of affairs. When there is no probability that any such repeal can be procured, it seems a bad method of compensating the injury done to certain classes of our people, to do another injury ourselves, not only to those classes, but to almost all the other classes of them. When our neighbours prohibit some manufacture of ours, we generally prohibit, not only the same, for that alone would seldom affect them considerably, but some other manufacture of theirs. This may no doubt give encouragement to some particular class of workmen among ourselves, and by excluding some of their rivals, may enable them to raise their price in the home-market. Those workmen, however, who suffered by our neighbours' prohibition will not be benefited by ours. On the contrary, they and almost all the other classes of our citizens will thereby be obliged to pay dearer than before for certain goods. Every such law, therefore, imposes a real tax upon the whole country, not in favour of that particular class of workmen who were injured by our neighbours' prohibition, but of some other class.

The case in which it may sometimes be a matter of deliberation, how far, or in what manner, it is proper to restore the free importation of foreign goods, after it has been for some time interrupted, is, when particular manufactures, by means of high duties or prohibitions upon all foreign goods which can come into competition with them, have been so far extended as to employ a great multitude of hands. Humanity may in this case require that the freedom of trade should be restored only by slow gradations, and with a good deal of reserve and circumspection. Were those high duties and prohibitions taken away all at once, cheaper foreign goods of the same kind might be poured so fast into the home market, as to deprive all at once many thousands of our people of their ordinary employment and means of subsistence. The disorder which this would occasion might no doubt be very considerable. It would in all probability, however, be much less than is commonly imagined, for the two following reasons:

First, all those manufactures, of which any part is commonly exported to other European countries without a bounty, could be very little affected by the freest importation of foreign goods. Such manufactures must be sold as cheap abroad as any other foreign goods of the same quality and kind, and consequently must be sold cheaper at home. They would still, therefore, keep possession of the home market, and though a capricious man of fashion might sometimes prefer foreign wares, merely because they were foreign, to cheaper and better goods of the same kind that were made at home, this folly could, from the nature of things, extend to so few, that it could make no sensible impression upon the general employment of the people. But a great part of all the different branches of our woolen manufacture, of our tanned leather, and of our hardware, are annually exported to other European countries without any bounty, and these are the manufactures which employ the greatest number of hands. The silk, perhaps, is the manufacture which would suffer the most by this freedom of trade, and after it the linen, though the latter much less than the former.

Secondly, though a great number of people should, by thus restoring the freedom of trade, be thrown all at once out of their ordinary employment and common method of subsistence, it would by no means follow that they would thereby be deprived either of employment or subsistence. By the reduction of the army and navy at the end of the late war, more than a hundred thousand soldiers and seamen, a number equal to what is employed in the greatest manufactures, were all at once thrown out of their ordinary employment; but, though they no doubt suffered some inconveniency, they were not thereby deprived of all employment and subsistence. The greater part of the seamen, it is probable, gradually betook themselves to the merchant-service as they could find occasion, and in the meantime both they and the soldiers were absorbed in the great mass of the people, and employed in a great variety of occupations. Not only no great convulsion, but no sensible disorder arose from so great a change in the situation of more than a hundred thousand men, all accustomed to the use of arms, and many of them to rapine and plunder. The number of vagrants was scarce any-where sensibly increased by it, even the wages of labour were not reduced by it in any occupation, so far as I have been able to learn, except in that of seamen in the merchant-service. But if we compare together the habits of a soldier and of any sort of manufacturer, we shall find that those of the latter do not tend so much to disqualify him from being employed in a new trade, as those of the former from being employed in any. The manufacturer has always been accustomed to look for his subsistence from his labour only: the soldier to expect it from his pay. Application and industry have been familiar to the one; idleness and dissipation to the other. But it is surely much easier to change the direction of industry from one sort of labor to another, than to turn idleness and dissipation to any. To the greater part of manufactures besides, it has already been observed, there are other collateral manufactures of so similar a nature, that a workman can easily transfer his industry from one of them to another. The greater part of such workmen too are occasionally employed in country labour. The stock which employed them in a particular manufacture before, will still remain in the country to employ an equal number of people in some other way. The capital of the country remaining the same, the demand for labour will likewise be the same, or very nearly the same, though it may be exerted in different places and for different occupations. Soldiers and seamen, indeed, when discharged from the king's service, are at liberty to exercise any trade, within any town or place of Great Britain or Ireland. Let the same natural liberty of exercising what species of industry they please, be restored to all his majesty's subjects, in the same manner as to soldiers and seamen; that is, break down the exclusive privileges of corporations, and repeal the statute of apprenticeship, both which are real encroachments upon natural liberty, and add to these the repeal of the law of settlements, so that a poor workman, when thrown out of employment either in one trade or in one place, may seek for it in another trade or in another place, without the fear either or a prosecution or of a removal, and neither the public nor the individuals will suffer much more from the occasional disbanding some particular classes of manufacturers, than from that of soldiers. Our manufacturers have no doubt great merit with their country, but they cannot have more than those who defend it with their blood, nor deserve to be treated with more delicacy.

To expect, indeed, that the freedom of trade should ever be entirely restored in Great Britain, is as absurd as to expect that an Oceana or Utopia should ever be established in it. Not only the prejudices of the public, but what is much more unconquerable, the private interests of many individuals, irresistibly oppose it. Were the officers of the army to oppose with the same zeal and unanimity any reduction in the number of forces, with which master manufacturers set themselves against every law that is likely to increase the number of their rivals in the home market; were the former to animate their soldiers, in the same manner as the latter enflame their workmen, to attack with violence and outrage the proposers of any such regulation; to attempt to reduce the army would be as dangerous as it has now become to attempt to diminish in any respect the monopoly which our manufacturers have obtained against us. This monopoly has so much increased the number of some particular tribes of them, that, like an overgrown standing army, they have become formidable to the government, and upon many occasions intimidate the legislature. The member of parliament who supports every proposal for strengthening this monopoly, is sure to acquire not only the reputation of understanding trade, but great popularity and influence with an order of men whose numbers and wealth render them of great importance. If he opposes them, on the contrary, and still more if he has authority enough to be able to thwart them, neither the most acknowledged probity, nor the highest rank, nor the greatest public services, can protect him from the most infamous abuse and detraction, from personal insults, nor sometimes from real danger, arising from the insolent outrage of furious and disappointed monopolists.

The undertaker of a great manufacture, who, by the home markets being suddenly laid open to the competition of foreigners, should be obliged to abandon his trade, would no doubt suffer very considerably. That part of his capital which had usually been employed in purchasing materials and in paying his workmen, might, without much difficulty, perhaps, find another employment. But that part of it which was fixed in workhouses, and in the instruments of trade, could scarce be disposed of without considerable loss. The equitable regard, therefore, to his interest requires that changes of this kind should never be introduced suddenly, but slowly, gradually, and after a very long warning. The legislature, were it possible that its deliberations could be always directed, not by the clamorous importunity of partial interests, but by an extensive view of the general good, ought upon this very account, perhaps, to be particularly careful neither to establish any new monopolies of this kind, nor to extend further those which are already established. Every such regulation introduces some degree of real disorder into the constitution of the state, which it will be difficult afterwards to cure without occasioning another disorder.

I have endeavoured to shew, even upon the principles of the commercial system, how unnecessary it is to lay extraordinary restraints upon the importation of goods from those countries with which the balance of trade is supposed to be disadvantageous.

Nothing, however, can be more absurd than this whole doctrine of the balance of trade, upon which, not only these restraints, but almost all the other regulations of commerce are founded. When two places trade with one another, this doctrine supposes that, if the balance be even, neither of them either loses or gains; but if it leans in any degree to one side, that one of them loses, and the other gains in proportion to its declension from the exact equilibrium. Both suppositions are false. A trade which is forced by means of bounties and monopolies, may be, and commonly is disadvantageous to the country in whose favour it is meant to be established, as I shall endeavour to shew hereafter. But that trade which, without force or constraint, is naturally and regularly carried on between any two places, is always advantageous, though not always equally so, to both.

By advantage or gain, I understand, not the increase of the quantity of gold and silver, but that of the exchangeable value of the annual produce of the land and labour of the country, or the increase of the annual revenue of its inhabitants.

If the balance be even, and if the trade between the two places consist altogether in the exchange of their native commodities, they will, upon most occasions, not only both gain, but they will gain equally, or very near equally: each will in this case afford a market for a part of the surplus produce of the other:

each will replace a capital which had been employed in raising and preparing for the market this part of the surplus produce of the other, and which had been distributed among, and given revenue and maintenance to a certain number of its inhabitants. Some part of the inhabitants of each, therefore, will indirectly derive their revenue and maintenance from the other. As the commodities exchanged too are supposed to be of equal value, so the two capitals employed in the trade will, upon most occasions, be equal, or very nearly equal; and both being employed in raising the native commodities of the two countries, the revenue and maintenance which their distribution will afford to the inhabitants of each will be equal, or very nearly equal. This revenue and maintenance, thus mutually afforded, will be greater or smaller in proportion to the extent of their dealings. If these should annually amount to an hundred thousand pounds, for example, or to a million on each side, each of them would afford an annual revenue in the one case of an hundred thousand pounds, in the other, of a million, to the inhabitants of the other.

If their trade should be of such a nature that one of them exported to the other nothing but native commodities, while the returns of that other consisted altogether in foreign goods; the balance, in this case, would still be supposed even, commodities being paid for with commodities. They would, in this case too, both gain, but they would not gain equally; and the inhabitants of the country which exported nothing but native commodities would derive the greatest revenue from the trade. If England, for example, should import from France nothing but the native commodities of that country, and, not having such commodities of its own as were in demand there, should annually repay them by sending thither a large quantity of foreign goods, tobacco, we shall suppose, and East India goods; this trade, though it would give some revenue to the inhabitants of both countries, would give more to those of France than to those of England. The whole French capital annually employed in it would annually be distributed among the people of France. But that part of the English capital only which was employed in producing the English commodities with which those foreign goods were purchased, would be annually distributed among the people of England. The greater part of it would replace the capitals which had been employed in Virginia, Indostan, and China, and which had given revenue and maintenance to the inhabitants of those distant countries. If the capitals were equal, or nearly equal, therefore, this employment of the French capital would augment much more the revenue of the people of France, than that of the English capital would the revenue of the people of England. France would in this case carry on a direct foreign trade of consumption with England; whereas England would carry on a round-about trade of the same kind with France. The different effects of a capital employed in the direct, and of one employed in the round-about foreign trade of consumption, have already been fully explained.

There is not, probably, between any two countries, a trade which consists altogether in the exchange either of native commodities on both sides, or of native commodities on one side and of foreign goods on the other. Almost all countries exchange with one another partly native and partly foreign goods. That country, however, in whose cargoes there is the greatest proportion of native, and the least of foreign goods, will always be the principal gainer.

It is a losing trade, it is said, which a workman carries on with the alehouse; and the trade which a manufacturing nation would naturally carry on with a wine country, may be considered as a trade of the same nature. I answer, that the trade with the alehouse is not necessarily a losing trade. In its own nature it is just as advantageous as any other, though, perhaps, somewhat more liable to be abused. The employment of a brewer, and even that of a retailer of fermented liquors, are as necessary divisions of labour as any other. It will generally be more advantageous for a workman to buy of the brewer the quantity he has occasion for, than to brew it himself, and if he is a poor workman, it will generally be more advantageous for him to buy it, by little and little, of the retailer, than a large quantity of the brewer. He may no doubt buy too much of either, as he may of any other dealers in his neighbourhood, of the butcher, if he is a glutton, or of the draper, if he affects to be a beau among his companions. It is advantageous to the great body of workmen, notwithstanding, that all these trades should be free, though this freedom may be abused in all of them, and is more likely to be so, perhaps, in some than in others. Though individuals, besides, may sometimes ruin their fortunes by an excessive consumption of fermented liquors, there seems to be no risk that a nation should do so. Though in every country there are many people who spend upon such liquors more than they can afford, there are always many more who spend less. It deserves to be remarked too, that, if we consult experience, the cheapness of wine seems to be a cause, not of drunkenness, but of sobriety. The inhabitants of the wine countries are in general the soberest people in Europe; witness the Spaniards, the Italians, and the inhabitants of the southern provinces of France. People are seldom guilty of excess in what is their daily fare. Nobody affects the character of liberality and good fellowship, by being profuse of a liquor which is as cheap as small beer. On the contrary, in the countries which, either from excessive heat or cold, produce no grapes, and where wine consequently is dear and a rarity, drunkenness is a common vice, as among the northern nations, and all those who live between the tropics, the negroes, for example, on the coast of Guinea. When a French regiment comes from some of the northern provinces of France, where wine is somewhat dear, to be quartered in the southern, where it is very cheap, the soldiers, I have frequently heard it observed, are at first debauched by the cheapness and novelty of good wine; but after a few months residence, the greater part of them become as sober as the rest of the inhabitants. Were the duties upon foreign wines, and the excises upon malt, beer, and ale, to be taken away all at once, it might, in the same manner, occasion in Great Britain a pretty general and temporary drunkenness among the middling and inferior ranks of people, which would probably be soon followed by a permanent and almost universal sobriety. At present drunkenness is by no means the vice of people of fashion, or of those who can easily afford the most expensive liquors. A gentleman drunk with ale, has scarce ever been seen among us. The restraints upon the wine trade in Great Britain, besides, do not so much seem calculated to hinder the people from going, if I may say so, to the alehouse, as from going where they can buy the best and cheapest liquor. They favour the wine trade of Portugal, and discourage that of France. The Portuguese, it is said, indeed, are better customers for our manufactures than the French, and should therefore be encouraged in preference to them. As they give us their custom, it is pretended, we should give them ours. The sneaking arts of underling tradesmen are thus erected into political maxims for the conduct of a great empire; for it is the most underling tradesmen only who make it a rule to employ chiefly their own customers. A great trader purchases his goods always where they are cheapest and best, without regard to any little interest of this kind.

By such maxims as these, however, nations have been taught that their interest consisted in beggaring all their neighbours. Each nation has been made to look with an invidious eye upon the prosperity of all the nations with which it trades, and to consider their gain as its own loss. Commerce, which ought naturally to be, among nations, as among individuals, a bond of union and friendship, has become the most fertile source of discord and animosity. The capricious ambition of kings and ministers has not, during the present and the preceding century, been more fatal to the repose of Europe, than the impertinent jealousy of merchants and manufacturers. The violence and injustice of the rulers of mankind is an ancient evil, for which, I am afraid, the nature of human affairs can scarce admit of a remedy. But the mean rapacity, the monopolizing spirit of merchants and manufacturers, who neither are, nor ought to be, the rulers of mankind, though it cannot perhaps be corrected, may very easily be prevented from disturbing the tranquillity of any body but themselves.

That it was the spirit of monopoly which originally both invented and propagated this doctrine, cannot be doubted; and they who first taught it were by no means such fools as they who believed it. In every country it always is and must be the interest of the great body of the people to buy whatever they want of those who sell it cheapest. The proposition is so very manifest, that it seems ridiculous to take any pains to prove it; nor could it ever have been called in question, had not the interested sophistry of merchants and manufacturers confounded the common sense of mankind. Their interest is, in this respect, directly opposite to that of the great body of the people. As it is the interest of the freemen of a corporation to hinder the rest of the inhabitants from employing any workmen but themselves, so it is the interest of the merchants and manufacturers of every country to secure to themselves the monopoly of the home market. Hence in Great Britain, and in most other European countries, the extraordinary duties upon almost all goods imported by alien merchants. Hence the high duties and prohibitions upon all those foreign manufactures which can come into competition with our own. Hence too the extraordinary restraints upon the importation of almost all sorts of goods from those countries with which the balance of trade is supposed to be disadvantageous; that is, from those against whom national animosity happens to be most violently inflamed. ●

43. On Foreign Trade

David Ricardo

Under a system of perfectly free commerce, each country naturally devotes its capital and labour to such employments as are most beneficial to each. This pursuit of individual advantage is admirably connected with the universal good of the whole. By stimulating industry, by rewarding ingenuity, and by using most efficaciously the particular powers bestowed by nature, it distributes labour most effectively and most economically: while, by increasing the general mass of productions, it diffuses general benefit, and binds together, by one common tie of interest and intercourse, the universal society of nations throughout the civilised world. It is this principle which determines that wine shall be made in France and Portugal, that corn shall be grown in America and Poland, and that hardware and other goods shall be manufactured in England.

In one and the same country, profits are, generally speaking, always on the same level; or differ only as the employment of capital may be more or less secure and agreeable. It is not so between different countries. If the profits of capital employed in Yorkshire should exceed those of capital employed in London, capital would speedily move from London to Yorkshire, and an equality of profits would be effected; but if in consequence of the diminished rate of production in the lands of England from the increase of capital and population wages should rise and profits fall, it would not follow that capital and population would necessarily move from England to Holland, or Spain, or Russia, where profits might be higher.

If Portugal had no commercial connection with other countries, instead of employing a great part of her capital and industry in the production of wines, with which she purchases for her own use the cloth and hardware of other countries, she would be obliged to devote a part of that capital to the manufacture of those commodities, which she would thus obtain probably inferior in quality as well as quantity.

The quantity of wine which she shall give in exchange for the cloth of England

Reprinted from *The Principles of Political Economy and Taxation* (London: J. M. Dent & Sons, Ltd., 1911), pp, 81-87.

is not determined by the respective quantities of labour devoted to the production of each, as it would be if both commodities were manufactured in England, or both in Portugal.

England may be so circumstanced that to produce the cloth may require the labour of 100 men for one year; and if she attempted to make the wine, it might require the labour of 120 men for the same time. England would therefore find it her interest to import wine, and to purchase it by the exportation of cloth.

To produce the wine in Portugal might require only the labour of 80 men for one year, and to produce the cloth in the same country might require the labour of 90 men for the same time. It would therefore be advantageous for her to export wine in exchange for cloth. This exchange might even take place notwithstanding that the commodity imported by Portugal could be produced there with less labour than in England. Though she could make the cloth with the labour of 90 men, she would import it from a country where it required the labour of 100 men to produce it, because it would be advantageous to her rather to employ her capital in the production of wine, for which she would obtain more cloth from England, than she could produce by diverting a portion of her capital from the cultivation of vines to the manufacture of cloth.

Thus England would give the produce of the labour of 100 men for the produce of the labour of 80. Such an exchange could not take place between the individuals of the same country. The labour of 100 Englishmen cannot be given for that of 80 Englishmen, but the produce of the labour of 100 Englishmen may be given for the produce of the labour of 80 Portuguese, 60 Russians, or 120 East Indians. The difference in this respect, between a single country and many, is easily accounted for, by considering the difficulty with which capital moves from one country to another, to seek a more profitable employment, and the activity with which it invariably passes from one province to another in the same country*

It would undoubtedly be advantageous to the capitalists of England, and to the consumers in both countries, that under such circumstances the wine and the cloth should both be made in Portugal, and therefore that the capital and labour of England employed in making cloth should be removed to Portugal for that purpose. In that case, the relative value of these commodities would be regulated by the same principle as if one were the produce of Yorkshire and the other of London: and in every other case, if capital freely flowed towards

---

* It will appear, then, that a country possessing very considerable advantages in machinery and skill, and which may therefore be enabled to manufacture commodities with much less labour than her neighbours, may, in return for such commodities, import a portion of the corn required for its consumption, even if its land were more fertile and corn could be grown with less labour than in the country from which it was imported. Two men can both make shoes and hats, and one is superior to the other in both employments; but in making hats he can only exceed his competitor by one-fifth or 20 percent., and in making shoes he can excel him by one-third or 33 per cent.; —will it not be for the interest of both that the superior man should employ himself exclusively in making shoes, and the inferior man in making hats?

those countries where it could be most profitably employed, there could be no difference in the rate of profit, and no other difference in the real or labour price of commodities than the additional quantity of labour required to convey them to the various markets where they were to be sold.

Experience, however, shows that the fancied or real insecurity of capital, when not under the immediate control of its owner, together with the natural disinclination which every man has to quit the country of his birth and connections, and intrust himself, with all his habits fixed, to a strange government and new laws, check the emigration of capital. These feelings, which I should be sorry to see weakened, induce most men of property to be satisfied with a low rate of profits in their own country, rather than seek a more advantageous employment for their wealth in foreign nations.

Gold and silver having been chosen for the general medium of circulation, they are, by the competition of commerce, distributed in such proportions amongst the different countries of the world as to accommodate themselves to the natural traffic which would take place if no such metals existed, and the trade between countries were purely a trade of barter.

Thus, cloth cannot be imported into Portugal unless it sell there for more gold than it cost in the country from which it was imported; and wine cannot be imported into England unless it will sell for more there than it cost in Portugal. If the trade were purely a trade of barter, it could only continue whilst England could make cloth so cheap as to obtain a greater quantity of wine with a given quantity of labour by manufacturing cloth than by growing vines; and also whilst the industry of Portugal were attended by the reverse effects. Now suppose England to discover a process for making wine, so that it should become her interest rather to grow it than import it; she would naturally divert a portion of her capital from the foreign trade to the home trade; she would cease to manufacture cloth for exportation, and would grow wine for herself. The money price of these commodities would be regulated accordingly; wine would fall here while cloth continued at its former price, and in Portugal no alteration would take place in the price of either commodity. Cloth would continue for some time to be exported from this country, because its price would continue to be higher in Portugal than here; but money instead of wine would be given in exchange for it, till the accumulation of money here, and its diminution abroad, should so operate on the relative value of cloth in the two countries that it would cease to be profitable to export it. If the improvement in making wine were of a very important description, it might become profitable for the two countries to exchange employments; for England to make all the wine, and Portugal all the cloth consumed by them; but this could be effected only by a new distribution of the precious metals, which should raise the price of cloth in England and lower it in Portugal. The relative price of wine would fall in England in consequence of the real advantage from the improvement of its manufacture; that is to say, its natural price would fall; the relative price of cloth would rise there from the accumulation of money.

Thus, suppose before the improvement in making wine in England the price of wine here were £50 per pipe, and the price of a certain quantity of cloth were £45, whilst in Portugal the price of the same quantity of wine was £45, and that of the same quantity of cloth £50; wine would be exported from Portugal with a profit of £5, and cloth from England with a profit of the same amount.

Suppose that, after the improvement, wine falls to £45 in England, the cloth continuing at the same price. Every transaction in commerce is an independent transaction. Whilst a merchant can buy cloth in England for £45, and sell it with the usual profit in Portugal, he will continue to export it from England. His business is simply to purchase English cloth, and to pay for it by a bill of exchange, which he purchases with Portuguese money. It is to him of no importance what becomes of this money: he has discharged his debt by the remittance of the bill. His transaction is undoubtedly regulated by the terms on which he can obtain this bill, but they are known to him at the time; and the causes which may influence the market price of bills, or the rate of exchange, is no consideration of his.

If the markets be favourable for the exportation of wine from Portugal to England, the exporter of the wine will be a seller of a bill, which will be purchased either by the importer of the cloth, or by the person who sold him his bill; and thus, without the necessity of money passing from either country, the exporters in each country will be paid for their goods. Without having any direct transaction with each other, the money paid in Portugal by the importer of cloth will be paid to the Portuguese exporter of wine; and in England by the negotiation of the same bill the exporter of the cloth will be authorised to receive its value from the importer of wine.

But if the prices of wine were such that no wine could be exported to England, the importer of cloth would equally purchase a bill; but the price of that bill would be higher, from the knowledge which the seller of it would possess that there was no counter bill in the market by which he could ultimately settle the transactions between the two countries; he might know that the gold or silver money he received in exchange for his bill must be actually exported to his correspondent in England, to enable him to pay the demand which he had authorised to be made upon him, and he might therefore charge in the price of his bill all the expenses to be incurred, together with his fair and usual profit.

If then this premium for a bill on England should be equal to the profit on importing cloth, the importation would of course cease; but if the premium on the bill were only 2 percent, if to be enabled to pay a debt in England of £100, £102 should be paid in Portugal, whilst cloth which cost £45 would sell for £50, cloth would be imported, bills would be bought, and money would be exported, till the diminution of money in Portugal, and its accumulation in England, had produced such a state of prices as would make it no longer profitable to continue these transactions.

But the diminution of money in one country, and its increase in another, do not operate on the price of one commodity only, but on the prices of all, and therefore the price of wine and cloth will be both raised in England and both lowered in Portugal. The price of cloth, from being £45 in one country and £50 in the other, would probably fall to £49 or £48 in Portugal, and rise to £46 or £47 in England, and not afford a sufficient profit after paying a premium for a bill to induce any merchant to import that commodity.

It is thus that the money of each country is apportioned to it in such quantities only as may be necessary to regulate a profitable trade of barter. England exported cloth in exchange for wine because, by so doing, her industry was rendered more productive to her; she had more cloth and wine than if she had manufactured both for herself; and Portugal imported cloth and exported wine because the industry of Portugal could be more beneficially employed for both countries in producing wine. Let there be more difficulty in England in producing cloth, or in Portugal in producing wine, or let there be more facility in England in producing wine, or in Portugal in producing cloth, and the trade must immediately cease.

No change whatever takes place in the circumstances of Portugal; but England finds that she can employ her labour more productively in the manufacture of wine, and instantly the trade of barter between the two countries changes. Not only is the exportation of wine from Portugal stopped, but a new distribution of the precious metals takes place, and her importation of cloth is also prevented.

Both countries would probably find it their interest to make their own wine and their own cloth; but this singular result would take place: in England, though wine would be cheaper, cloth would be elevated in price, more would be paid for it by the consumer; while in Portugal the consumers, both of cloth and of wine, would be able to purchase those commodities cheaper. In the country where the improvement was made prices would be enhanced; in that where no change had taken place, but where they had been deprived of a profitable branch of foreign trade, prices would fall.

This, however, is only a seeming advantage to Portugal, for the quantity of cloth and wine together produced in that country would be diminished, while the quantity produced in England would be increased. Money would in some degree have changed its value in the two countries; it would be lowered in England and raised in Portugal. Estimated in money, the whole revenue of Portugal would be diminished; estimated in the same medium the whole revenue of England would be increased.

Thus, then, it appears that the improvement of a manufacture in any country tends to alter the distribution of the precious metals amongst the nations of the world: it tends to increase the quantity of commodities, at the same time that it raises general prices in the country where the improvement takes place.

To simplify the question, I have been supposing the trade between two countries to be confined to two commodities — to wine and cloth; but it is well known that many and various articles enter into the list of exports and imports. By the abstraction of money from one country, and the accumulation of it in another, all commodities are affected in price, and consequently encouragement is given to the exportation of many more commodities besides money, which will therefore prevent so great an effect from taking place on the value of money in the two countries as might otherwise be expected. ●

44. Restraint of Trade

Frédéric Bastiat

Mr. Protectionist* (it was not I who gave him that name; it was M. Charles Dupin) devoted his time and his capital to converting ore from his lands into iron. Since Nature had been more generous with the Belgians, they sold iron to the French at a better price than Mr. Protectionist did, which meant that all Frenchmen, or France, could obtain a given quantity of iron *with less labor* by buying it from the good people of Flanders. Therefore, prompted by their self-interest, they took full advantage of the situation, and every day a multitude of nailmakers, metalworkers, cartwrights, mechanics, blacksmiths, and plowmen could be seen either going themselves or sending middlemen to Belgium to obtain their supply of iron. Mr. Protectionist did not like this at all.

His first idea was to stop this abuse by direct intervention with his own two hands. This was certainly the least he could do, since he alone was harmed. I'll take my carbine, he said to himself. I'll put four pistols in my belt, I'll fill my cartridge box, I'll buckle on my sword, and, thus equipped, I'll go to the frontier. There I'll kill the first metalworker, nailmaker, blacksmith, mechanic, or locksmith who comes seeking his own profit rather than mine. That'll teach him a lesson!

At the moment of leaving, Mr. Protectionist had a few second thoughts that somewhat tempered his bellicose ardor. He said to himself: First of all, it is quite possible that the buyers of iron, my fellow countrymen and my enemies, will take offense, and, instead of letting themselves be killed, they might kill me. Furthermore, even if all my servants marched out, we could not guard the whole frontier. Finally, the entire proceeding would cost me too much, more than the

---

* In French, "M. Prohibant:" this ironic term for a protectionist, coined, as Bastiat says, by Charles Dupin, could be roughly translated as "Mr. Restrainer-of-Trade" or "Mr. Protectionist." — Translator.

Reprinted from *Selected Essays on Political Economy*, translated by Seymour Cain and edited by George B. de Huszar, pp. 25-30. Copyright © 1964 by The William Volcker Fund. Reprinted by permission of the Institute for Humane Studies at George Mason University, Fairfax, VA.

result would be worth.

Mr. Protectionist was going to resign himself sadly just to being free like everyone else, when suddenly he had a brilliant idea.

He remembered that there is a great law factory in Paris. What is a law? he asked himself. It is a measure to which, when once promulgated, whether it is good or bad, everyone has to conform. For the execution of this law, a public police force is organized, and to make up the said public police force, men and money are taken from the nation.

If, then, I manage to get from that great Parisian factory a nice little law saying: "Belgian iron is prohibited," I shall attain the following results: The government will replace the few servants that I wanted to send to the frontier with twenty thousand sons of my recalcitrant metalworkers, locksmiths, nail-makers, blacksmiths, artisans, mechanics, and plowmen. Then, to keep these twenty thousand customs officers in good spirits and health, there will be distributed to them twenty-five million francs taken from these same blacksmiths, nailmakers, artisans, and plowmen. Organized in this way, the protection will be better accomplished; it will cost me nothing; I shall not be exposed to the brutality of brokers; I shall sell the iron at my price; and I shall enjoy the sweet pleasure of seeing our great people shamefully hoaxed. That will teach them to be continually proclaiming themselves the precursors and the promoters of all progress in Europe. It will be a smart move, and well worth the trouble of trying!

So Mr. Protectionist went to the law factory. (Another time, perhaps, I shall tell the story of his dark, underhanded dealings there; today I wish to speak only of the steps he took openly and for all to see.) He presented to their excellencies, the legislators, the following argument:

"Belgian iron is sold in France at ten francs, which forces me to sell mine at the same price. I should prefer to sell it at fifteen and cannot because of this confounded Belgian iron. Manufacture a law that says: 'Belgian iron shall no longer enter France.' Immediately I shall raise my price by five francs, with the following cᵒ .sequences:

"For each hundred kilograms of iron that I shall deliver to the public, instead of ten francs I shall get fifteen; I shall enrich myself more quickly; I shall extend the exploitation of my mines; I shall employ more men. My employees and I will spend more, to the great advantage of our suppliers for miles around. These suppliers, having a greater market, will give more orders to industry, and gradually this activity will spread throughout the country. This lucky hundred-sou piece that you will drop into my coffers, like a stone that is thrown into a lake, will cause an infinite number of concentric circles to radiate great distances in every direction."

Charmed by this discourse, enchanted to learn that it is so easy to increase the wealth of a people simply by legislation, the manufacturers of laws voted in favor of the restriction. "What is all this talk about labor and saving?" they said. "What good are these painful means of increasing the national wealth, when a decree will do the job?"

And, in fact, the law had all the consequences predicted by Mr. Protectionist, but it had others too; for, to do him justice, he had not reasoned *falsely*, but *incompletely*. In asking for a privilege, he had pointed out the effects *that are seen*, leaving in the shadow those *that are not seen*. He had shown only two people, when actually there are three in the picture. It is for us to repair this omission, whether involuntary or premeditated.

Yes, the five-franc piece thus legislatively rechanneled into the coffers of Mr. Protectionist constitutes an advantage for him and for those who get jobs because of it. And if the decree had made the five-franc piece come down from the moon, these good effects would not be counterbalanced by any compensating bad effects. Unfortunately, the mysterious hundred sous did not come down from the moon, but rather from the pocket of a metalworker, a nailmaker, a cartwright, a blacksmith, a plowman, a builder, in a word, from James Goodfellow, who pays it out today without receiving a milligram of iron more than when he was paying ten francs. It at once becomes evident that this certainly changes the question, for, quite obviously, the *profit* of Mr. Protectionist is counterbalanced by the *loss* of James Goodfellow, and anything that Mr. Protectionist will be able to do with this five-franc piece for the encouragement of domestic industry, James Goodfellow could also have done. The stone is thrown in at one point in the lake only because it has been prohibited by law from being thrown in at another.

Hence, *what is not seen* counterbalances *what is seen*; and the outcome of the whole operation is an injustice, all the more deplorable in having been perpetrated by the law.

But this is not all. I have said that a third person is always left in the shadow. I must make him appear here, so that he can reveal to us a *second loss* of five francs. Then we shall have the results of the operation in its entirety.

James Goodfellow has fifteen francs, the fruit of his labors. (We are back at the time when he is still free.) What does he do with his fifteen francs? He buys an article of millinery for ten francs, and it is with this article of millinery that he pays (or his middleman pays for him) for the hundred kilograms of Belgian iron. He still has five francs left. He does not throw them into the river, but (and this is *what is not seen*) he gives them to some manufacturer or other in exchange for some satisfaction — for example, to a publisher for a copy of the *discourse on Universal History* by Bossuet.*

---

*   Jacques Bénigne Bossuet (1627-1704), bishop of Condom and of Meaux, was the outstanding pulpit orator of his day, his funeral orations for members of the royal family ranking as brilliant examples of French classical style and power. As tutor to the heir apparent, the son of Louis XIV, he wrote his *Histoire universelle*, one of the classics on which French school children were raised for generations. His vigorous stand against Protestantism and his successful leadership of the Gallican movement, which brought increased independence to the French Catholic Church, reveal him as an important ecclesiastical, as well as literary, figure. — Translator.

Thus, he has encouraged *domestic industry* to the amount of fifteen francs, to wit:

10 francs to the Parisian milliner

5 francs to the publisher

And as for James Goodfellow, he gets for his fifteen francs two objects of satisfaction, to wit:

1. A hundred kilograms of iron

2. A book

Comes the decree.

What happens to James Goodfellow? What happens to domestic industry.

James Goodfellow, in giving his fifteen francs to the last centime to Mr. Protectionist for a hundred kilograms of iron, has nothing now but the use of this iron. He loses the enjoyment of a book or of any other equivalent object. He loses five francs. You agree with this; you cannot fail to agree; you cannot fail to agree that when restraint of trade raises prices, the consumer loses the difference.

But it is said that *domestic industry* gains the difference.

No, it does not gain it; for, since the decree, it is encouraged only as much as it was before, to the amount of fifteen francs.

Only, since the decree, the fifteen francs of James Goodfellow go to metallurgy, while before the decree they were divided between millinery and publishing.

The force that Mr. Protectionist might exercise by himself at the frontier and that which he has the law exercise for him can be judged quite differently from the moral point of view. There are people who think that plunder loses all its immorality as soon as it becomes legal. Personally, I cannot imagine a more alarming situation. However that may be, one thing is certain, and that is that the economic results are the same.

You may look at the question from any point of view you like, but if you examine it dispassionately, you will see that no good can come from legal or illegal plunder. We do not deny that it may bring for Mr. Protectionist or his industry, or if you wish for domestic industry, a profit of five francs. But we affirm that it will also give rise to two losses: one for James Goodfellow, who pays fifteen francs for what he used to get for ten; the other for domestic industry, which no longer receives the difference. Make your own choice of which of these two losses compensates for the profit that we admit. The one you do not choose constitutes no less a *dead loss*.

Moral: To use force is not to produce, but to destroy. Heavens! If to use force were to produce, France would be much richer than she is. ●